Publication description:

# Brigham Young's United Order:
# A Contextual Interpretation

## Volume 1 – Main Presentation

The United Order was Brigham Young's collection of policies and plans for overcoming the many economic and legal problems the Saints faced in their Western territory. Having been denied through federal malice for many decades the normal benefits of state and local self-government, including an effective criminal law system and mechanisms for property ownership and conducting business, the Saint's creating of a vigorous society and economy was very difficult and required much ingenuity until statehood and legal independence were finally achieved. It was necessary for the first 50 years in Utah to create temporary substitutes for normal criminal systems, property ownership, and conducting corporate business.

On a more personal note, what does the term "United Order" mean to you? Have you ever worried whether you might have to join a communal enterprise, and surrender all your worldly goods to gain salvation? Some of the LDS traditions seem to support such a possibility.

You may be pleased and surprised to learn that Brigham Young was strongly against the idea of any required communal ownership of property or the equal distribution of the proceeds.

> You take some ... who want us all to be of one heart and of one mind, and they think we cannot be so unless we all have the same number of houses, farms, carriages, horses, and the same amount in greenbacks. There are plenty in this Church who entertain such a notion .... but let such ... guide and dictate, and they would soon accomplish the overthrow of this Church and people. JD 12:61 June 16, 1867 SLC.
> I do not wish for one moment to recognize the idea that in order to establish the United Order our property has to be divided equally among the people ... JD 18:353-7 April 6, 1877 St. George.

So where did all the unusual ideas and projects come from that have helped spawn the troubling traditions? The hostile terrain and political climate meant that the Saints were required to be in a "wagon train" or military mode, a version of martial law, for the first thirty years they were in Utah, and this explains almost everything.

Armies must coordinate all aspects of their lives and operations to survive and be effective. In peacetime, such discipline is usually counterproductive. We surely do not wish to hold up the military life as the epitome of religious devotion and temporal felicity, thus letting past persecutors determine our view of future possibilities.

Many of the harsher aspects of that early political and temporal setting have been glossed over to help heal the breach with the rest of the country. However, without an understanding of those stressful circumstances, one can never hope to understand the many economic, political, and doctrinal anomalies that are found among the historical fossils from the Brigham Young period.

## Volume 2 – Related Anomalies and Side Issues

These chapters were separated from the original unabridged edition to facilitate a more economical publishing process and to lessen the complexity level of the original study. Those people who have a very active interest in the history of the united order and related ideas, and wish to go beyond the central issue into various levels of related historical and doctrinal sub-issues, should find these supplemental chapters of interest. The multiple conflicting views of early church leaders on the united order, blood atonement, one-man power, Adam-God, polygamy, theocracy, and Christ's infinite atonement are among the many topics analyzed using opinions expressed in the *Journal of Discourses* – the original conference reports.

# BRIGHAM YOUNG'S
# UNITED ORDER
# ORDER

# BRIGHAM YOUNG'S
# UNITED
# ORDER

## A Contextual Interpretation

### Kent W. Huff

VOLUME 1 — MAIN PRESENTATION

**Publication history:**

First ebook edition, volume 1 of 2
Published by Theological Thinktank, Orem, Utah
Copyright © 2020 by Kent W. Huff
Distributed by Amazon
ISBN: 978-0-9755831-6-6

Second paperback edition, volume 1 of 2
Published by Theological Thinktank, Orem, Utah
Copyright © 2020 by Kent W. Huff
Distributed by Amazon
ISBN: 978-0-9755831-5-9

First paperback edition, volume 1 of 2
Copyright © 1998 by Kent W. Huff
ISBN-10: 1-55517-393-4
ISBN-13: 978-1-5551739-3-7
Published by: Bonneville Books, Springville, Utah
Cover design and page layout by Corinne A. Bischoff
Printed in the United States of America

Original hardback edition, all text in a single volume, less than 100 copies
Copyright 1994 by Kent W. Huff. No ISBN

To my mother,
Kathryn Isaac Huff,
who has always been the source of much
unity and order in our family

# Table of Contents

## Volume 1 — Main Presentation

# PREFACE

In this day when Marxism-Leninism has been bereft of its world-wide power, largely because its moral and philosophical bankruptcy has finally become clear to a larger and more enlightened middle class, it seems anachronistic to still find LDS church members either secretly fearing or secretly awaiting and promoting the implementation of a church-sponsored system which many of them imagine to be much like the socialism/communism that is being discredited and dismantled elsewhere. It required a 70-year period of waste, suffering, terror, and destruction to finally prove communism wrong. One scholar worried concerning the possible aftermath of the collapse:

> No doubt if a brilliant new utopian theory were to appear, promising salvation at the cost of enslavement, countless intellectuals would rush to accept it all over the world, and new revolutions would come to recreate revived forms of totalitarianism that would themselves take decades to erode.[1]

I would be chagrined if LDS misunderstanding of history and principle could somehow contribute to further social disasters. LDS people should surely be far more sophisticated on these matters than the Russian peasants conquered by Lenin and his ideas. One of my friends who escaped the communist rule of Castro in Cuba shows a remarkable ability to spot even the slightest tendency toward accepting those ideas in the U.S. context. Hopefully, we will not need to repeat her unpleasant experiences to gain a similar sensitivity.

While the united order idea seems to have little practical application in the church today, and so may be considered of little consequence, I fear that this mostly dormant idea still has the power to cause confusion at points where the church may find it necessary to make an incremental change in its temporal program.

In the relevant historical commentaries I have read, there is usually much that is assumed about the doctrinal infrastructure of the united order. Our current scriptures contain only a few fragments on the topic, hardly enough to construct a complete constitution for such a major social revision. In fact, as one scholar demonstrated,[2] if you ask fifty knowledgeable people what the United Order is or means, you will likely get fifty different answers, each depending to a large extent on each person's preferences and interpretations.

I have tried to attack directly the problem of amorphous and widely differing assumptions by going straight to the words of those most involved, and have found some striking things as I have explored the literature. Most striking of all is Brigham Young's rejection and denunciation of the "all things common" scriptural allusions which have become part of the Christian tradition (see chapter 11). Joseph Smith also rejected and denounced those ideas.[3] Today's leaders have rejected or at least avoided them as well.

I find much confusion and misinformation in the various myths and traditions that have come down to us. These spurious traditions often conflict with more permanent doctrinal elements of the church, particularly when they imply the use of force in a gospel that decries all types of force. This conflict of principles causes confusion.

I believe that I have discovered for myself a plausible explanation for the united order idea and other related troubling traditions and doctrinal anomalies of the past, which explanation both preserves the inspired standing of past leaders, and confirms the wisdom of the choices made by current leaders.

Among other things, I wish to show that **the <u>Law of Consecration is a principle without an attached organization.</u>** It can be lived and exercised in an infinite number of settings and ways. We need to be aware that as the political, economic, technological, moral and spiritual social context of the saints changes because of changes in the world, the course that the saints as individuals and the church as a whole should follow will change accordingly. For example, where banding together in many economic matters was a great solution to the Utah problems, that same kind of banding together today could have many negative consequences and could stop us from carrying on the church's mission. The church could not be leaven if its members could not freely mix with the populace.

## Difficult Material

To create this book, it has been necessary to touch on topics which some people find disturbing. So before going on to address in detail specific historical or doctrinal questions, I wish to affirm that I consider myself a member of the LDS church in good standing, orthodox in all the things that matter, and that I accept and reaffirm that the church has been and continues to be led by inspired men, prophets who receive revelation from God in carrying out their duties. Joseph Smith was a prophet, Brigham Young was a prophet, and so the line has continued until today, and will continue. Dissenters and apostates often seem to be the ones bringing up some of the topics I wish to deal with, and I want to make it clear that I do not consider myself among that group.

## Motivation

I have always been curious about the general topic of economics and religion, but one of the original impulses toward actually writing a book was a statement by one of my lawyer friends that the current-day welfare state in the United States was leading us to the united order. I was so shocked and distressed by that statement that I determined to do something about it. That was 15 years ago, and I am finally delivering on the last part of this self-assignment.

Another lawyer friend expressed the opinion that many of the practical commercial laws of today would need to be in effect under almost any economic system, even the united order. This struck me as quite sensible, but certainly was in contrast with the myths and traditions of the utopian united order, giving me another puzzle to untangle. I am happy to report evidence that her intuition was correct.

## Thesis of the Joseph Smith Book

This book is a continuation of my earlier work, *Joseph Smith's United Order; A Noncommunalistic Interpretation* (JSUO). The two books were conceived as a single research project, but were later separated because of the sheer size of the project. It is recommended that JSUO be read first or consulted along with this book, lest some aspects of this book seem incomplete or insufficiently supported or explained.

That earlier book demonstrated that Joseph was adamantly against any socialist programs. His "united order," usually called the "united firm," was merely a business partnership, limited to eleven church leaders, which was the predecessor of today's Corporation of the President as the property-holding, publishing, business unit of the church. The general body of the church had no part in the small "united firm," although they benefitted much from its activities.

## Response to First Book

In response to my first book, JSUO, the leader of a breakoff church that considers the pooling of property to be a critical, mandatory, gospel doctrine, wrote to tell me I was wrong in my thesis that Joseph Smith did not sponsor, support or require such mandatory pooling, but actively fought it. I was happy to hear that my message had got out to that particular kind of audience. One important reason for writing both books has been to combat the misconceptions, the misrepresentations, and the misuse of property concepts, especially by religious groups, to keep current-day people under a form of bondage.

## Reading the Book

I have wanted very much for the reading of this book to be an historical experience, not just an academic inquiry or exercise. This study is based to a large extent on the text of the *Journal of Discourses*. It would be highly desirable for the interested reader to read large amounts of the *Journal*, to be sure to catch all the context cues. However, publishing costs have placed limits on what could be included in the book itself. I hope that those who read this will also have access to a copy of the *Journal of Discourses* and will refer to it often for the readings indicated. This will help make the experience less like a quick bus tour and more like living there for a while. In choosing what to print, I have tried to hit a balance between summaries and quotes that will neither burden the reader will too much text, nor leave him without confidence in my interpretations.

If one were to read only one chapter of the book, I recommend chapter 11 entitled "Brigham Young Rejected the Acts 'All Things Common' Tradition." That should present an adequate challenge to the usual traditions on the topic and lead a person to reconsider the whole area. Brigham Young himself tried to get rid of the tradition which we today often (incorrectly) attribute to him.

## Methodology, Content, and Limitations

One early reviewer observed that this book is less thorough than it might be as far as historical events are concerned since it relies on a fairly narrow set of sources, largely the *Journal of Discourses* and the other standard published histories of the Church. That is a weakness, but the cost to remedy it is beyond my current means. Hopefully there will be a way to extend the search in the future. Perhaps this can serve as a treasure map to highlight the possible historical information treasures.

This is a book of theory much more than a historically time-sequenced work. Therefore, the placement of the chapters may seem a bit arbitrary. The book tries to set out the problems the united order ideas were designed to solve, and then to discuss the nature of the solutions. There are many subsidiary points grouped around the main points to help create the feeling of context that is the overall goal of the book. One might say this book is organized more like a flower arrangement than like a graph of history. Many chapters give their own separate view of the thirty-year period of Brigham Young's church leadership. The major unusual teachings of the Brigham Young era are grouped and interrelated in a network of ideas.

## Intellectual History

Rather than being oriented to historical events and outcomes, this book is an attempt at intellectual history -- getting at the thoughts, plans, reasoning and intentions of those involved. Intellectually and doctrinally, intent and desire may be more important (and interesting) than actual results in a particular case, since practical problems may greatly skew the final visible results. In the military intelligence business, assets and behavior of the opponent may be known, but the intent of the enemy may be far more important than anything observable, and yet it is the hardest thing to get data on. For example, who accurately knew Saddam Hussein's intentions, a few days before he moved his tanks into Kuwait in 1990? Or who knew the intentions of the Mainland Chinese before they attacked in North Korea in 1950?

## Acknowledgements

Anyone who has a family and tries to write a major book outside of normal work hours will know that family members suffer for this activity, regardless of any direct involvement in the project. I wish to acknowledge that my wife's patience was sufficient to keep her from divorcing me during the years of this book's gestation. She has made many sacrifices in the sense that she has taken on extra family and household tasks and foregone numerous other more interesting activities where my involvement would have been required, but where I had locked myself in the den. Others have also contributed both directly and indirectly, but I believe most would be happy to have their contributions remain anonymous, especially since they have had little control over the final content of this somewhat controversial project.

I would have preferred to have this be a more collegial project, or to have had clerical or research assistance in its preparation. However, my isolation in Saudi Arabia and Mexico did not allow close cooperation with others with similar interests during the last fifteen years. In retrospect, this isolation may have been a blessing in disguise, since it allowed me, indeed required me, to take an independent view of the matter with little constraint from any conventional wisdom.

Perhaps my main source of outside help was the *Journal of Discourses* in computer readable and indexed form, published by Information Solutions, Inc., of Salt Lake City. Without that assistance it is questionable whether I could have finished the effort in one lifetime. With the good fortune to have the *Journal* available on computer, I hoped to be among the first to mine its depths and get some good data to the marketplace of ideas.

## Notes to abridged edition (Volume 1 - Main Presentation)

The goal of the original research project was to identify and explain every one of the significant doctrinal and policy issues or problems that arose in the Brigham Young period and have come down to us by myth and tradition in various, usually garbled, forms. The result was a rather large book. The reactions of reviewers indicated that few people had the interest, patience, or the academic preparation to work through all 60 of the resulting chapters/topics and to integrate that huge mass of information into a coherent view.

It has been suggested that the entire book should be restructured and re-written to make it more comprehensible. I don't disagree, but merely lack the many months of strenuous editing time it would take to make such a major revision. The best I can offer is a separation of the core materials from the extensive peripheral issues, the separation of the central idea from its much larger web of related ideas.

Thus, the original and unabridged edition (the "Casebook Edition"), at 650 letter-sized pages of small print, was considered too large and complicated for practical publication. Sixty percent of the contents dealt with topics other than the main presentation on the united order. These other topics come from the same milieu and have many interactions with the united order topic. For my own purposes, I considered it necessary to cover these other topics in detail to fully demonstrate that my underlying theory was accurate and well corroborated. However, many readers may be less interested in these sides issues and may be content to examine just the central issue, itself complicated enough. Some of the side issues and their interpretations may also appear to be more controversial than the main united order issue.

For those who wish to explore all aspects of the approach I have taken, including some discussion of disagreements with other writers, I have prepared a second volume to contain this extra material. Those interested may order the 450-page *Brigham Young's United Order, A Contextual Interpretation; Volume 2 - Related Anomalies and Side Issues* [from Amazon.com starting in about August 2020.] [Obsolete note: "[order] by sending $40.00 to: The Huff Residence, 1224 West 7300 South, Spanish Fork, Utah, 84660. If the number of orders proves large enough, a more economical edition may be possible."]

As another alternative, copies of the original complete work have been placed in the special collections of major libraries such as those at Brigham Young University, the University of Utah, and the Church Historian's Office.


## Chapter notes

[1] David Chirot, ed., *The Crises of Leninism and the Decline of the Left: The Revolutions of 1989* (Seattle: University of Washington Press, 1991). xiv.

[2] Stephen Thornley Evans, *Voluntary Redistribution of Wealth Under Capitalism: The Future United Order*, Arizona State University, D.B.A. 1979 (Ann Arbor Michigan: University Microfilms International, 1979).

[3] Kent W. Huff, *Joseph Smith's United Order: A Non-Communalistic Interpretation* (Orem, Utah: Cedar Fort, Inc., 1988), hereinafter identified as JSUO.

# BRIGHAM YOUNG'S UNITED ORDER:
## A Contextual Interpretation

### Volume 1 — Main Presentation

### CHAPTER SUMMARIES

### INTRODUCTORY SECTION

## Preface
An incorrect understanding of church history can cause problems today.

## 1. Interpreting History and Economics.
"Intellectuals, politicians, and journalists rob leaders of choice when they consecrate policy as doctrine." (cited in chapter.)

## 2. Introduction to the United Order.
The united order represented locally created societal substitutes for the missing state and local government powers and processes, and the missing economic and business structures. Having these substitutes was necessary for the survival of the saints.

## THE PROBLEM

## 3. The World's Hostility
Religious persecutions have always succeeded if the persecuted were temporally weak. Brigham Young knew this well from his experience in Missouri and Illinois. The world hated the Mormons for the very fact that they were so righteous and cooperated together so well, and that they were so capable economically and threatened the political and economic power of the people they lived among. They were also easy to steal from and so they suffered more perhaps than if they had been a ferocious people (and therefore worse Christians). The fulsome doctrines of the saints contrasted sharply with the competing, far less defined religions of those around them, especially the southerners.

## 4. A Strategic Overview
The saints could not stay in the borders of the United States without being exterminated. They were reluctant to go further west, but were finally given no choice in the matter. After reaching Utah, they had a prize piece of real estate astraddle the lines of communication to California and the west coast. They had the mountains and prairies to protect them even from a federal army. The saints' holding of both a very desirable and a very defensible location, gave the easterners the incentive to claim the place as their own, but prevented them from doing so by force, leaving only negotiation as a realistic solution to the "Mormon" problem.

## 5. Overview of Political Power Relationships

The saints were usually quite weak in relation to the easterners while they were within the United States, although there were a few times of apparent strength, or at least ability to control their own environment. They did not accept the slave culture of the South and so were in conflict with that group. After they reached Utah they were more protected, but could have been swept off again with the coming of the railroad had not the Civil War devastated the entire eastern portion of the American continent. After that time, the saints had reached a substantial size, one that could not be swept away by the powers of brute force that the US could then muster.

## 6. Slavery and the Territories

The settling of Utah occurred at a time of great national conflict over the slavery issue, which ended in the Civil War. Utah could have become a slave state.

## 7. The Utah War

The reasons for sending a federal army to Utah in 1857 are not terribly clear, except that easterners for various reasons wanted to get complete control of the strategic Utah area and dispossess the saints again. The army's Southern general and the Southern governor to be installed probably had the additional goal of making Utah a slave state.

## 8. Weaknesses in Territorial Government: Utah as a Third World Country

Utah was treated much as the British treated the American colonies as far as their granting of local government, etc. In spite of this unfair treatment, Brigham Young managed to control the land, resources, and money of the people there, and engaged in economic development activities in much the same way other third world countries today keep control of their own resources and destiny. Trade restrictions, immigration restrictions, currency controls, and controls on acquisition of property were among the techniques used.

## THE RESPONSE—BRIGHAM YOUNG'S UNITED ORDER

## 9. An Historical Overview of the United Order in Utah

There were many manifestations of the united order concept, teachings and practices. Among the earliest was the assistance rendered to each other in moving to Missouri, then to Nauvoo, and then to Utah. It became a more formal idea in 1854, was re-emphasized in 1864 and 1869, and in 1874 reached its most complex form. The urban forms and the rural forms were quite different.

*Building the City of God*[1] deals mostly with the 1874 version of the united order, but that is merely one manifestation, and perhaps not even the most important. Many preceded it.

## 10. The Original Concept/Impulse: A British Institution.

Brigham Young was impressed by the English international corporate forms where government and business combined their "imperial" interests, such as the British East India Company. He thought it would be a suitable model for the Mormons in Utah.

## 11. Brigham Young Rejected the Acts "All Things Common" Tradition.

Contrary to most current traditions, Brigham Young was strongly against the idea of the "all things common" societies and their sharing of property described in the Bible and Book of Mormon. He no more wanted socialism than Joseph Smith did, but he did want economic success, and worked hard to teach people how to do it and to create institutions that could assist.

## 12. Explanation of "All Things Common" References.

The scriptural cases of "all things common" are explained as tribal survival techniques necessitated by extreme physical hardship, deprivation, scarcity, and danger.

## 13. United Order Types.

The largest form conceived of was the 1874 version explained by Erastus Snow. Smaller ones such as Orderville existed as well. In all cases, coordination, specialization, and efficiency were the most important concepts, not communal ownership and leveling.

## 14. Brigham Young's Temporal Philosophy.

Brigham Young used some doctrinal and much practical persuasion in his arguments for cooperative efforts. But he was actually in the middle ground between such men as Orson Pratt and George Q. Cannon who took strongly ideological views on these matters, and John Taylor, the consciously non-ideological person who took a practical view wherever possible, and resisted any hint of socialism/communism.

Brigham Young might better be compared with today's Dr. Deming who taught the Japanese about cooperation and quality in a large corporate setting. Brigham Young had some success in introducing the principles of modern bureaucracy among the unsophisticated Mormons.

## 15. Comparing the Brigham Young and Joseph Smith United Orders.

Many imagine that the organizations of Joseph Smith and Brigham Young were quite similar. They were not, but their goals and teachings were similar. Contrary to common tradition, both were strongly anti-socialist.

## 16. Multiple Contemporary Viewpoints.

The leading brethren were not all in agreement on the nature of the economic problems, their solutions, or the applicable principles.

## 17. The Judgement of History.

As President, John Taylor rejected the united order tradition, and later leaders did not re-embrace it.

## 18. The Mystical Nature of the United Order Tradition.

No one can understand and or explain the united order traditions, yet people cling to them, even though many mortal centralized institutions are destructive of both freedom and economic success.

### 19. Gini Ratios, Equality, and Developmental Economics.

Brigham Young had little interest in making people economically equal, although he encouraged equality in educational opportunities. His policies tended to make people unequal, as the more talented controlled more resources. This is consistent with current research on economic development of third world countries.

### 20. Poverty and Inequality - Reason and Cure.

Brigham Young had no desire to encourage poverty by subsidizing it. His plan was to give the poor every incentive and opportunity to improve their own economic status. He would teach them and help them learn useful skills. Equality of opportunity through schooling was his goal.

### 21. Rich Men and the United Order.

Creating wealth was far more important than redistributing it, and men of talent were needed. Brigham Young found rich men easier to work with in reaching his goals.

### 22. Treasure and Heart.

The phrase "where your treasure is, there will your heart be also" was given a new meaning with overtones of force when it was proposed to cause a man to place his treasure in centralized administrative circumstances so that he would then be compelled to join the group and attend to "his" property.

### 23. Tithing and the United Order

Some united order organizations were used to enforce the payment of tithing, recognizing tithing as a higher law.

### 24. The United Order and Communism.

Brigham Young apparently never mentioned any connection between the united order and communism, and far as the Journal of Discourses goes. John Taylor was firmly against any idea or practice from the communist/socialist school of thought. George Q. Cannon seemed willing to accept their ideas and goals to some extent. After Brigham Young's death, one person specifically denied that the united order was French Communist, but still seemed to accept a few of its concepts.

Note: Two other chapters were originally intended to be placed here, but because the materials are already disseminated throughout the book, they were not consolidated in this edition.

### United Order and Territorial Legal Considerations.

Governmental and legal matters had enormous effects on the saints. Laws regarding property titles, corporate organizations, other economic organizations, taxes, anti-polygamy laws, limits on church property holdings, and powers of the territorial legislature were among the most important.

**Traditions.**

The saints inherited many religion-related traditions, both good and bad, and Brigham Young and others created some of their own Some inherited traditions caused problems, and even some of Brigham Young's own teachings returned to cause him difficulties.

MODERN INTERPRETATIONS OF TEMPORAL ISSUES AND TERMS.

**25. Latter-day Prophets on Welfare Topics.**

All principles of the gospel, including consecration, can be lived within the boundaries of the current church programs.

SUMMARY AND CONCLUSIONS

**26. Summary and Conclusions.**

The united order traditions from the 1800s are not accurate doctrine. The difficult problems caused by the church's enemies made improvised solutions necessary. We should not let our past enemies and hardships define the ideal future for us.

# Chapter notes

[1] Leonard J. Arrington, *et al, Building the City of God; Community and Cooperation Among the Mormons* (Salt Lake City, Utah: Deseret Book Company, 1976), hereinafter identified as BCG.

CHAPTER 1

# Interpreting History and Economics

It can be difficult work interpreting the words and actions of past prophets. The Brigham Young era is close enough in time that we may think we should be able to understand it easily, and yet the circumstances were far outside the experience of most of today's church members. There is a great deal that can be "lost in the translation" when we do not know the exact context in which words were spoken and actions taken. "Likening the scriptures (or history) unto us" can be carried too far. In the most general matters such as faith and repentance there may be little difficulty, but when we come to less important or more detailed or complicated teachings or administrative matters, the difficulty may be great. The Brigham Young era produced numerous words and actions that are puzzling to many still. The term "anomaly" is sometimes used to describe these instances, although there may not be complete agreement on which are "anomalies" and which are not.

There seems to be a general tendency in all religions to transform into doctrine what was only ad hoc reaction to circumstances at the time of the statement or event. If we lack all the data to fully evaluate historical events (as we always do) we may wish to err on the side of extreme caution. Where personal salvation is at stake one might hedge his bets and err on the side of excessive orthodoxy lest he be charged with ignoring or trivializing some important doctrine or event.

This seems to be the approach of the law of Moses: Where the mind can not or will not discover or grasp the general principles involved, safety is sought in exhaustive detail of requirements and action, where rituals replace thought.

## Internal versus External History

The thesis of this book, that Brigham Young's programs were, by necessity, aimed at survival, is greatly at odds with the usual interpretation of those events. Most writers on the subject have assumed that the behavior was not driven by pressing external factors, but was engaged in for its own sake, perhaps as a means of self-flagellation or self-improvement, as a test of obedience, as an encouragement of humility, or fulfilling some obscure commandment. I believe that is an error and that only by being aware of the external factors and pressures is there any consistent way of explaining what happened and why.

In other words, the church history that Brigham Young created was largely a consequence or result of external history. Church historians may do us a disservice by making the internal church history the only history or even the most important history.

For the most part, I have not tried specifically to refute the logic or conclusions of other writers. It seemed more useful to concentrate on presenting the alternative view. Perhaps later a comparison study can be prepared. Nonetheless, a few comparisons will be found throughout the book, such as in the chapter dealing with the welfare programs of the 1930s.

## Interpreting History

An interesting current events newspaper article of December 10, 1992, may serve to make my general point concerning the incorrect interpretation of church history:

### The Somali Plan is No Bush Doctrine.

As President Bush on Friday explained his dispatch of U.S. forces to Somalia, he sounded eerily similar to President Harry Truman justifying massive new U.S. aid to Greece and Turkey more than 45 years ago.

Within days, Truman's carefully crafted language became raw meat for ideologues casting about for something to worship or hate and for journalists eager to make government policies far clearer and more momentous than their authors intended.

Over time, they elevated his address into the Truman Doctrine and stripped away its distinctions and qualifications. If economic aid went to Greece and Turkey to stop communism, they came to ask, why not military aid to Vietnam, Nicaragua, or anywhere else for that same noble purpose? With intellectuals, politicians and journalists now clamoring again for simple answers and proclaiming "turning points" and "watersheds," Bush will have difficulty explaining the limits of his Somali decision. It could easily assume the dimensions of a Bush Doctrine with unfortunate consequences for Bill Clinton.

For of future presidents it will be asked: If Somalia, why not Bosnia, Liberia, Armenia and all countries drowning in civil wars and humanitarian disasters?

The last Cold War president clearly had such thoughts in mind while fashioning his announcements about Somalia. He may even have reread the March 1947 speech of the first Cold War president.

Bush spoke of "starvation" and "anarchy" in Somalia. Truman said Greece lacked the essentials "for bare subsistence" and was threatened by "terrorist activities."

Bush explained that righting the situation in Somalia was beyond the means of the U.N. Truman said he had decided that the U.N. was incapable of "immediate action" and "not in a position to extend help of the kind that is required."

Bush insisted that "America must act." Truman said that the U.S. "must supply ... assistance," and that "there is no other country to which democratic Greece can turn."

Truman sensed the trap in his own words: Justifying aid to these two countries might spark demands to contain the spread of communism worldwide by any means, indiscriminately.

Dean Acheson, his secretary of state, rushed to head off just such interpretations. He told Congress that all future aid requests would be judged "according to the circumstances of each specific case." But these central and fine points soon vanished in the political intellectual maelstrom.

Bush's intent is also limited to use force to end starvation in Somalia. But he, too, knows he is opening the door to pressures for humanitarian intervention everywhere. He walked this line Friday as best he could:

"I understand the United States alone cannot right the world's wrongs, but we also know that some crises in the world cannot be resolved without American involvement."

Defense Secretary Dick Cheney also scrambled to underline the "case by case" nature of the president's decision.

Whenever policy makers try to do something creative or deal with a new challenge, they cross traditional lines. Truman did so by asking for foreign aid to halt communism. Bush did so when he justified military intervention on humanitarian grounds.

But by crossing lines and establishing new policies on Greece or Somalia, neither wished to tie his own hands. On the contrary, each meant to give himself fresh choices for new circumstances.

Intellectuals, politicians and journalists rob leaders of choice when they consecrate policy as doctrine.

Policies provide general direction and yet allow flexibility on ends and means. Doctrines virtually eliminate choice: either intervention is always called for or it is never permitted. Doctrines demand consistency over good sense.

They demand answers in advance, where there can be only questions.

To me, Bush made the right decision in Somalia; but he is wrong not to back greater force in Bosnia.

Yet his choices on Somalia and Bosnia should have little bearing on what Bill Clinton should do in Somalia, Bosnia, Haiti, Liberia or Central Asia.

Presidents should always set directions but, especially in a messy world, retain the leeway to choose. It is pundits, not presidents, who carve new policies into doctrinal stone. It is the nation that pays for this orthodoxy.[1]

How does this quotation relate to the distant past of church history? Historians and other authors, normally not general authorities, have evidenced a strong inclination to build up some of Brigham Young's economic policies into a rigid doctrine and requirement, and, unfortunately, the writers have been quite successful in their efforts (perhaps because of lack of competition), even though in recent times the real leaders have been careful not to make the rigid statements that the writers would like to see.

Incidentally, near the beginning of the quote there is a potential play on words concerning the phrase "consecrate policy as doctrine." If we rephrased it in church terms to "consecration of consecration," we would have an interesting recursive statement that contributes to my point.

It is my opinion that the long term meaning and effect of the economic materials from the Brigham Young period has generally been misinterpreted by historians and others, and given meanings that are inconsistent with the Gospel, with the then-contemporary interpretations of the Brigham Young era itself, and with interpretations of those same matters by church leaders today.

For example, if church members are led to believe that socialism and communism and the gospel have much in common or are identical, then much damage will be done. The idea of doctrinally required pooling of property under a single leader has been used in our time as a means of exercising unrighteous dominion and exploitation and caused apostasy and confusion.

These bad effects of incorrect historical interpretation should be counteracted. Perhaps this book can bring a little competition into the marketplace of ideas on this topic.

## External Factors

One interesting "external factor" may help start the process of seeing the world as Brigham Young saw it. The physical location of the Utah settlers had many important consequences. The great distances back to the "states" provided a strong defense, but also imposed corresponding economic costs. A current article arguing for an expanded communication infrastructure describes the economic effects of the railroads which may help illustrate one of the technology factors of Brigham Young's time:

> As Kevin Costner was told in [the movie] Field of Dreams, "if you build it [a baseball field in a corn field], they will come."
>
> If you doubt that article of faith, consider the effects of the other public infrastructure this nation has built.
>
> The railroads united this nation by making it possible to traverse the continent. And they ushered in the Industrial Age.
>
> I've done some reading about railroads, and one author's analysis struck me. He made the point that before railroads, the cost of transportation was such that, after moving something just 150 miles, the transportation cost grew higher than that of the article itself.
>
> Railroads changed that equation and permitted us to tap this nation's vast natural resources. They spurred the development, manufacture and distribution of products no one could have imagined at the time those rails were first laid on the ground.
>
> As with railroads, I envision the government's role in this information infrastructure as facilitator, not builder.[2]

From the beginning, Brigham Young wanted economic gains and profits for the saints on the scale illustrated and made possible by the railroads. Although he might have feared the negative social effects of the coming of the railroad, he actively supported their construction, presumably seeing far more gain than loss to the saints, as, for example, the costs and dangers decreased for bringing in immigrant converts.

His greatest united order proposal came just at the time that the saints could truly be integrated economically into the national economy and did not need to suffer (any more) the problems of the usual third world country (isolated by expensive transportation) that exports only raw materials and must pay very dearly for the few imports it receives, is subject to mercantilist practices, etc.

On the other hand, before the railroads came, the enormous costs of importing goods made it imperative that, if the saints were to maximize their wealth (and thus strengthen their defenses), they should not spend it on outrageously expensive transport, but create needed products themselves. With the main manufacturing centers 1,500 land miles away (implying up to a ten-fold increase in price due to transport), the resulting huge "import tax" of transport gave a great economic incentive to create local industries. If the large transport costs were paid to support and attract outsiders (and potential enemies), the result was doubly bad.

Brigham Young was trying to amass as much surplus as possible to gather more saints, build up industries, and ensure survival. With the high transport cost, members could expend most of their year's wheat crop on a few trinkets from the East. This would be a great loss to the church as a whole, where feeding newcomers had a much higher social value. Brigham Young wanted to go far beyond hillbilly subsistence farming, but many members did not see the need.

At the same time, before the railroads, any army moving toward Utah would face the same enormous transport costs. This was the great barrier that gave relative safety to the saints for their first 20 years there.

One of the assumptions of this book is that there is no such thing as a magical mystical earthly economic system that can make people better and richer, but wherein the people need not understand it, but only need to "follow the rules" in a Law of Moses or Pied Piper style. I contend that only if people thoroughly understand the economic consequences of their acts (and everyone else's' acts) and choose wisely based on the use of that knowledge, can an unusually successful economic order be built up.

"You can't cheat an honest man" is an old aphorism. My interpretation of it is that in order to be thoroughly honest, a man must be thoroughly experienced and familiar with every aspect of a transaction that might go awry or that might offer a chance for one to take advantage of the other. With that deep knowledge, plus a determination to do right, then the man can be very honest, and also, as a byproduct, be a difficult man to trick or deceive.

As a small example of attempting to analyze economic plans and programs, here are some notes on a current event:

In January of 1993, one of President Clintons' first acts after inauguration was to seek passage of and sign a law requiring employers to grant family leave benefits to their employees. Although that particular law does not require salary to be continued, there are still many costs involved, such as continuing all other benefits such as health insurance, etc. There may be overtime payments for other employees required to keep up with an unchanged workload, lost business because of disruption of contacts and work flow, extra training costs to temporarily prepare a substitute, putting a generalist into a specialist slot, etc.

In this family leave plan, if ten are working and one takes off, then the remaining nine are paying for the tenth's benefits and doing his work. If salary were required, then they would be paying that also. Even without the salary, the government is here requiring the employer to enforce this transfer payment, possibly under threat of fine or other punishment. One might think that if the government thought this was an important benefit, it ought to provide for it itself, as it does now for unemployment. In order to do that it would have to explicitly tax someone to raise the funds, thus running the risk of taxpayer ire. Instead, it puts the burden of the taxing and transfer payment on the employer. The government takes the credit for the perceived gain to workers at no apparent tax cost. Of course, there is a tax cost, but an ignorant (or grasping) public does not see this or chooses not to see it. Another "soak the rich" plan goes into effect, and charitable impulses are subverted by the force-based solution imposed by the government.

There can be many benefits from cooperation at all levels of society, but governments typically seem to want to have the gain and benefit of them all or to seem the author of all of them. Such governments are quite willing to force people into cooperation and then take the credit and a large part of the gain. The government goal is not "uplift the downtrodden" but to increase the power and fame of those in control. They are enjoying social engineering which really means "do it my way."

Although they often argue otherwise, governments do not have a patent on the idea and benefits of cooperation. However, they can require or prevent cooperation, and then extract the loss of one group for the benefit of another, taking credit for that transfer payment. They usually subscribe to the labor union logic of using force to get gain (a topic mentioned frequently in the Book of Mormon). There are a multitude of other ways that cooperation can be instigated, at family, church, neighborhood, and city levels, etc.

Since the church today is a large organization and might conceivably expand and take on broad governmental roles, people in the church today may have the same impulse or desire to use the church to enforce transfer payments. (Of course, we already have transfer payments within the church, but they are both modest in size and voluntary.) If it were not otherwise directed, the church today might have the same impulse, that is, to do or promote something that may benefit some people, but to then take or claim credit for all or nearly all of those benefits for itself. Or as Brigham Young seems to have considered, if all money goes through the church, then it should be easier to get the tithing flowing to it more reliably. This could be like the church today deducting tithing from the pay stubs of its employees. Would that be a convenience to make sure no one forgets, or would it be a coercion? If the church took on a larger economic role, questions like this would surely multiply rapidly.

## Chapter Notes

[1] "The Somali Plan is No Bush Doctrine," *The News* of Mexico City, Mexico, December 10, 1992, p. 24. (vol. vliii No.157.)

[2] John Young, "The Coming Information Age: Computing and Communication as Ubiquitous as Electricity," *Washington Technology*, Dec. 3, 1992, vol. 7 No. 17., p. 13.

CHAPTER 2

# Introduction to the United Order

The previous book in this series, *Joseph Smith's United Order: A Non-communalistic Interpretation*, shows that Joseph Smith was against communal economic systems. In contrast, most people think of Brigham Young as promoting communal economic systems. Why do we have this contrast?

After Joseph died, it was many years before the Brigham Young united order was taught and begun. The new teachings and programs began in 1854. This was 10 years after Joseph Smith's death and seven years after the saints had arrived in the Salt Lake Valley. We might wonder why it was delayed so long and what was its purpose.

We might begin by referring to the single canonized revelation that was given to Brigham Young, that he was to form companies and assign captains of hundreds, fifties and tens (D&C 136:3) and march them to the West. In that setting the wagon train master was the leader for nearly all purposes. It seems that Brigham's command lasted for the thirty years that he was president of the church, and, perhaps better than any single reason or text, explains his actions and teachings during that 30 years. Brigham Young had lived through several of the mobbings that occurred in Ohio, Missouri, and Illinois, and if there was one thing he was aware of, it was the hostility of the world towards the saints. As the "trail boss," his main concern was to keep the saints safe from any further displacement and devastation as they had had in the past. This was an overriding concern in his life; perhaps we could even call it an obsession. In his mind, the prime goal was to build up the saints in numbers and economic, political, and military power at a rate sufficient to keep them protected from the world. He often despaired that the saints would ever learn to care for themselves. He seemed to feel entrusted with a bunch of welfare cases!

As the East grew larger and extended its reaches west, the danger to the saints from the clash in cultures would increase, but if the saints grew in strength sufficiently, they could always be just one step ahead of the Easterners and therefore survive. On September 13, 1847, when Brigham Young had been in Utah only a few weeks, he expressed the thought "Give us 10 years and we will be able to fend off the easterners without help".[1] He had a chance just ten years later to test his statement when an army was sent out to put down a supposed rebellion. As he said then, the only problem the saints had was that they had three or four times as many men as it would take to "use up" that army. In Utah, they were in a very defensible position, not only because of the rough terrain getting into the mountains and the many places for guerrilla fighters to hide in the mountain valleys, but also because there were huge stretches of prairie to cross. At that early time the logistics of taking an army to Utah were very difficult. For one thing, it was not possible for an ox-drawn wagon to take enough food along to feed the oxen all the way to Utah. Obviously, if the wagons were to carry any cargo for an army, the oxen must be fed from other sources. It was fairly easy for raiding parties to burn up the fodder that was available on the plains, or to interfere with supply depots, destroy wagons, or steal draft animals, as the army soon found out. A thousand-mile-long supply system was simply impossible to defend without an unbelievably large expenditure of resources.[2] Brigham Young seemed to sense all the parameters that made up the strength which would keep the saints safe from extermination by a hostile East. He had a simple but powerful program of bringing in as many immigrant saints as possible, while encouraging those who were already in Utah to grow much grain and save it to feed those newcomers. The high rate of immigration caused many difficulties to all involved, but it was an important undertaking. A small group of saints might be scattered and few in the world would notice or care (as had happened before), but displacing a large group is not so easy, especially when the cost of sending an official mob was so expensive.

On the occasion of the coming of Johnston's army, Sam Houston in Texas had observed that if, instead of sending 5,000 troops, they had sent 50,000, then all that would have done is cost the government 10 times as much; they still would not have accomplished anything more than they did, which was nothing. When the army arrived there, its existence was at the mercy of the saints. There was no way that that organization could feed itself. They had to rely on purchasing goods from the saints to survive. Later on, of course, with the coming of the railroad, those logistics problems were changed, but by that time the saints were much larger and, of course, the railroad itself enabled a larger number of the saints to be transported out there quickly.

The railroad also allowed more easterners to visit Utah and determine for themselves the conditions there. They could not be fooled by hostile rumormongering as before. For example, President Grant, after seeing the families and children of the Mormons, noted that he had been deceived in the reports he had received.

This goal of improving public relations through "tourism" was a goal in Nauvoo as well as in Utah. The saints were told to build the Nauvoo House hotel in Nauvoo, but they failed to build it as soon as they should have. Its purpose was to allow men of influence to come and determine for themselves that the saints were peaceful, decent people and ought not to be persecuted and driven.

The graph in chapter 5 entitled "Relative Power" is intended to portray the fact that Brigham Young finally accomplished his purpose of creating an immovable object. The saints could not be dislodged from their place by the time of his death. Easterners could continue to harass them and cause various troubles, but extermination or removal was no longer a question. When the Vice President of the United States asked "Will he fight?" everyone knew the answer was "Yes," and Brigham Young would either win, or exact a dreadful price from his attackers.

The extermination order in Missouri was a simple matter to carry out, with the government directing its forces to disarm the saints under color of law for supposedly peaceful purposes, and then allowing the same army in the form of mobs to harass and drive them out, taking all their property and some of their lives.

When Brigham Young spoke in Utah of the saints' failure to live the "united order" in Missouri, it is likely that what he really meant was that they had not reached the advanced military/political/economic order and discipline necessary to hold their ground. Later at Nauvoo they made up for much of that lack, and held off attacks for some time, but finally were forced to withdraw lest they face the entire might of the westernmost states and the Federal army itself. In making that criticism of the early Missouri saints, Brigham Young was trying to get the Utah saints to unite and avoid a similar fate.

So if we look at Brigham Young's philosophy on these questions, his main thrusts were, first, that he should be the leader of the people for all purposes, as Joseph Smith had been, and, second, that property and men should be matched up in the most efficient combination to gain the largest growth, to be the most economical, and so on. He actually seemed to care little for the philosophical questions of equality and other matters which were much more discussed by his counselors and others than by him. If one attempts to find a consistent doctrinal or ideological pattern in any of his teachings, other than maximum growth and strength, it will be a difficult task.

Throughout his life in Utah, Brigham Young accumulated much property, directed factories, and was the overseer of many business operations. His great practical skills were put to extensive use. His property was more or less matched with his skills, and he accomplished much with it; this was actually what he preferred that others do as well. Some of them, then and now, imagined that his holding of property rather than putting it into some communal order was inconsistent with his teachings, but it was not. It may have been inconsistent with some of the teachings of others around him, but not his own.

As described in JSUO, Joseph Smith did accomplish some mighty feats in organizing and financing the gathering of the saints on the western boundaries of the United States, and preparing a people for the next stage of the church's movement and growth. He did not spend his time and exercise his gifts quite as much in those practical areas as did Brigham Young, but he had and exercised many other gifts. His clear, consistent, thorough, philosopher's view of everything allowed him to be the conduit for pure eternal truth.

Brigham Young put a tremendous stress on his position as leader of the church. It takes some special understanding of the circumstances to see why that was so. Though for a short time he was governor of the territory, during most of his time there he had no constitutionally authorized power over the people. For the saints to have any semblance of an effective administrative society, a single person had to have all the constitutional powers informally vested in himself much like a tribal chieftain. Brigham Young was that person, the lawgiver for all purposes.

This is in stark contrast with the conditions in Nauvoo where Joseph Smith was legally and constitutionally elected as mayor of the city, was the general of the army, the Nauvoo Legion, and was the president of the church which was legally recognized and organized under the laws of the state. Joseph Smith held all of these positions of power in a perfectly constitutional and legally recognized way. He even ran for president of the United States legally.

We do have the exception of Joseph Smith leading the Zion's camp "irregular" unit under the Lord's direction, but we might wonder how Joseph Smith would have fared in Brigham Young's place, trying to improvise a whole society with no legal basis, often having to act in direct conflict with "legal" institutions. It could be a difficult and untidy business. As Wilford Woodruff's journal records, Brigham Young found it necessary to campaign for what might be termed "political" support, going ward by ward, swearing people into the united order. In this way we might say he was organizing an unofficial but controlling political party.

Again, all of the normal, legally recognized structures were denied to Brigham Young. It appears that much of the unusual organization which he proposed for the church members in Utah was related directly to this question of creating effective organizations there, independent of the obviously weak and inadequate and even hostile territorial government. A state organization would have allowed them to solve most of their legal and governmental problems, but since the saints were largely denied self-governmental powers, for 50 years they had to use other means.

Without that key thought concerning lack of a constitutional basis for organizational action, there is probably no way to understand much of what was said and done. For example, what about the very basic process of acquiring, improving, and transferring property? For the first 22 years in Utah there was no provision for holding title to property. That was surely disruptive in managing practical affairs. As another example, how did they defend themselves against Indians and other hostile groups? The Nauvoo Legion, headed by a counselor to Brigham Young was THE military organization for twenty-five years in Utah. Now, what was the constitutional basis for the Nauvoo Legion? There was none at all. It was an organization outside of any legally constituted program, no more than a citizens' militia.

What did they use for a corporate law to allow them to replace weak and unstable partnerships and associations with organizations which could accumulate large amounts of property and use it efficiently? There was no legally available way to do that. Therefore, other organizations known as "orders" were created for that purpose. The common law partnership is a tenuous mechanism. Many economic projects were unsuccessful partly because, with no stable law under which to operate, anyone having contributed property could then easily cause the organization to be dissolved under some partnership theory. As a result, there could be no long-term planning -- they could not know how long an economic unit might be in existence. That was a severe economic handicap.

There surely was some temptation to re-interpret and re-use the "deed that cannot be broken" scriptural language to help solve these major economic/legal problems. It might seem to be the means of holding capital together for an extended period. Of course, even a corporation can be dissolved, but it is usually more difficult than with a partnership, requiring at least a majority vote, where a partnership may be dissolved by a single partner. The problem with using the "deed that cannot be broken" concept (besides the fact that there was no such thing as a legal deed until 1869) is that the term in its scriptural use applied to quite a different and less complicated situation. During the Joseph Smith period it merely covered, in a few cases, farm land that was given to the church, either to assist the poor to have a temporary place to live and earn a living, or in exchange for other land to be provided by the church at the end of one of its migrations. The "cannot be broken" part was to make sure that the transfer was legal and final, and that the land could not later be reclaimed at a disruptive time. It only applied to land that ultimately was held and owned by individuals, and involved no major improvements such as factories, etc.

Another way to view the "orders" is as a means of creating an oath-based or religion-based organization as a substitute for the missing legal basis. The risk of loss of salvation becomes the "consideration," the force for keeping the organization intact. It is the furthest from gold as a "consideration" for business transactions as one can get. It is an unmeasurable, uncertain quantity which is non-transferable, non-fungible, and non-divisible. With no certain enforcement techniques, it becomes a blunt and unrefined tool for attempting to organize sophisticated economic activities. It has some *in terrorem* value, but its incentive value is unpredictable and unreliable.

No force of state law and regulation would be available to control the use of this "spiritual currency." A bishop's court is probably not well suited to the task either. The result becomes more of a tribal kind of entity with their "favors and bartering" economies. Tribes are notoriously unable to accumulate capital, so the wisdom of using such a mechanism is questionable, except as a last resort. The same might be said for most communal organizations.

How about a system of criminal and civil law -- for crimes and contract problems? There was no court system available to the saints that would allow these things to be settled in a reasonable way. There were courts in existence, but they were often either not available to church members or they were hostile. So another system had to be invented using local authorities, the bishops.

Joseph Smith was able to hold a mayor's court or a meeting of the city council or other court such as a justice of the peace to enforce the law in an orderly fashion. Brigham Young was denied that power.

We might wonder whether one reason state government was denied to the Utah saints was BECAUSE of the success of the Nauvoo Charter, which gave the saints in Illinois safety and order for a time. Joseph Smith carefully crafted those legal arrangements for just that purpose. See later materials on civil war incidents for other explanations for the delay in statehood.

How about organizing cities? Without a state it is difficult to have an incorporated city which has powers to operate. Therefore, you have again the problem of empowering some kind of government, the bishops again being the most available magistrates to exercise those powers. This might be done by consent of the governed, but not through any law of the land that sustained it. Since direct enforcement was not possible, there would be a temptation to invent dire religious consequences for the deviants.

One interesting episode which illustrates the unofficial but real government of Utah occurred during the Civil War when there was a need to have someone protect the telegraph wires in the western area. There was a constituted governor of the territory from whom President Lincoln might have requested assistance. But, of course, the practical, real authority in the area was Brigham Young, acting in his unofficial, let us say non-constitutional, role as head of the people there. He was the real governor. Rather than go through an obvious figurehead, Pres. Lincoln communicated directly with President Young and asked him for assistance in the matter, and of course it was given and handled with dispatch.

The slave/free question of the time likely had a hand in the federal army coming to Utah in 1857-1858, with a southerner as general. The southerners would especially have a reason to want to keep Utah from becoming a free state. A review of the five years leading up to the civil war would be useful, including the Dred Scott case with its overturning of the Missouri Compromise, the Kansas Act, etc. See chapter 6 for more on this topic. The army which came out in 1857-1858 had been greatly humbled by the loss of supplies and the spending of a very cold winter in the mountains of Wyoming. It stayed for just a few years, and then in 1861 at the outbreak of the Civil War, left Utah and returned to the States. Some of the officers from the Utah army were killed while fighting for the south.

The Civil war caused about two million casualties, including 600,000 dead, which meant that hardly a family was untouched. Perhaps one out of three men of military age were casualties of some sort in the war. This surely weakened the country a great deal and probably greatly lessened the easterners' desire to wage civil war of any sort again, and surely was a great assistance in protecting the saints.

Soon after the end of the Civil War, the railroads came west and the access of the easterners to Utah was much easier and faster. Those impenetrable barriers of prairie and mountain were no longer very effective. But where the original expedition against the Mormons had been started seemingly almost on a whim and on false information, in the new postwar social setting such a blatant attack on the nation's own citizens could probably not be begun so easily without a public outcry. This less bellicose reaction might be somewhat akin to the Vietnam syndrome of our own age.

In 1896, when Utah was finally granted statehood, it was reported there were 240,000 people in the territory. That very respectable number is four times the minimum necessary in other cases to form a state. The Mormons had shown themselves to be such a durable, tenacious, and incessantly growing group, that it was useless to make further attempts to break them up or wrest political control from them through either force or chicanery.

In summary then, the united order, or, rather, the united orders, since there were so many different kinds, can probably best be explained by a desire for maximum efficiency for the saints for their own protection. In other words, these orders were not created for some separate or independent doctrinal reason which would require the saints to organize in a preset pattern regardless of the circumstances they found themselves in. In many circumstances, accepting such extensive church control over our economic matters might give some substance to a charge of being a "cult."

In reality, and in the context of Brigham Young's time, the problem or the circumstances which confronted the saints also defined the organization (or lack of it) necessary to react to the problem. From this we might conclude that the rule would be the same today, that the saints would have an organization which would suit their needs at the time, with no rigid preconceptions as to what was required. If they are able to live without conflict among the Gentiles, then they will be allowed to do so and no particular organization will be necessary except for dealing with welfare problems ("the poor are always with you") and questions of common interest such as buildings -- chapels and temples. However, if social matters deteriorated greatly, so that it was a matter of physical survival as it was in Utah (or in the small civil war in "Bleeding Kansas"), then perhaps the centralized economic, even semi-military organization of Brigham Young's time might then be re-created for the same reasons. But that, we would hope, would be a very unusual situation, for defensive purposes only. It might be noted that the church is part of the "Israel program" and our own and biblical history indicates that we might have problems like the Jews, being driven and persecuted. It could happen again.

I believe this need for defense for physical survival explains the other instances in the scriptures and in the histories where communal living was required. Required communal living is a partial description of a military organization, complete with a quartermaster corps and a military procurement system. It applies as well to a semi-military organization such as a tribe where there are warrior and worker roles, and resources are shared, because without the sharing there would be suffering and hunger and death for the whole group. The subsistence lives of many tribes are examples of this.

In the following chapters I hope to demonstrate in greater detail the central theme of Brigham Young's awareness of the massive security problem the Saints had, and of his strenuous efforts to solve it in a very sensible and practical way. Along the way, while striving with these mighty problems, Brigham Young always seemed to understand what needed to be done and how to do it. The purpose or the goal of different activities always seemed to be quite clear to Brigham Young. However, it seems that some of his explanations to others about the reasons for doing certain things sometimes were not so clear. There is a class of teachings or comments from him and his contemporaries which have in later years been shown to be simply untrue, not part of the Gospel. Some of these, what I shall call "anomalies," will be dealt with in later chapters. It will be shown that the reasons for them can logically be traced to Brigham Young's concern about carrying out his role as leader of the people, as the prophet, as the commander of the armies of God, as he viewed it. Nearly all these "anomalous" teachings were associated with improving his power to lead them, or the power of the people to control their own destinies and their own growth.

This survival drive and the associated need to accumulate power wherever possible, is really the central theme, the unifying theme for Brigham's life and teachings. Those who read on may find some difficulty in dealing with those instances where what Brigham Young said has since proved incorrect or has been retracted by others. However, distressing those topics may be, it appears that they must be dealt with because otherwise we can't really understand all the story. But lest that become a stumbling block, the reader should focus on and remember the mighty mission which Brigham Young carried out. Once we can see the situation with the same fear and trembling that he held, the same life and death concern over the Saints, and the creative aspects of his solutions, we can appreciate the amazing work which he did. The other matters will fall aside as interesting side issues, but nothing which interferes with our view of him as a mighty man and a prophet of God. He was human and therefore less than perfect, but a mighty man indeed, the Lion of the Lord, as he was called.

It seems that many of the saints did not share Brigham Young's vision, did not understand the circumstances they were in. They perhaps wished to just go into some nice mountain valley and forget the world that had caused them so much trouble. But they weren't allowed that luxury. If they and everyone were to survive this 30-year ordeal, they had to work together, they had to set strenuous goals and accomplish them. Much of what Brigham Young said was to stir them up, to get them going in the right direction, to convince them of the need to act, even if delivering a few hell, fire, and damnation threats was necessary to get their attention. Different versions of the "general orders" to the saints were presented in the 1850's, the 1860's, and the 1870's as conditions and needs changed.

One of his early techniques was presenting "wave of history" arguments dealing with the requirements and conditions of the future, both in heaven and on earth, and linking the two together. This kind of rhetoric has proven to be effective in stirring up people and societies to action. As an example, Marx was a contemporary of Brigham Young's and taught his own materialistic version of a millennial vision which has certainly affected many nations since. Almost every group has such a vision, whether it is accurate or not. It is interesting to find that one of the brethren felt he had to declare that his version of an economic plan was not French Communism. There is nothing terribly wrong with Brigham Young and others using this rhetorical technique for influencing the saints, except that it leaves many puzzles for those who come later, read his words, and try to relate them to their own time.

The most all-encompassing statement of his economic goals was made in 1874, and included centrally directing and coordinating all the property and labor in the entire territory. The 1875 visit to Salt Lake City of Baron Rothchild, the European banker to kings and ministers, who met with Brigham Young, probably shows a desire on the part of church leaders to get funding for some large scale development, using some kind of taxing or "tithing" scheme as a means of repaying the loans, with property or mortgages held centrally and given as collateral, that property having been accumulated by "consecration." WWJ 7:253. The 1870 visit to Salt Lake City of the President of the Bank of England, including several meetings with the church leaders, probably was part of the same kind of effort. WWJ 6:572.

It should be useful to review the economic arrangements of Joseph Smith's time and compare them with the Brigham Young period. Joseph Smith had a need for an organization to solve a serious church problem, and he carried it out under the Lord's direction in the context of the social/cultural/legal context of his time. He created a central church business organization that was able to function until the Twelve and more formal corporate means were able to be brought into use.

In a similar way, Brigham Young also used various temporary means, but to a far larger extent than Joseph Smith ever had to resort to. He used temporary "extra-legal" means to run the entire state, all the affairs of the church and its people, including civil, criminal, military, and economic matters. Later, after his death, as constitutional means became available, other more normal ways were be used to carry out these things. So as these normal, constitutional means became available, Brigham Young's temporary kingdom and its associated united order mechanisms were no longer necessary to replace those parts that were missing.

In the same way we might expect in the future that if there are major failures in our society, if our social, criminal, military or economic areas fail, at that point, substitute measures might need to be created and operated much as Brigham Young did. (This brings to mind the World War II situation where the Germans were subject to blockades and had to resort to creating substitutes for many needed materials. The German term Ersatzmittel (substitute) describes this process from which we have adopted the term "ersatz" to describe a substitute or "make-do" replacement). In each case where a change was needed the solution would depend on the problem at the time. As one example, the church has various welfare farms which are used for normal crop growing, dairy cattle, etc. At one time it was thought that in the event of serious social disruption, some of the welfare farms might be used as safe-havens. In the event of a serious problem, the farm would be large enough so that church members could flee there and survive in a stressful situation. The land would then be worked to produce food products directly for people, support gardens and so on. Whether that emergency plan is still in effect I don't know. The church in some areas may be too large at this point for that. But that was a thought within my lifetime, in and concerning the Virginia and Maryland Saints.

Perhaps the point of greatest interest and greatest concern, the lesson we might learn from this, is that we can live the law of consecration, we can live all the laws of God, without being yoked to an arbitrary organization determined from some past social time. We might compare this situation to the charge often made against the nation's army -- the generals are always getting ready to re-fight the last war -- so that when a crisis comes, the plans, methods, and reactions are inappropriate and even disastrous. Hopefully we will not suffer from that problem of backward-looking rigidity. One humorous example is the army artillery practice of assigning men to hold the horses before each artillery round was fired, which practice continued even after horses had been replaced with trucks. Rather than being driven to instigate some arbitrary organization which might take away our freedom and property for some inappropriate goal, perhaps just for the purpose of humiliating us, we should expect an enlightened view, an enlightened direction in what we should do to adapt to each changing situation.

In today's world, where the technology is different, the society is different, all the nations are different, we would never expect or desire to have to retrace the steps of Brigham Young, except in a most unusual chain of events. For that reason, we should not be in too much of a hurry to return to yesteryear, or to assume today that every small change in church administration or church policy is somehow the signal that this ancient order, whatever it may be, is about to be dropped on us.

There may still be reasons to keep alive this fear or this tradition, this preprogrammed response, to encourage instant obedience without having to explain what is going on. But hopefully no one would ever try to make use of that psychological power over the people, or if there is actually a need, that it be a very short-term matter, an intense emergency. Breakoff groups from the church today regularly use that technique to maintain power over people in an unrighteous manner. There would have to be strong justification to use that lever today.

To keep our perspective on this whole matter, we should again remember that Joseph Smith was against this kind of program, that is, required socialism in any form. To him an "order" was any kind of social organization or program whether it was tithing, priesthood quorums, or the Gilbert and Whitney store. He used an "order" as much as he needed to for church business reasons, but otherwise was against commanding the saints to create any particular economic organizations.

After Brigham Young's death, John Taylor was the next president of the church, and the question of what programs to begin or continue was his to answer. After wrestling with this problem, he circulated a letter in which he stated essentially that, <u>he didn't know if there was such a thing as a required united order, but even if there was, whatever Brigham Young did wasn't it</u>. In other words, as far as he could tell, there were no doctrinally required organizations, or at least none which should be continued. There may have been an original impelling economic or social need, but if so, it had passed. He did not continue those earlier programs, perhaps because at the time of his presidency, a large number of the problems that the saints had been struggling with were overcome.

It should be clear to anyone who thinks about the saints today, if they were to organize into a tight economic block for what they took to be their own benefit, this would almost certainly be perceived to be to the detriment of other groups of people. It would cause envy and friction and would be counterproductive in the saint's mission as leaven in the loaf, spreading the Gospel to the world. In fact, as you might suspect, the brethren have cautioned us not to do that, one instance being in the 1970's. In that case, we were not to join together economically in a way that would be the least threatening or disruptive to local retail businesses. Wards handling large food supply orders for their members was one example. As a tax-exempt organization, the church's relationship with the Internal Revenue Service may also have been a factor.

We might say that our relationship to the world today is the exact opposite of what it was in Brigham's day. We can join them instead of being forced to fight them. As to living the law of consecration in these times, a discourse by President Kimball in the October 1977 *Ensign* (quoted in a later chapter) seems to be a well thought out and integrated statement on how we should view welfare and consecration today. It should be noted that in the discourse there are no overtones of any specific required forms of organization involved.

A few comments about the governmental aspects of the united orders might be interesting. In the Utah territory, it was often hard to tell the difference between territorial taxes and church tithing. Many inhabitants thought of tithing as a tax. Some united order organizations were required to pay tithing for their members, much like the way income taxes are withheld by companies today. This makes tithing a corporate or governmental function rather than the more individualized approach we use now.

One consequence might be that people cease to feel the responsibility (or get the blessings) themselves. One of the reasons for such a program was that the individuals were not paying an adequate tithing. Ironically, the "greater law" of the united order was thus instigated as the means of enforcing the "lesser law" of tithing. A successful tithing program would have obviated at least that portion of the stop-gap "united order" device.

The united order was not the only mechanism for unifying the saints. Other elements used to bind the saints together included age-old tribal mechanisms such as the giving of daughters in marriage. It was a 300-mile trip from Salt Lake City to St. George by wagon or horseback which obviously could involve many days of travel, and therefore would tend to very limited communications and very loose control of that remote area by the church center in Salt Lake. Therefore, when the presiding authority in St. George, Wilford Woodruff, is given in marriage the daughter of the President of the Church, Brigham Young, one might reasonably speculate that there was some organizational purpose involved. Any means of binding that important outpost closer to the center would be useful. The binding together of distant leaders through marriage makes it look like a Biblical kingdom such as Solomon's.

Of course, there were other power principles involved, such as polygamy, which is a power principle in the sense of its making sure that the reproductive powers of the saints are put to the best possible use. Those bachelors who are left without a wife are encouraged to find one, converting one from outside the church if necessary.

The ward, then and now, has some of the elements of a tribal unit. There is a single head for all administrative purposes, the bishop. The unit is sized small enough to allow everyone to know each other and assist each other, and yet large enough to allow some economies of scale in building, activities, etc.

St. George was one of the first places to try the 1870's style corporate form of the united order. Perhaps St. George was the most likely place for starting a large agri-business or plantation style facility. Perhaps that is why Brigham Young was so interested in it. Wilford Woodruff was greatly interested in agricultural matters, and would have made a good overseer for that area. In other parts of Utah there were ranges for cattle which were only profitable by using a very low per-acre productivity, but doing it over a large area. There were other areas that were suitable for only individual farming. They would not sustain high output, labor intensive crops, and so would not be tempting places to try the ideas attempted in St. George.

The united order and polygamy ideas are both power doctrines. If one cannot instigate all power doctrines at once, which do you do first? Logically you would do polygamy first. It takes little central organization, or any organization at all, for that matter, and so should be easy to install. One of the desired results, conservation of women, needs to start immediately. The other goal, more children, is a "long lead-time item," to use today's military procurement jargon, and so should be started as soon as possible.

Of course, although the practical aspects of starting polygamy are very simple -- simply pair them up and marry them -- it may be quite another matter to convince people to do it. How much pressure and rhetoric was needed and devoted to polygamy to get it started? Was it enough to use up seven years of time, from 1847 when they reached Utah, to 1854 when the united order ideas were first announced? Polygamy was formally announced in 1852, but that was not the first use of it.

The united order, meaning the economic stimulation, rationalization and integration of labor and capital for maximum efficiency, required a much more complex level of social organization. Was the heavy preaching load required to get polygamy started enough to delay the introduction of united order organizations and associated teachings? Does it take even more preaching to get the united order started? It seems to, probably because the people must change the way they work and interact with everyone else.

Perhaps another reason for delaying the introduction of the united order ideas was that during the first seven years until 1854 they were already so bound together in their pioneer activities that it was redundant -- Brigham Young would have been preaching to the choir. John Taylor alludes to this idea of spontaneous assistance to each other based on early circumstances.

Perhaps after the saints had been in Utah for 7 years, they had reached the end of their initial spontaneous cooperation, and were starting to miss opportunities for large economic benefits through cooperation. They may have been comfortable themselves, but they were perhaps not creating enough excess output to fund the huge number of emigrants Brigham Young wished to be transported to Utah and supplied with food, clothing and shelter during their initial time there.

In 1854 an early version of the united order was introduced, in 1864 it was reemphasized, and in 1874 there was another revival of the idea. At least for the 1874 version, we have notes from Wilford Woodruff's journal which show that besides the conference talks which we have in the *Journal of Discourses*, we also know that the brethren went from ward to ward committing people to become members of the united order. This ward to ward visitation sounds like political grass roots campaigning, and might be called "stumping" in any other setting. I don't know exactly what those ward level commitments meant or contained. It would be nice if we had a copy of the oath if they took one, or of the talks that were given. What were these people committing to do? The most likely thing was that they were simply committing to follow the leadership of the prophet, and do whatever he said. That would give him maximum power, and therefore give the saints the maximum power, because they would be organized and coordinated.

We should note that some of the more extreme doctrines that were presented along with the united order were taught by such men as Orson Pratt, who wrote *The Seer* and *The Equality and Oneness of the Saints* in which he talked about the ideas of union of property, equality, and related things. Brigham Young really didn't talk about those ideas very much. He apparently encouraged other people to speak on those topics at times, but he didn't really articulate those same ideas in the same way. George Q. Cannon was another who was often pressing for organizations, being quite pleased in several cases where groups had joined together to do their farm work. He was very optimistic about it, and tended to glide over any errors of judgement and any foolish projects, saying that even if they made mistakes, they were better off together than separate, which, of course, isn't necessarily true. It is standard procedure in third world, communist, or authoritarian counties to carefully exclude accidents, errors, crimes, etc., from the news, lest the government be embarrassed, or the people learn of these things and feel less accepting and supportive of the government. The myth of progress, justice, efficiency, perhaps even omnipotence, etc., is supposedly kept alive that way.[3] There seems to be some of that same spirit (of, dare I say, propaganda?) with some of George Q. Cannon's statements where the message was often "Don't give me no bad news!" He seemed to ignore problems and liked to say that only a "want of system" prevented success. That, of course, can be an enormous "want." By that same logic, it was only a "want of system" that kept us from having mass-produced automobiles during the middle ages.

In contrast, we had such men as John Taylor who received the doctrines with skepticism. Because it was the prophet speaking, they accepted it, at least the actions expected, but they never really accepted the implied ideology. Others did the same; they thought it sounded like an interesting idea, good for some purposes, but they weren't sure they wanted to do it. Centralization, especially ideologically-driven centralization, might have good effects, but it might also have some bad effects. John Taylor avoided ideological reasoning and preferred to use other more common and observable practical economic reasons or needs to explain certain behavior or economic programs. And, ultimately, when he became president of the church, he rejected the unique doctrinal nature of it and discontinued the united order teachings and programs, although he probably retained the idea that members should always be willing to do what the prophet says.

The full implementation or the full vision of the last, 1874, united order, contemplated the joinder of all property (or at least some significant level of property rights held in central trust) so that it could be used as the basis for borrowing money for development. This is exactly the way third world countries do today, using government debt to fund economic development. They even had Baron Rothschild, the financier from Europe, to Utah for a visit on November 1, 1875, good timing if one were serious about using united order property for loan collateral. I presume they discussed the possibility of doing some of the normal development transactions, which would normally include making plans to use the tax base to repay the loans. However, in the Utah situation, with no church control of the legal system and thus the tax base, it was more likely that the property would be mortgaged to reach the same result.

Third world countries normally rely on a taxing power to repay debt. Brigham Young probably had no reliable way to legislate and enforce taxes. But this may partially explain why units were set up which paid corporate tithing to Salt Lake. This would serve much the same purpose as withholding taxes do today in meeting government revenue needs, including bond interest payments.

Having explored the background history, we might consider some specific programs. Brigham Young first implemented his 1874 program in St. George by starting an agribusiness and trying to build essentially a corporate organization with long-term commitment of properties. He had been trying for many years to find ways to keep properties intact within a corporate framework. There were other examples such as Lehi where it was recommended that valid common law measures be used such as articles of association or deeds of trust be used with the appointment of trustees to manage the property. The result would be a pseudo-corporate form.

There was Brigham City where most of the economic operations of the city were directed and controlled by just a few very able administrators. That was the practice -- finding very able men and empowering them, assigning property to them, and allowing them to direct the city's labor force. They became for most purposes like the salaried professional managers of today's corporate form. The pseudo-corporations of the time replaced the banking/finance/venture capital/stock market functions of today which lodge property ownership where it can be most productive and reach its highest potential and use. They were striving for efficiency; that was the common goal.

One of the goals of their leaders apparently was to accumulate as much capital as possible to build up the city businesses. Today's corporate property holding and accounting methods accomplish much the same goals. It would be useful to have all available convertible currency in the hands of the "corporation," so that special equipment might be purchased from outside sources. If they let the city residents be paid in real dollars, there was the risk that the concentration of investment in the city's businesses could not be maintained as people spent their earnings elsewhere. So they used their own form of nonconvertible currency or scrip. Later, the city was fined and greatly damaged economically by a hostile U.S. government for inventing and using their own form of currency or scrip.

They were attempting to do something like was done later in Russia. By owning all property and having a nonconvertible ruble, the Russian leaders could control or prevent nearly all exchanges with the outside world, and maximize their internal economic powers. They could direct the economy in the way they wished. To the rest of the world, their citizens could do no more than carry on a tribal barter economy. Even inside the system, barter would be the basis for much trade activity. There have been many "company towns" with similar regimes since Brigham City in the 1800's, but most have not had to contend with such a hostile government as existed in Utah.

Even Orderville seemed to have that same nature, that is, combining property into a corporate form to achieve efficiency through specialization. However, they went somewhat beyond the secular efficiencies visibly provided by such an organization, and employed doctrinal or ideological arguments to support their particular organization and property ownership form, making it "required" in a moral sense. Living and eating in communal arrangements and wearing the same clothes provided early economic efficiencies. However, making those temporary efficiencies into a required doctrinal sameness went too far. This doctrinal sameness was rejected later as being inappropriate, but perhaps it may have been encouraged at that time just to see the effects, as an experiment. It did promote the goal of a corporate (or corporate-tribal) framework for property accumulation, utilization, and exploitation.

Their version of a closed system was found to be an error, and they were counselled to change the form to a more open system. This would avoid rigidity and the tendency of the first owners to keep control of all the property without any market-based or merit-based transfer to the younger generation. One might say that they had added tribal or feudal elements to the corporate form, somewhat like the Japanese of today.

We should note that later on, probably after Orderville and similar events, the brethren had to undo some of their past claims. They had to say over and over again that diversity was good, perhaps to undo some of the harm done to the program by the excess conformity of Orderville and similar places. By overdoing the unity idea they seemed to get a backlash. The young people in the Orderville community felt squelched and did not expect to be able to get a share of the system. Perhaps the oldsters thought they owned all the "stock" and would not share with the younger generation. This might be compared to excess tribalism, where the chief owns it all, in a feudal structure like the international communist movement of recent years.

Some of these ideas and specific projects such as Orderville and Brigham City seemed to be mixtures (or admixtures) of both cooperation and coercion, good and bad, good impulses and bad impulses, all mashed into one. This merging of one system with another was done with a sloppy intellectual basis, perhaps an "inspired ignorance" or "muddling through." This is in sharp contrast with the precision of Joseph Smith on doctrinal and ideological matters. Perhaps it was necessary to have a person like Brigham Young who was willing to "break a few eggs to make an omelet." Joseph Smith might have found it distasteful, however necessary it may have been.

In today's large corporation we usually have the elements of management, labor, ownership, and debt financing mostly separated and compartmentalized. We might also find these elements integrated at any percentage level. The separation options were not possible in Brigham Young's time. Without money systems, ownership systems, and supporting laws and institutions, building complex and differentiated organizations is extremely difficult to do. Instead, they had to do it all in bootstrap fashion, the workers also being the owners and financiers, with managers chosen from among them. Methods of societal "status" were relied on more than "contract."

If we had sufficient data on all these early organizations and the processes by which they were formed, we might find a general pattern. Perhaps the various types of units were tried partly to see which would get the best corporate efficiency results, since apparently no one knew exactly how best to do it.

It is interesting that early in the ideological discussions, in 1852 and 1857, John Taylor gave talks which showed the folly of communism. He had obviously studied it very thoroughly, and felt many aspects of it were clearly wrong. Apparently, to Brigham Young it was less clear that communism was wrong. He neither praised nor condemned it, but rather seemed to avoid discussion of it altogether. Of course, any philosophy that accomplished the combination of capital for economic efficiency, especially if done voluntarily, would be a very powerful growth enabler and a potential source of strength to the saints. Some version of communism may have seemed to promise that result. Karl Marx, a contemporary of Brigham Young, propounded various theories about historical progressions concerning communism and capitalism, with great expectations of economic plentitude at the end. One historical rumor has it that Karl Marx actually visited Salt Lake City.

Many of the orders that were formed, as in Richfield and other places, were organized for only one or two years, and then discontinued. Although the usual practice seems to be to condemn these efforts as failures simply because of their relatively short life, there may be another explanation for some of them. If one is only interested in promoting some particular ideological position or result, then an apparently abortive attempt to institutionalize that ideology might be viewed as a failure. However, if only pure economic progress is measured, then some of these projects might be found to be significant successes.

For example, there would be large and clear payoffs in fencing land in a group to save efforts, or in combining efforts for building irrigation systems and so on, but once these initial infrastructure projects were finished, then the military togetherness would be less valuable. These methods might prove efficient for a time, but might become inefficient where each person would be best employed as a steward over his own lands, caring for them, and seeing that they were producing well.

It is interesting that the outlying areas, those areas away from Salt Lake City, were the most likely to have the most intense communal efforts. Perhaps the more remote they were, the more need for togetherness there was, the more they were like a pioneer company and needed a semi-military organization. Orderville was pretty remote. Such places were somewhat like today's kibbutzes [kibbutzim] in Israel, with their farming/military/tribal organization.

It is possible that the people in the far-out places might feel religiously superior to the city folk if they felt they were living a higher law. They were in fact contributing greatly to the security of the city dwellers of the Salt Lake area. Perhaps they ought to have some psychic rewards for their greater risk and hardship.

In the larger settled areas such as Salt Lake City and others, the intense communal sort of behavior was generally not engaged in, and of course, there was no particular reason that they should. They were not in nearly such hostile conditions, and could turn their attention to such things as trade and manufacturing which people in more remote areas could never do. In settled areas, the skilled people could be more efficient working in facilities created just for them and their economic needs, their factories and shops, etc. Except in times of fires or attack, there would be no particular reason for them to be rigidly coordinated in their activities by some central command and control center.

Some of the ideological confusion of the Brigham Young era might be partially explained by a recent newspaper article about Jonas Savimbi, the leader of an anticommunist rebel group, UNITA, in Angola, Africa:

He is sophisticated enough to understand the irony in the fact that he practices socialism in Jamba while advocating a market economy for Angola. "We are an army at war," he shrugs, "not a normal society."[4]

If we realize that Brigham Young was in a war mode much of the time, we may better be able to understand what his real intents and purposes were, and not be confused by any particular event or statement.

There are several things we might learn by comparing Brigham Young's problems and solutions with those of the Soviet Union from 1917 to 1989. The two societies had some similarity of problems and strengths, both ideological and practical. The basic problem in each case was to take an unsophisticated people and introduce industry to maximize economic growth and power. The direction of the people had to be drastically changed. Each leader wanted to charge up the masses to move in the direction he foresaw was best, that is, toward development of industry among a largely peasant population. The two basic means available were ideology (a positive method) and force (a negative method). Both ideologies promised to change the world, the Soviets with their transnational view of communism taking over the world, by force if not by conversion, and the LDS expectation that the gospel would reach everyone before the millennium, with no force on the part of the saints, but some assistance from heavenly intervention.

Brigham Young could use ideology to keep down consumption and maximize economic growth and emigration of new people. He could attempt to direct the energies of the people to meet the strategic goals set by him, often quite contrary to the natural inclinations of the people. He would want strong central control of the economy and to ensure its contribution to the center's resources. He needed income through taxes, tithing, profits, contributions or any other means. Brigham Young could not use much negative repression, but he could use negative ideology to scare people about their salvation and their future status in heaven.

Stalin used force and deception to collect the maximum from the peasants to invest in industrial progress. He used ideology where possible, but when that waned as an effective influence, he and his successors turned almost solely to police repression to control the people and the resources they produced. In 1920 40% of the soviet citizens were illiterate. They knew little and could be made to believe almost anything. In that case a command economy worked fairly well. A time finally came when there was no more illiteracy, and the government had to meet the needs of a better educated people, who could see and understand many options, alternatives, and points of view, and who rejected one-dimensional policies. The resources collected before had been used to build a large version of already outdated German heavy industry technology, which, when completed, would be very much out of date.

Some observations from a book on the Soviet Union might be enlightening and further help to draw some parallels between the two societies' buildups to be ready for conflict with outsiders. The first comment is on the backwardness of many of the people involved in the Soviet case:

> In any case the Muslim peoples of Soviet Central Asia and the Caucasus were then still so backward that their identity was defined by family, tribe, clan and religion rather than nationality; in other words, they were in a prenationalist stage.[5]

Many of the Utah people seemed to lack the sense of "national" cohesion necessary to accomplish the church's (or kingdom's) mission.

> In some cases, centrally controlled economies have an efficiency advantage:
>
> ...
> [C]entral planning could indeed serve well in wartime to produce arms and ammunition in response to fixed specifications and quantity targets, but that it could not channel the right amounts of the right resources into the very many, very varied and always changing paths of peacetime economic development.[6]
>
> ...
> Actually superior to any free enterprise system in a warlike environment in which the goal is the supply of a few essentials for civilians and the maximum output of a fully specified range of products for the armed forces, ... the Soviet economy becomes less and less effective as its setting is further and further removed from that of a war economy.[7]

In the Utah case, grain, shelter, forts, and clothing were the things needed to get emigrants there and care for them. Getting those emigrants to Utah was a large part of the "war" they were fighting. Brigham Young surely sensed the efficiencies involved in centrally controlled, focused cooperative behavior, and wished to exploit it. But it was tough to get people into the warlike mood without actual conflict. (Anciently, Enoch was at war with the world, probably making it easy to get conformance and sacrifice). Could Brigham Young get the same support from the saints as the communists got, but without using force? What sort of preaching or propaganda is necessary to get people into that mode? The Russians used Draconian punishments to force the people and get results. It is hard for us to recognize the efficiencies without also getting confused by the ideology. Brigham Young used a version of the "we'll take over the world" logic and stimulation to get an effect on the Utah populace similar to the stimulation of the early transnationalist ideas of the Soviets, before they abandoned that logic and again glorified Russian nationalism.

## Chapter notes

[1] The actual statement was "...ten years ago on this ground I stated that we would not ask any odds of our enemies in ten years from that date ...". JD 5:234. Sept. 13, 1857. SLC.

[2] JD 5:234. Recently, in an unusual opinion article in a Utah newspaper, someone commented that a guerrilla war against the saints would still be a very hard thing.

[3] For notes on the force of ideology in Soviet television, its enthusiasm and its careful exclusion of any accidents, mishaps, or errors, see Ellen Mickiewicz, *Split Signals, Television and Politics in the Soviet Union* (New York: Oxford University Press), 1988.

[4] Jeane Kirkpatrick, "Still Moscow's Satellites," *The Washington Post*, Monday, June 18, 1990. page A13.

[5] Edward M. Luttwak, *The Grand Strategy of the Soviet Union* (New York: St. Martin's Press, 1983), p. 8.

[6] Ibid., p. 24.

[7] Ibid., p. 38.

*Introduction to the United Order*

CHAPTER 3

# The World's Hostility

Brigham Young had the opportunity to prove both the negative and positive portions of John Stuart Mill's observation on persecution in his *On Liberty*:

> [T]he dictum that <u>truth always triumphs over persecution</u> is one of those pleasant falsehoods which men repeat after one another till they pass into commonplace, but which <u>all experience refutes</u>. History teems with instances of truth put down by persecution. If not suppressed for ever, it may be thrown back for centuries. To speak only of religious opinions: the Reformation broke out at least twenty times before Luther, and was put down. Arnold of Brescia was put down. Fra Dolcino was put down. Savonarolo was put down. The Albigeois were put down. The Vaudois were put down. The Lollards were put down. The Hussites were put down. Even after the era of Luther, wherever persecution was persisted in, it was successful. In Spain, Italy, Flanders, the Austrian Empire, Protestantism was rooted out; and, most likely, would have been so in England, had Queen Mary lived, or Queen Elizabeth died. <u>Persecution has always succeeded, save where the heretics were too strong a party to be effectually persecuted</u>. No reasonable person can doubt that Christianity might have been extirpated in the Roman Empire. It spread, and became predominant, because the persecutions were only occasional, lasting but a short time, and separated by long intervals of almost undisturbed propagandism. It is a piece of idle sentimentality that truth, merely as truth, has any inherent power denied to error of prevailing against the dungeon and the stake. Men are not more zealous for truth than they often are for error, and a sufficient application of legal or even of social penalties will generally succeed in stopping the propagation of either. The real advantage which truth has consists in this, that when an opinion is true, it may be extinguished once, twice, or many times, but in the course of ages there will generally be found persons to rediscover it, until some one of its reappearances falls on a time when from favourable circumstances <u>it escapes persecution until it has made such head as to withstand all subsequent attempts to suppress it</u>.[1]

Brigham lived through the early and unsuccessful attempts to withstand persecution, and, with great power and conviction, saw to it that in Utah the saints were finally strong enough to withstand it once and for all.

Unless we grasp the depth of the mortal threat to the saints, and the desperate need for the defensive responses crafted by Brigham Young, we can never understand the meaning of the teachings and policies related to those defenses. The term "united order" and a dozen other related ideas from that time can only be understood in this "martial law" setting. What follows is not a history of the times, but only a partial listing of events which showed the unreasoning and implacable hatred of the saints' enemies.

As the Saints were being expelled from Missouri, the Governor, who issued the Extermination Order, informed his military commander that he preferred that they all be killed, including women and children, but he left the final choice to that commander. (JD 5:337 BY OCT 18, 1857 SLC). Luckily, the commander chose not to obey that suggestion.

The saints were thrown out of three more intervening places before they reached Nauvoo, where they finally had a time to recuperate and consolidate. The arrest of Joseph Smith was contrived using his enemies' favorite, but always disproved, charge of treason. (Treason, if proven, would probably have the convenient result of leading to a death sentence.) The Governor of Illinois, having been warned many times and having heard the boasts of the mob, was fully aware that his leaving Carthage was the signal to kill the Mormon leaders.

The government required the saints to leave Nauvoo under pain of death. As the Saints were preparing to move west, they were required, again under penalty of death, to provide 500 men to fight in the war with Mexico. The loss of the help of those men was a direct threat to the already precarious lives of the five-times-dispossessed and struggling saints. Having been cruelly expelled from the boundaries and protection of the United States, it was a wicked blow to then threaten their lives again if they did not assist that country in its wars.

The saints had difficulty in finding any way they would be allowed to support themselves on Indian or government land. It was obvious that the organized state and federal governments wished that the saints would perish by the elements instead of directly by the hand of those governments. They were left alone in Utah under the assumption that they would probably perish there, and that was nearly the outcome, prevented only by divine intervention.

The coming of the Federal army in 1857 could hardly have been for any but the most hateful reasons. The standard charge of treason was mentioned again (implying death to the leaders of the "uprising"). The original commander of the army, General Harney, was known as the "Squaw Killer" for his massacres of Indian villages. The final commander, General A. Sidney Johnston, was from the slaveholding south. He later led one of the southern armies in the Civil War and was killed in battle.

The decision to send the army was made in secret, and the mails were immediately stopped in an effort to prevent those in Utah from becoming aware of their impending fate, and to prevent any defensive preparations. No attempt was made to investigate any of the rash charges made against the Mormons. A bit of irony occurred when Brigham Young, having received no official notice (because the army had stopped the mails) of his being discharged as Governor of the territory, declared that the approaching army was a mob and would be dealt with as such. (JD 5:336)

A combination of factors, including bad timing, snow storms and Mormon raiders, conspired to give the army a long and unpleasant winter in Wyoming. This helped the Mormons make it very clear that the army, with its very long supply lines, could never survive an attack on the Mormons. Others might come to avenge them, but that particular army would be annihilated. Based on that logic, the army did not carry out its oft-repeated boasts concerning the destruction of the saints. There would be no more surrenders to a hostile government, leading to the slaughter of the leaders as occurred in the Joseph Smith case, and to another dispossession or destruction of the body of the saints. The line had been drawn in the sand, and Brigham did not blink.

When the army left in 1861 to join in the War Between the States, mostly on the southern side, they were under instructions to destroy all weapons and supplies that might be of any use to the saints. This shows a continuing war footing and hostility.

(It should be noted that the territories all supported the North, so if it had been a Northern army, the materials might have been left. The southern makeup of the army may explain part of the antipathy. In other words, did Lincoln give the order or was it the local (southern) commander's idea?)

Later, in 1869, there was other talk of more armies, but by that time the saints had grown immensely in size, and the intervening devastation of the Civil War probably would have made another attack on a "seceding" state subject to very close scrutiny by an exhausted and better-informed public.

Through all this, Brigham Young's goal was to accumulate the people, land, and economic and political strength to deflect any attacks made against them. Finally, that was accomplished, and the saints were allowed to merge with the rest of the population and move to a new stage of growth and development.

Let me make it clear that I have no interest in bringing up these old animosities for any other reason than to show the mindset of the Mormons in the 1800's. Their condition gave rise to certain policies and ideas that cannot be understood without a clear understanding of their setting as they perceived it. Hopefully, clarifying these points will actually contribute to even more peaceful relations today by showing that Mormons have undergone extreme persecution in the past but have done no more than defend themselves when there were no other options open to them.

There are numerous discourses in the *Journal of Discourses* commenting on the hostility of the eastern gentile establishment for the "Mormons." One of the better examples is an address by Brigham Young in August 1862:

A KNOWLEDGE OF GOD OBTAINED ONLY THROUGH
OBEDIENCE TO THE PRINCIPLES OF TRUTH.
Remarks by President BRIGHAM YOUNG made in the Bowery,
Great Salt Lake City, August 3, 1862
REPORTED BY G. D. WATT.

The way of life and salvation is mapped out so plainly in the Old and New Testaments that any man may read and understand, yet people do not understand. The most approved geography and map fail to give a description and delineation of any people or country so perfectly as to exclude all possibility of more being known by personally visiting and examining the country or people described. A mere geographical description has a claim only upon our belief, but to gain a perfect knowledge of the country or people described it is necessary to visit that country and people; having obtained this knowledge, you in turn become a witness to others of what you have seen, heard, handled, or felt. So it is with the Gospel.

We may read the history of the life of Christ, admire his moral and religious teachings, be impressed with awe by the description of the character and works of the Father and God of the universe, be made acquainted with the means he has devised to prepare mankind to enter his presence, but it is necessary that we should follow Christ, put into actual practice the lessons of Christ, and obey the ordinances of Christ, to know for ourselves the saving effects they produce in mankind. A mere theory amounts to but little, while practice and obedience have to do with stern realities. In this way the ancients obtained a knowledge of the true God. "And we know that the Son of God, is come, and hath given us an understanding, that we may know him that is true; and we are in him that is true, even in his Son Jesus Christ. This is the true God, and eternal life."

Although the character of God is plainly described in the Scriptures, yet mankind do not understand it, but have imagined to themselves a God without form or location. It is written in the Scriptures, "God is a Spirit: and they that worship him, must worship him in spirit and in truth." Again, "But the natural man (or as we now use the language, the fallen or sinful man) receiveth not the things of the Spirit of God: for they are foolishness unto him; neither can he know them, because they are spiritually discerned. But he that is spiritual judgeth all things, yet he himself is judged of no man." In no other way can the things of God be understood. Men who are destitute of the influence of the Holy Ghost, or the Spirit of God, cannot understand the things of God; they may read them, but to them they are shrouded in darkness.

We try to tell the people how to be saved; and if we have not the fulness of the Gospel, it is not upon the face of the earth. If we have not the Priesthood of Heaven, it is not possessed by any people upon earth. The Priesthood of the Son of God to the children of men is a perfect system of government — a heavenly institution among men — designed to bring them back into the presence of God to partake of the fulness of his glory. The power of all truth dwells in the bosom of our Father and God, which he dispenses to his children as he will, by the means of his eternal Priesthood. He is enthroned in the light, glory and power of truth. He has abided the truth, and is thereby exalted, and his power, light and glory are eternal. The Gospel and the Priesthood are the means he employs to save and exalt his obedient children to the possession with him of the same glory and power, to be crowned with crowns of glory, immortality and eternal lives.

"We alone have the words of life," is a great saying; who can bear it? "If you Latter day Saints are the only people who have the words of life, why are you so despised, hated? Why have you been under the necessity of leaving your homes and possessions?" For no other reason than the following: — "God ministered unto him (this first Elder) by an holy angel, whose countenance was as lightning, and whose garments were pure and white above all other whiteness; and gave unto him commandments which inspired him; and gave him power from on high, by the means which were before prepared, to translate the Book of Mormon, which contains a record of a fallen people, and the fulness of the Gospel of Jesus Christ to the Gentiles and to the Jews also, which was given by inspiration, and is confirmed to others by the ministering of angels, and is declared unto the world by them, proving to the world that the Holy Scriptures are true, and that God does inspire men and call them to his holy work in this age and generation, as well as in generations of old, thereby showing that he is the same God yesterday, to day, and for ever. Amen." This is all the reason that I know of.

"Have the Mormons been persecuted for their evil deeds?" If they have, shame on their persecutors, for if any Latter day Saint breaks the law of his country he is amenable to that law, and it provides a suitable penalty. The latter day Saints live and always have lived in a land of law, and if they have transgressed the law, shame on a community, like the people that live under the Government of the United States, to persecute them instead of prosecuting them. An instance cannot be found upon the records of any court in the United States where the leaders of this people have been legally convicted of a breach of law and order.

Joseph Smith was arraigned before Judge Austin A. King, on a charge of treason. The Judge inquired of Mr. Smith, "Do you believe and teach the doctrine that in the course of time the Saints will possess the earth?" Joseph replied that he did. "Do you believe that the Lord will raise up a kingdom that will fill the whole earth and rule over all other kingdoms, as the Prophet Daniel has said?" "Yes, sir, I believe that Jesus Christ will reign king of nations as he does king of Saints." "Write that down, clerk; we want to fasten upon him the charge of treason, for if he believes this, he must believe that the State of Missouri will crumble and fall to rise no more." Lawyer Doniphan said to the Judge, "damn it, Jud[g]e, you had better make the Bible treason and have done with it."

I was not in Missouri at the first of our people's going there, but I have searched diligently to find whether any of the Latter day Saints have ever been convicted in any of the courts of Missouri for transgressing the law, and, so far as I could learn, such an instance cannot be found on the court records of that State, "Then why are you persecuted?" Because the Lord has committed unto us the words of eternal life to deliver to the world, which, if they will obey, will bring them back into the presence of the Father and the Son.

The world will not receive the Gospel, unless they can have it on their own terms, and will persecute the few that do receive it. We preach the truth as it is in Christ Jesus, and this gives offence to the wicked; they become angry with God, with Jesus Christ, and with his Saints; God and Christ they cannot reach, but the Saints they can persecute as long and as much, as they are permitted.

"But were you not persecuted for teaching that odious doctrine called Polygamy?" No. We were planted in these valleys before it was publicly made known to the people. Only a few of Joseph Smith's intimate friends knew it previous to its being published to the world, which was several years after his death. We have not been driven from our homes since it was published.

Do you not aggravate your enemies by your close communion habits?" I speak for myself; I acknowledge that I do not fellowship much of their conduct, nor do I expect to, unless it is better than some of it has been; and I will say further, it is hard for me to fellowship the conduct of some who profess to be Latter day Saints.

Polygamy in Utah and polygamy among the Christian nations of the world at the present day are very different. Polygamy in Utah is an honourable transaction for we marry our wives, and openly acknowledge them and their children. It is a very different matter elsewhere; women are seduced and secretly kept as mistresses as long as they please their unprincipled seducers, when they are cast off to meet, if it were possible, a worse fate; their children are not acknowledged, but are thrown upon the world unprotected, and left exposed to be carried away by the dark and turpid stream of crime, to end their wretched lives in prison, upon the gallows, or in some other violent manner.

Did the Devil believe that Joseph Smith was an impostor? He knew that Joseph Smith was a true Prophet. Did the first priest who persecuted Joseph Smith, when Joseph was about nineteen years of age, believe that Joseph was an impostor? No. The Devil and his emissaries are not afraid of an impostor; for the world is full of imposition. Men who lecture against God, Jesus Christ, and the Bible, are not persecuted, but figure in what is called the best society. This proves one saying of the Saviour, that the world loves its own; and those that the Lord has chosen out of the world, they hate and persecute. Infidelity, under some popular name, makes it way to the altars of Christian sanctuaries, and its supporters receive the honour of this world. But when Joseph Smith came before the world bearing testimony that Jesus lived, than he had seen him, declaring that he was his witness, and that Jesus was the Saviour of the world, that he had spoken from the heavens and had revealed in these days the fulness of the Gospel for the salvation of men, that the Old and New Testament were true and contained the plan of human redemption, he was cast out, and the cry —— "False Prophet, false Prophet, away with him," was almost universal.

Who can justly say aught against Joseph Smith? I was as well acquainted with him, as any man. I do not believe that his father and mother knew him any better than I did. I do not think that a man lives on the earth that knew him any better than I did; and I am bold to say that, Jesus Christ excepted, no better man ever lived or does live upon this earth. I am his witness. He was persecuted for the same reason that any other righteous person has been or is persecuted at the present day.

The world have the Gospel preached o [to] them, but they do not receive it, and they wish to drive the Priesthood and its supporters from the earth. Blessed are they which are persecuted for righteousness sake: for theirs is the kingdom of heaven. Blessed are ye when men shall revile you, and persecute you, and shall say all manner of evil against you falsely, for my sake. Rejoice and be exceeding glad: for great is your reward in heaven: for so persecuted they the prophets which were before you." Had Jesus Christ been an impostor and of the world, the world would have loved its own. Had Joseph Smith been an impostor and of the world, the world would not have hated him, but would have loved its own. Had Joseph Smith made political capital of his religion and calling, and raised up a political party, he doubtless would have become celebrated and renowned in the world as a great man and as a great leader.

The world fears a concentration of feeling and union of action. We say that we live in a Republican Government, and we hold that we have the best national constitution in the world; but a wicked people will corrupt themselves and do wickedly under any government, and, in so doing, will sooner or later be destroyed. The most excellent human or divine laws are of no use to earthly or heavenly beings, unless they are faithfully observed. Law is for the protection of the law abider; and the penalty of the law is for the lawbreaker. God cannot acknowledge a divided government as his, wherein some are of Paul, some of Apollos, &c.

The Church of Jesus Christ could not exist, and be divided up into parties. Where such disunion exists in any government, it ultimately becomes the means of the utter overthrow of that government or people, unless a timely remedy is applied. Party spirit once made its appearance in heaven, but was promptly checked "And there was war in heaven: Michael and his angels fought against the dragon; and the dragon fought and his angels, and prevailed not; neither was their place found any more in heaven. And the dragon was cast out, that old serpent, called the Devil, and Satan, which deceiveth the whole world; he was cast out into the earth, and his angels were cast out with him." They were cast out; and if our Government had cast out the Seceders, the war would soon have been ended. This placed the Spirit of Evil on the earth. Those evil spirits are not permitted to receive tabernacles of their own, and that is their condemnation and punishment. They have been known to take possession of the bodies of men and women, and rather than to be without a body, they have entered the bodies of brutes. All such spirits and all embodied spirits who violate wholesome laws and abuse the rights and privileges guaranteed unto them will be hurled down to hell.

The people in the States have violated the Constitution in closing their ears against the cries of the oppressed, and in consenting to shedding innocent blood, and now war, death and gloom are spread like a pall over the land, which state of things will sooner or later spread all over the world. The world is at war against the truth, and against those who propagate it. Are they opposed to canting hypocrites in the garb of parsons? No. Will they ridicule a black attired blackguard and pelt him with mud and rotten eggs, even though he should lecture against God, Christ, and the Holy Scriptures? No, but they will fight against the truth which has been revealed from heaven, "and this is the condemnation that light has come into the world, and men loved darkness rather than light, because their deeds were evil." The wicked hate the light because it maketh manifest their evil deeds, and they love to dwell in darkness, thinking to cover their sins from the public gaze and from the eye of God; but in the due time of the Almighty their deeds will be exposed upon the house tops. This is the reason why the religious and political factions of this land united their energies to slay the Prophet Joseph Smith, and to banish the religion of Jesus, because they saw that it would instruct, inform, and unite the people.

It may be said that the Roman Catholics are as much united as the Latter day Saints, but is it in righteousness? No. I have not read that the Roman Catholics of late years have taken patiently the spoiling of their goods and suffered the loss of all things for their religion. Though this may not be positive proof of the truth of any religion, for it well known that fanatics will suffer horrible torture for a false and foolish religion, more than is required of the Lord for true Christian to suffer for their religion, except in cases when his providences may require for certain wise purposes. Votaries of false systems of religion will at times court persecution, with a view to establish their religion and give it notoriety. The most effectual way to establish the religion of Heaven is to live it, rather than to die for it: I think I am safe in saying that there are many of the Latter day Saints who are more willing to die for their religion than to faithfully live it. There is no other proof can be adduced to God, angels, and men, that a people faithfully live their religion, than that they repent truly of their sins, obey the law of baptism for the remission of sins, and then continue to do the works of righteousness day by day.

Some few who profess to be Latter day Saints have been unruly and froward, not respecting the rights and property of others. The army that was quartered in our vicinity introduced more corruption and iniquity than had been made manifest for years. Whether to be thankful or sorrowful for this, sometimes I am at a loss to know. The wicked that were among us have been made manifest, and many of them have left; this is a result we have no cause to mourn over. There are still a few who are impatient of control, will go their own way, will steal, lie, swear, get drunk, &c. Their works make them manifest, and we know them. We also know upon whom we can depend in a time of trouble; a good sailor is always found at his post, both in calm and storm. The good soldier is ready to resist the enemy, and not to shake hands with him and be tamely taken prisoner. The time of storm, and trouble is the time to prove ourselves to God and to one another.

We desire to be a great deal better than we are as individuals and as a people, and if we are faithful, we shall be. Praise to the faithful Latter day Saints, who are striving to serve God with all their hearts. Let all Latter day Saints learn that the weaknesses of their brethren are not sins. When men or women undesignedly commit a wrong, do not attribute that to them as a sin. Let us learn to be compassionate one with another; let mercy and kindness soften every angry and fretful temper, that we may become long suffering and beneficent in all our communications one with another. No man can ever become a ruler in the kingdom of God, until he can perfectly rule himself; then is he capable of raising a family of children who will rise up and call him blessed. On the other hand, if the Elders of Israel do not pay attention to this and improve themselves in every possible way, their families will see their weaknesses and follies, can have no confidence in them as leaders, and will scatter away from them and join themselves to more substantial, wise, and reliable fathers and leaders.

Shall we as a people ever become popular in the world? Yes, when righteousness reigns triumphantly on the earth. In the end, when the judgment is set and the Judge of all the earth makes his appearance, he will place upon his right hand Abraham and Abraham's seed, and all those who have obeyed the Gospel of his Son, and they will inherit the earth and its fulness, while the sinner and the ungodly will be cast into prison to pay the uttermost farthing.

May the Lord help us to live so that we may be accounted worthy of all the glory our Heavenly Father has in store for us. Amen. JD 9:329

This discourse explores the reasons for the hostility of the eastern establishment. In discussing the united order programs in the 1800's it is important to begin with the perceptions of the saints' problems held by the leaders. Even if their perceptions of hostility were incorrect, it is still the thought processes of these leaders and their guidance under certain assumed conditions that is important. The goal here is to understand church behavior and teachings under stress, real or perceived.

,Of course, faulty communication could conceivably have caused the saints to misunderstand some of the East's actions. Later historical writers such as B. H. Roberts seemed to understate in some areas the level of conflict and eastern aggression, perhaps to "paper over" the past and to lessen current conflicts with the world.

Having said all that, it still seems to the author that Brigham Young's grasp of the physical problems of the saints and the intentions of their enemies was quite accurate. Note that Brigham Young seems to have had good intelligence sources and pursued them actively. He at least knew that the 1857 army's orders were sealed (JD 5:154 JT AUG 23 1857 SLC), tending in the circumstances to indicate that their intentions were hostile to the Mormons. We cannot tell from his comments about the Missouri Exterminating Order whether he learned early or late about the Missouri army/mob's orders (they are now widely published documents), but he certainly made it his business to learn of and understand such treachery as soon as possible.

The brethren seemed to follow current events carefully, including the Crimean War, and commented on the politics, military maneuvers, etc.:

> **Crimean War**, the war of October 1853 - February 1856, fought mainly on the Crimean Peninsula between the Russians and the British, French, and Ottoman Turkish.... In September 1854 the allies landed troops in Russian Crimea, on the north shore of the Black Sea, and began a year-long siege of the Russian fortress of Sevastopol. ... Finally, on September 11, 1855, three days after a successful French assault on the Malakov, a major strongpoint in the Russian defenses, the Russians blew up the forts, sank the ships, and evacuated Sevastopol.[2]

It is likely that Brigham Young considered this and other military history experiences in planning his Utah War strategy, as when he spoke of leaving the enemy "nothing but heaps of ashes and ruins," a possible allusion to Sevastopol. Brigham Young had a good idea of what guerrilla war was all about (JD 5:338 BY Oct 18, 1857), and no doubt was prepared to use it.

## Chapter notes

[1] John Stuart Mill, *Utilitarianism; On Liberty; Essay On Bentham* (New York: The New American Library, Inc, 1962), pp. 154-155.

[2] "Crimean War," *Encyclopaedia Britannica*, 15th ed., 30 vols. (Chicago: Encyclopaedia Britannica, Inc., 1981).

CHAPTER 4

# A Strategic Overview

In 1861, George A. Smith recalled that

> When James K. Polk, President of the United States, was told that the "Mormons" had
> occupied the Great Basin, and were making settlements on the borders of the Great Salt
> Lake, "Why," said he, "that is the key of the continent." JD 9:109 GAS Sept 10, 1861 Logan.

Polk was President from 1845 to 1849, and presumably made this comment during
that time. The saints arrived in Utah in 1847, so it was obvious to everyone, at least
shortly after the fact, that the saints had chosen an important spot to call their own,
ensuring continual attention, good or ill, from the nation's leaders and press.

It was not generally expected that the saints would settle in such a strategic location
(or that if they did so, they would survive). They discussed going to Oregon or
Vancouver or California or Texas. (There appears to have been some secrecy and
perhaps a little deception, something like the secrecy surrounding the trip to Missouri
and the exact spot to purchase land there). The saints going to one of those other
places would have been less threatening to the nation's leaders. Going to Vancouver,
Canada, would put them out of the US altogether, and out of the politician's hair. If
they were in the US, most locations were already partially settled and would have
governments that would surely have been able to control and even overpower the
saints. Oregon was also jointly claimed by Britain and the US, leaving open the
possibility that moving there might ultimately mean that the saints would be outside the
US. On the other hand, their presence there might help strengthen the US claim to
Oregon. (Most thought Oregon would eventually become US territory.) California
already had some "old settlers" to help control the Mormons. Texas was a slave area
and had many settlers.

The main criteria for finding a new location for the saints were that it had to be
defensible, and not be too desirable to others. The first location in Missouri was too
nice a place, too much milk and honey. The saints were told they could get rich by
going there. It was true, but so was it true for others who had larceny in their hearts.
John Taylor had these descriptions:

> For instance we lived in a rich land back in Missouri. Everything there seemed to grow at a
> very rapid rate, everything increased very fast. I have heard some people tell such big stories
> about the productiveness of that country that I have sometimes been afraid to tell what I
> myself knew of it, for fear that people would not believe me. For instance, I have seen fields
> of corn that a regiment of soldiers could ride into and they would be out of sight; and I have
> seen beans grow where corn had been planted where the corn stalks have served as bean
> poles; and I have seen pumpkins and squash grow among them, three crops growing the
> same year and at the same time. JD 23:11-13 JT Nov 9, 1881 SLC.

Of course, the richness of the land did draw the saints out to the edge of the United States, making it easier eventually to move them the rest of the distance to Utah.

It should be noted that before the saints left Illinois for the west, and they were trying to decide where to go, several places were considered, based on maps and other data then available. It was clear enough that the US government was neither willing to help defend them on their trip or at their destination, nor did the government want the Mormons to be able to acquire any significant control of any place they might move to. For example, in the Mormon Battalion incident, the government took pains to make sure that the LDS soldiers could not settle in such numbers or concentrations in California as to actually control any particular part of it. CHC 3:75.

It must therefore have come as a small shock to the church's enemies that the Mormons had chosen to stop in a strategic location such as what is now known as the "Crossroads of the West." They were in Utah far ahead of the building of the transcontinental railroad, but they had chosen well. It may have seemed like a nearly barren wasteland to others, but it had great possibilities that apparently many overlooked.

Some of the recorded information about how the Mormons made their choices of location should be interesting here. Brigham Young thought that they could not stay in California, presumably because of the many people already there, or who would come, who would mob them again. The gold rush of 1849 certainly confirmed Brigham Young's concerns. Incidentally, the gold rush probably raised the value of California to the US, and therefore the value of Utah, because of the need for travelers to pass through Utah. It certainly caused many to get better acquainted with the Mormons and to appreciate their help to travelers through trade, protection, etc. The Nauvoo House was meant to get people to come to Nauvoo and meet the Mormons; the gold rush probably did a much better job for Utah.

The following September 1857 address by Brigham Young deals with the general location question including the California option. The address was given in the context of the federal army approaching Utah, with one of its officers in Utah attempting to prepare the way.

> If you do your duty in this respect, you need not be afraid of mobs, nor of forces sent out in violation of the very genius of our free institutions, holding you till mobs kill you. Mobs? Yes; for where is there the least particle of authority, either in our Constitution or laws, for sending troops here, or even for appointing civil officers contrary to the voluntary consent of the governed? We came here without any help from our enemies, and we intend to stay as long as we please.
>
> They say that their army is legal, and I say that such a statement is as false as hell, and that they are as rotten as an old pumpkin that has been frozen seven times and then melted in a harvest sun. Come on with your thousands of illegally-ordered troops, and I will promise you, in the name of Israel's God, that you shall melt away as the snow before a July sun.

There is one thing that I want, for the satisfaction of Captain Van Vliet. One of our old senators, Stephen A. Douglas, recently said before his constituents in Illinois, that nine-tenths of our people were aliens. We have a larger proportion of foreigners in this city than in any other part of the Territory, and there are a good many here to-day who have just come in from the Plains. I want those who are native born and naturalized American citizens to raise their right hands. (Over two-thirds of the congregation raised their hands.) You who have not yet received your naturalization papers will please manifest it in the same way. (Less than a third of the congregation raised their hands.) Now, Captain, you can see yourself that over two-thirds of this congregation are either native born or naturalized American citizens.

I have called this vote that Captain Van Vliet may be able to do as he always does — speak the truth boldly, and tell them of it next winter in Washington; and that he can, if he sees Senator Douglas in Washington, tell his that he statement was false, for he has seen for himself.

If it were any use, I would ask whether there is ONE person in this congregation who wants to go to the United States; but I know that I should not find any. But I will pledge, myself that if there is a man, woman, or child that wants to go back to the States, if they will pay their debts, and not steal anything, they can go; and if they are poor and honest, we will help them to go. That has been my well-known position all the time.

Brother Taylor has said that he bantered the United States for a trade, and promised them that if they would send all to Utah that wanted to come, we would send all to the States that wanted to go. We would get our thousands to their one, if they would make that trade. But no — they must keep on lying, howling, and trying to oppress and kill the innocent.

When some went away last spring, I told them to go in peace, and they did so. What are they doing now? Many of them are struggling to get back, and the rest are wishing that they had never left here. It is a kind of dear business to apostatize every year. I would rather stick to the old ship Zion.

When I was written to in Nauvoo by the President of the United States, through another person, enquiring, "Where are you going, Mr. Young?" I replied that I did not know where we should land. We had men in England trying to negotiate for Vancouver's Island, and we sent a shipload of Saints round Cape Horn to California. Men in authority asked, "Where are you going to?" "We may go to California, or to Vancouver's Island." When the Pioneer company reached Green River, we met Samuel Brannan and a few others from California, and they wanted us to go there. I remarked, "Let us go to California, and we cannot stay there over five years; but let us stay in the mountains, and we can raise our own potatoes, and eat them; and I calculate to stay here." We are still on the backbone of the animal, where the bone and the sinew are, and we intend to stay here, and all hell cannot help themselves.

We are not to be persecuted as we have been. We can say, "Come as a mob, and we can sweeten you up right suddenly." They never did anything against Joseph till they had ostensibly legalized a mob; and I shall treat every army and every armed company that attempts to come here as a mob. (The congregation responded, "Amen.") You might as well tell me that you can make hell into a powder-house as to tell me that you could let an army in here and have peace; and I intend to tell them and show them this, if they do not keep away. By taking this course, you will find that every man and woman feels happy, and they say, "All is right, all is well;" and I say that our enemies shall not slip the bow on "Old Bright's neck" again.

God bless you. Amen. JD 5:230 BY Sep 13, 1857 SLC

Apparently, before the saints left Nauvoo, a specific agreement was made about the saints settling California. The following October 1863 address by Brigham Young touches on that point and related issues:

I now wish to present a few questions to the congregation, for I think there is no harm in asking questions to elicit information. Do the Government officials in Utah, civil and military, give aid and comfort to and foster persons whose design is to interrupt and disturb the peace of this people? and are they protected and encouraged in this ruinous design by the strong arm of military power, to do what they will, if they will only annoy and try to break up the "Mormon" community? Does the general Government, or does it not, sustain this wicked plan? Is there in existence a corruption-fund, out of which Government jobbers live and pay their travelling expenses while they are engaged in trying to get men and women to apostatize from the truth, to swell their ranks for damnation? Is this so, or is it not so? Those who understand the political trickeries and the political windings of the nation, can see at once that these are political questions. Who feeds and clothes and defrays the expenses of hundreds of men who are engaged patroling the mountains and kanyons all around us in search of gold? Who finds supplies for those who are sent here to protect the two great interests —— the mail and telegraph lines across the continent-while they are employed ranging over these mountains in search of gold? And who has paid for the multitude of picks, shovels, spades and other mining tools that they have brought with them? Were they really sent here to protect the mail and telegraph lines, or to discover, if possible, rich diggings in our immediate vicinity, with a view to flood the country with just such a population as they desire, to destroy, if possible, the identity of the "Mormon" community, and every truth and virtue that remains? Who is it that calls us apostates from our Government, deserters, traitors, rebels, secessionists? And who have expressed themselves as being unwilling that the "Mormons" should have in their possession a little powder and lead? I am merely presenting a few plain questions to the Latter-day Saints, which they or anybody else may answer, or not, just as they please. Who have said that "Mormons" should not be permitted to hold in their possession fire-arms and ammunition? Did a Government officer say this, one who was sent here to watch over and protect the interest of the community, without meddling or interfering with the domestic affairs of the people? I can tell you what they have in their hearts, and I know what passes in their secret councils. Blood and murder are in their hearts, and they wish to extend the work of destruction over the whole face of the land, until there cannot be found a single spot where the Angel of peace can repose.

The waste of life in the ruinous war now raging is truly lamentable. Joseph the Prophet said that the report of it would sicken the heart; and what is all this for? It is a visitation from heaven, because they have killed the Prophet of God, Joseph Smith, jun, Has not the nation consented to his death, and to the utter destruction of the Latter-day Saints, if it could be accomplished? But they found that they could not accomplish that.

Before we left Nauvoo, members of Congress made a treaty with the Latter-day Saints, and we agreed to leave the United States entirely. We did so, and came to these mountains, which were then Mexican territory. When we were ready to start on our pilgrimage west, a certain gentleman, who signed himself "Backwoodsman," wished to know on what conditions we would overcome and settle California. He gave us to understand that he had his authority from headquarters, to treat with us on this matter. I thought that President Polk was our friend at that time; we have thought so since, and we think so now. We agreed to survey and settle California — we drawing the odd numbers, and the Government the even numbers; but I think the President was precipitated into the Mexican war, and our prospective calculations fell through, otherwise we should have gone into California and settled it. Many of you were not aware of this.

Joseph said that if they succeeded in taking his life, which they did, war and confusion would come upon the nation, and they would destroy each other, and there would be mob upon mob from one end of the country to the other. Have they got through? No, they have only just commenced the work of wasting life and property. They will burn up every steamboat, every village, every town, every house of their enemies that comes within their reach; they will waste and destroy food and clothing that should feed and comfort women and children, and leave them destitute and beggars, without homes and without protectors, to perish upon the face of all the land, and all to satiate their unhallowed and hellish appetite for blood; and this awful tornado of suffering, destruction, woe and lamentation, they would hurl upon us, if they could, but they cannot, and I say in the name of Israel's God, they never shall do it. We will have peace if we have to fight for it. They have not power to destroy Israel, neither will they have. The time will come when he who will not take up his sword against his neighbor must flee to Zion. JD 10:254 BY Oct 6, 1863 SLC.

In this deal for settling California, the saints were offered the odd sections of land, the government getting the even. The problem was that they could expect to lose control of the general area as others moved in. They would lose their culture, freedom of religion and homes as in Missouri. Their being the "old settlers" would not be enough.

In a June 25, 1871, address, Brigham Young comments on the major contribution to the US made by the saints by settling Utah and claiming it from Mexico (at least that is how they saw it). However, the fact that they had it all to themselves was a great irritation to the US government.

Speaking of persecutions, neglects, slights and insults, was it an insult for the President of the United States, after calling upon our men to redeem this land from a foreign government, which we did, so far as the whole of Upper California is concerned, for it was acquired by the Latter-day Saints from the Mexican Government; and over it we hoisted the American flag, and have maintained it ever since; and then for our Chief Magistrate to make war upon the people who had actually added so much to the public domain and placed it under the banner and flag of their Government, to send an army to waste us away and destroy us, was it generous? Did it evince brotherly kindness? Was it according to Christian light? Was it according to the New Testament, the sayings of the Savior, or the acts of the wise and the good? We leave everybody to judge. Still they did not do it, no, nor they will not do it either.

What did we do when we came here? A few words upon this. Did we manifest to the world that we knew how to take care of ourselves? What did we bring with us? Five times have I been broken up and left a fine property behind. I never looked after it, for I knew that the earth was the Lord's and the fullness thereof, and that he could give me what he pleased, hence I never looked behind, but marched forward, right ahead five times. What did we bring here? Nothing; we came here comparatively, as the old saying is, naked and barefoot. We have lived here twenty-four years, and now we are told that if we can convince the people of the United States that we can actually govern, control and sustain ourselves, why, we can have a State Government, so as to get us a little land to school our children and help ourselves a little. I suppose from this that they wish to imply that up to this time we have not proved that; we can sustain and govern ourselves. What is necessary, judging by the standard of civilization, to prove this? What does it take to constitute a people capable of governing and controlling themselves? Now, mark, in the estimation of civilization it requires a settlement, territory and subjects for this territory; and then it requires certain ingredients within this community, to constitute civilization. Where shall we begin? We will build a grogshop, that will be the first thing, and have a few groceries; and we will bring on the liquor. The description of an outfit to the mines in early days will answer to illustrate and fill up the picture. The first thing was a barrel of whisky, then ten pounds of dried beef, and a box of crackers; what next? A ten gallon keg of whisky and four pounds of cheese, ten of butter, then another barrel of whisky, next ten pounds of dried beef, two sacks of flour, and so on. Now after we get a parcel of grogshops and can see, every Saturday, men drinking in the streets, hurrahing, running their horses, having children run over, and perhaps get to fighting and somebody's head broken, or some one shot down, and have some gambling saloons, then we are ready for a meeting house, and here comes the priest through the streets mourning over the sins of the people, crying and "Oh what a wretched place this is." That is civilization. You will excuse me, this is no overdrawn picture, but is a representation of what is misnamed civilization. But is it so in the eyes of Heaven? No, it is civilization in the eyes of filth and corruption, that is what it is.

To call this civilization is like saying to a kind, judicious and loving mother, "You are not capable of taking care of your children, we will put them out." What is the matter, mother? And the mother says, "Why, my children obey me. I make no request of them but what they comply with; and they are willing and obedient. I teach them morning and evening to pray; I teach them to read the Bible, to be good, not to tell falsehoods, but to be truthful and honest, and not to take a pin's worth from their neighbors; not to contend with each other about the toys. " And this mother is kind, loving and agreeable, and her children love her, and in the morning run with open arms and salute her with, "Mamma, how glad I am to see you, are you well? " And at night when going to bed the mother says, "Good night, my darlings, come and let me give you a kiss." But this mother is not worthy of her children, and they must be taken from her and put out she is too kind to them, and has perfect control over them. That is what they are afraid of. And the father, when he comes from his work, his store or mechanics' shop, is met with smiling faces, and "good evening, father, or papa," and he has a kiss for each of them, and has a kind good night for all, and perfect love and peace reign in their midst. But that mother and father are unworthy of those children; the way they have trained them is not civilization. Whip them, teach them to quarrel, fight, knock each other down, and finally kick them out of doors! That is civilization according to the notion of the world. This is a comparison and it may be a strong one; but lay it in the balance and see how it will weigh. Will they among whom such manners and principles prevail be prepared for the celestial kingdom, or for a terrestrial or telestial kingdom, no matter who they are? I think not. They will have to abide a kingdom where there is no glory. JD 14:153 BY June 25, 1871 SLC

The saints' goal was to find a place that they could control against all comers, so they could not be dispossessed again. Brigham Young appears to have made every possible effort to get a complete north/south swath of land under his control, from the borders of Canada to Mexico. He may have had many reasons, including getting agricultural land in every climate so that a wide range of products could be grown, and land that might hold minerals for industrial use. The original state of Deseret was many times larger than the final state of Utah, and perhaps would have had the space and resources to be a more self-sustaining unit.

In all this, Brigham Young surely did not overlook the strategic value of holding potential control of all east-west traffic on the continent. Anyone traveling through, as in a wagon train going to Oregon or on a railroad train to California, or installing and using an east-west telegraph system, would be going through HIS territory. That situation could be used at least as a bargaining chip when it came to dealing with the Easterners. If nothing else, it was used as a source of cash income as the Mormons traded with the westbound travelers and built large sections of the railroad roadbed and supplied needed materials. As a practical matter, when the Mormons reached a certain size they really did control that area. Although their ability to own legal title to land was delayed for 22 years after their arrival, probably for the very reason that the East wished to prevent their control of the area, when they did come to own title to the land by patience and vigilance against aggressive squatters, they did finally accomplish their goal, and the government had to try other methods to scare them off, disrupt them or more directly attempt to dispossess them.

Even without legal title, their possession and control claims plus a good posse (counter mob) to enforce it, allowed them to handle most hostile claims. Of course, controlling the way immigrants traveled, and not letting them stop, catching them at the very beginning, was one good policy for preventing land ownership disputes.

By being peaceful, in the past the saints had lost to evil men who had no compunctions. Without obvious miraculous intervention, good can only win when it is stronger. In the Utah case, good was stronger. There were many smaller or less obvious miracles which made them stronger, perhaps more in the nature of just happening to choose the right place, have enough people willing to travel there, growing enough food, having enough snow to delay the army, etc. The sum total was the same as if Enoch had sealed the mountain passes for the entire length of the Wasatch range, but was not so obvious to the uninformed onlooker. In an address dated September 13, 1857, Brigham Young reviewed the high points of the saints' strategic location, preparations, and intentions:

> Suppose that our enemies send 50,000 troops here, they will have to transport all that will be requisite to sustain them over one winter; for I will promise them, before they come, that there shall not be one particle of forage, nor one mouthful of food for them, should they come. They will have to bring all their provisions and forage; and though they start their teams with as heavy loads as they can draw, there is no team that can bring enough to sustain itself, to say nothing of the men. If there were no more men here than there are in the Seminole nation, our enemies never could use us up; but they could use up themselves, which they will do. The Seminoles —— a little tribe of a few hundred in Florida —— have cost our government, I suppose, in the neighbourhood of 100,000,000 dollars; and they are no nearer being conquered than when the war commenced. And what few have removed have been induced to do so by compromise; and it would be far cheapest for the Government to pay the debts they honestly owe us, and leave us unmolested in the peaceful enjoyment of our rights.
>
> Would not our enemies feel well in going to the kanyons for wood the first night to cook their suppers with? The idea puts me in mind of an anecdote told by one Brown about the man who took the first barrel of whisky up the Missouri river on a log-raft.
>
> They might stay amid blackened desolation till they had ate up what they had brought, and then they would have to go back. JD 5:233 BY Sep 13, 1857 SLC.

In Utah, they were in a very defensible position, not only because of the rough terrain getting into the mountains and the many places for guerrilla fighters to hide in the mountain valleys, but also because there were huge stretches of prairie to cross. At that early time the logistics of taking an army to Utah were very difficult. For one thing, it was not possible for an ox-drawn wagon to take enough food along to feed the oxen all the way to Utah. Obviously, if the wagons were to carry any cargo for an army, the oxen must be fed from other sources. It was fairly easy for raiding parties to burn up the fodder that was available on the plains, or to interfere with supply depots, destroy wagons or steal draft animals, as the army soon found out. A thousand mile long supply system was simply impossible to defend without an unbelievably large expenditure of resources. JD 5:234 BY Sept 13, 1857 SLC. (Recently, in an unusual opinion article in a Utah newspaper, someone commented that a war against the saints would still be a very hard thing, assuming the saints adopted guerrilla tactics as before.)

In an October 18, 1857, address, Brigham Young discussed the use of guerrilla tactics, and made it clear he knew what he was doing:

> We have sought for peace all the day long; and I have sought for peace with the army now on our borders, and have warned them that we all most firmly believe that they are sent here solely with a view to destroy this people, though they may be ignorant of that fact. And though we may believe that they are sent by the Government of the United States, yet I, as Governor of this Territory, have no business to know any such thing until I am notified by proper authority at Washington. I have a right to treat them as a mob, just as though they had been raised and officered in Missouri and sent here

expressly to destroy this people. We have been very merciful and very lenient to them. As I informed them in my unofficial letter, had they been those mobocrats who mobbed us in Missouri, they never would have seen the South Pass. We had plenty of boys on hand, and the mode of warfare they would have met with they are not acquainted with.

I would just as soon tell them as to tell you my mode of warfare. As the Lord God lives, we will waste our enemies by millions, if they send them here to destroy us, and not a man of us be hurt. That is the method I intend to pursue. Do you want to know what is going to be done with the enemies now on our borders? If they come here, I will tell you what will be done. A[s] soon they start to come into our settlements, let sleep depart from their eyes and slumber from their eyelids until they sleep in death, for they have been warned and forewarned that we will not tamely submit to being destroyed. Men shall be secreted here and there and shall waste away our enemies, in the name of Israel's God.

I have thought that perhaps the Lord designs to furnish us a little clothing and ammunition; and if he does, he will permit our enemies to try to come in here; but if he sees that that would be an injury to us, he will turn them another way.

I intend to publish the communications between the army and myself; for I wish the whole United States to understand it.

Colonel Alexander complains of our mode of warfare. They have two or more field-batteries of artillery with them, and they want us to form a line of battle in an open plain and give them a fair chance to shoot us. I did not tell the Colonel what I thought; but if he had a spark of sense, he must be a fool to think that we will ever do any such thing. I am going to observe the old maxim ——

> "He that fights and runs away
> Lives to fight another day."

Should our enemies venture upon violent measures, I design to so manage affairs that none of our boys will be killed; and in my answer to the Colonel, I have told him pretty plainly what we shall do under certain contingencies.

Did he not granny it off admirably about the prisoners, when he wrote, "I need not assure you that not a hair of their heads will be hurt?" He dare not hurt them, neither has he the first particle of reason for hurting them. He has released and sent in the younger brother with an express, under the alleged consideration of his having a wife and three children entirely dependent upon him. I wonder that the Colonel had not a young officer to send with him.

The boys report their order of march to be the 10th Infantry in front, the baggage in the centre, the 5th Infantry in the rear, and several flanking companies travelling through the brush as best they can. Don't you think they would look well coming from the United States in that way? That is the way in which they were travelling at our last advices, and it was said that their picket-guard declared they would not watch.

If the soldiers knew the facts in the case as do their officers, they would probably nearly all leave the army; but the officers keep the soldiers in the dark. The last report is that the officers had been telling the men that I had written a very favourable letter to Colonel Alexander, and that they were intending to come in.

When I think, Are they in your houses? Are they in your fields? I can answer, No: they are in the mountains; they are in the cold and snow; and if they continue, as those officers appear to intend to, upon the side of despotism and mobocracy, they justly ought to be served as we would serve all mobocrats. But we are here and we are free, as brother Kimball has said —— just as free, in one sense, as we ever shall be. We need not think that we are always going to be unmolested by the efforts of mobs, until wickedness is swept from this earth. If we live, we shall see the nations of the earth arrayed against this people; for that time must come, in fulfilment of prophecy. Tell about war commencing! Bitter and relentless war was waged against Joseph Smith before he had received the plates of the Book of Mormon; and from that time till now the wicked have only fallen back at times to gain strength and learn how to attack the kingdom of God.

Colonel Alexander preached to me a little, stating in his letter, "I warn you that the bloodshed in this contest will be upon your head." But that warning gave me no thought. But if the blood of those soldiers is shed, it will be upon the heads of their officers.

What they will do I neither know nor care; for it will be just as the Lord God wills it. If he sees that we need their substance, he will turn things to that end; and if he designs them to be wiped out, he will either cause them to undertake to come here or will overrule some other plan to accomplish that end.

Another year I am going to prepare for the worst, and I want you to prepare to cache our grain and lay waste this Territory; for I am determined, if driven to that extremity, that our enemies shall find nothing but heaps of ashes and ruins. We will be so prepared that in a few days all can be consumed. I shall request the Bishops to see that the people in their wards are provided with two or three years' provisions. There is already enough raised in many places this season to supply the people from two to three years, and I wish them to take care of it; though I expect that in all probability we will raise a great many crops before our enemies again attempt to come here to disturb us; and I expect that we are fully able to defend ourselves, and that our enemies will not be able to come within a hundred miles of us. I know that ten men, such as I could name and select, could stop them before they got to Laramie. And if we had seen fit to have sent such men this season, they alone could very easily have so stopped our enemies that they never would have got through the Black Hills. I count five such men equal to twenty-five thousand, and believe that two of them could put ten thousand to flight. I believe we are now where that could be done. I will take five or ten such as I can name; and if two can put ten thousand to flight, I am sure that ten are perfectly able to do it.

Who has sought for war? Have we? No. We have preached the Gospel to Saints and strangers, when strangers would come and tarry long enough to hear it. We do not want to stand here and talk about war. There is nothing so repugnant to my feelings as to injure or destroy. But what is upon us? Nothing, only another manifestation of the opposition of the Devil to the kingdom of God. War has been declared against the Saints over twenty-seven years, and our enemies have only fallen back so as to gain strength and pretexts for making another attack. Will that spirit increase? If it does, and we love our religion, let me tell you that we will increase faster than our enemies will. This Territory and people are perfectly able to defend themselves, with the help of our God. They are perfectly able to set apart men of the right stripe and maintain a standing army that can keep off the armies of our enemies. And if the world combine against us, so we are but one, then all will go on well and work together for our good.

Our enemies, in the last treaty they made with us, should have stipulated that we should have gone only a short distance, so that we would not be out of their reach. They had better have made that stipulation; but they did not have wisdom, or they would have stopped us from going so far away. They drove us away from their society and allowed us to travel so far over the sage plains, that it is impossible for an army to bring provisions enough to last them here. JD 5:338 BY Oct 18, 1857 SLC.

Brigham Young seemed to sense all the parameters that made up the strength which would keep the saints safe from extermination by a hostile East. He had a simple but powerful program of bringing in as many immigrant saints as possible, while encouraging those who were already in Utah to grow much grain and save it to feed those newcomers. The high rate of immigration caused many difficulties to all involved, but it was an important undertaking. A small group of saints might be scattered and few in the world would notice or care (as had happened before), but displacing a large group is not so easy, especially when the cost of sending an official mob was so expensive.

As the "Utah War" showed, if military activities were started against them under any pretext, they could defend themselves rather well. If the East wanted to reach the west coast and tie up with the pacific ocean ports and with the California gold mining and so on, then they had to go through more or less on Brigham Young's terms. Note that the services of providing food for travelers and keeping the Indians and bandits in check, were probably valuable and enlightening enough to enough travelers to provide a partial check on the falsehoods and designs of the Eastern power brokers in their attempts to dispossess the saints.

The Mormons quickly reached a point where they could not be easily crushed militarily, and so the East had to more or less negotiate with them on different issues, using lesser means of force, as in their anti-polygamy campaigns. It seems clear enough that such strategic considerations were in the minds of both sides of the struggle, even though it may not have been discussed openly very much.

To summarize, in their previously unsettled, uninhabited mountain home they were clearly in control and nothing short of massive armed force would remove their ability to control their own society. Dislodging them from their mountain fortress proved to be an impossible task. Any travelers crossing the continent would do so by their leave, and usually only with their help. Much profitable trade occurred with California-bound gold seekers. Trails, railroads and telegraphs had to pass through their sphere of influence. The Indians were held in check largely by the Mormon influence. All this surely angered the national leaders while also giving them reason to bargain with the saints. If they could not be displaced, they must ultimately be incorporated.

## Joseph Smith and the Move West

Joseph recorded a prophecy in Nauvoo in August 1842, two years before his death:

I prophesied that the Saints would continue to suffer much affliction and would be <u>driven</u> to the Rocky Mountains, many would apostatize, others would be put to death by our persecutors or lose their lives in consequence of exposure or disease, and some of you will live to go and assist in making settlements and build cities and see the Saints become <u>a mighty people in the midst of the Rocky Mountains</u>. (DHC 5:85 Saturday, August 6, 1842)

It is interesting to try to reconstruct the statements and actions of Joseph Smith concerning staying in Nauvoo versus going west. The saints in general seemed much against it, and Joseph Smith himself appears to have vacillated, but mostly to have tried to stay in Nauvoo, at least until the very last moment. The discussion about moving further west from Illinois was certainly a major strategic issue. There were many factors involved. It appears however, that in the last resort, they would not leave of their own volition, or on the basis of counsel, but would only take action at gun point, and after suffering the disaster of losing their prophet.

It appears that they could not grasp the strategic situation they found themselves in, and so let their wishes for quiet settlement overcome their political sense of what was actually possible. (The same problem occurred again in Utah. The saints still did not grasp the nature of their peril and the actions necessary, even with Brigham Young telling them continually.) In Nauvoo, they did not even make proper preparation until it was almost too late. Their (and Joseph's) pugnacity in attempting to defend their constitutional rights cost them a great deal.

Although Joseph had the vision and made the prophecy concerning the move to the Rocky Mountains, it appears from other statements that he did not desire to be the one to lead the saints west. Note that he anticipated that they would be *driven* there rather than having a more gradual move. The unfair and evil treatment of the saints and himself by the government and inhabitants of the US, and the undoing by them of much that he had wrought, such as the Nauvoo Charter and the building up of Nauvoo, and the pressure for the saints to leave Nauvoo to yet another spot, seemed to give him such a sense of outrage and despair that he seemed to consider the move west as something that could only come much later than it did, and perhaps at a more leisurely and controllable pace. By not pursuing that option with more vigor, the persecutors were perhaps given all the more reason to put great pressure on the saints. If the saints were already leaving in numbers, the local anti-Mormon hatred and paranoia might have been lessened. The Mormons would be making a statement that they did not desire to accumulate even more economic and political power in Illinois and Missouri.

Of course, the move into the great unknown of the west was a daunting project, fraught with peril as Joseph foresaw. And it is possible that, without direct and specific revelation, they might have made a bad choice as to location. It is possible that the revelation cited above might have been sufficient, but, more likely, something repeated with more force and detail would have been necessary. On the other hand, the saints were clearly not ready to execute such a plan, even less so than the prophet.

Once they were pushed out of Nauvoo, the apparent options may have narrowed a great deal, so that only Utah was a serious candidate. It would be even clearer to them that they would not be welcome or successful in any of the already settled areas. The continuing overt US government hostility would have made that point clear.

The following address by Joseph Smith perhaps shows us a side of Joseph that we do not often hear about. His fiery defense of his city, its charter, and his rights, and his apparent willingness to go to war over them is intriguing. He was fed up with the wars on the Mormons by the Missourians, and released the saints to make war on the mobbers. As we shall see later, apparently at the last moment he changed his opinion on whether fight or flight was better, but by then it was too late to execute an orderly "flight" movement.

THE CONSTITUTIONS OF THE UNITED STATES AND ILLINOIS — NAUVOO CHARTER AND MUNICIPAL COURT — WRIT OF HABEAS CORPUS.

An Address by President Joseph Smith, Delivered on the evening of his arrival from Dixon, June 30, 1843, in the Grove, near the Temple, Nauvoo; about eight thousand people having hastily assembled, under the most intense excitement, in consequence of the attempt of Sheriff Reynolds, of Jackson County, Missouri, to kidnap him to Missouri, by preventing him from obtaining a writ of Habeas Corpus.

(REPORTED BY DR. WILLARD RICHARDS AND ELDER WILFORD WOODRUFF.)

The congregation is large; I shall require attention. I discovered what the emotions of the people were on my arrival at this city, and I have come here to say, "How do you do?" to all parties, and I do now at this time say to all, "How do you do?" I meet you with a heart full of gratitude to Almighty God; and I presume you all feel the same. I am well — I am hearty. I hardly know how to express my feelings — I feel as strong as a giant. I pulled sticks with the men coming along, and I pulled up with one hand the strongest man that could be found: then two men tried, but they could not pull me up; and I continued to pull mentally until I pulled Missouri to Nauvoo. But I will pass from that subject.

There has been great excitement in the country since Joseph H. Reynolds and Harmon Wilson took me; but I have been cool and dispassionate through the whole. Thank God, I am now a prisoner in the hands of the Municipal Court of Nauvoo, and not in the hands of Missourians.

It is not so much my object to tell of my afflictions, trials, and troubles; as to speak of the writ of Habeas Corpus, so that the minds of all may be corrected. It has been asserted by the great and wise men, lawyers and others, that our municipal powers and legal tribunals are not to be sanctioned by the authorities of the State and accordingly *they* want to make it lawful to drag away innocent men from their families and friends, and have them put to death by ungodly men for their religion! Relative to our city charter, courts, right of Habeas Corpus, &c., I wish you to know and publish that we have all power; and if any man from this time forth says anything to the contrary, cast it into his teeth. There is a secret in this; if there is not power in our charter and courts, then there is not power in the State of Illinois, nor in the Congress or Constitution of the United States, for the United States gave unto Illinois her constitution or charter, and

Illinois gave unto Nauvoo her charters, ceding unto us our vested rights, which she has no right or power to take from us; all the power there was in Illinois she gave to Nauvoo; and any man that says to the contrary, is a fool. The Municipal Court has all the power to issue and determine writs of Habeas Corpus, within the limits of this city, that the Legislature can confer. This city has all the power that the State Courts have, and was given by the same authority — the Legislature.

I want you to hear and learn, O Israel! this day, what is for the happiness and peace of this city and people. If our enemies are determined to oppress us, and deprive us of our constitutional rights and privileges as they have done; and of the authorities that are on the earth will not sustain us in our rights, nor give us that protection which the laws and constitution of the United States, and of this State, guarantee unto us, then we will claim them from higher power — from Heaven — yea, from God Almighty.

I have dragged these men here by my hand, and will do it again; but I swear I will not deal so mildly with them again; for the time has come *when forbearance is no longer a virtue*; and if you or I are again taken unlawfully, you are at liberty to give loose to blood and thunder. But be cool, be deliberate, be wise, act with almighty power, and when you pull, do it effectually — make a *sweepstakes* for once!

My lot has always been cast among the warmest hearted people; in every time of trouble, friends, even among strangers, have been raised up unto me, and assisted me.

The time has come when this vail is torn off from the State of Illinois, and its citizens have delivered me from the State of Missouri; friends that were raised up unto me would have spilt their life's blood, to have torn me from the hands of Reynolds and Wilson, if I had asked them; but I told them not. I would be delivered by the power of God, and generalship; and I have brought these men to Nauvoo, and committed them to her from whom I was torn, not as prisoners in chains, but as prisoners of kindness. I have treated them kindly, I have had the privilege of rewarding them good fur evil. They took me unlawfully, treated me rigorously, strove to deprive me of my rights and would have run with me into Missouri to have been murdered, if Providence had not interposed; but now they are in my hands, and I have taken them into my house, set them at the head of my table, and placed before them the best which my house afforded; and they were waited upon by my wife, whom they deprived of seeing me when I was taken. I have no doubt but I shall be discharged by the Municipal Court: were I before any good tribunal I should be discharged, as the Missouri writs are illegal, and good for nothing — they are "without form and void."

But before I will bear this unhallowed persecution any longer — before I will be dragged away again, among my enemies for trial, *I will spill the last drop of blood in my veins, and will see all my enemies* IN HELL! To bear it any longer would be a sin, and I will not bear it any longer. Shall we bear it any longer? (One universal "No!" ran through all the vast assembly, like a loud peal of thunder.)

I wish the lawyer who says we have no powers in Nauvoo may be choked to death with his own words. Don't employ lawyers, or pay them money for their knowledge, for I have learnt they don't know anything. I know more than they all.

Go ye into all the world, and preach the Gospel; he that believeth in our chartered rights, may come here and be saved, and he that does not shall remain in ignorance. If any lawyer shall say there is more power in other places and charters, with respect to Habeas Corpus, than in Nauvoo, believe it not. I have converted this candidate for

Congress (pointing to Cyrus Walker, Esq.), that the right of Habeas Corpus is included in our charter. If he continues converted, I will vote for him.

I have been with these lawyers, and they have treated me well; but I am here in Nauvoo, and the Missourian too. I got here by a lawful writ of Habeas Corpus, issued by the Master in chancery of Lee County, and made returnable to the nearest tribunal in the Fifth Judicial District having jurisdiction to try and determine such writs: and here is that tribunal, just as it should be.

However indignant you may feel about the high hand of oppression which has been raised against me by these men, use not the hand of violence against them; for they could not be prevailed upon to come here till I pledged my honor and my life that a hair of their heads should not be hurt. Will you all support my pledge, and thus preserve my honor? (One universal "Yes!" burst from the assembled thousands.) This is another proof of your attachment to me. I know how ready you are to do right; you have done great things, and manifested your love towards me in flying to my assistance on this occasion. I bless you, in the name of the Lord, with all the blessings of heaven and earth you are capable of enjoying.

I have learned we have no need to suffer as we have heretofore — we can call others to our aid. I know the Almighty will bless all good men — He will bless you; and the time has come when there will be such a flocking to the standard of liberty as never has been, or shall be hereafter. What an era has commenced! Our enemies have prophesied that we would establish our religion by the sword; *is it true?* No, but if Missouri will not stay her cruel hand in her unhallowed persecutions against us, I restrain you not any longer: I say, in the name of Jesus Christ, by the authority of the Holy Priesthood, I this day turn the key that opens the heavens to restrain you no longer from this time forth. I will lead you to battle; and if you are not afraid to die, and feel disposed to spill your blood in your own defence, you will not offend me. Be not the aggressor — bear until they strike you on the one cheek; then offer the other, and they will be sure to strike that; *then defend yourselves*, and God will bear you off, and you shall stand forth clear before His tribunal.

If any citizens of Illinois say we shall not have our rights, treat them as strangers and not friends, and let them go to hell and be damned! Some say they will mob us; let them mob and be damned! If we have to give up our chartered rights, privileges, and freedom, which our fathers fought, bled, and died for, and which the Constitution of the United States, and of this State, guarantee unto us, we will do it only at the point of the sword and bayonet.

Many lawyers contend for those things which are against the rights of men, and *I can only excuse them because of their ignorance.* Go forth and advocate the laws and rights of the people, ye lawyers; if not, don't get into my hands, or under the lash of my tongue.

Lawyers say the powers of the Nauvoo charter are dangerous; but I ask, is the Constitution of the United States, or of this State, dangerous? No; neither are the charters granted unto Nauvoo by the Legislature of Illinois dangerous, and those who say they are, are fools. We have not enjoyed unmolested those rights which the Constitution of the United States of America, and our charters grant. Missouri and all wicked men raise the hue and cry against us, and are not satisfied. Some political aspirants of this State also are raising the hue and cry that the powers in the charters granted unto the city of Nauvoo are dangerous; and although the General assembly have conferred them upon our city, yet the whine is raised —— "Repeal them, take them away" like the boy who swapped off his jackknife, and then cried, "Daddy, daddy, I have sold my jack-knife, and got sick of my bargain, and I want to get it back again." But how are they going to help themselves? Raise mobs? And what can mobocrats do in the midst of Kirkpatrickites? No better than a hunter in the claws of a bear. If mobs come upon you any more here, dung your gardens with them. We don't want any excitement; but after we have done all, we will rise up, Washington-like, and break off the hellish yoke that oppresses us, and we will not be mobbed.

The day before I was taken at Inlet Grove, I rode with my wife through Dixon to visit some friends, and I said to her, "Here is a good people." I felt this by the Spirit of God. The next day I was a prisoner in their midst, in the hands of Reynolds of Missouri, and Wilson of Carthage. As the latter drove up, he exclaimed, "Ha, ha, ha, by God we have got the Prophet now!" He gloried much in it; but he is now our prisoner. When they came to take me, they held two cocked pistols to my head; and saluted me with "God damn you, I'll shoot you! I'll shoot you, God damn you;" repeating these threats nearly fifty times from first to last. I asked them what they wanted to shoot me for. They said they would do it if I made any resistance. "O very well," I replied, "I have no resistance to make." They then dragged me away, and I asked them by what authority they did these things. They said, "By a writ from the Governors of Missouri and Illinois." I then told them I wanted a writ of Habeas Corpus. Their reply was, "God damn you, *you shan't have it.*" I told a man to go to Dixon, and get me a writ of Habeas Corpus. Wilson then repeated, "God damn you, you shan't have it; I'll shoot you." When we arrived at Dixon, I sent for a lawyer, who came, and Reynolds shut the door in his face, and would not let me speak to him, repeating "God damn you, I'll shoot you." I turned to him, opened my bosom, and told him to "shoot away; I have endured so much persecution and oppression that I am sick of life; why then don't you shoot, and have done with it, instead of talking so much about it?" This somewhat checked his insolence. I then told him that I *would* have counsel to consult; and eventually I obtained my wish. The lawyers came to me, and I got a writ of Habeas Corpus for myself, and also a writ against Reynolds and Wilson for unlawful proceedings and cruel treatment towards me. Thanks to the good citizens of Dixon, who nobly took their stand against such unwarrantable and unlawful oppression, my persecutors could not get out of town that night; although, when they first arrived, they swore I should not remain in Dixon five minutes; and I found they had ordered horses accordingly to proceed to Rock Island. I pledged my honor to my counsel that the Nauvoo city charter conferred jurisdiction to investigate the subject; so we came to Nauvoo, where I am now prisoner in the custody of a higher tribunal than the circuit court.

The charter says that "the city council shall have power and authority to make, ordain, establish, and execute such ordinances, not repugnant to the Constitution of the United States, or of this State, as they may deem necessary for the peace, benefit, and safety of the inhabitants of said city;" and also that "the Municipal Court shall have power to grant writs of Habeas Corpus in all cases arising under the ordinances of the city council." The city council have passed an ordinance "that no citizen of this city shall be taken out of this city by any writ, without the privilege of a writ of Habeas Corpus." There is nothing but what we have power over, except where restricted by the Constitution of the United States. "But," say the mob, "what dangerous powers!" Yes, dangerous, because they will protect the innocent, and put down mobocrats. The Constitution of the United States declares that the privilege of the writ of Habeas Corpus shall not be denied. Deny me the right of Habeas Corpus, and I will fight with gun, sword, cannon, whirlwind, and thunder, until they are used up like the Kilkenny cats.

We have more power than most charters confer, because we have power to go behind the writ, and try the merits of the case.

If these powers are dangerous, then the Constitution of the United States, and of this State, are dangerous; but they are not dangerous to good men; they are only so to bad men who are breakers of the laws. So with the laws of the country, and so with the ordinances of Nauvoo; they are dangerous to mobs, but not to good men who wish to keep the laws.

We do not go out of Nauvoo to disturb anybody, or any city, town, or place; why then need they be troubled about us? Let them not meddle with our affairs, but let us alone. After we had been deprived of our rights and privileges of citizenship, driven from town to town, place to place, and State to State, with the sacrifice of our homes and lands, our blood has been shed, many having been murdered; and all this because of our religion — because we worship Almighty God according to the dictates of our own consciences. Shall we longer bear these cruelties, which have been heaped upon us for the last ten years in the face of heaven, and in open violation of the Constitution and laws of these United States, and of this State? God forbid! *I will not bear it:* if they take away my rights, I will fight for them manfully and righteously until I am used up. We have done nothing against the rights of others.

You speak of lawyers; I am a lawyer too, but the Almighty God has taught *me* the principle of law; and the true meaning and intent of the writ of Habeas Corpus is to defend the innocent, and investigate the subject. Go behind the writ, and if the form of one that is issued against an innocent man is right, he should not be dragged to another State, and there be put to death, or be in jeopardy of life and limb, because of prejudice, when he is innocent. The benefits of the Constitution and Laws are alike for all; and the great Eloheim has given me the privilege of having the benefits of the Constitution, and the writ of Habeas Corpus, and I am bold to ask for this privilege this day; and I ask, in the name of Jesus Christ, and all that is sacred, that I may have your lives and all your energies to carry out the freedom which is chartered to us. Will you all help me? If so, make it manifest by raising the right hand. (There was a unanimous response, a perfect sea of hands being elevated.) Here is truly a committee of the whole.

When at Dixon, a lawyer came to me as counsel; Reynolds and Wilson said I should not speak to any man, and they would shoot any man who should dare to speak to me. An old grey-headed man came up, and said I should have counsel, and he was not afraid of their pistols. The people of Dixon were ready to take me from my persecutors and I could have killed them notwithstanding their pistols; but I had no disposition to kill any man, though my worst enemy — not even Boggs: in fact *he* would have more hell to live in the reflection of his past crimes than to die. After this, I had lawyers enough, and I obtained writ for Joseph H. Reynolds, and Harmon Wilson, for damage, assault, and battery, as well as the writ of Habeas Corpus.

We started for Ottoway, and arrived at Pawpaw Grove, thirty-two miles, where we stopped for the night. Squire Walker sent Mr. Campbell, Sheriff of Lee County, to my assistance, and he came, and slept by me. In the morning, certain men wished to see me, but I was not allowed to see them. The news of my arrival had hastily circulated about the neighborhood and very early in the morning the largest room in the hotel was filled with citizens, who were anxious to hear me preach, and requested me to address them. Sheriff Reynolds entered the room, and said, pointing to me, "I wish you to understand this man is my prisoner, and I want you should disperse; you must not gather round here in this way." Upon which an aged gentleman who was lame, and carried a large hickory walking-stick, advanced towards Reynolds, bringing his hickory upon the floor, said, "You damned infernal puke; we'll, learn you to come here and interrupt gentlemen: sit down there, (pointing to a very low chair,) and sit still, don't open your head till General Smith gets through talking; if you never learned manners in Missouri, we'll teach you that gentlemen are not to be imposed upon by a nigger driver: you can *not* kidnap men here, if you do in Missouri; and if you attempt it here, there is a committee in this Grove that will sit on your case; and, sir, it is the highest tribunal in the United States, *as from its decision there is no appeal.*" Reynolds, no doubt aware that the person addressing him was at the head of a committee, who had prevented the settlers on the public domain from being imposed upon by land speculators, sat down in silence, while I addressed the assembly for an hour and a half on the subject of marriage; my visitors having requested me to give them my views of the law of God respecting marriage.

My freedom commenced from that hour. We came direct from Paw-paw Grove to Nauvoo, having got our writ directed to the nearest court having authority to try the case, which was the Municipal Court of this city.

It did my soul good to see your feelings and love manifested towards me. I thank God that I have the honor to lead so virtuous and honest a people, to be your leader and lawyer, as was Moses to the children of Israel. Hosannah! *Hosannah!! HOSANNAH!!* to Almighty God, who has delivered us thus from out of the seven troubles! I commend you to His grace, and may the blessings of heaven rest upon you, in the name of Jesus Christ. Amen.

(President Smith then introduced Mr. Cyrus Walker to the assembled multitude; and remarked to him) —— These are the greatest dupes, as a body of people, that ever lived, or I am not as big a rogue as I am reported to be. I told Mr. Warren I would not discuss the subject of religion with you. I understand the Gospel, and you do not; you understand the quackery of law, and I do not.

(Mr. Walker then addressed the people to the effect that from what he had seen in the Nauvoo city charter, it gave the power to try writs of Habeas Corpus, &c. After which President Smith continued as follows —— )

If the Legislature have granted Nauvoo the right of determining cases of Habeas Corpus, it is no more than they ought to have done, or more than our fathers fought for.

Furthermore, if Missouri continues her warfare, and to issue her writs against me and this people unlawfully and unjustly as she has done, and to take away and trample upon our rights, I swear in the name of Almighty God, and with uplifted hands to heaven, I will spill my heart's blood in our defence. They shall not take away our rights; and if they don't stop leading me by the nose, I will lead them by the nose; and if they don't let me alone, I will turn up the world —— I will make war. When we shake our own bushes, we want to catch our own fruit.

The lawyers themselves acknowledge that we have all power granted us in our charters that we could ask for —— that we had more power than any other court in the state; for all other courts were restricted, while ours was not; and I thank God Almighty for it. I will not be rode down to hell by the Missourians any longer; and it is my privilege to speak in my own defence; and I appeal to your integrity and honor, that you will stand by and help me, according to the covenant you have this day made. JD 2:163 JS June 30, 1843 Nauvoo.

It appears that Joseph didn't himself understand and accept the need to get to Utah as a final refuge against the mobs and fighting. Is that part of why he was killed? Apparently neither he nor the saints could accept that one more arduous and dangerous move. Joseph said "To bear it any longer would be a sin, and I will not bear it any longer." Did the Lord want Joseph to "sin" by going west? I expect so, but the Lord would probably have viewed it differently than Joseph did, and perhaps would have preferred that result, as a late inspiration to Joseph seems to have indicated. On his way to Carthage, Joseph remarked, "little do they know the trials that await them." (DHC 6:554). Perhaps some of those trials could have been avoided, if the saints had been more ready to follow that inspiration of Joseph's.

In early 1844, the saints had sought government sponsorship to assist them in their move to the west, apparently suggesting that a military unit of volunteers be created out of Mormons. The following letter shows that there was little hope of any such help:

Letter: Elder Orson Hyde's Report of Labors in Washington: President Smith's Memorial for Western Movement Before Congressmen.
Washington, April 25, 1844
....
Mr, Hoge thought the bill would not pass, from the fact that there already exists between England and America a treaty for the joint occupancy of Oregon, and that any act of our government authorizing an armed force to be raised, and destined for that country, would be regarded by England as an infraction of that treaty, and a cause of her commencing hostilities against us.
....
I will now give you my opinion in relation to this matter. It is made up from the spirit of the times in a hasty manner, nevertheless I think time will prove it to be correct: -- That Congress will pass no act in relation to Texas or Oregon at present. She is afraid of England, afraid of Mexico, afraid the Presidential election will be twisted by it. The members all appear like unskillful players at checkers -- afraid to move, for they see not which way to move advantageously. All are figuring and play round the grand and important questions. In the days of our Lord the people neglected the weightier matters of the law, but tithed mint, rue, anise and cummin; but I think here in Washington they do little else than tithe the *mint*.
....
Most of the settlers in Oregon and Texas are our old enemies, the mobocrats of Missouri. If, however, the settlement of Oregon and Texas be determined upon, the sooner the move is made the better; and I would not advise any delay of the action of our government, for <u>there is such jealousy of our rising power already, that government</u>

will do nothing to favor us. If the Saints possess the kingdom I think they will have to take it; and the sooner it is done the more easily it is accomplished.

Your superior wisdom must determine whether to go to Oregon, to Texas, or to remain within these United States, and send forth the most efficient men to build up churches, and let them remain the time being; and in the meantime send some wise men among the Indians, and teach them civilization and religion, to cultivate the soil, to live in peace with one another and with all men. But whatever you do, don't be deluded with the hope that government will foster us and thus delay an action for which the present is perhaps is the most proper time that ever will be.

Oregon is becomming a popular question: the fever of emigration begins to rage. If the Mormons become the early majority, others will not come; if the Mormons do not become the early majority, the others will not allow us to come. DHC 6:372.

In a second letter dated April 26, 1844, Orson Hyde, in Washington DC, suggested a route for moving the saints to Oregon, and mentioned a map of great value:

Judge Douglas has given me a map of Oregon, and also a report on an exploration of the country lying between the Missouri River and the Rocky Mountains on the line of Kansas and great Platte rivers, by Lieut. J. C. Fremont, of the corps of Topographical Engineers. On receiving it I expressed a wish that Mr. Smith should see it. Judge Douglas says "It is a public document, and I will frank it to him." I accepted his offer, and the book will be forthcoming to you. The people are so eager for it here that they have even stolen it out of the library. ... I was not to tell any one in this city where I got it. The book is a most valuable document to any one contemplating a journey to Oregon. The directions I have given may not be exactly correct, but the book will tell correctly. DHC 6:375

It is hard to tell just how much the saints knew about the western lands and settlement options, but this paragraph indicates that not much was generally known, and so the planning for a large move could not be too far advanced.

A short summary of the last nine days of Joseph's life should help make a point about the issue of moving west. On Tuesday, June 18, 1844 (DHC 6:498), Joseph addressed the Nauvoo Legion and again spoke of standing to the death against the mobs. On Saturday June 22, Joseph had his inspiration that if Hyrum and he went west, all would be well, and no harm would come to the saints. (DHC 6:545). The two men crossed the Mississippi river that evening. Horses were to be brought to them the next evening. On Sunday, June 23, his wife and friends sent a letter and messengers to call him back. (DHC 6:549). In reality they were attempting to save themselves, as they supposed, by sacrificing their prophet. Joseph was called a coward for wishing to leave. Joseph returned to Nauvoo that evening. He told everyone multiple times that he would be killed, but no one seemed to be concerned about it, apparently because of their own fears. On Monday, June 24, Joseph and Hyrum went to Carthage with a group. They spent the night in Carthage and on Tuesday, they surrendered themselves to the constable. (DHC 6:561). On Thursday, June 27, they were killed. (DHC 6:618).

48

There was some basis for the saints' worries. They had had threats from the Illinois Governor and his troops, and their state-owned arms were taken from them (DHC 6:555), prompting some to wonder if another Missouri Massacre would occur. (DHC 6:557). The Missourians were in fact sending troops and weapons into Illinois. (DHC 6:564, 565; CHC 2:238).

If Joseph and Hyrum had left, the mobs might reasonably have assumed that all the saints might move west also, and so would leave them alone. This is partially corroborated by the mobs seeming to offer some safety to saints outside Nauvoo while those in Nauvoo were being expelled. (CHC 2:238).

As noted above, Joseph was defiant of mob action until almost the very end. A portion of his Nauvoo speech of Tuesday, June 18, 1844 follows:

### The Last Speech of President Smith to the Legion.

It is thought by some that our enemies would be satisfied with my destruction; but I tell you that as soon as they have shed my blood they will thirst for the blood of every man in whose heart dwells a single spark of the spirit of the fullness of the Gospel. The opposition of these men is moved by the spirit of the adversary of all righteousness. It is not only to destroy me, but every man and woman who dares believe the doctrines that God hath inspired me to teach to this generation.

....

Will you all stand by me to the death, and sustain at the peril of your lives, the laws of our country, and the liberties and privileges which our fathers have transmitted unto us, sealed with their sacred blood? ("Aye!" shouted thousands.) He then said, "It is well. If you had not done it, I would have gone out there (pointing to the west) and would have raised up a mightier people."

....

[Drawing his sword, and presenting it to heaven, he said] I call God and angels to witness that I have unsheathed my sword with a firm and unalterable determination that this people shall have their legal rights, and be protected from mob violence, or my blood shall be spilt upon the ground like water, and my body consigned to the silent tomb. While I live, I will never tamely submit to the dominion of cursed mobocracy. DHC 6:498 Tuesday, June 18, 1844 Nauvoo.

It appears that Joseph Smith thought that with pluck enough, they could stay in Nauvoo. At the same time, however, a move west was being contemplated. Apparently, he just did not think the time had come yet. When he finally had the answer, the saints would not believe and follow him.

Perhaps Joseph was still not fully learned as to RealPolitic and survival. He was bombastic at first, then used discretion later. Brigham Young also did a little of this. But in hindsight, Nauvoo was the wrong place to fight an all-out battle; Utah provided a much better place. There the odds were in the saints' favor, and they were able to avoid bloodshed and useless battle. If they had left sooner, perhaps they could have kept more of their military weapons.

Note that it was another charge of treason that was to take Joseph to Carthage for trial. That was the usual charge that he had faced many times before and won.

It was on a Saturday night, June 22, 1844, just five days before his martyrdom that he finally received the inspiration that he should leave for the west. The following excerpts describe the events of Saturday and Sunday:

> I had a consultation for a little while with my brother Hyrum, Dr. Richards, John Taylor and John M. Bernhisel, and determined to go to Washington and lay the matter before President Tyler.*
>
> About 7 p.m. I requested Reynolds Cahoon and Alpheus Cutler to stand guard at the Mansion, and not to admit any stranger inside the house.
>
> At sundown I asked O. P. Rockwell if he would go with me a short journey and he replied he would.

> [Abraham C. Hodge says that soon after dusk, Joseph called Hyrum, Willard Richards, John Taylor, William W. Phelps, A. C. Hodge, John L. Butler, Alpheus Cutler, William Marks and some others, into his upper room and said, "Brethren, here is a letter from the Governor which I wish to have read. After it was read through Joseph remarked, "There is no mercy -- no mercy here." Hyrum said, "No; just as sure as we fall into their hands we are dead men." Joseph replied, "Yes; what shall we do Brother Hyrum?" He replied, "I don't know." All at once Joseph's countenance brightened up and he said, "The way is open. It is clear to my mind what to do. All they want is Hyrum and myself; then tell everybody to go about their business, and not to collect in groups, but to scatter about. There is no doubt they will come here and search for us. Let them search; they will not harm you in person or property, and not even a hair of your head. We will cross the river tonight, and go away to the West." He made a move to go out of the house to cross the river. When out of doors he told Butler and Hodge to take the *Maid of Iowa*, (in charge of Repsher) get it to the upper landing, and put his and Hyrum's families and effects upon her; then go down the Mississippi and up the Ohio river to Portsmouth, where they should hear from them. He then took Hodge by the hand and said, "Now, Brother Hodge, let what will come, don't deny the faith, and all will be well."]

> *I told Stephen Markham that if I and Hyrum were ever taken again we should be massacred, or I was not a prophet of God. I want Hyrum to live to avenge my blood, but he is determined not to leave me.*

* "At this juncture the council was interrupted by the withdrawal of President Smith to give an interview to two gentlemen ... The project of laying the case before President Tyler was abandoned. Joseph had received an inspiration to go west and all would be well." (Ibid.). DHC 6:545 Saturday, June 22, 1844

Saturday, June 22, 1844. -- About 9 p.m. Hyrum came out of the Mansion and gave his hand to Reynolds Cahoon, at the same time saying, "A company of men are seeking

to kill my brother Joseph, and the Lord has warned him to flee to the Rocky Mountains to save his life. Good-by, Brother Cahoon, we shall see you again." In a few minutes afterwards Joseph came from his family. His tears were flowing fast. He held a handkerchief to his face, and followed after Brother Hyrum without uttering a word.
....

Sunday, 23.--At daybreak arrived on the Iowa side of the river. Sent Orrin P. Rockwell back to Nauvoo with instructions to return the next night with horses for Joseph and Hyrum, pass them over the river in the night secretly, and be ready to start for the Great Basin in the Rocky Mountains.

....

At 1 p.m. Emma sent over Orrin P. Rockwell, requesting him to entreat of Joseph to come back. Reynolds Cahoon accompanied him with a letter which Emma had written to the same effect, and she insisted that Cahoon should persuade Joseph to come back and give himself up. ...

Reynolds Cahoon informed Joseph what the troops intended to do, and urged upon him to give himself up, inasmuch as the Governor had pledged his faith and the faith of the state to protect him while he underwent a legal and fair trial. Reynolds Cahoon, Lorenzo D. Wasson and Hiram Kimball accused Joseph of cowardice for wishing to leave the people, adding that their property would be destroyed, and they left without house or home. Like the fable, when the wolves came the shepherd ran from the flock, and left the sheep to be devoured. To which Joseph replied, "If my life is of no value to my friends it is of none to myself." DHC 6:547 Saturday, June 22, 1844

The threats the saints were hearing probably seemed real enough:

The Governor "threatened that if General Smith did not give himself up at that time, Nauvoo would be destroyed and all the men, women, and children that were in it." DHC 6:552 Sunday June 23, 1844

The saints feared for their lives and property. They did not believe Joseph in his claim that no harm would come to them if he simply left. Their own cowardice and lack of understanding of their situation was the cause of his death. They called him a coward and he let them have their way. Apparently, the Lord had to allow the prophet to be sacrificed to prove to the people they had to move again. This appears to be a test of faith for the saints which they failed.

How do we reconcile the feeling that Joseph had that if he left for the west, all would be well, with the governor's threat of annihilation of Nauvoo if he did not allow himself to be arrested? It is possible that the most severe threats were made to frighten the saints into forcing Joseph to surrender. If Joseph had not been there, but was already on his way west, the saints could not as easily be held accountable for not delivering him. Even though the state arms had been surrendered and the Nauvoo Legion disbanded, the mob would probably not come away unscathed from a direct attack on the city. Notice that after Joseph's murder the mob dispersed quickly fearing they might be caught by an avenging group of Mormons, whom they apparently assumed would have adequate weapons for the task.

Joseph's leaving might have been a sufficient signal to the mobs that the saints also intended to leave, and their animosity and jealousy might have been dampened enough to avoid the threatened slaughter. The saints' unwillingness to follow him in this dangerous time may have caused him to "resign" as their prophet.

Perhaps there was a fear on the part of the saints that if they ran, the wolf pack might just run that much faster after them. However, note that they were not attacked in Winter Quarters where they were probably more vulnerable than in built-up Nauvoo. They were on their way west, so their enemies could see that the Mormons were licked and might well die in the wilderness even without any interference from their enemies.

Apparently even Brigham Young thought the saints could stay in Nauvoo for an extended period. Similar to his later Utah initiatives, he tried the "home manufacture" theme there as a means of building up economic strength.[1] However, about one and one-half years after Joseph's death, the saints finally had changed direction and were preparing in earnest to move west.

> Saints in Nauvoo gave further evidence of the benefits of specialization. They divided the construction of wagons into specialized tasks and constructed over 2000 wagons during the winter of 1845 and 1846. This was an incredible feat since one man skilled in wagon construction and working alone could hardly build one wagon every three months.[2]

## Polygamy as a Strategic Issue

As discussed in the chapter on polygamy, polygamy served the obvious purposes of protecting their women from outsiders and maximizing the size of the next generation. It may have left some bachelors who were them obliged to bring in women from outside as wives, and so further increase the membership. These were surely the big strategic effects of polygamy. However, it is possible that there were other more esoteric purposes that polygamy fulfilled. It obviously provided a good deal of world-wide free publicity. It was not made illegal until long after it had become a well-entrenched practice, but did surely catch the eye of nearly every reader, male or female.

Is it possible that besides increasing church growth rates from births to members, it also had a positive effect on the conflict with the hostile outside? I have a feeling that it did, although I cannot offer much proof at this point.

In a way I cannot completely articulate, the polygamy situation strikes me as a stroke of pure strategic genius. The polygamy policy not only made it easier to expand the population at a higher rate, but also, by leaving no unattached women around, made it more difficult for any outside adventurers (and potential mobbers) to find any easy entry into the local society. Later, as the saints were getting ready for a merger with the larger society, the polygamy policy had outlived its usefulness. However, that is the very time that the government was conducting a major campaign to break up the Mormon influence through using the polygamy issue to inflame anti-Mormon passions, leading to persecutions.

At the peak of this frenzy, the polygamy issue was taken away by the manifesto (D&C Official Declaration 1). Many in the government were probably quite depressed about the manifesto announcement. They surely hoped that the saints would hold out to the bitter end on this religious point, providing continuous excuses for escalating destruction. This announcement left the government with an empty and useless issue on their hands, constructed at great cost over many years. It was simply impossible at that point to find another issue which could be used as a club against the saints on the same scale. Any attempt to fabricate another issue of that magnitude would clearly show that all their previous moral outrage had been nothing but partisan posturing. Having met all the apparent conditions for entry into the mainline society, that entry could no longer be denied them, however much their enemies gnashed their teeth.

The ploy is like a football quarterback's faking right, and then left. You get your opponent to think he has the perfect issue to kill you with - an issue you will happily cling to and die for. You get him to focus all his energy on that one "fatal weakness," then you fake left and go around him, leaving him standing grasping air.

The church's enemies were left with the sound of one hand clapping. It is very possible that, after polygamy was abandoned, their enemies made up rumors about polygamy continuing, at the endowment house, etc., simply for the purpose of attempting to keep up national antagonism against the saints to try to use this as a means to hurt them further.

This is an indication that hurting the saints was the main goal, with polygamy being the most convenient means, with the church's enemies going to desperate lengths to try to keep using that carefully crafted club.

What alternative issues might the church's enemies have passed up in pursuing the polygamy issue? It is hard to say without having lived during that time. The cry of "treason" was the favorite of their enemies from the beginning. But perhaps after the Civil War, in which there were 2 million casualties including 600,000 dead, all laid on the alter of "treason," perhaps further cries of "treason" concerning the saints would have been counterproductive, if it caused large groups within the nation, now more skeptical of such claims, to focus in detail on the saints and their behavior. Such scrutiny might have shown the saints in too favorable a light, and so their enemies would not wish to encourage such scrutiny. However, the polygamy issue, along with appropriate misinformation and claims of illegal behavior, could probably be used to outrage much of the population (although the males and females may have had different views as to how deplorable it was). Nonetheless, it allowed the politicians to posture as though they were saving the country from a great sin when they attacked the saints through this means.

This "throw-away issue" may have actually protected the saints from attacks on some other doctrinal or practical point that would have been harder to give up, and thus could have caused more real damage.

## Chapter notes

[1] The musical program presented at the Nauvoo visitors center in 1990 contained the tidbit that Brigham Young encouraged home manufactures there.

[2] Lindon J. Robison, "Economic Insights from the Book of Mormon," *Journal of Book of Mormon Studies* (Provo, Utah: Foundation for Ancient Research and Mormon Studies), Volume 1, Number 1, Fall 1992, p.38.

CHAPTER 5

# Overview of Political Power Relationships

A major theory of this book is that the changes in relative power of the eastern people and the Mormons was an important factor in determining the actions and programs of the church to strengthen and protect itself. By power, I really mean the relative ability of the saints or their enemies to determine the choices and actions of the saints. The accompanying chart entitled "RELATIVE POWER -- Saints versus Easterners" portrays a subjective estimate of these power relationships over time. The X axis shows dates from 1830 to 1900, while the Y axis has no specific scale, except that higher is better for the saints' control of their own lives. This chart shows only the differences, so both lines are shown as nearly horizontal, the line representing the saints finally ascending beyond the line representing the United States in general. Of course, the absolute power of the saints was always only a tiny fraction of that of the U.S., and any difference in relative power (made possible by isolation, etc.,) was probably very small. The graph shows the differences to be large only so that they can be placed on a graph. The most important point to be taken from the graph is that Brigham Young was able to prevent the recurrence of the negative swing pattern shown twice in the early times.

The other two charts present some of the more quantifiable comparisons. As shown in the chart entitled "Church Population versus United States Population," both groups were continually growing. The last chart entitled "Church Percentage of United States Population" highlights the fact that the church rate of growth was greater than that of the general population during most of the 1800s, with the apparent exception of the period from about 1850 to 1860. Assuming the data are correct, the cause of the dip presumably was related to the hardships of the initial pioneer movement to Utah. Some fell away, some died from exposure, and some probably delayed their migration to Utah until life there was more secure. It is possible that the data I have are inaccurate in that they may exclude many faithful saints who were in the east or in England or Europe who wisely delayed their move until they could be absorbed into Utah society in an orderly fashion.

Having seen the destructive consequences of the saints' early political weaknesses, when Brigham Young became the church's leader, he did everything he could to keep the saints ahead of the easterners in relative power - in the ability to do as they wished or felt called to do by the gospel. The leverage of the great distances over the plains was the major factor which finally allowed the saints the advantage they needed in the continuing conflict with their enemies.

The saints at first seemed successful in their move to the frontier state of Missouri. However, after only two years the reaction of the old settlers forced them to leave their first settlement. A second try in the nearly uninhabited area of Nauvoo was more successful and lasted longer, but the inhabitants of the state later organized to eject them after 7 years. Only by moving to totally uninhabited land (and apparently uninhabitable by eastern standards) far from any present or future "neighbors" could the saints hope to find any long-term respite. Even at that, an army was on the way 10 years after the first Utah settlement. This time the blow was deflected because of the vast distance the army had to travel and over which it had to supply itself. The saints made it perfectly clear that if the army remained belligerent, it would find not a morsel of food for man or beast anywhere near Utah.

It should be noted that the saints as a body apparently did not normally understand their strategic situation. Perhaps if they had they would have been so discouraged that they would have given up at the thought of moving into the wilds of what became Utah. Even though in retrospect it was clear that they could never stay in Missouri or Nauvoo, they were willing to project themselves that far in hopes of finding long-term prosperity. It seems clear enough that Joseph understood their long-term situation. He made some efforts to get the saints to move further west before they were forced to do so. However, few, if any, would accept his vision and conclusion. As it turned out, when they were forced by their neighbors to make a choice, many preferred to abandon their religion rather than face the difficulties and uncertainties of the move to the mountain west. Joseph probably realized that his own death would be the shock necessary to get the saints mentally prepared for the next stage.

Even after the saints had established a base in Utah, the saints continued to be largely unaware of the dangers to them and their religious culture. Their own subsistence seemed to be as far as they could see, ignoring the need for group preparations for future conflicts. That was the genius of Brigham Young. He was perhaps the only one who could grasp their situation in its entirety and press for the necessary actions to keep them one step ahead of disaster. It is only in that context that the programs and teachings of the Utah period can be fitted into a consistent whole.

## Notes on "Relative Power" Chart

The accompanying chart is a subjective estimate of the relative power of the saints versus the easterners at various points in the history of the saints. Some of those important historical points are as follows:

| Historical notes on "Relative Power" Chart | |
|---|---|
| 1830 | The church is organized |
| Early 1831 | Many saints (about 1000) move to Kirtland. CHC 1:250 |
| Spring 1831 | The saints begin their move to Jackson County. CHC 1:256 |
| Fall 1833 | The saints are driven out of Jackson County. CHC 1:340 |
| Jan. 1838 | Prophet leaves Kirtland. CHC 1:407 |
| Spring 1838 | Saints move to Far West. CHC 1:424. |
| Oct. 1838 | Missouri Extermination Order. CHC 1:465. |
| Dec. 1838 | 12,000 Saints turned out of Missouri, driven from Far West. CHC 1:453, 515. |
| 1839 | Saints move to Nauvoo. CHC 2:18 |
| 1844 | Prophet killed, 27 June 1844. CHC 2:288. |
| 1845 | Nauvoo City Charter repealed, Jan 21, 1845. CHC 2:469. |

| 1845 | Church organization operated in place of the repealed civil laws. CHC 2:470. |
| 1846 | 30,000 Saints driven from Nauvoo. Feb. CHC 3:40 |
| 1846 | 500 men taken for Mexican war ("Mormon Battalion"). July. CHC 3:83. Saints were in Winter Quarters, still close to their enemies. |
| 1847 | Saints arrive in Utah. Isolated from enemies by large distances but small in number and weak in food. July 24. CHC 3:224. |
| 1857 | Johnston's army approaches Utah. |
| 1858 | Army enters Utah. |
| 1861 | Start of Civil War, April 13, 1861. |
| 1861 | Army leaves Utah. |
| 1865 | End of Civil War, April 9, 1865. Two million casualties including 600,000 dead. |
| 1869 | Land titles finally available in Utah. CHC 5:283. |
| 1869 | Completion of railroad, May 10. CHC 5:242. |
| 1869 | Vice President Schuyler Colfax visits SLC Oct 3, 1869, to consider war, only five months after railroad completed. CHC 5:282-6. |
| 1877 | Death of Brigham Young, Aug. 29, 1877. CHC 5:509. |
| 1890 | Repeal of Polygamy by the church, Oct. 6, 1890. D&C Off. Decl. - 1 |
| 1896 | Utah receives statehood, 4 Jan 1896. CHC 6:337. No serious hope of overtaking or changing the saints. |

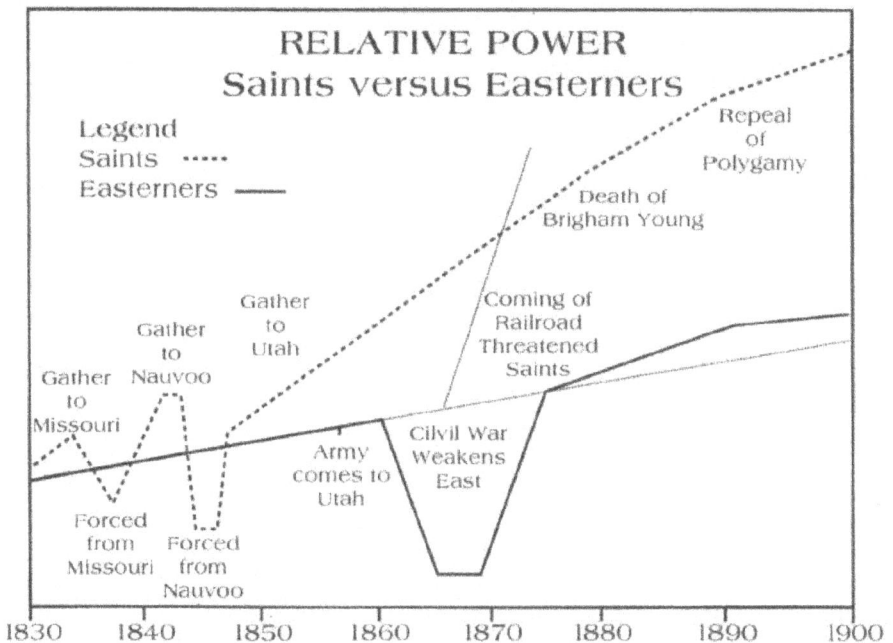

RELATIVE POWER Saints versus Easterners

## Church Population versus U.S. Population
### 1830 - 1910

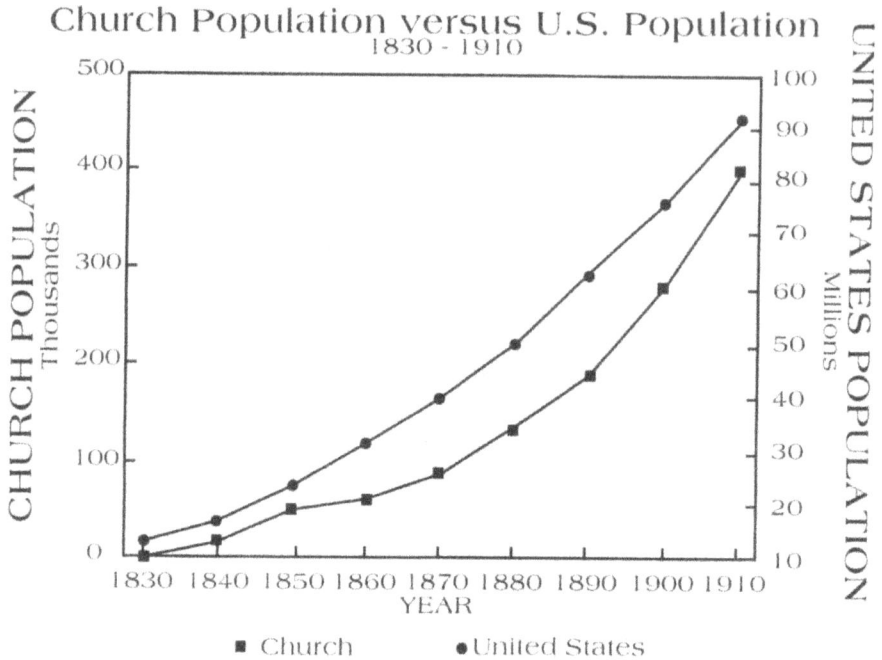

| | Church Population 1830-1910 | | United States Population 1830-1910 | |
|---|---|---|---|---|
| | 1830 | 6 | 1830 | 12,866,020 |
| | 1840 | 17,000 | 1840 | 17,069,453 |
| | 1850 | 52,000 | 1850 | 23,191,876 |
| | 1860 | 61,000 | 1860 | 31,443,321 |
| | 1870 | 90,000 | 1870 | 39,818,449 |
| | 1880 | 133,000 | 1880 | 50,155,783 |
| | 1890 | 188,000 | 1890 | 62,947,714 |
| | 1900 | 283,000 | 1900 | 75,994,575 |
| | 1910 | 400,000 | 1910 | 91,972,266 |

Some of the many factors that determined the relative decision-making power of the saints, or factors in the power relationship, are as follows: distance between the two groups (time and cost of transportation), relative population sizes, and the mood or inclination of the populations. This "mood" factor is of course much more difficult to quantify. Before the Civil War, the southerners were bellicose and arrogant (See General Johnston's writings during the Utah War episode, CHC 4:311.)

# Church Percentage of United States Population
## 1830-1910

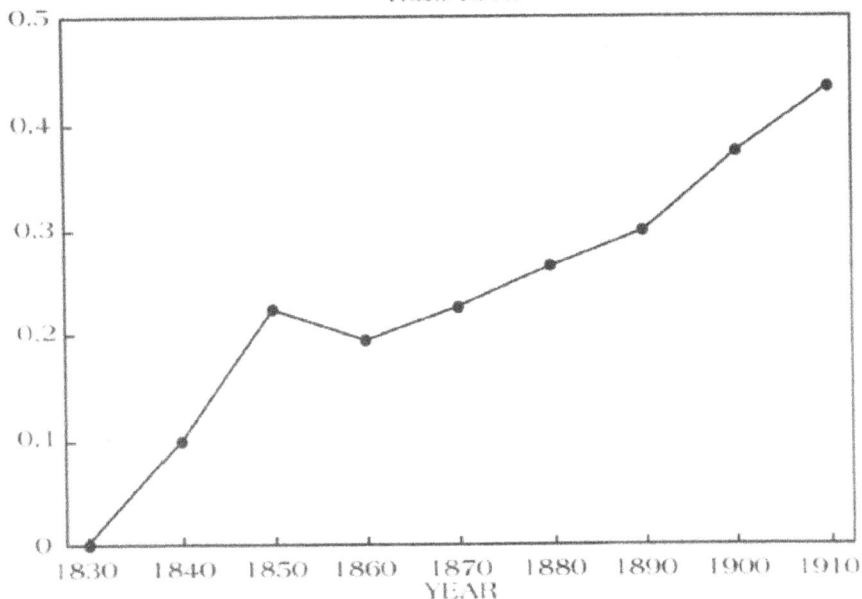

## CHURCH AS PERCENT OF
## UNITED STATES POPULATION
## 1830 - 1910

| | |
|---|---|
| 1830 | 0.00 |
| 1840 | 0.10 |
| 1850 | 0.22 |
| 1860 | 0.19 |
| 1870 | 0.23 |
| 1880 | 0.27 |
| 1890 | 0.30 |
| 1900 | 0.37 |
| 1910 | 0.43 |

The South seemed to want to keep control of Utah and other areas. After the war, the South lost control of all governmental functions, and was subjected to carpetbaggers, as they had helped impose on Utah. They got a taste of "territorial" government themselves. Their loss of power and governmental suffering may have made them less likely to try to impose territorial style governments on other states.

There surely was a tiredness of and disgust for war. They had seen the death and destruction caused by immorality and the war spirit. After the war, there may have been more accurate information available to the public. The public level of tolerance for each other and the "spirit of constitution" (due process, equal protection, and freedom of religion) may have increased. The Civil War may have changed the standards by which secession, treason, etc., were judged. These had always been the charges hurled against the saints by their enemies. After the Civil War, there were only free men, no slaves, so that slave-state issue was gone. The saints had never attempted to create another nation.

The chart has an associated table showing some of the historical events which help illustrate the ebb and flow of power relationships. Some of the major events noted on the chart deserve a brief discussion.

1. The settling of Missouri and Nauvoo and the forced expulsion from each is familiar history and needs no extra comment here.

2. The first major conflict after the saints left Nauvoo occurred at Winter Quarters in 1846, while the saints were still fairly close to their enemies. They were approached about sending 500 men to fight in the Mexican War. Later historians have put a good face on this event, emphasizing only some of the good results, while overlooking the sinister aspects and the saints' less than enthusiastic contemporary reactions. Brigham Young's comment in 1857 on that transaction (as the army was approaching Utah) sets the tone:

> There cannot be a more damnable, dastardly order issued than was issued by the Administration to this people while they were in an Indian country, in 1846. Before we left Nauvoo, not less than two United States' senators came to receive a pledge from us that we would leave the United States; and then, while we were doing our best to leave their borders, the poor, low, degraded curses sent a requisition for five hundred of our men to go and fight their battles! That was President Polk; and he is now weltering in hell with old Zachary Taylor, where the present administrators will soon be, if they do not repent. JD 5:231-2 BY Sept 13, 1857 SLC.

John Taylor made similar comments about the saints' treatment. He spoke of these two senators despoiling and disenfranchising 30,000 saints (JD 5:151 JT Aug 23, 1857 SLC), and making war on the sick and infirm (JD 7:122-3 JT Jan 10, 1858 SLC).

In the CHC an optimistic view is taken of this situation, saying that the US government had finally extended some help to the saints, arguing that the pay for the men would be enough to get their families to Utah. CHC 3:81 July 1846. However, the brethren did not at first view it that way. The CHC treatment puts a minimal focus on Brigham Young's words, but a more extensive coverage of Elder Little's work in Washington. This seems to have put quite a different twist on things; "spin doctors" are not a recent government invention.

Apparently, the saints had requested that they be enlisted to go California or Oregon to help protect an area where they thought they might live, but they had not requested that they go south to participate directly in the war with Mexico.

The officers delivering the requisition for men were accompanied by three companies of dragoons. That military contingent seems much larger than might be required if it were truly an offering of charity. Had the saints not complied, they might well have been charged once again with treason and some of them imprisoned and killed. John Taylor was of the opinion that the whole thing was a trap which failed to work because they complied with the request. JD 5:144 Aug 23, 1857.

The logic in requesting 500 men rather than some other number is itself an indication of the government's unfriendly attitude toward the saints. The officers making the request were told that the Mormons were not to be permitted to contribute more than 500 men, so that the total military force to be sent was not more than one-third Mormon, (perhaps to make sure they did not mutiny), and so that they would not be able to have a chance at being a majority population in any part of California (granted statehood in 1850). These restrictions do not sound wholly sympathetic to the saints.

Brigham Young did console the men with the fact (prophetic insight) that they would not have to fight. (It is unlikely that the non-Mormons were as sure as Brigham Young that there would be no fighting involved.)

But still the loss to the saints of these men was probably never made up for by the money received. At least Brigham Young did not think so. The money would have little value in Utah.

There are other indicators of a non-charitable intent. The rather obvious issue of where the families would reside during the years of army duty had not been addressed by the president before the "offer" was made, showing that little concern was held for the welfare of the saints. The "impress gang" finally made a weak and temporary, tentative offer, unauthorized by the president, of allowing them to use Indian lands until the men could return for their families. By not making arrangements and commitments in advance, the president could still delay and finally offer them nothing on the land issue.

Some good did come of the Mormon Battalion episode, but certainly not because of the good intentions of the US government. It was good only because the Lord turned it to good.

A note on personalities: President Polk was from North Carolina and Tennessee, and was obviously in sympathy with southern opinions. The two senators included Senator Douglas, supposedly a past friend, now opportunistically turned persecutor.

3. The Utah War will be dealt with in its own separate chapter. The main point is that for political, economic, and strategic factors, the east could not project a military force to Utah with sufficient strength to intimidate or overpower the saints. The Civil War caused the army to leave.

4. The civil war was a major factor in protecting the saints. The eastern state's will to fight was greatly weakened after many casualties and much destruction. The

civil war gave the saints the long-term edge they needed. It blasted southern power and bigotry against Mormons.

The pre-Civil War South seems to have had much greater antipathy for the Mormons than did the Northerners. One reason related to the slave state/free state issue. The South had lost California, but perhaps wished to claim Utah. It is probably significant that General A. Sidney Johnston was one of the few men willing to lead the 1857 expedition against the Mormons. He was a southerner as were some of his officers. They left Utah in 1861 to fight in the Civil War on the South's side. General Johnston died in that war.

Before the war there were 15 slave states and 19 free states and eight territories. In the war, 11 slave states withdrew from the union and formed the Confederate States. The remaining 23 states and the territories, including Utah, fought for the union. The civil war put a great dent in the easterners' power to persecute the saints. There were two million casualties including 600,000 dead. One third (260,000) of the south's adult white male army of about 780,000 were killed (out of about 1 million men of military age, 15-40). Total southern population was about 9 million including 3.5 million blacks.

In the north, one-sixth of the soldiers (360,000) died out of an army of about 2,160,000. About 4 million northern men were of military age out of a total population of about 22 million.

Put in other terms, two-thirds of all soldiers suffered some kind of casualty, and 40% of all military age men were casualties of the war. This probably means nearly every family in the country felt some direct consequences of the war. The sheer size of the tragedy surely drained off much of the desire for further internal violence.

The *World Book Encyclopedia* article on the Civil War contains this statement:

With the loss of Southern control of the national government, the more traditional Southern ideals no longer had an important influence over government policy. The Yankee Protestant ideals of the North became the standard for the United States. However, those ideals, which stressed hard work, education, and economic freedom, helped encourage the development of United States as a modern, industrial power.[1]

This intriguing statement deserves further study. To the extent it is true, it helps provide further explanations for the effects of the Civil War on the success of the saints. The South was the saints' greatest enemy, and the Civil War crushed it.

A second possible reason for the South's greater antipathy against the Mormons was the conflict and competition of two major American religions. The Southern Baptist church has been called the catholic church of the south. By the same token, the Mormon church is the catholic church of the west and southwest. The Baptist church of the time was pro-slavery, anti-freedom, and inefficient economically. The Mormons were anti-slavery, for freedom, and efficient economically. The Baptists were an almost creedless "no-religion" religion, in contrast with the Mormons' precise and complete revealed religion. The intellectual ties between the Baptist church and the Civil War are discussed in Harold Bloom's *The American Religion.*[2]

The Civil War was a religious war in that it was driven by two opposing moralities. The same could probably be said of the 1857 Utah War, wherein the morals of the South fought the morals of the North at the periphery of the country.

There are several indications that the South was more hostile to the Mormons than the North, and that the Civil War which crushed the South had many lasting good results for the saints, besides the more immediate weakening of the nation and enforcing a long preoccupation with survival, leaving no time or strength to bother with the Mormons. At this critical time perhaps Abraham Lincoln's comment about the Mormons described the attitude of the whole nation in its time of great travail. He is reported to have said, "If the Mormons let him alone, he would let them alone." CHC 5:310.

As noted above, there was a moral and cultural change that resulted from the North winning the Civil War. Politically, it appears that the South was largely Democratic, so that joining with the northern Democrats gave them a large amount of power in the national government. The political power held by the South before the Civil War seemed to have a large negative effect on the saints. We can start with the fact that the three US presidents who presided over the saints' worst disasters were Democrats, elected with the help of the strongly Democratic south (and presumably bound to implement the views and preferences of their southern supporters, including a hatred of the Mormons). The Democratic presidents who drew curses from the saints and the disasters they allowed or ordered were as follows: Van Buren and the expulsion from Missouri; Polk and the expulsion from Illinois and the requisition of Mormon troops for the Mexican War; Buchanan and the Utah Expedition. These experiences might be reason enough for Utah to tend to support Republican leaders.

A short history of the Democratic party will help show its many connections with Southern viewpoints:

> Although the party was from the outset a strong opposition force in Congress, it did not win control of the administration until Jefferson became president in 1801. For the next 40 years, however, a Democratic president was continually in office.
>
> ....
>
> Between 1837, when Jackson retired, and 1860, four Democratic presidents-- Martin Van Buren, James K. Polk, Franklin Pierce, and James Buchanan--were elected. The party history of this period was dominated by the slavery issue, and in 1860, on the eve of the Civil War, the party split into Northern and Southern factions. The Republican Party then won decisive victories until 1876, when a close presidential election opened an era of fairly even struggle between the parties. The Democrats triumphed temporarily when Grover Cleveland won the presidency in the elections of 1884 and 1892, but in 1896 they split over the issue of the free coinage of silver.[3]

On the Democratic Party's position in the northern states, the *World Book* article on the Civil War makes this comment:

> Opposition to the war and Lincoln's policies came chiefly from the Democratic party, especially from a group known as the Peace Democrats, who wanted the war stopped. Republicans considered the Peace Democrats disloyal and treacherous and called them Copperheads, after the poisonous snake.[4]

In other words, for only 8 out of 60 years before the Civil War was there a non-Democratic president. And even then, for 5 of those 8 years, the Whig president was from Virginia, a southern state. Obviously, these men could not have been president without the support of the south, and thus they had to represent much of the antipathy of the south toward the Mormons.

We may assume that Lincoln, a Republican, would have been more tolerant of the Mormons even without the Civil War to divert his attention. Four years after the War, Ulysses Grant, also a Republican, did consider military action against the saints, but did not carry it out, even though by Civil War standards it would have been a small operation (see above).

The one Democrat who did become president (twice) after the Civil War and before Utah's statehood, Grover Cleveland, may have had views more like the then-current Republicans than the Pre-Civil-War Democrats.

This has been a very brief overview, and one might like to see here a whole book's worth of information devoted to the national politics of the time and the saints' place within it. However, the only goal here has been to show ties between the saints' persecutors and the viewpoints of the pre-Civil War South, plus the changes caused by the Civil War.

Besides the general political conflicts, there are the more individualized conflicts felt by those who visited the South, including southern-controlled Missouri. The Church's problems in Missouri are well known. In other parts of the South there were occasions where Mormon missionaries were mobbed and killed. Of course, there was mob violence in the North as well, but it seems that the North was more tolerant than the South and required far more stimulus to reach the point of killing people. Missouri might be thought an exception, but it was really a southern stronghold. (See the chapter on blood atonement for comments on the death of missionaries in the South, and related social commentary.)

It appears that slave systems generally cannot compete economically with free systems, at least not in the long term. In a growing society, slave systems must extend tyranny to wider and wider groups or lose relative power themselves. The Mormons were a powerful force for freedom in the "new territories" (border areas and potential new states), and the south seemed to hate them passionately. Apparently, they saw them as having huge power to thwart the southern plan to make all new states slave states. The Mormons apparently had far more political power in this area than their numbers might otherwise indicate.

The question of slavery in the territories was a lively one and came up several times. In the Missouri Compromise of 1820-21 Congress said there was to be no slavery in the territories. The 1857 Dred Scott Supreme Court decision said slavery must be allowed in the territories. The Congress in 1862, during the Civil War, banned slavery in the territories;[5] on January 1, 1863, President Lincoln issued the Emancipation Proclamation, freeing the slaves in the Southern states; and in 1865 the Thirteenth Amendment abolished slavery in the entire United States.

5. Had the Civil War not happened, the saints may easily have been crushed with the coming of the railroad. This possibility is represented by the sharply rising dotted line that begins at about 1865 and intersects the saints' line at about 1870. This is not idle speculation. Just five months after the completion of the railroad, Vice President Tyler Colfax was in Utah to see whether a second federal military campaign against the saints might be successful. CHC 5:282-6.

The Cullom bill, before Congress in 1870, proposed to punish bigamy and break up homes where multiple marriages existed. 40,000 troops were to be used to accomplish this. The press predicted war if the bill were passed. The bill was finally defeated, partly because of the great and long-lasting blow to interstate commerce it would mean. Surely the first thing to be destroyed by the resisting saints would be the railroad system to keep out the armies and their supplies. A two or three year war was contemplated at a cost of $600 million, with a 20 year period to rebuild what was lost. All this for an institution that would probably die out on its own in due time. CHC 5:314-5.

In 1871, the government, including President Grant was still considering war with the saints, although nothing happened. WWJ 7:3, 36. Later, in Oct. 1875, President Grant actually visited Salt Lake City in a friendly mood, and at least his family were disabused of some of the many falsehoods then circulating about the saints. WWJ 7:249. After that time, war seemed not to be an option seriously considered. President Grant served as president for two terms, 1869 to 1877.

6. The death of Brigham Young brought a change in the power factors, an apparent loss for the saints. The "Lion of the Lord" was gone, and the past levels of group organization and resistance could probably never be the same again. The East pressed hard against the church at that time, apparently trying to exploit what they hoped would be a weak point.

However, his death probably came at a time when a different strategy was required by the saints. The saints had reached a critical mass that could not be snuffed out by the pressures of their enemies. It was time to end the confrontation phase and start the reconciling process so that the saints could merge with the main society and have an opportunity to act as a leaven.

7. The 1890 repeal of polygamy was another important development. This probably weakened the saints slightly because of possible lowered birth rates, and the greater ability of foreigners to marry in among the saints. But it also weakened the east significantly because they lost what may have seemed the perfect club to beat the saints and seek their destruction. Losing that club was a great blow to their evil plans. After 1890, the saints' ability to win converts might well have gone up enough to more than offset the loss of growth through a lower birth rate.

The war on the saints based on the polygamy issue, 1862-1890, is summarized in detail in such historical works as Smurr, *Territorial Constitutions*.[6]

8. The granting of statehood to Utah in 1896 finally signaled the end of the official government policy of persecution of the Mormons. The dates that the other western states were admitted to the union are interesting. The fact that California was admitted in 1850, Oregon in 1859, and Nevada in 1864, while Utah was kept out, is evidence of specific eastern antipathy against the Mormons. Utah had four times the required population when it was finally admitted. The others needed far fewer to enter. Letting in a small-population state like Nevada may have been done as much to restrict Utah's future size as for any other reason.

## Chapter Notes

[1] "Civil War," *The World Book Encyclopedia,* 22 vol. (Chicago: World Book, Inc., 1992), vol. 4, p. 634.

[2] Harold Bloom, *The American Religion; The Emergence of the Post-Christian Nation* (New York: Simon and Schuster, 1992).

[3] "Democratic Party," *Encyclopaedia Britannica*, 15th ed., 30 vols. (Chicago: Encyclopaedia Britannica, Inc., 1981).

[4] "Civil War," *World Book.*

[5] Smurr, John Welling, *Territorial Constitutions; A Legal History of the Frontier Governments Erected by Congress in the American West, 1787-1900.* Indiana University, Ph.D., 1960 (Ann Arbor, Michigan: University Microfilms, Mic 60-2846).

[6] Smurr, Chapter III, "The Bill of Rights in the Territories," pp. 89-193, especially pp. 108-127.

The following table shows the U.S. presidents holding office during the long period of the saint's struggle to find a place of refuge. The granting of statehood to Utah represented the achievement of safety for the saints and their integration with the United States on favorable terms.

| U.S. Presidents | | | |
|---|---|---|---|
| **President** | **Years in Office** | **Birth State** | **Party** |
| 1. George Washington | 1789-1797 | Va. | none |
| 2. John Adams | 1797-1801 | Mass. | Federalist |
| 3. Thomas Jefferson | 1801-1809 | Va. | Democratic-Repub. |
| 4. James Madison | 1809-1817 | Va. | Democratic-Repub. |
| 5. James Monroe | 1817-1825 | Va. | Democratic-Repub. |
| 6. John Quincy Adams | 1825-1829 | Mass. | Democratic-Repub. |
| 7. Andrew Jackson | 1829-1837 | S.C. | Democratic |
| 8. Martin Van Buren | 1837-1841 | N.Y. | Democratic |
| 9. William H. Harrison | 1841 | Va. | Whig |
| 10. John Tyler | 1841-1845 | Va. | Whig |
| 11. James K. Polk | 1845-1849 | N.C. | Democratic |
| 12. Zackary Taylor | 1849-1850 | Va. | Whig |
| 13. Millard Fillmore | 1850-1853 | N.Y. | Whig |
| 14. Franklin Pierce | 1853-1857 | N.H. | Democratic |
| 15. James Buchanan | 1857-1861 | Pa. | Democratic |
| 16. Abraham Lincoln | 1861-1865 | Ky. | Republican |
| 17. Andrew Johnson | 1865-1869 | N.C. | Natl. Union (Republicans and War Democrats). Johnson was a Democrat. |
| 18. Ulysses S. Grant | 1869-1877 | Ohio | Republican |
| 19. Rutherford B. Hayes | 1877-1881 | Ohio | Republican |
| 20. James A. Garfield | 1881 | Ohio | Republican |
| 21. Chester A. Arthur | 1881-1885 | Vt. | Republican |
| 22. Grover Cleveland | 1885-1889 | N.J. | Democratic |
| 23. Benjamin Harrison | 1889-1893 | Ohio | Republican |
| 24. Grover Cleveland | 1893-1897 | N.J. | Democratic |
| 25. William McKinley | 1897-1901 | Ohio | Republican |

Source: *World Book*, "President of the United States"

Utah's neighboring states and their dates of admission to statehood are listed below:

| | |
|---|---|
| California | 1850 |
| Oregon | 1859 |
| Nevada | 1864 |
| Colorado | 1876 |
| Wyoming | 1890 |
| Utah | 1896 |
| New Mexico | 1912 |
| Arizona | 1912 |

## CHAPTER 6

# Slavery and the Territories

The settling of Utah occurred at a time of great national conflict over the slavery issue, which ended in the Civil War. This national conflict had many effects on the Mormons, both before and after the move to Utah. It would be valuable to have access to a thorough study of the political setting of Utah as it related to slavery and other major issues of the time. Perhaps someone has already done it, but I do not have the benefit of that data. What follows is a cursory survey of that historical political setting, consisting of readings plus a summary and conclusion.

Slavery was prohibited in the territories outside the original thirteen states by the Northwest Ordinance of 1785, and the law was reaffirmed when the U.S. Constitution was adopted in 1787. Twelve of the original thirteen states were slave states at the time they entered the union,[1] but by 1858 some, such as New York, had abolished slavery, and some new states such as Illinois (1803)[2] had abolished slavery (1848). Maine and Ohio are also mentioned as having abolished slavery by 1858.[3]

**Northwest Ordinances** (1785, 1787), in U.S. history, the major accomplishment of the Congress under the Articles of Confederation, establishing the prototype for development of all subsequently acquired territory. The ordinances outlined the method for survey and sale of the vast territory north of the Ohio River and set aside land for public schooling in each township. Further provision was made for the franchise, self-government, a bill of rights, and the prohibition of slavery, thereby establishing an important precedent in a sensitive area of sectional differences.[4]

The Northwest Ordinances also established a population threshold for admission as a state. Utah reached the 60,000 threshold before 1860, and perhaps as early as 1857.

Article V.

....

And, whenever any of the said [prospective] states shall have <u>sixty thousand free inhabitants</u> therein, such state shall be admitted, by its delegates, into the Congress of the United States on an equal footing with the original states in all respects whatever, and shall be at liberty to form a permanent constitution and state government: provided, the constitution and government so formed shall be republican.[5]

The Northwest Ordinances policy on slavery was modified by congressional action under the popular sovereignty concept:

**popular sovereignty**, generally, rule by the people; in pre-Civil War U.S. history, a controversial political doctrine that the people of federal territories should decide for themselves whether their territories would enter the Union as free or slave states. Its enemies, especially in New England, called it "squatters sovereignty." It was first applied in organizing the Utah and New Mexico territories in 1850; its most crucial application came with the passage of Sen. Stephen A. Douglas' Kansas-Nebraska Act of 1854, which repealed the prohibition of slavery north of latitude 36 degrees 30 minutes (established in the Missouri Compromise of 1820). The violent struggle that followed for control of the Kansas Territory (*see* Bleeding Kansas) illustrated the failure of popular sovereignty as a possible ground for agreement between pro-slavery and anti-slavery factions in the country.[6]

One of the results of "popular sovereignty" was the Kansas conflict:

**Bleeding Kansas** (1854-59), small civil war in the U.S. fought between pro-slavery and anti-slavery advocates for control of the new territory of Kansas under the doctrine of popular sovereignty. Sponsors of the Kansas-Nebraska Act (May 30, 1854) expected its provisions for territorial self-government to arrest the "torrent of fanaticism" that had been dividing the nation regarding the slavery issue. Instead, free soil forces from the North formed armed emigrant associations to populate Kansas, while pro-slavery advocates poured over the border from Missouri. Regulating associations and guerrilla bands were formed by each side, and only the intervention of the governor prevented violence in the Wakarusa War, launched in December 1855 over the murder of an anti-slavery settler. "Bleeding Kansas" became a fact with the Sack of Lawrence (May 21, 1856) in which a pro-slavery mob swarmed into town, wrecking and burning the hotel and newspaper office in an effort to wipe out this "hotbed of abolitionism." Three days later, an anti-slavery band led by John Brown retaliated in the Pottawatomie Massacre (*q.v.*). Periodic bloodshed along the border followed as the two factions fought battles, captured towns, and set prisoners free. Rivalry moved into politics with the struggle over the Lecompton Constitution (*q.v.*; 1857), reaching as far as the halls of Congress and the presidency. The question was finally settled when Kansas was admitted as a free state in January 1861, but meanwhile "Bleeding Kansas" had furnished the newly formed Republican Party with a much-needed antislavery issue in the national election of 1860. Claims for $400,000 in damages sustained in the border war were later approved by territorial commissioners.[7]

The Dred Scott decision removed all congressional and statutory protections against slavery in the territories, and, by implication, threatened to remove prohibitions against slavery in the states as well. Note that this decision was issued just before the federal army left for Utah.

**Dred Scott decision** (March 6, 1857), ruling of the U.S. Supreme Court that made slavery legal in the territories, thus adding fuel to the bitter sectional controversy and pushing the nation along the road to civil war. Though each member of the Supreme Court wrote a separate opinion, that of Chief Justice Roger B. Taney is usually referred to as the opinion of the court. This opinion is most widely known for its obiter dicta, or further observations about the case, uncalled for by the technical ruling. The decision declared that: (1) Negroes were not citizens and therefore could not sue in the federal courts; (2) a slave's residence in a free state did not make him a free man; and (3) the Missouri Compromise of 1820, which had forbidden slavery in that part of the Louisiana Purchase (except Missouri) lying north of latitude 36□ 30' was an unconstitutional exercise of congressional power.

The case concerned the status of a black man, Dred Scott, who in 1834 had been taken by his master from Missouri, a slave state, to Illinois, a free state, and later to Ft. Snelling in the Minnesota Territory. In 1846, with the help of anti-slavery lawyers, Scott sued for his own and his family's freedom in the Missouri state courts on the ground that his residence in a free state and a free territory had made him a free man. The court did not agree and held that Congress had no power to forbid slavery in the territories, because slaves were property and property rights were protected by the Constitution. This case was the first since *Marbury v. Madison* (1803) in which the Supreme Court had declared an act of Congress unconstitutional.

The Dred Scott decision dealt a serious blow to the anti-slavery forces that had hoped to keep slavery out of the territories, and particularly to Sen. Stephen A. Douglas' doctrine of "popular sovereignty." The slavery issue was not put to rest by the decision, as the court had hoped, but was the polarizing issue in a four-year civil war, after which the Thirteenth and Fourteenth Amendments to the Constitution were ratified, giving slaves freedom and citizenship.[8]

It should be noted that the saints were in Missouri when Dred Scott was taken out by his master, and were still in Nauvoo at the time his court action began.

The army's move to Utah immediately after the Dred Scott decision looks surprisingly like a Southern move to make Utah a slave state, either in practice by bringing in a slave culture, or if popular sovereignty still had any strength, by control of the government.

Chief Justice Roger Brooke Taney was the author of the Dred Scott decision.

**Taney, Roger Brooke** Roger Brooke Taney, fifth chief justice of the Supreme Court of the United States, is principally remembered for the decision in the Dred Scott case, with which the court's majority opinion set back the cause of the antislavery forces by many years. Yet Taney was more than merely a rigid supporter of states' rights; in many important cases he advanced, in strict accordance with the Constitution, the power of the federal government.

....

But the majority opinion that Taney delivered 20 years later, on March 6, 1857, in *Dred Scott v. Sanford* is the one for which he became famous. In essence, the decision argued that Scott was a slave and as such was not a citizen and could not sue in a federal court. Taney's further opinion that Congress had no power to exclude slavery from the territories and that Negroes could not become citizens was bitterly attacked in the Northern Press. The Dred Scott decision probably created more disagreement than any other legal opinion in U.S. history; it became a violently divisive issue in national politics and dangerously undermined the prestige of the Supreme Court.[9]

Stephen A. Douglas was a man whose career paralleled that of the saints and he interacted with them at many points. His name appears in the History of the Church several times.

**Douglas, Stephen A(rnold)** (b. April 23, 1813, Brandon, Vt. -- d. June 3, 1861,

Chicago, U.S. orator and Democratic leader who espoused the cause of popular sovereignty (local choice) in relation to the issue of slavery in the territories before the Civil War (1861-65). He was re-elected senator from Illinois in 1858 after a series of debates with the Republican candidate, Abraham Lincoln, to whom he lost the presidency two years later.

Douglas left New England at the age of 20 to settle in Jacksonville, Ill., where his affinity for politics quickly propelled him into a position of leadership in the Democratic Party. A number of judicial and administrative positions (1835-43) broadened his experience and led to his election to the U.S. House of Representatives (1843). One of its youngest members, Douglas gained early prominence as a dedicated worker and gifted speaker. Heavy-set and only five feet four inches tall, he was dubbed the "Little Giant" by his contemporaries.

He embraced a lifelong enthusiasm for national expansion, giving consistent support to the annexation of Texas (1845), the Mexican War (1846-48), a vigorous stance toward Great Britain in the Oregon boundary dispute (1846), military protection for Western settlements, government land grants to promote transcontinental railroad construction, and a free homestead policy for settlers.

Douglas was elected in 1846 to the U.S. Senate, in which he served until his death; there he became deeply involved in the nation's search for a solution to the slavery problem. He was immediately placed in the strategic position of chairman of the Committee on Territories; as such, for the following 14 years, he introduced all bills organizing Western territories and admitting them as states to the Union. Douglas was particularly prominent in the bitter debates between North and South on the extension of slavery westward. Trying to remove the onus from Congress, he developed the theory of popular sovereignty (originally called squatter sovereignty), under which the people in a territory would make the slavery decision themselves. Douglas himself was not a slaveholder, though his wife was. He was influential in the passage of the Compromise of 1850 (which tried to maintain a congressional balance between free and slave states), and the organization of the Utah and New Mexico Territories under popular sovereignty was a victory for his doctrine.

COMMENT: We may speculate that the army went to Utah to take advantage of that political "victory."

The climax of Douglas' theory was reached in the Kansas-Nebraska Act (1854); more than any other, it influenced the course of U.S. history by substituting local option toward slavery in the Kansas [Bloody Kansas] and Nebraska territories for that of congressional mandate, thus repealing the Missouri Compromise of 1820. Its passage was largely a triumph for Douglas, who was bitterly condemned and vilified by anti-slavery forces. A strong contender for the Democratic presidential nomination in both 1852 and 1856, he was too outspoken to be chosen by a party that was still trying to bridge the sectional gap.

The Supreme Court struck directly at the popular sovereignty concept in the Dred Scott decision (1857), which held that the prohibition of slavery in the free states or territories was unconstitutional. The following year Douglas engaged in a number of widely publicized debates with Lincoln in a close contest for the Senate seat in Illinois, and although his followers received fewer electoral votes than those of Lincoln,

Douglas was elected 54 to 46 by a favorable legislature. In the debates, Douglas spelled out his continued support of popular sovereignty, denying that it contradicted the court's decision, with the result that Southern opposition to him intensified, and he was denied reappointment to his committee chairmanship in the Senate.

When the "regular" (Northern) Democrats nominated him for president in 1860, the Southern wing broke away and supported a separate ticket headed by John C. Breckinridge of Kentucky. Although Douglas received only 12 electoral votes, he was second to Lincoln in the number of popular votes polled. Douglas then urged the South to acquiesce in the results of the election.

At the outbreak of the Civil War, he denounced secession as criminal and was one of the strongest advocates of maintaining the integrity of the Union at all costs. At Lincoln's request, he undertook a mission to the Border States and to the Northwest to rouse the spirit of Unionism. Partly as a result of these exertions, he died unexpectedly in Chicago, where he had made his home since his election to the Senate.[10]

Douglas was one of the political leaders who helped push the saints out of Illinois, his home state. Politically that would help him since he was pro-slavery, and the saints were anti-slavery. Getting that large group of anti-slavery people out of the state would improve the proportion of voters inclined to vote for him. He was obviously interested in keeping the southern pro-slavery people happy so he could be president. He was upset when they seceded, but perhaps it was more because that ended his opportunity to benefit from supporting them, and they him, than from any genuine concern about the Union. Perhaps to him, retaining the Union simply meant he could be president of a larger group.

He may also have argued that the saints' going west served the nation's (and his) goals of territorial expansion, even if their rights as citizens were destroyed in the process. Of course, anybody who went west for any reason might serve that purpose. But there is no particular reason to think he would protect them or their institutions or their freedom once they had arrived and claimed and tamed some new land. He would probably take their gains from them as quickly as the next man when it served his larger purposes, just as he did in Nauvoo.

Before the Dred Scott decision, Douglas may have wished to see the saints pushed into the territories as an aid to his plan for "popular sovereignty," which really meant an opportunity to override the previous prohibitions against slavery in the territories. The popular sovereignty concept was first used in 1850 in setting up the Utah and New Mexico territories. The saints had not been effective in the past in stopping the slavery people, so perhaps they would also be a pushover again in the West. The southern forces may have seen it the same way, and planned to take over the state at the opportune time just as it first became ripe for statehood, as indicated by the army's movement to Utah in 1857, preceded by some Missourians, such as those involved in the so-called Mountain Meadow Massacre.

The second use of his popular sovereignty concept was in Kansas, and led to the "Bleeding Kansas" episode, indicating either he did not understand or chose to ignore the destructive forces he was dealing with.

The Lincoln-Douglas debates took place in the year that the federal army arrived in

Utah. The debates portray the issues and tensions of the era, and took place in Illinois, a part of the nation familiar to the Mormons. The importance of the territories to the whole free/slave issue is illustrated. The territories were the battleground, either in actual violence, as in Kansas, or in rhetoric, as in these debates.

## The Lincoln-Douglas Debates

The debates between Abraham Lincoln and Stephan A. Douglas for the U.S. Senate seat from Illinois in 1858 constitute one of the most famous political dialogues in American history. A man of great ability with a magnificent voice, Douglas had served in the Senate since 1847, and was generally regarded as a certain presidential candidate in 1860. Lincoln's voice was high-pitched; he tended to speak indifferently at first, but then to warm to his subject. Riding into town on a wagon, he played to the hilt the contrast with Douglas' splendid entourage, which included a private railroad car. In the end, Lincoln narrowly lost the election through inequitable apportionment, but acquired a national reputation.

....

## Lincoln's Reply

Well, then, let us talk about popular sovereignty. What is popular sovereignty? Is it the right of the people to have slavery or not have it, as they see fit, in the territories? I will state -- and I have an able man to watch me -- my understanding is that popular sovereignty, as now applied to the question of slavery, does allow the people of a territory to have slavery if they want to, but does not allow them *not* to have it if they *do not* want it.

I do not mean that if this vast concourse of people were in a territory of the United States, any one of them would be obliged to have slave if he did not want one; but I do say that, as I understand the Dred Scott decision, if any one man wants slaves, all the rest have no way of keeping that one man from holding them.

....

In the first place, what is necessary to make the institution national? Not war. There is no danger that the people of Kentucky will shoulder their muskets, and, with a young "nigger" stuck on every bayonet, march into Illinois and force them upon us. There is no danger of our going over there and making war upon them. Then what is necessary for the nationalization of slavery? It is simply the next Dred Scott decision. It is merely for the Supreme Court to decide that no state under the Constitution can exclude it, just as they have already decided that under the Constitution neither Congress nor the territorial legislature can do it. When that is decided and acquiesced in, the whole thing is done.

This being true, and this being the way, as I think, that slavery is to be made national, let us consider what Judge Douglas is doing every day to that end. In the first place, let us see what influence he is exerting on public sentiment. In this and like communities, public sentiment is everything. With public sentiment, nothing can fail; without it nothing can succeed. Consequently, he who molds public sentiment goes deeper than he who enacts statutes or pronounces decisions. He makes statutes and decisions possible or impossible to be executed.

....

I hold that the proposition that slavery cannot enter a new country without police regulation is historically false. It is not true at all. I hold that the history of this country shows that the institution of slavery was originally planted upon this continent *without* these "police regulations" which the Judge now thinks necessary for the actual establishment of it. Not only so, but is there not another fact: How came this Dred Scott decision to be made? It was made upon the case of a Negro being taken and actually held in slavery in Minnesota Territory, claiming his freedom because the act of Congress prohibited his being so held there. *Will the Judge pretend that Dred Scott was not held there without police regulations?* There is at least one matter of record as to his having been held in slavery in the territory, not only without police regulations but in the teeth of congressional legislation supposed to be valid at the time. This shows that there is vigor enough in slavery to plant itself in a new country even against unfriendly legislation. It takes not only law but the *enforcement* of law to keep it out. That is the history of this country upon the subject.

....

This is but an opinion, and the opinion of one very humble man; but it is my opinion that the Dred Scott decision, as it is, never would have been made in its present form if the party that made it had not been sustained previously by the elections. My own opinion is that the new Dred Scott decision, deciding against the right of the people of the states to exclude slavery, will never be made if that party is not sustained by the elections. I believe, further, that it is just as sure to be made as tomorrow is to come, if that party shall be sustained. ...

....

The real issue in this controversy -- the one pressing on every mind -- is the sentiment on the part of one class that looks upon the institution of slavery as a wrong and of another class that does not look upon it as a wrong. The sentiment that contemplates the institution of slavery in this country as a wrong is the sentiment of the Republican Party. It is the sentiment around which all their actions, all their arguments, circle -- from which all their propositions radiate. They look upon it as being a moral, social, and political wrong; and, while they contemplate it as such, they nevertheless have due regard for its actual existence among us and the difficulties of getting rid of it in any satisfactory way and to all the constitutional obligations thrown about it. Yet, having a due regard for these, they desire a policy in regard to it that looks to its not creating any more danger. They insist that it should, as far as may be, *be treated* as a wrong, and one of the methods of treating it as a wrong is to *make provision that it shall grow no larger*. They also desire a policy that looks to a peaceful end of slavery at some time as being wrong. ...

And if there be among you anybody who supposes that he, as a Democrat, can consider himself "as much opposed to slavery as anybody," I would like to reason with him. You never treat it as a wrong. What other thing that you consider as a wrong do you deal with as you deal with that? Perhaps, you *say* it is a wrong, *but your leader never does, and you quarrel with anybody who says it is wrong*. Although you pretend to say so yourself, you can find no fit place to deal with it as a wrong.

You must not say anything about it in the free states, *because it is not here*. You must not say anything about it in the slave states, *because it is there*. You must not say anything about it in the pulpit, because that is religion and has nothing to do with it. You must not say anything about it in politics, *because that will disturb the security of "my place."* There is no place to talk about it as being wrong, although you say yourself it *is* wrong.

But, finally, you will screw yourself up to the belief that if the people of the slave states should adopt a system of gradual emancipation on the slavery question, you would be in favor of it. You would be in favor of it. You say that is getting it in the right place and you would be glad to see it succeed. But you are deceiving yourself.

You all know that Frank Blair and Gratz Brown, down there in St. Louis, undertook to introduce that system in Missouri. They fought as valiantly as they could for the system of gradual emancipation, which you pretend you would be glad to see succeed. Now, I will bring you to the test. After a hard fight they were beaten, and when the news came over here, you threw up your hats and *hurrahed for democracy.* More than that, take all the argument made in favor of the system you have proposed, and it carefully excludes the idea that there is anything wrong in the institution of slavery. The arguments to sustain that policy carefully exclude it.

Even here, today, you hear Judge Douglas quarrel with me because I uttered a wish that it might sometime come to an end. Although Henry Clay could say he wished every slave in the United States was in the country of his ancestors, I am denounced by those pretending to respect Henry Clay for uttering a wish that it might sometime, in some peaceful way, come to an end. ...

I was glad to express my gratitude at Quincy, and I reexpress it here to Judge Douglas, -- *that he looks to no end of the institution of slavery.* That will help the people see where the struggle really is. It will hereafter place with us all men who really do wish the wrong may have an end. And whenever we can get rid of the fog which obscures the real question, when we can get Judge Douglas and his friends to avow a policy looking to its perpetuation, we can get them out from among that class of men and bring them to the side of those who treat it as a wrong. Then there will soon be an end of it, and that end will be its "ultimate extinction." Whenever the issue can be distinctly made and all extraneous matter thrown out so that men can fairly see the real difference between the parties, this controversy will soon be settled, and it will be done peaceably, too.

There will be no war, no violence. It will be placed again where the wisest and best men of the world placed it. Brooks of South Carolina once declared that when this Constitution was framed, its framers did not look to the institution existing until this day. When he said this, I think he stated a fact that is fully borne out by the history of the times. But he also said they were better and wiser men than the men of these days; yet the men of these days had experience which they had not, and, by the invention of the cotton gin, it became a necessity in this country that slavery should be perpetual.

I now say that, willingly or unwillingly, purposely or without purpose, Judge Douglas has been the most prominent instrument in changing the position of the institution of slavery which the fathers of the government expected to come to an end ere this -- *and putting it upon Brook's cotton gin basis --* placing it where he openly confesses he has no desire there shall ever be an end of it.

## Douglas' Reply

Mr. Lincoln tries to avoid the main issue by attacking the truth of my proposition, that our fathers made this government divided into free and slave states, recognizing the right of each to decide all its local questions for itself. Did they not thus make it? It is true that they did not establish slavery in any of the states or abolish it in any of them; but, finding thirteen states, twelve of which were slave and one free, they agreed to form a government uniting them together as they stood, divided into free and slave states, and to guarantee forever to each state the right to do as it pleased on the slavery question. Having thus made the government and conferred this right upon each state forever, I assert that this government can exist as they made it, divided into free and slave states, if any one state chooses to retain slavery.

He says that he looks forward to a time when slavery shall be abolished everywhere. I look forward to a time when each state shall be allowed to do as it pleases. If it chooses to keep slavery forever, it is not my business, but its own; if it chooses to abolish slavery, it is its own business, not mine. I care more for the great principle of selfgovernment, the right of the people to rule, than I do for all the Negroes in Christendom. I would not endanger the perpetuity of this Union, I would not blot out the great inalienable rights of the white men for all the Negroes that ever existed. Hence, I say, let us maintain ths government on the principles that our fathers made it, recognizing the right of each state to keep slavery as long as its people determine, or to abolish it when they please.

But Mr. Lincoln says that, when our fathers made this government, they did not look forward to the state of things now existing, and therefore he thinks the doctrine was wrong; and he quotes Brooks, of South Carolina, to prove that our fathers then thought that probably slavery would be abolished by each state acting for itself before this time. Suppose they did; suppose they did not foresee what has occurred -- does that change the principles of our government? They did not probably foresee the telegraph that transmits intelligence by lightning, nor did they foresee the railroads that now form the bonds of union between the different states, or the thousand mechanical inventions that have ellevated mankind. But do these things change the principles of the government? Our fathers, I say, made this government on the principle of the right of each state to do as it pleases in its own domestic affairs, subject to the Constitution, and allowed the people of each to apply to every new change of circumstances such remedy as they might see fit to improve their condition. This right they have for all time to come.

Mr. Lincoln went on to tell you that he does not at all desire to interfere with slavery in the states where it exists, nor does his party. I expected him to say that down here. Let me ask him, then, how he expects to put slavery in the course of ultimate extinction everywhere if he does not intend to interfere with it in the states where it exists? He says that he will prohibit it in all territories, and the inference is, then, that unless they make free states out of them, he will keep them out of the Union; for, mark you, he did not say whether or not he would vote to admit Kansas with slavery or not, as her people might apply (he forgot that, as usual, etc.); he did not say whether or not he was in favor of bringing the territories now in existence into the Union on the principle of Clay's Compromise Measures on the slavery question. I told you that he would not.

His idea is that he will prohibit slavery in all the territories and thus force them all to become free states, surrounding the slave states with a cordon of free states and hemming them in, <u>keeping the slaves confined to their present limits while they go on multiplying, until the soil on which they live will no longer feed them; and he will thus be able to put slavery in a course of ultimate extinction by starvation</u>. He will extinguish slavery in the Southern States as the French general exterminated the Algerines when he smoked them out. He is going to extinguish slavery by surrounding the slave states, hemming in the slaves and starving them out of existence, as you smoke a fox out of his hole.[11]

The famous statement by William M. Seward, concerning an "irrepressible conflict," was made in the fall of the year the federal army arrived in Utah. It restates Lincoln's concerns and arguments. The Civil War broke out two and one-half years later in 1861. The Utah army and its leaders returned to fight with the South. The territories, including Utah, all supported the Union. As the army left Utah, it destroyed most of its military material rather than leave it in the hands of the "opposition."

### William M. Seward: An Irrepressible Conflict

October 25, 1858.
Shall I tell you what this collision means? They who think that it is accidental, unnecessary, the work of interested or fanatical agitators, and therefore ephemeral, mistake the case altogether. It is an *irrepressible conflict* between opposing and enduring forces, and it means that the United States must and will, sooner or later, become either entirely a slaveholding nation or entirely a free-labor nation. Either the cotton and rice fields of South Carolina and the sugar plantations of Louisiana will ultimately be tilled by free labor, and Charleston and New Orleans become marts for legitimate merchandise alone, or else the rye fields and wheat fields of Massachusetts and New York must again be surrendered by their farmers to slave culture and to the production of slaves, and Boston and New York become once more markets for trade in the bodies and souls of men. It is the failure to apprehend this great truth that induces so many unsuccessful attempts at final compromise between the slave and free states, and it is the existence of this great fact that renders all such pretended compromises, when made, vain and ephemeral.[12]

It is difficult to follow the twist and turns of the decisions and statutes on territories and slavery, but perhaps a short outline will help.

1. The Northwest Ordinances (1785, 1787) established the prototype for development of all subsequently acquired territory. Provision was made for the prohibition of slavery, thereby establishing an important precedent in a sensitive area of sectional differences.

2. The Missouri Compromise of 1820 declared there was to be no slavery above latitude 36□ 30', thus partially repealing the Northwest Ordinances as to slavery. Utah's southern border is exactly at 37□, and is thus clearly in the northern "free" area.

3. California was allowed into the Union as a free state in 1850. It is both below and above the 36□ 31' line, so it is not clear what statutes or logic was used.

4. The concept of "popular sovereignty" was first used in 1850 in creating the Utah and

New Mexico territories (Utah is above the line and New Mexico is below the critical latitude), thus, as to Utah, removing the congressional prohibition against slavery in a piecemeal fashion. The Missouri Compromise of 1820 was still in effect, but apparently overridden or ignored in this case. The 1850 action also overrode the Northwest Ordinances. This allowed Utah to become a slave state if it chose, and New Mexico to not become a slave state if it chose. The reality was that Utah could become a slave state by infiltration as Lincoln suggested, there being no defense against such an event.

5. The process of creating the Kansas and Nebraska Territories in 1854 using "popular sovereignty," further eroded any claim to congressional statutory protection against slavery.

6. In 1857, the Dred Scott decision went further and said no statutory act of Congress could constitutionally protect territories from being slave areas. It explicitly overruled the Missouri Compromise of 1820, and, by implication, removed the territories' protection from slavery from the Northwest Ordinance. A second "Dred Scott" decision, feared by Lincoln if the Democrats won the presidency in 1860, might have gone the last step and prevented the states themselves from prohibiting slavery within their borders.

One source shows that in 1860, there were about 61,000 church members. So in 1857, the population of Utah must have been at or near the 60,000 mark needed for statehood. That would make it the next possible state to be admitted to the Union, and thus of special interest to the South and others as to the terms on which it might be admitted. Was it the next state to be a test case in the slave/free struggle? The South would want to be sure that there were strong pro-slavery forces in residence there. Having a southern general install a southern governor would surely help the process. (Governor (previously Colonel) Alfred Cumming was from Georgia, and General Albert Sidney Johnston was from Kentucky. General Johnston was killed in 1862 at Shiloh, Tennessee, in a battle against General Grant's forces.)

So, at the time of the coming of the army, it appears that Utah, as a territory, was not forbidden to have slavery by any still-current Congressional action, and the Dred Scott decision had said it could not have any such Congressional protection. Under the terms under which it became a territory, it explicitly had the authority, on becoming a state, to decide either way itself, under the "popular sovereignty" idea. As a state it could forbid slavery. But according to Lincoln's reading of the Dred Scott case, as a territory, it could not prevent anyone from bringing in slaves and continuing to keep them in slavery.

It may not have been clear what would have happened if the territory had chosen to try legislatively to exclude slavery from its boundaries. The Dred Scott case probably did not go that far. It may only have said that Congress could not prevent slavery in the territories, but may have said nothing about what the territories themselves may do, especially those with an explicit "popular sovereignty" clause in their enabling legislation, such as Utah. As a state it was still clear that Utah could exclude slavery, so why not as a territory? That would have been consistent with the "states rights" preferences of Judge Taney and others.

A southern political strategist of the time might have concluded that with a southern government in control of the territory, supported by an army, it would never be able exclude slavery through any legislative action of its own (it is not clear whether it could legally have taken such a step). Slaves might be brought in using the Dred Scott logic (they could not be excluded or freed), and when it came time for the statehood question, a strong southern presence there might cause the state to go slave, especially if the Mormons could be driven out and replaced with others, or had the right to vote taken from them. Thus Utah appears to have been a pawn in the national fight about the future of slavery. This may help explain the coming of Missouri people to Utah, and the saints' (and Indians') violent reaction to them, as in the so-called Mountain Meadow Massacre incident.

There is an intriguing possibility that the South wished to try to use polygamy to promote slavery, by disenfranchising the Mormons because of polygamy, and then slipping in slavery by the vote of only a small portion of the residents. That would have been a fiendishly clever use of one "bad" thing to promote something even worse.

## Chapter notes

[1] "The Lincoln-Douglas Debates," *The Annals of America*, 20 vols. (Chicago: Encyclopaedia Britannica, Inc., 1976), vol. 9, p. 9.

[2] "Illinois," *Encyclopaedia Britannica*, 15th ed., 30 vols. (Chicago: Encyclopaedia Britannica, Inc., 1981), vol. 9, p. 236.

[3] *Annals*, vol. 9, p. 10-11.

[4] "Northwest Ordinances," *Encyc. Brit.*

[5] W. Cleon Skousen, *The Making of America; The Substance and Meaning of the Constitution* (Washington, DC: The National Center for Constitutional Studies, 1985), p. 635.

[6] "popular sovereignty," *Encyc. Brit.*

[7] "Bleeding Kansas," *Encyc. Brit.*

[8] "Dred Scott decision," *Encyc. Brit.*

[9] "Taney, Roger Brooke," *Encyc. Brit.*

[10] "Douglas, Stephen A.," *Encyc. Brit.*

[11] *Annals*, vol. 9, pp. 8, 13, 14, 19, 26, 28-31.

[12] *Annals*, vol. 9, p. 33.

CHAPTER 7

# The Utah War

The "Utah War" was perhaps the greatest potential threat by the eastern establishment to the survival of the Mormons as a culture and a people that occurred during the Utah period. The army traveled across the plains into the Rocky Mountain range in the summer and fall of 1857. It remained in Wyoming for the winter and came into Utah in the Spring of 1858 in a peaceful manner. It did later cause some small disturbances, but left in 1861 after the beginning of the Civil War in the East.

Reproduced below are samples of the many discourses on the war and related topics, coming from the summer and fall of 1857 as the U.S. army under the command of General A. Sidney Johnston was approaching Utah. The discourses contain many valuable comments on the history of the saints' dealings with the U.S. government, on constitutional questions and interpretations, and on the attitude of the saints toward the approaching army. The *Journal of Discourses* contains 125 discourses given in 1857, by far the highest number of discourses reported in one year. The war was obviously a compelling topic and brought forth much worth reporting. The next highest year was 1860 with 92 discourses, and the third highest was 1862 with 64. The intense Utah War and Civil War threats presumably had much to do with the numbers of discourses given and reported. Brigham Young's discourse on September 13, 1857, describes the nation's crimes of the past and exhibits great determination to never again submit to mobbing:

> Movements of the Saints' Enemies -- The Crisis.
> Remarks by President Brigham Young,
> made in the Bowery, Great Salt Lake City,
> Sunday Afternoon, September 13, 1857.

I would like very well to hear some of the rest of the brethren speak, if I had entirely got over being angry and had patience to sit and hear. I think, however, that I shall be able to calm and control my feelings, though I do not expect to become entirely settled until the affairs around me are settled.

It is a pretty bold stand for this people to take, to say that they will not be controlled by the corrupt administrators of our General Government. We will be controlled by them if they will be controlled by the Constitution and laws; but they will not. Many of them do not care any more about the Constitution and the laws that they make than they do about the laws of another nation. That class trample the rights of the people under their feet, while there are also many who would like to honour them. All we have ever asked for is our constitutional rights. We wish the laws of our Government honoured, and we have ever honoured them; but they are trampled under foot by administrators.

There cannot be a more damnable, dastardly order issued than was issued by the Administration to this people while they were in an Indian country, in 1846. Before we left Nauvoo, not less than two United States' senators came to receive a pledge from us that we would leave the United States; and then, while we were doing our best to leave their borders, the poor, low, degraded curses sent a requisition for five hundred of our men to go and fight their battles! That was President Polk; and he is now weltering in hell with old Zachary Taylor, where the present administrators will soon be, if they do not repent.

Liars have reported that this people have committed treason; and upon their lies, the President has ordered out troops to aid in officering this Territory: and if those officers are like many who have previously been sent here, (and we have reason to believe that they are, or they would not come when they know they are not wanted,) they are poor, miserable blacklegs, broken-down political hacks, robbers, and whoremongers - men that are not fit for civilized society; so they must dragoon them upon us for officers. I feel that I won't bear such cursed treatment, and that is enough to say; for we are just as free as the mountain air.

I do not lift my voice against the great and glorious Government guaranteed to every citizen by our Constitution, but against those corrupt administrators who trample the Constitution and just laws under their feet. They care no more about them than they do about the Government of France; but they walk them under their feet with impunity. And the most of the characters they have sent here as officers cared no more about the laws of our country and of this Territory than they did about the laws of China, but walked them under their feet with all the recklessness of despots.

I do not want to be angry, nor to have my feelings wrought up; but I cannot keep quiet under the continued outrageous tyranny of the wicked.

I have said that if the brethren will have faith, the Lord will fight our battles, and we will have the privilege of living here in peace. I have counted the cost to this people of a collision with our enemies; but I cannot begin to count the cost it will be to them.

I have told you that if this people will live their religion, all will be well; and I have told you that if there is any man or woman that is not willing to destroy anything and everything of their property that would be of use to an enemy, if left, I wanted them to go out of the Territory; and I again say so today; for when the time come to burn and lay waste our improvements, if any man undertakes to shield his, he will be sheared down; for "judgement will be laid to the line and righteousness to the plummet." Now the faint-hearted can go in peace; but should that time come, they must not interfere. Before I will suffer what I have in times gone by, there shall not be one building, nor one foot of lumber, not a stick, nor a tree, nor a particle of grass and hay, that will burn, left in reach of our enemies, I am sworn, if driven to extremity, to utterly lay waste, in the name of Israel's God.

I know that the Saints, both the brethren and sisters, pray that our enemies may not come here; for their entrance is designed by our Government to be the prelude to the introduction of abominations and death. And you cannot talk to a brother, or even to a sister, but that she will tell you that, if she consents in her feelings to have our enemies come here, she feels uncomfortable, and her heart sinks within her. If I consent in my feelings to have them come here, my heart sinks within me, my buoyant spirits are gone, and I have no comfort; for I know the hellish designs concealed under the present movement. But we are free, and every man says, "Stand by the kingdom." When this is the case, every man is like a troop; they are like lions.

Admit of corrupt administrators sending troops here, and what would be the result? All hell would follow after. I naturally dislike to have any trouble, and would not, were I not obliged to; but we are obliged to defend ourselves against the persecution of our oppressors, or have our constitutional rights rent from us, and have ourselves destroyed. We must either suffer that, or stand up and maintain the kingdom of God on the earth.

We have known all the time that the kingdoms of darkness were opposed to the kingdom of God -- that the powers of earth and hell were combined against it. Christ and Baal cannot make friends with each other: you cannot mix oil and water, righteousness and wickedness. This is the kingdom of God; all others are of [the] Devil. They never can be united in this world, nor in any other: there is no possibility of the two kingdoms becoming one. Those who believe and obey the Gospel of the Son of God, and forsake all for its interests, belong to the kingdom of God, and all the rest belong to the other kingdom. There is a distinction, and the line must be drawn; and you and I have to stand up to it, even though it may take from us our right eyes and right hands. We must stand up to the line and maintain the kingdom of God, or we will all go to destruction together.

I am perfectly willing that the brethren should stop all improvements, if they choose, and spend a few years in seeing what our enemies will do; though their efforts against us will only tend to use them up faster. If the people prefer it, they may stop their improvements and take care of their wheat, and cache a supply of grain, flour, &c., where no other persons can find it; though we can raise grain here all the time, -- yes, all the time.

Suppose that our enemies send 50,000 troops here, they will have to transport all that will be requisite to sustain them over one winter: for I will promise them, before they come, that there shall not be one particle of forage, nor one mouthful of food for them, should they come. They will have to bring all their provisions and forage; and though they start their teams with as heavy loads as they can draw, there is no team that can bring enough to sustain itself, to say nothing of the men. If there were no more men here than there are in the Seminole nation, our enemies never could use us up; but they could use up themselves, which they will do. The Seminoles -- a little tribe of a few hundred in Florida -- have cost our government, I suppose, in the neighbourhood of 100,000,000 dollars; and they are no nearer being conquered than when the war commenced. And what few have removed have been induced to do so by compromise; and it would be far cheapest for the Government to pay the debts they honestly owe us, and leave us unmolested in the peaceful enjoyment of our rights.

Would not our enemies feel well in going to the kanyons for wood the first night to cook their suppers with? The idea puts me in mind of an anecdote told by one Brown about the man who took the first barrel of whisky up the Missouri river on a log-raft.

They might stay amid blackened desolation till they had ate up what they had brought, and then they would have to go back.

It has been asked, "Have you counted the cost?" Yes, for ourselves; but I cannot begin to count it for our enemies. It will cost them all they have in this world, and will land them in hell in the world to come, while the only trouble with us is that we have two or three times more men than we need for using up all who can came here to deprive us of our rights.

As I said this morning, ten years ago on this ground I stated that we would not ask any odds of our enemies in ten years from that date; and the next time that I thought of it was ten years afterwards to a day. "They are now sending their troops" was the news; and it directly occurred to me, "Will you ask any odds of them?" No; in the name of Israel's God we will not; for as soon as we ask for odds, we get ends -- of bayonets. When we have asked them for bread, they have given us stones; and when we have asked them for meat, they have given us scorpions; and what is the use in asking any more? I do not ask any odds of those who are striving to deprive us of every vestige of freedom and to destroy us from the earth.

Suppose that we should now bow down, and they should order their troops back, and then send a Governor and other officers here, how long would it be before some miserable scamp would get into a fuss with the Indians in Utah County, or in some other county, and get killed? Then the Governor would order out the Militia -- probably two or three hundred men -- to kill off those Indians. Well, the brethren, knowing that the aggressor is a white man, do not want to turn out and, like Gen. Harney, kill the squaws; and they say, "We shall not go." Then the Governor would say, "They have committed treason;" and it would be "Send an army here, and shoot and hang them." Our enemies are determined to bring us into collision with the Government, so that they can kill us; but they shall not come here.

If the troops are now this side of Laramie, remember that the Sweetwater is this side of that place. They must have some place to winter, for they cannot come through here this season. We could go out and use them up, and it would not require fifty men to do it. But probably we shall not have occasion to take that course, for we do not want to kill men. They may winter in peace at some place east of us; but when spring comes, they must go back to the States, or at any rate, they must leave the mountains.

We have no desire to kill men, but we wish to keep the devils from killing us. If you hear that they are near the upper crossing of the Platte, they will probably stay there till they can collect 50,000 troops. We will say that 9 and 3 equal 17; and if that is so, how long will it take to get those troops here? Let an arithmetician figure out how long it will be before 9 and 3 will make 17; for that will just be as soon as our enemies will get 50,000 troops here.

We have got to be called treasoners by our enemies. Joseph was taken up six times, if I remember rightly, on the charge of treason. Once he was brought into a court by some enemies who thought they could prove that he had committed adultery, and that they termed treason. At another time our brethren wanted to vote in Davies County, Missouri, and said they would cast their votes and have their rights with other citizens; whereupon Joseph was taken up for treason. Another time, he was taken up on a charge of high treason; and when he came before the grand jury, his enemies wanted to prove that he had more than one wife, asserting that that was high treason.

Our enemies are constantly yelling "Rebellion! treason!" no matter how peaceful, orderly, and loyal we may be. And now to come out in open opposition to their cursed, corrupt practices, will of course be counted treason. But let me tell you that the real, actual treason is committed in Washington, by the administrators of our Government sending an army to take the lives of innocent citizens. Every man is allowed by the Constitution to have what religion he pleases and to profess what religion he pleases. That liberty is guaranteed by the Constitution; "but you, 'Mormons,' an army must be sent against you, because you are Latter-day Saints." Yes, an army must be sent to drive us from the earth.

There is high treason in Washington; and if the law was carried out, it would hang up many of them. And the very act of James K. Polk in taking five hundred of our men, while we were making our way out of the country under an agreement forced upon us, would have hung him between the heavens and the earth, if the laws had been faithfully executed. And now, if they can send a force against this people, we have every constitutional and legal right to send them to hell, and we calculate to send them there.

When I get over being angry, I may preach something else; but the past travels and sufferings of this people through mobocracy are before me.

I am not speaking of the Government, but of the corrupt administrators of the Government. They make me think of a sign in New York, upon which was lettered, "All manner of twisting and turning done here." It is just so in Washington city; they can twist and turn in any and every way, to suit their hellish appetites.

Were I an officer sent to Utah for the purpose of aiding the unhallowed oppression of the innocent, (and in this connection I disclaim all personalities,) I would know the facts in the case before I would make any hostile move; and sooner than side with tyranny and murder, I would resign my commission, and say, "Take it and stick it in your boot, and go to hell, and I will go my way." And I would rather go and raise my own potatoes for my wives and children than to hold office under such a set of administrators and bow down to their wicked designs; though, if I were of the world, I should probably do as the rest do.

I have already told you that the main cause of an army being now sent here is a political scheme for the purpose of getting money out of the United States treasury. Politicians and traders combine to lay plans, no matter how devilish, for getting their hands into the treasury of the United States, that they may have money with which to sow corruption and gratify their debauched natures.

Some men do not realize what they are doing. I said, a few weeks ago, that the deeds of some men are out of sight. Our merchants here have fanned the flame, and what for? To peddle off my blood and yours for gold and silver. Although that design may have been out of their sight, yet such is the case; but they will not make money by the operation. Should the crisis come, they will find themselves in poor pasture, with nothing but greasewood and sage to feed upon. It will not do for them to sell us for money; for we are worth more than the Methodist society was sold for in Canada, where they were sold at three cents a head.

I am aware that you will want to know what will be the result of the present movement against us. "Mormonism" will take an almighty stride into influence and power, while our enemies will sink and become weaker and weaker, and be no more; and I know it just as well now as I shall five years hence. The Lord Almighty wants a name and a character; and he will show our enemies that he is God, and that he has set to his hand again to gather Israel, and to try our faith and integrity. And he is saying, "Now, you, my children, dare you take a step to promote righteousness, in direct and open opposition to the popular feelings of all the wicked in your Government? If you do, I will fight your battles."

Our enemies had better count the cost; for if they continue to job, they will want to let it out to sub-contractors, before they get half through with it. If they persist in sending troops here, I want the people in the west and in the east to understand that it will not be safe for them to cross the Plains.

It has cost the Government hundreds of thousands of dollars more for the Indians in other territories than it has in this; and I have saved the Government hundreds of thousands of dollars, by keeping the Indians peaceable in Utah. Hundreds of miles have the Indians travelled to see me, to know whether they might use up the emigrants, saying -- "they have killed many of us; and they damn you and damn us, and shall we stand it?" I have always told them to hold on, to stop shedding blood and to live in peace. But I have been told that the first company of packers that went through here this season, on their way from California to the States, shot at every Indian they saw between Carson Valley and Box Elder; and what has been the result? Probably scores of persons have been killed; animals have been taken from nearly all the emigrants that have passed on that road; and the Indians in that region have now more stock than they know how to take care of; and they come into settlements with their pockets full of gold. The whites first commenced on the Indians; and now if they do not quit such conduct, they must stop travelling through this country; for it is more than I can do to keep the Indians still under such outrageous treatment. The people do not realize what they have done by driving us into the midst of the Lamanites. They prevented Joseph from associating with the Indians; but they, through their ignorance, thought that we were going to Vancover's Island, or on the borders of the Pacific; but lo! they have driven us into the midst of the Lamanites. These Lamanites begin to have a knowledge of their forefathers, and they are cultivating the earth. Here were the most degraded classes of Indians to be found; but now there is not a tribe so enlightened, nor one that has so good a knowledge of its real position and standing before the Lord as have some of these Utah Indians. It is now very different with them to what it was when we first came here. It is now becoming a universal practice with them to punish the guilty, and not the innocent: they have been taught that from the time we first came here. Talk with them and you will learn that they have a good deal of knowledge. They must be saved for they are the children of Abraham.

The Lord in his mercy has suffered our enemies to do that which we could not have accomplished for many years; and, let a war commence, and there is no knowing where we shall next land in Jackson County, Missouri. They will learn that "Mormonism" is a living creature.

COMMENT: Brigham Young's reference to the loss of Missouri seems calculated to give the saints a symbol to keep them going and fighting - the lost land, etc. At the moment, it doesn't really matter if they ever get there or not, since meeting the present conflict is so important.

> All the world have to learn that the Lord is God, and that he is the God of his children. He will protect his annointed; he will defend his own family; and all we have to do is to do his will; and every man, woman, and child ought to seek to learn the will of God and do it. When that is the case, we need not fear all earth and hell. Do not offend God by not doing as he wants you to.
> May the Lord God bless you, brethren and sisters. Amen. JD 5:231-236.

If these comments by Brigham Young strike the reader as excessively emotional or unreasonable, then the likely answer is that the reader does not as yet grasp the setting and the issues. When Brigham's words begin to make sense, then the reader will have made the trip back in time to see things as Brigham and the saints saw them. That will then allow more insight into the cooperative efforts of the times.

References to President Polk appear five times in the *Journal of Discourses*. In this discourse, Brigham Young mentions President Polk twice, neither in a complimentary way, because of his involvement in the pressing into service of the 500 men for the Mormon Battalion. Brigham Young expands on this tale in JD 8:335 (Feb. 17, 1861 SLC, quoted infra) and shows the depth of treachery and duplicity of the U. S. government. In JD 9:109 (Sep 10, 1861) George A. Smith quotes Polk as saying that Utah is the key to the continent. In puzzling contrast, in JD 10:255 (Oct 6, 1863) Brigham Young, speaking of the 1846 discussion about the saints going to California to settle government land, said "I thought that President Polk was our friend at that time, we have thought so since, and we think so now."

John Taylor also expressed anger in his powerful discourse of August 23, 1857, but in the process, he makes some valuable comments on historical and constitutional matters, including the Declaration of Independence, the constitutional status of the saints and the coming army, plus the political interplay of slavery and polygamy.

IGNORANCE AND LOW CONDITIONS OF THE WORLD. — PAST
EXPERIENCE, PRESENT POSITION, AND FUTURE PROSPECTS
OF THE SAINTS.
A Discourse by Elder John Taylor, delivered in the Bowery,
Salt Lake City, August 23, 1857.

> In listening to the remarks made by President Kimball this morning, I felt myself very much edified, very much instructed, and very much blessed. In fact, where the Spirit of the Lord is, and the oracles of God dwell, there must of necessity be truth, intelligence, and certainty. Many of those things, as he justly remarked, that seem light and trivial, and of little importance to many, are pregnant with meaning are full of interest, and are of the utmost importance to the Saints that dwell in these valleys, and to the world of mankind, if they would only pay attention to and be governed by them.
> Mankind are, more or less, fond of paraphernalia, show, pomp, and parade; but the

kingdom of God does not always come with "observation," as the Scripture says. The great and precious principles of eternal truth, like pearls and precious gems, are often hid from the view of the human family.

What is the reason that the world of mankind do not appreciate the principles that are so plain and so manifest to us? How is it that all of our friends, relatives, and associations, and the neighbourhoods where we have resided have not fallen in with the Gospel of Jesus Christ? Why is it that all these things have not been received and appreciated by the millions of the human family who have had precisely the same opportunities that we have had? It is because they do not appreciate them — because they cannot see and understand. The light shone in darkness and it comprehended it not; but to those who received it, it was life and salvation.

Why is it that a swine cannot discern the value of pearls, and tramples them under its feet? Because it does not understand, — it has not the intelligence, and does not comprehend the difference between the filth that surrounds it and precious gems. You might cast a precious jewel at a hog, and it would turn and rend you; but throw that to a man of understanding and intelligence, and he would ask for more. That is the difference. God has so ordained that strait shall be the gate, and narrow the way that leads to life; and but few there are that find it."

If the men of the world, if the princes and potentates of the earth, if the statesmen and great men among the nations could comprehend things as we comprehend them, could understand the Gospel as it has been revealed to us, — if they could know anything of our high calling's glorious hope, and of the principles that animate our bosoms, they would, many of them, lay down their honours and their thrones, and come down and ask for admission into this kingdom. But they have got to receive the kingdom of God like a little child, just the same as you and I, or they cannot enter it; they have got to enter by the door into the sheepfold; and hence there is a test for every man to try him by; and hence the difference between us and them, and therefore a difference in regard to our views and position, which necessarily produce a difference in our feelings. They think differently, they speak differently, they look upon things in a different point of view to what we do. They look upon us as being enthusiastic, foolish, wild, and visionary, and among the rest as being polluted; and they would, forsooth, sympathize with us, some of them, and think we are in the most dreadful position of any people under the face of the heavens — that we are degraded and fallen. But they know not the spirit that animates our or bosoms; they know not the hope that God has inspired in our hearts; they know not the things pertaining to the kingdom of God; they are as ignorant of them and of their own destiny as the brute beast which is "made to be taken and destroyed."

It was a very correct figure that the Apostle made use of formerly, when he spoke of men being as ignorant as brute beasts, which were made to be taken and destroyed. Man, holding a relationship with things that have been, with things that are, and with things, that are to come, being an eternal being, having existed before, existing now, and destined to exist while endless ages shall endure, — when he understands his relationship to God, how he is associated with his progenitors, the position in which he stands to the Church and kingdom of God on the earth, the blessing he is able to seal on his posterity, worlds without end, and the great things he is destined to enjoy, if faithful, — there is as much difference between his views and the world of mankind in general as there is between midnight darkness and the light of the sun in its meridian glory.

Men that are in darkness do not understand why it is that we think as we do, that we act as we do, that we endure as we do, that men can be united as we are, that people will leave their homes and traverse seas, oceans, deserts, mountains, plains, and sterile wastes, in order to meet with a people so much despised by a great majority of mankind. They do not know why it is, because they do not understand the counsels of God. How is it in relation to them? They have no revelation, no knowledge of God; and hence they are like the brute beasts, and know nothing but what they know naturally, as beasts obtain their knowledge, &c. They know nothing of their own position, or of their relationship to God; they know nothing about their progenitors, of their own destiny in the future, of what is within their reach while here on the earth, or how to secure blessings on their posterity; in fact, they are ignorant of all the great and vital principles which have a tendency to animate, enliven, and give vitality and power to all the acts of the sons of God; and hence they are like the brute beasts.

You can take an ox, or a hog, and put it into a stable, and feed it, and it will get fat there. What for? For the knife. If you could only give it a little revelation — if you could only make that ox or hog understand that it was being prepared to be killed and eaten, I wonder how fat you could make it? It is just so with the world; they are ignorant of their position, and they glory in their own shame, just as much as a hog does in wallowing in the mire; and they are just as ignorant of their destiny. This is the position of the world, and that is the reason you see things as they are — why there is so much darkness; and I only wonder there is so much light among them as there is.

You wonder why men act so much like fools. I wonder they have as much intelligence as they have; and the only reason why they have so much is, that the Spirit of God is not entirely withdrawn from them.

In regard to principles of science, mechanism, &c., they possess a great deal of information; but they do not know that "every good and perfect gift" proceeds from God, and they won't acknowledge it or him; and hence the little light they enjoy relative to religious matters, in relation to eternity, to their present real position and destiny, and to the things which God has communicated to us.

Is it to be wondered at, then, that men acting in that way should feel strange and act strangely? You cannot expect the conduct of a gentleman to proceed from a brute beast; you cannot expect anything but a grunt from a hog: it is their nature; and it is the nature of the wicked to act as they have done and as they are doing; and if you see animosity, hatred, evil, strife, vicious feelings bad practices, lasciviousness, corruption of every grade, and every kind of abomination prevailing, it is because of their nature. One of those little hymns composed by Watts for children describes it right: —

"Let dogs delight to bark and bite, for God hath made them so:
Let bears and lions growl and fight; it is their nature too."

Not desirous to retain God in their knowledge, they have given themselves up to every kind of evil, and are led captive by the Devil; and the Scriptures say, "His servants ye are whom ye list to obey."

Now, what is it that enlightens our minds? We were like them precisely. Is there any man here who knew anything about God until it was revealed to him? Is there a man or woman here who understood even the first principles of the Gospel of Christ until they were revealed to them?

I have travelled great deal, and been in different nations, and I have never yet met with a man that did. To what are we indebted for that knowledge? To the administration of an angel, which made manifest the order of God to Joseph Smith, and he revealed it unto others to that we are indebted for the first principles of the Gospel.

Can you find anybody, anywhere, in any part of the earth, who professes to teach religion, that will tell the people to repent of their sins, be baptised in the name of Jesus Christ for the remission of them, and receive the imposition of hands for the gift of the Holy Ghost? And who dare promise them that they shall receive it in its power, as the Apostles did formerly? I cannot. I have not met with such a people nor have you.

I was well versed in the Scriptures myself when this Gospel came along, but I was as ignorant as a brute about these things, and so is everybody else. I have not come in contact with a man who understood correct principles in relation to the principles of the Gospel, or who knew the way to enter into the kingdom of God. Who could know it without God revealing it? And it is to that revelation that we are indebted for the intelligence we have received concerning these matters, and to the spirit of prophecy and revelation that has been communicated with it.

Brother Kimball said he did not profess to be a Prophet of God. I bear testimony that he is a Prophet of God; and why do I do that? Because I have known many things that I could relate here, that I heard him prophesy years ago, that have been fulfilled to the very letter. And I bear testimony of it on another ground: any man that has the testimony of Jesus has the spirit of prophecy; for "the testimony of Jesus is the spirit of prophecy" so says the old Bible; and consequently, such a man is prophet.

Concerning the first principles of the Gospel, at first they came by revelation; they were communicated to a young man who did not possess what is termed worldly wisdom, education, or intelligence; but he came and told it out just as God told it to him.

Was there anybody that could controvert it? No. It was not because it was in the Bible that he taught it, but because God had communicated it to him; and he went and told the things which he had received. Did you ever meet with a man anywhere that could controvert the principles Joseph Smith taught? Did you ever find a theologian, or priest, of any description, that could contradict these things successfully? Did I? I never did. I have never met with a man under the heavens that could successfully contradict one principle of it — never; NO, NEVER; and I do not expect ever to be able to.

Why is it that people cannot contradict it? Because it is the eternal truth of heaven, and emanated from the great Eloheim, and is one of those eternal principles of truth which God has communicated to the human family; and truth, like God, is unchangeable, and cannot be controverted. Darkness flees before it, and error hides its head wherever it appears.

It was so in regard to the first principles of the Gospel, and it has been so in regard to principles that have been revealed and communicated from time to time, both by Joseph Smith, by President Young, by brother Kimball, and by all the authorities of this Church who have been inspired by the Holy Ghost.

In relation to the position we now occupy, the things that were spoken this morning are as correct, as true, and as incontrovertible as anything that could be adduced by any man — I do not care where he comes from, nor what may be his intelligence, — I do not care whether he is king, president, potentate, or statesman, of any description, or what his intellectual qualifications: it matters not.

The principles that were spoken here are, in and of themselves, correct; and I want to speak a little in relation to some of these things, in order that men who have not examined them may understand them more minutely. You believe the principles because you heard them, of course; and so do I; so do we all; and every truth recommends itself to the minds of the human family; yet, at the same time, we are not all of us at all times prepared to judge of the correctness of all these matters.

The things we have heard this morning might sound to some croakers and ignoramuses, who have never examined the subject, and do not understand principle, like treason, as though we were in open rebellion against the United States and opposed to the Government we are associated with — as though we were going to trample down all law, rule, and order. No such thing. We are the only people in these United States, at the present time, who are sustaining them. I can prove this, and that it is others who are trampling them under foot, and not us. Whilst they are committing acts, themselves, that are treasonable in their nature, and pursuing a course opposed to the Constitution and the very genius of the institutions of the United States, they want to lay the sin at our doors that they themselves are guilty of.

Would I, as a citizen of the United States, come out in rebellion against the United States, and act contrary to my conscience? Verily no. Would brother Young? Verily no. Would brother Kimball, or brother Wells? Verily no.

Are they not true patriots — true Americans? Do they not feel the fire of '76 burning in their bosoms? Assuredly they do. Would they do a thing that is wrong? No; and they will also see that others do not do it. That is the feeling, the spirit, and principle that actuate them.

There are thousands of you who are Americans, who have been born in this land, whose fathers fought for the liberties we used to enjoy, but have not enjoyed for some years past. There are thousands of such men here who feel the same spirit that used to burn in their fathers' bosoms — the spirit of liberty and equal rights — the spirit of according to every man that which belongs to him, and of robbing no man of his rights.

Your fathers and grandfathers have met the tyrant when he sought to put a yoke on your necks; as men and true patriots, they came forward and fought for their rights and in defence of that liberty which we, their children, ought to enjoy. You feel the same spirit that inspired them; the same blood that coursed in their veins flows in yours; you feel true patriotism and a strong attachment to the Constitution and institutions bought by the blood of your fathers, and bequeathed to you by them as your richest patrimony.

There are others of you that have taken the oath of allegiance to the United States; and some of you, not understanding correct principles, may, perhaps, feel qualms of conscience, and think, probably, that if we undertake to resist the powers that are seeking to make aggression upon us, we are doing wrong. No such thing. You let your conscience sleep at ease; let it be quiet: it is not us who are doing wrong; it is others who are committing a wrong upon us.

What was the case in Missouri? Let me draw your attention briefly to some of the circumstances that have transpired in our history as a people. Whom did we interfere with in the State of Missouri? Did we rebel against the United States, or against the State in which we lived? Verily no; and I am at the defiance of that State of Congress, with all the world at their backs, to prove that we did rebel in one iota. Did they give unto us the protection of American citizens? They did not; and they perjured themselves in not doing it. They perjured themselves before God and all honest men.

Whom did we rebel against in Illinois?

Let me mention one circumstance in the State of Missouri. How much land did we purchase there from the United States, and pay for, which they promised to warrant and defend us in the possession of? Did they protect us in the right they guaranteed unto us? No; they allowed us to be robbed and plundered with impunity. And how many suffered death in consequence of their recklessness, carelessness, and barefaced iniquity? Thousands. I have seen their condition when many thousands were driven from their lands and homes, were persecuted, harassed, and driven like felons without redress, robbed, plundered, imprisoned, and put to death; and thousands of men, women, and children wandered houseless and homeless exiles in their own land, and fugitives flying from the rage of a lawless rabble, infuriated banditti, and bloodthirsty miscreants and murderers. I saw then a whole people robbed and disfranchised, and this too in the middle of winter. Did the State authorities yield us any redress? No. They were foremost in the mob. Did the United States? No.

Many of my brethren around me also witnessed these things, and know the misery, destitution, and death caused by those bloodhounds, when they first fled to Nauvoo, resting where the mud was knee deep — the only position they could get — with three or four little sticks put up, and a counterpane thrown over them, and there left to die.

Brother Wells was in Nauvoo at the time. After the excitement was over, there was not

*The Utah War*

enough of well folks to wait on the sick.

I was off on a mission to England at this time, and all my family were sick; and my son George, who has been away and returned with me, being quite a little boy, not able to draw water, and nobody in the house able to get it, had to go and wait at the well, with a little bucket, for somebody to come and draw him a little water to carry hole to the sick, to quench the parching tongue and allay the raging fever occasioned by these Missouri demons.

Brother Brigham, brother Kimball, George A. Smith, and the Twelve here, and everybody, almost, was down sick; and in this condition, feeble, faint, and half dead, they started off a mission, because we were commanded to go. We went to fulfill the word of the Lord. Did the United States step forward and yield us any redress? No; but they stood there, and were willing to see us imposed upon and robbed of our property and rights; and we have obtained no redress for it to the present day.

Who are the transgressors? Are we? Martin Van Buren, the then President of the United States, acknowledged the injustice done to us when he said, " Your cause is just, but we can do nothing for you." And we endured it.

We staid in Illinois, lived there as peaceable citizens, and had a city charter, and under its protection improved our city, and had in a short time, by our energy, industry, and enterprize, built one of the best cities in the western country, and had one of the most peaceable societies that existed anywhere, without exception.

The first thing they did to aggravate us was to rob us of our city charter; and this very Judge Douglas, of whom we have heard so much as being our friend, was one of the first movers for its repeal. The first time I ever met with him was in a hotel in Springfield, Illinois, the time they were trying Joseph Smith before Judge Pope. He told me that they had a right to do it, and that the Judges had decided so. I said, I did not know anything about the Judges.

I did not know who he was at the time, and it would not have made much difference if I had. I told him, It is no matter to me what the judges decided about charters; the Legislature had given us our charter for perpetual succession; and for them to take away a charter with these provisions proved them either to be knaves or fools.

They were knaves if they did it knowingly, to give what they knew they had not power to do; and if they did not know it, they were fools for giving us a thing they had not power to give. Did they do it? Yes. And that State robbed us of the rights of freemen; and the only chance we had then, when they sent their scamps and rogues among us, was to have a whittling society and whittle them out. We could not get them out according to law, and we had to do it according to justice and there was no law against whittling, —— so we whittled the scoundrels out.

I remember that one of the legislators who had annulled our charter, named Dr. Charles, went to President Young, and says he, "Mr. Young, I am very much imposed upon by the people around here; there are a lot of boys following me with long knives, and they are whittling after me wherever I go; my life is in danger."

Brother Young replied, "I am very sorry you are imposed upon by the people: we used to have laws here, but you have taken them away from us: we have no law to protect you. "YOUR CAUSE IS JUST, BUT WE CAN DO NOTHING FOR YOU." Boys, don't frighten him, don't."

They deprived us of the rights of law to protect ourselves, and in doing it, they deprived us of the power of protecting them; and we could not help them when they wanted help.

(Voice: "We still have whittling societies.")

Yes, we still have whittling societies, as brother Kimball says.

Why did we leave Nauvoo? Had we killed anybody? Had we broken any law? Had we trampled upon the rights of any people? Had we done anything that the law of the United States or of that State could interfere with us for? If we had, they would pretty soon have dragged us up.

The people wanted us to leave; and because the people were dissatisfied —— because there were a lot of religious enthusiasts, political aspirants, blacklegs, and scoundrels, who wanted to possess our property, all bound together to rob us of our rights, we must go away, of course.

Judge Douglas, General Harding, Major Warren, and some of the prominent men from Springfield met together in my house in Nauvoo, and these men could go to work and talk deliberately (and there was no less than two United States' Senators among them at the time,) about removing thousands of people, and letting them be disfranchised and despoiled, as coolly as they would cut up a leg of mutton.

(Voice: "And you told them of it.")
Yes, I did.

Now, then, whom did we injure? What law did we break? Whose rights did we trample upon? Did we dispossess anybody of his land, rob anybody, interfere with anybody's rights? Did we transgress any State's law, national law, or any other law? We did not; and they never have been able to prove one item against us, and we stand clear. We maintained the law and tried to make it honourable.

What must we go away for? Why, they had murdered our Prophet and Patriarch under the sacred pledge of the Governor of the State and of his officers, all combined, and we could obtain no redress; and because they had done one injury, they must heap a thousand on the back of it.

That is the only reason I know of. They were murderers, and sanctioned the practice, and those men have got to atone for these wrongs yet. (Voices: "Amen.") The debt has got to be paid.

(Voice: "Douglas is not a bit better than the rest of them.")
Not a particle.

What is our position at the present time? Why are we here, gentlemen and ladies? Answer me, ye sons of the ancient patriots —— ye sons of those fathers who fought for the rights and liberties this nation boasts so much of. Answer me —— Why are you here? Because you could not go anywhere else —— because you could not be protected in those rights that your fathers bled and died for. That is the reason you are here, gentlemen.

We are here, because we are exiled and disfranchised, because we are robbed of our rights, because we could not possess equal rights with other American citizens —— rights that the Constitution guaranteed to every citizen of the Union.

We had to fly from the face of civilization, and found a refuge among the red men of the forest; we had to seek that mercy from the hands of the savage that Christian civilization denied us.

We are talking now about rights, laying aside religion. If we come to talk about the kingdom of God, that is another matter. We are talking now about our rights as American citizens, or rather our wrongs, —— the rights we have been robbed of.

We are here, then, under these circumstances. Have we broken any law here? No. I defied the whole Eastern country, when I was there, to prove that we have broken any law, and have not found a man that dare take up the gauntlet —— not one, because they could not

*The Utah War*

do it. Why could they not? Because we have done no wrong.

What did we do on the road here? Right in the midst of difficulties, in the midst of exile, when we were journeying to this place, this Government called upon us for 500 soldiers to go and fight their battles, when they were literally allowing us to be driven from our homes and to be robbed of millions of property without redress.

Did we send the soldiers? We did. Was it our duty to comply with such a requisition at such a time, and under such circumstances? I don't know. I think it was one of those works of supererogation which the Roman Catholics talk about. I do not think any law of God or man would have required it at our hands; but we did it; and I suppose it was wisdom and prudent, under the circumstances, that we should take that course, because our enemies were seeking to entangle and destroy us from the earth. They laid that as a trap, thinking to catch us in it; but it did not stick.

What did we do when we came here? We framed a Constitution and a Provisional Government, and reported our doings to the United States again, right on the back of all the insults, robbery, and fraud which we had endured. We still went constitutionally to work.

Afterwards, we petitioned for a Territorial Government. Did they give it to us? They did. Is there any step that we have taken that is contrary to law? There is not? They have appointed our Governor, our Secretaries, our Judges, our Marshals; they have done to us the same in this matter as they have done with other Territories.

I do not believe in their right constitutionally to appoint our officers. Still they have done it, and we have submitted to it. And they have sent some of the most cursed scoundrels here that ever existed on the earth. Instead of being fathers, they have tried every influence they could bring to bear in order to destroy us.

Such have been our protectors. These have been the men who have been sworn to fulfil their public duties; but they have foresworn themselves in the face of high heaven.

What law have we transgressed? None. They trump up every kind of story that it is possible to conceive of, but have always been and are now unable to substantiate any of their barefaced assertions; and I declare it before you and the world, that this people are the most peaceable, law-abiding, and patriotic people that can be found in the United States.

What have they been doing in Kansas, in California, in Oregon? What in Cuba, in Nicaragua, and at present in New York, if you please? They have been filibustering in Cuba and in Nicaragua; and officers of every grade and condition, both civil and military, have winked at it and suffered those things to go on, right under their noses.

The position of affairs in Kansas has been anything but flattering; it has been North against South, and South against North, and Kansas has been the battle-ground.

The people there are not, perhaps, much worse than the rest of the people; they are principally emigrants from the North and South, who are arrayed against each other, whilst Kansas is the greatest Sebastopol, where the battle is fought. The inhabitants there are the representatives of Eastern, Western, Southern, and Northern civilization and Christianity, all combined.

Are they traitors? O, no! They are only a little excited. We must try and get a Governor who will try and get a Governor who will try and compromise matters between the parties, and we will get things straightened out by-and-by. They send one Governor —— he fails; and another, and he fails; and they have sent another; but whether he will fail or not, time must determine.

What are they doing in New York? The Legislature of New York passed laws interfering with the city of New York, and the city is in rebellion against the State of New York, and it was raging at the time I left. The State says, "I won't submit," and the city says, "I won't submit." And they had two different classes of officers there to regulate matters in the emporium of the United States: it is the mercantile emporium at least.

They are very peaceable; they are good citizens; there is no harm in that; it is only a little family trouble that we have to settle; and in doing so, we must use any pacific measure we can.

What is the matter with us? Have we broken any law? James Gordon Bennett, a man who is quarrelling with everybody, comes out at last, and says, "The Mormons" have the advantage of us, and they know it." And out of all he could hatch up and scrape together against the "Mormons," there is only one thing that seems even in his eyes to supply <u>any pretext</u> for hostilities against them, and that is, the charge of <u>burning some 900 volumes of United States' laws</u>; and this charge is also false. <u>Bennett is one of the most rabid "Mormon"-eaters you can find, with the exception of Greeley.</u>

What are they sending an army here for? I had thought things were a little different until I got here; but I have found, in conversing with President Young, that he knows more about things as they exist in the Eastern country than I did, who had just come from there. I had read all the newspapers, examined the spirit of the times, and tried to get at all the information I could; and I find, from the information I have received since then, that be understood things more correctly than I did.

I thought it was a kind of a pacific course which the Administration was taking, in order to pacify the Republicans, that they might have a reasonable pretext to have fulfilled their duties' for I do know that they were apprised of the unreliable character of some of their informants. <u>When I heard that the troops now on their way here had sealed orders, were coming with cannon, and had stopped the mail, it argued that there was the Devil behind somewhere.</u>

I will give you my opinion about their present course. <u>The Republicans were determined to make the "Mormon" question tell in their favour.</u> At the time they were trying to elect Fremont, they put two questions into their platform-viz., opposition to the domestic institutions of the South and to polygamy. The Democrats have professed to be our friends, and they go to work <u>to sustain the domestic institutions of the South and the rights of the people [slavery]</u>; but when they do that, the Republicans throw <u>polygamy</u> at them, and are determined to make them swallow that with the other. This makes the Democrats gag, and they have felt <u>a strong desire to get rid of the "Mormon" question.</u>

Some of them, I know, for some time past, have been concocting plans to <u>divide up Utah among the several Territories around</u>; and I believe a bill, having this object in view, was prepared once or twice, and came pretty near being presented to Congress; but that was not done.

Now, they go to work and <u>send out an army with sealed orders</u>, and, if necessary, are prepared to commit anything that the Devil may suggest to them; for they are under his influence. <u>They wish now to steal the Republicans' thunder, to take the wind out of their sails, and to out Herod Herod.</u>

Say they, "<u>We</u>, who profess to be the friends of the 'Mormons,' and support free institutions, squatter sovereignty, and equal rights, <u>will do more to the 'Mormons' than you dare do</u>; and we will procure offices by that means, and save our parties;" and, as Pilate and Herod could be made friends over the death of Jesus, so they go to work and plan our sacrifice and destruction, and make up friends on the back of it. <u>They would crucify Jesus Christ, if he were here, as quick as the Scribes and Pharisees did in his day, and the priests would help them.</u>

<u>President Young says they shall not come here and destroy us; and I say, Amen.</u> (The congregation shouted, "Amen.")

I have not quoted a great deal of Scripture to-day, but I will quote some. It says there was the opening of the "first seal;' so we will open this seal for them. <u>We will declare their orders</u> —— a thing they have not manhood to do. They are too sneaking and underhanded, and have not manliness enough to declare their mind to a handful of people —— the poor, pusillanimous curses. We dare do it; and, I thank God, that I live among a people that dare; for I do despise this sneaking, miserable, cowardly tribe, that are obliged to act underhanded in all their ways. Why? For fear of something to come. We dare declare our intentions, and risk the consequences.

Now, I want to touch upon a principle which I spoke about awhile ago. We have submitted to their sending officers here; that is all right enough, if we have a mind to. We are citizens of the United States, and profess to support the Constitution of the United States; and wherein that binds us, we are bound; wherein it does not, we are not bound.

They have sent Judge after Judge, and many times we have been without them: their loss, however, was not felt. They have sent their officers, and we have treated them well; and for the good treatment we have received curses, bitterness, wrath, lying, and destruction in return. They have sought to destroy our reputation —— to rob us of our rights. They have sought to injure us in every possible way that men could be injured, as patriots, Christians, and moral men. They have lied about us in every conceivable way.

We have borne it and borne it over and over again. Are we bound to bear it for ever? That is the question that necessarily arises. Are we bound to suffer their abuse and oppression continually? And if we are, upon what principle? If there is any man in this congregation, or anywhere else, that will show me one principle or one piece of instruction or authority in the Constitution of the United States that authorizes the President of the United States to send out Governors and Judges to this Territory, I would like to see it.

I cannot find such authority. I will admit that a usage of that kind has obtained —— that it is quite customary for the President of the United States, by and with the consent of the Senate, to appoint Governors, Judges, Marshals, Secretaries of State, and all of those officers that you have had here. But it is a thing that is not authorized by the Constitution, —— much less to force them upon us by an armed soldiery. There is no such authority existing.

I wish to quote to you one little thing. If I had the Constitution here, I would read it to you. It is to the effect, "That the powers not delegated to the United States by the Constitution, nor prohibited by it to the States, are reserved to the States respectively, or to the people."

No matter, therefore, whether the people live in States or Territories, they possess constitutional privileges alike. The most that is said in regard to Territories and the authority of the President and Congress is, that "The Congress shall have power to dispose of and make all needful rules and regulations respecting the territory or other property of the United States." That is speaking of it as land; and some of the most prominent statesmen of the United States have so construed it. It is property as land —— territory as land they have a right to interfere with, not territory as regards the people.

I published this in the "Mormon" long ago, and said the Missouri compromise was unconstitutional. By-and-by, the United States' Judges gave the same decision. I gave mine, however, before they gave theirs.

It is a true principle, they have not the authority. If they have it at all, it is in the people ceding it to them, and not what they possess by the Constitution of the United States. They have sent scoundrels amongst us from time to time. If they had sent decent men, would we have opposed them? No: we would have respected them. But will we submit to such infernal scoundrels? Never; no, never!!

So far as right is concerned, then, they have no right to appoint officers for this or any other Territory; and I will defy any man to prove that there is any such right in the Constitution.

I conversed with a Judge Black, who was coming up to Nebraska Territory on a steam-boat, —— an intelligent man, a Democrat, of course. When talking about these principles to him, which he acceded to, I put my hand on his shoulder, and said, "Judge, what are you doing here?" "I am here," said he, "according to the usage that has obtained; but if the people do not want me, all they have to do is to empress it, and I will go away again." I wish we had only half such decent men as that sent here.

He tried to take another tack, which is this: He pointed out in the Constitution where the Supreme Court of the United States was made one of the branches of the Government, and the President has the appointment of its Judges. That is true —— he possesses the power to appoint the greater, but not the less. How do you make that appear? Simply because one is mentioned in the Constitution, and the other is not. The United States' Supreme Court is a co-ordinate branch of the Government, and there is provision made by the Constitution for the election and appointment of its officers.

This is not the case in regard to the officers of a Territory. Out of courtesy we, as citizens of the United States, may say, "Mr. President, if you have a mind to appoint discreet persons to fill those offices, all well and good; but if you don't, you had better take them back; for we won't have them: we stand on our reserved rights as citizens of the United States."

We are not lacking for men in the United States, at the present time, who want to make it appear that the United States have a right to lord it over the Territories, the same as the British Government used to do over their colonies.

Thousands of you before me were citizens of the United States, where you came from. You had the right of franchise —— had a right to say who should be your Governor, and who should be your Municipal and State officers. You came out here by thousands or by tens of thousands. By what right or upon what principle are you disfranchised? Can anybody tell me? Say some, "You need not have come out here unless you had a mind to." Of course not. But we had a mind to; we were American citizens before we came out, and we have transgressed no law in coming; and by what rule are we deprived of our citizenship? If we had a right then to vote for anything, we have a right now; and nobody has a right to cram this or that man upon us without our consent, —— much less have they a right to dragoon us into servility to their unconstitutional exactions.

What was the great cause of complaint at the time the Constitution was framed? In the Declaration of Independence, it was stated that the people had rulers placed over them, and they had no voice in their election. Read that instrument. It describes our wrongs as plainly as it did the wrongs the people then laboured under and discarded.

Our Government are doing the very things against us that our fathers complained of. "They send armed mercenaries among us, to subjugate us," &c. What is our Government doing? The same thing.

As American citizens and patriots, and as sons of those venerable sires, can we, without disgracing ourselves, our fathers, and our nation, submit to these insults, and tamely bow to such tyranny? We cannot do it, and we will not do it. We will rally round the Constitution, and declare our rights as American citizens; and we will sustain them in the face of High Heaven and the world.

No man need have any qualms of conscience that he is doing wrong. You are patriots, standing by your rights and opposing the wrong which affects all lovers of freedom as well as you; for those acts of aggression have a withering, deadly effect, and are gnawing, like a canker-worm, at the very vitals of religious and civil liberty. You are standing by the Declaration of Independence, and sustaining the the constitution which was given by the inspiration of God; and you are the only people in the United States this time that are doing it —— that have the manhood to do it. You dare do it, and you feel right about the matter as the vox populi.

According to the genius and spirit of the Constitution of the United States, we are pursuing the course that would be approved of by all high-minded, honourable men; and no man but a poor, miserable sneak would have any other feeling.

I lay these things before you for your information, that you may feel and act understandingly. I have carefully criticised these matters, and examined the views of many of those who are said to be our greatest statesmen on this subject; for I have desired to comprehend the powers of the Government and the rights of the people; and I have watched with no little anxiety the encroachments of Government and the manifest desire to trample upon your rights. It is for you, however, to maintain them; and if those men that are traitors to the spirit and genius of the Constitution of the United States have a mind to trample under foot those principles that ought to guarantee protection to every American citizen, we will rally around the standard, and bid them defiance in the name of the Lord God of Israel.

In doing this, we neither forget our duties as citizens of the United States, nor as subjects of the kingdom and cause of God; but, as the Lord has said, if we will keep His commandments, we need not transgress the laws of the land. We have not done it; we have maintained them all the time.

When we talk about the Constitution of the United States, we are sometimes apt to quote —— "Vox populi, vox Dei;" that is, The voice of the people is the voice of God. But in some places they ought to say, VOX POPULI, VOX DIABOLI; that is, the voice of the people is the voice of the Devil.

We are moved by a higher law. They talk sometimes about a higher law in the States. Greeley is a great man to talk about a higher law, which means, with him, stealing niggers. We do not care anything about that. We want to do something better —— something higher and more noble. That is rather too low for us; consequently, they need not be afraid of our stealing their niggers: we will let them have all the benefits of them as one of the grand institutions of Christians, together with the amalgamating process as another of the institutions of Christianity. And another grand institution they have among them is prostitution.

Well, thank God, we do not know anything about such things. A very respectable gentleman in Philadelphia said to me a while go, in talking over some of these matters —— "Suppose a <u>Mahommedan</u> should come into the city of <u>Philadelphia</u>" —— that is one of the puritanical cities, where they profess to be so good, the city of brotherly love —— and walk through our streets in the evening, and see a number of ladies walking alone, being informed that it was usual for respectable ladies to be protected, he would necessarily enquire what was the meaning of this. Being informed that these were <u>prostitutes,</u> he would very naturally say, "Then I suppose this is <u>one of the institutions of Christianity</u>?" This is the conclusion he would come to at once. Well, so it is; and this <u>niggerism in the South</u> is about the same kind of thing, only a change of colour.

These are all moral, all legal, all truly Christian. Men East may have one or a dozen misses, keep part of their children, and turn the other out as paupers. In the South, they buy them body and soul, prostitute them at pleasure, and sell their own children. Yet these men talk of our morals, and send out armies to chastise us for our corruptions, when God knows, and they know, that they are a thousand times more corrupt than we are.

We are not taking any steps contrary to the laws and the Constitution of the United States, but in everything we are upholding and sustaining them. Gentlemen, hands off: We are free men; we possess equal rights with other men; and if you send your sealed orders here, we may break the seal, and it shall be the opening of the first seal.

In relation to the kingdom of God, that is another matter. You before me understand about it —— its laws, priesthood, principles, and influences, and the things that are about to transpire. God has set His hand to accomplish His purposes, to roll on His great designs, and bring to pass the things spoken of by all the holy Prophets since the world began, that should take place in the latter days, to establish His kingdom on the earth, that shall become mighty and prevail over all other kingdoms. You know all about this.

We are established here, and have the oracles of God in our midst, and the principles of truth revealed. This is the kingdom of God. The stone cut out of the mountain without hands has got to roll forth and become a great mountain, and fill the whole earth.

Satan has held dominion, and rule, and power, over the human family, for generations and generations; and God is gathering together a little nucleus here —— a band of brethren clothed upon with the Holy Priesthood and the Spirit of God, by which they will be able to roll back the cloud of darkness that has overwhelmed the inhabitants of the earth, and plant the principles of truth, and establish the kingdom of God. That is what we are engaged in, and what we mean to accomplish by the help of the Lord; and in regard to any little thing that may be transpiring around us, in regard to their little armies they are sending here, great conscience! it is comparatively nothing; there will be thunder and lightning and the bellowing of earthquakes, in comparison with that, before we get through. Thrones will be cast down, and desolation, war, and bloodshed will spread abroad in the earth, and desolate nations and empires, and God win turn and overturn until the kingdoms of this world shall become the kingdoms of our God and His Christ, and he will reign for ever; and we are going to have part in it, and our children and our children's children.

It is for us to act as the sons of the living God, magnify our calling, honour our God and His Priesthood, and live as men and as God's true children on the earth, accomplish His purposes here, and then join with the redeemed that have gone before to help to roll on weightier matters in the upper world.

I do not know but I have been talking long enough. I feel well. I am happy. All is right; and if it thunders, let it thunder; let the lightnings flash and the earthquakes bellow; let them rage: there is a God in heaven that can hold the children of men, and He will do it, and His work will spread, His kingdom increase, and His power be made manifest among us and among all nations, and Zion will spread and go forth, and every creature in the heavens, and on the earth, and under the earth will be heard to say, "Blessing and power, might and majesty be ascribed to Him that sitteth upon the throne and to the Lamb for ever and ever."

Brethren. God bless you, in the name of Jesus Christ. Amen. JD 5:155 JT Aug 23, 1857 SLC.

In a February 17, 1861 address, Brigham Young tells more about the saints' enemies who sought to destroy them, especially the Mormon Battalion episode in which a trap was laid for the saints if the 500 men were not produced:

When I hear of the brethren and sisters going after gold —— the riches and wealth of the earth —— I think that if they had it in the spirit-world they could not do anything with it there. There are no merchants there with their merchandise —— no grog-shops there in which to spend money. Those who possess wealth must leave it here for the Saints, and the Saints will become heirs of it; and we wish the people to be ready to receive these and all blessings the Lord has in store for them. Be ready. We were ready when King James Buchanan sent his friends here to initiate us into Christianity. If we had not been ready, your heads and mine might have been cold ere to-day. We were ready, and we said, "Stop —— stay your sad career, until you think."

Did Thomas H. Benton aid in gathering the Saints? Yes, he was the mainspring and action of governments in driving us into these mountains. He obtained orders from President Polk to summon the militia of Missouri, and destroy every "Mormon" man, woman, and child, unless they turned out five hundred men to fight the battles of the United States in

Mexico. He said that we were aliens to the Government, and to prove it he said —— "Mr. President, make a requisition on that camp for five hundred men, and I will prove to you that they are traitors to our Government." We turned out the men, and many of them are before me to-day; among whom is father Pettigrew —— a man that ought to have been asked into the Cabinet to give the President counsel; but they asked him to travel on foot across the Plains to fight our country's battles against Mexico. We turned out the men, and Mr. Benton was disappointed. He went to his grave in disgrace, and shame covered him. Was he a man of influence in his last days —— in the latter portion of his career in public life? When he could not be President, nor be returned again to the Senate, after much exertion he succeeded in being elected a member of the House of Representatives, and at the close of his public career, because the hands of the clock in the Representatives Hall were turned back, and the hands of his watch did not agree with it when at twelve o'clock, said he, "Mr. Speaker, I am not a member of this legislative body." The Speaker said, "Sergeant-at-Arms, show that gentleman to the door," and there was scarcely a man in the House that so much as turned his eyes to look. The ground he walked on was disgraced by his step, and his acquaintances shunned him: and so it will be with others.

Brother Kimball says that King James [Buchanan] will have to pay the debt he has contracted. He has more on his hands than he will settle for many generations. You will see the old man go down to the grave in disgrace. He has cast off his political friends, and they will all cast him off as a thing of naught, and he will become a hiss and a by-word, and has already.

The London Times speaks of the old man's being incapable of magnifying the office bestowed upon him. They complain of him now; but, when he was minister from our Government to England, did they not in secret council induce him to pledge himself to destroy the "Mormons," if they would assist in electing him President? Did they not connive with Buchanan to destroy the "Mormons" from the earth? Did they not send their armies to the north to head us in our retreat, provided King James succeeded in routing us from our homes? I spoke of this to Captain Van Vleit, when he was here. I merely ask these questions, that those who are acquainted with political moves may draw their conclusions upon the workings of governments. But the Lord has given his people power to elude the grasp of our enemies; for he led them in a way they knew not, turned them hither and thither, diverted the blow aimed at our heads, and brought disgrace and ruin on those who sought to bring ruin and destruction upon us. It will take them a great while to pay the debt they have contracted. That Government known as the United States' has become like water spilled on the ground, and other governments will follow.

"Kings become nursing fathers," indeed? Not King James: no. Queens become nursing mothers?" Will Queen Victoria become a nursing mother to the Saints? I have not one word of fault to find with her as an individual; but the Government holds her; she is fettered. She is a good woman, but she will never nurse the Saints. Will the Queen of Spain? Never. But the kings and queens I am looking upon to-day will belong to that class; they will be the fathers and mothers to the lost sheep of the house of Israel. There are many sheep on the earth that we have not yet found. We consider ourselves the flock of God —— the kingdom of God; and when you travel upon the islands of the sea and among the nations who have never heard the Gospel, you will learn that there are thousands and millions of the sheep that have not heard the voice of the Good Shepherd. They are to be entered into the fold, and we have it to do. JD 8:335 BY Feb 17, 1861 SLC.

There are many intrigues revealed here that historians seem to have skipped over. The existence of a British army on the north waiting to assist Buchanan's army in crushing the saints is a chilling thought. This is further evidence that if we do not understand the enormous and mortal pressures on the saints, we cannot possibly understand some of the actions they took, and least of all can we try to apply the policies and actions of those times to our own times.

An October 1868 discourse of George A. Smith discusses more of the reasons for the war and its results, including its bringing in merchants who plagued the saints for many years thereafter:

### HISTORICAL ADDRESS BY PRESIDENT GEORGE A. SMITH

...

As soon as it was known in Christendom that the Latter-day Saints were not dead, but that they were alive and flourishing, and were gathering their people to the mountains at the rate of from two to five thousand a year, and that they had succeeded in reclaiming the desert, and in making grain and grass grow where nothing would grow before, it seemed as though all hell was aroused again. Federal officers were sent here, and they thought it policy to join in the general hue and cry, or at least some of them; there were a few honorable exceptions. But the majority of them raised a hue and cry against us, and it was thought so much of, that one of the rotten planks in the platform of the great rising party which contested the elevation of James Buchanan to the Presidency, was the destruction of polygamy. This brought to our country immense armies, more men being concerned in the matter than in some of the principal battles of the revolution, or even in the war of 1812. Some six thousand regulars were marched in this direction, while teamsters and hangers on increased this number to about seventeen thousand. There were also several thousand freight wagons, and everything on the face of the earth, seemingly, that could be done to hurl into this country destruction and vengeance, was done. But God overruled it. when they got here they found that they really had been deceived. They went and established themselves at Camp Floyd, and spent their time in destroying arms and ammunition, and breaking up the property of the United States, until forty million dollars, the reported cost of the expedition, had been wasted. The armies then scattered to the four winds of the heaven. This expenditure of the Government money laid the foundation of these outside mercantile establishments which have been nursed by us to so great an extent from that time to this.

It has been believed that great benefit, financially, accrued to the Saints through this expedition; but I think that as a whole it has been a hindrance to our real progress. Very little of the money came into the hands of the Saints, but some merchandize at high prices, which might have been a temporary convenience. But it caused our people to relax their energies in producing from the elements what they needed, such as flax, cotton and wool; and also turned their attention from the manufacture of iron. The burning of wagons, the bursting of shell, and the destruction of arms, furnished much of the latter at comparatively nominal prices; hence a present benefit worked a permanent injury. The speculators who made vast fortunes at the expense of the nation soon squandered them, and part of this army, and even its commander, and many of the officers were soon found arrayed against the flag of our country, and taking an active part in the terrible war between the North and South, the results of which are being so severely felt at the present time.

Scandalous sheets have been issued here for years, and, as far as possible, sent to all parts of the world, filled with lies, defamation and abuse, and everything that would tend to rouse the indignation of the Christian world against us, and to get up an excuse for our annihilation. These sheets have been sustained by men in the mercantile business whom we have sustained by our trade, and consequently have been supported indirectly by our money. I have been horrified at such a use of our means, and have felt that it was our duty, as Saints, to stop supporting these slanders, lest, peradventure, should they continue until they produced the designed effect, our blood should be upon our own heads.

What did we cross the Plains for? To get where we could enjoy peace and religious liberty. Why did we drag hand-carts across the Plains? That we might have the privilege of dwelling and associating with Saints, and not build up a hostile influence in our midst, and place wealth in the hands of our enemies, who use it to spread abroad defamation and falsehood, and to light a flame that will again have the direct result, unless overruled by the almighty power of God, of bringing upon the Latter-day Saints here the same sorrow, distress and desolation that have followed them elsewhere. For my part I do not fellowship Latter-day Saints who thus use their money. I advise the Saints to form co-operative societies and associations all over the Territory and to import everything they need that they cannot manufacture, and not to pay their money to men who use it to buy bayonets to slay them with; and to stir up the indignation of our fellow-men against us. Our outside friends should feel contented with the privilege of paying us the money for the products of our labor, and we should exact it at their hands, a due reward for our exertions in producing the necessaries of life in this desert. JD 13:123 GAS Oct. 8, 9 1868 SLC.

In the Utah War as in many other situations, Brigham Young's constant concern and fear was that the eastern establishment would again be able to crush the "Mormons" as they had so many times before. He sought through every means available to bring the Saints to a level of economic, political, and even military power such that they could never again be dislodged, plundered, and destroyed. This was the problem that he addressed for thirty years in Utah until his death in 1877. All his programs were focused on solving that one large problem.

It is probably not too extreme to state that regardless of what other reasons Brigham Young may have given for "united order" programs, at bottom the real reason was related to the survival of the saints as a culture and a religion. He was eminently successful in that effort, and although the easterners were able at various times to harass the saints to some extent, they were never able to begin to break up or even noticeably weaken the saints. By the time of Brigham Young's death, there could be no more serious thought of another "extermination order" as had occurred in Missouri, regardless of the continued existence of numerous enemies who would prefer a repeat performance.

## Mountain Meadow Massacre

The Mountain Meadow Massacre has been a much talked about event. However, most accounts seem not to put the event completely in the context of the times. Taken alone, it seems bizarre and unbelievably cruel and grisly, but in the context of the war it was part of, it is not so much different than many other war-related atrocities. With the tension and suspicion, even paranoia, of the Vietnam war where even little children carried grenades that could kill a soldier or his friends, everyone except one's closest buddies were potential mortal enemies. Apparently, something like that same tension existed in the "Utah War" setting.

One should first realize that the Mountain Meadow Massacre event happened in September 1857, as the federal army was marching toward Utah, with its soldiers muttering threats that they were going to annihilate the Mormons. In effect, it might be considered the first battle of the Utah war, and as it turned out, luckily, it was the only battle in which anyone was killed on either side. As evidenced by a historical trivia game question, some have gotten the history backwards, saying that the Mountain Meadow Massacre was the cause of the army's coming to Utah, rather than one of the results.

One must remember who these people were and what they had done. This party of about fifty to sixty men and their families claimed to be from Missouri and to have participated in the mobbings and expelling the Mormons from that state. They had been explicitly told not to travel south through Utah, if they were going to California as they claimed. They would be allowed to use the westbound Oregon trail only. They went south anyway, and, besides being generally offensive and obnoxious, it is reported that by poisoning a spring and the meat of a dead ox, they caused the death of about ten Indians and one Mormon, injured one Mormon, and caused the death of many animals. Another similar group had shot and wounded an Indian, and had been spared from massacre by the Indians only by army assistance. In fact, by saving one group, the army put itself in the wrong location to save the other group.

The party of Missourians had

> threatened to stop at some convenient point, and fatten their stock, that when the United States troops should arrive, the emigrants would have plenty [of] beef to feed them with, and would then help to kill every 'God damned Mormon' that there was in the mountains.
>
> This course of conduct on their part, coupled with the rumor which they spread, that some four or five hundred Dragoons were expected through on the Fremont trail, whom they would join, caused them to be regarded by the settlers with a feeling of distrust. (CHC 4:163).

Some of the local Mormons even sent out search parties to locate the Dragoons that never appeared.

So here we have a hostile force taking up positions within the Mormon space. It was clear to the Mormons that they could not let outsiders begin to take over parts of Mormon territory, lest they have a repeat of Missouri. If one group had been allowed to stay and occupy land, others would surely have come also. The other emigration party that had a brush with the Indians, and were also threated with massacre, continued on to California through Las Vegas, but this group seemed to be planning to stay and fight it out. Perhaps the only apparent alternative for the Mormons was to escort them on to Las Vegas as well, even if against their will. But of course, in doing so, the Mormons risked taking casualties themselves, especially if the claim that Dragoons were coming proved to be true. Apparently, the emigrant wagon train outnumbered the few Mormons that lived in the area. When finally consulted, Brigham Young said to leave them alone, but surely they could not be allowed to take up permanent residence in southern Utah if they continued their hostile attitude.

Based on the legal status of Utah, it is possible that these people may have come on their own or explicitly been sent there to turn Utah into a slave-holding area, and to dispossess the Mormons again. No one has mentioned any such connections, but it is possible. Certainly, the local Mormons had reason to assume the worst on those points. That would be so repugnant and threatening, that it probably would be considered a life-and-death matter to the saints. The coming of an army with southern leadership right behind the coming of the Missourians would add credence to the slave-state plot theory. Was the army there to support the next group of Missouri slavers coming in? Who could be sure at the time? The army came in secrecy, with no statement as to its purpose. There had been no proper investigations of any of the wild charges made against the saints. The saints would be justified in expecting the worst. Even if the exact reason was unclear, allowing the Missourians to stay in Utah posed a real danger to the saints. Brigham Young had many fears, most of them justified, and he apparently passed them on to the saints quite successfully, perhaps a little too successfully in this case.

However strange it may seem, the incident may have done more good than harm. The group had reportedly caused the deaths of about eleven people, so the attack on them may not have been without justice. It may have actually saved many lives. For one thing, it is likely that no more emigrants tried the southern route against the advice of the Utah leaders. The Indians were probably the main original danger, but the Mormons as well were not to be trifled with by deceptive or larcenous outsiders. Keeping out nonmember outsiders with evil intent was a necessary part of keeping control of the territory and preserving a haven for the saints.

For another thing, it may have showed the approaching army that the days of pushing the "gentle" Mormons around were over. It should have helped make quite clear to the army that the Mormons, or at least some of them, were quite able to snuff out their lives if it came to that, and that they would likely have some Indians to help them. With that point made perfectly clear, the army would not likely be so foolish as to play at deception or go back on their word and attempt to attack or extort the saints as soon as they had been permitted into the valley. The saints were fully prepared to see that not a man left alive, if it came to that, and it was useful for the army to know it. The Mormons had probably learned a little something about guerrilla warfare from the Indians, had prepared food, supplies, weapons, etc., and were certainly able to use their knowledge and control of the mountains to make the army pay a very high price for aggression. "Let them come up the canyon for firewood," was one comment, implying that few would return.

The army had to make many promises before they were allowed the privilege of entering the valley. The original Mormon intent was not to let them in under any circumstances. The Missouri emigrants had made moves to stay in Utah, and to bring in yet another army to defend them in their criminal intents. They had been snuffed out, and the lesson was there for anyone to learn. There was a limit to how far the Mormons could be pushed, and they had just found out where it was.

The Mountain Meadow Massacre, while certainly a brutal deed, and damaging to the saints' public image, nonetheless is a useful indicator of the realities and attitudes and sentiments of the times. Many of the saints believed they were locked in mortal combat with the world. It had been a life and death struggle in Missouri, and they were not willing to have mobbers again gain such power over them.

## CHAPTER 8

# Weaknesses in Territorial Government: Utah as a Third World Country

Utah had many of the characteristics and problems of today's third world, colonial or ex-colonial countries. By making some of those comparisons, it may help us to understand some of the pressures and concerns of the 1800s and the wisdom of some of the actions taken. It may also help to de-mystify some of the "doctrinal" emanations from that time. Utah's situation was not completely unique in the history of the world, and many books have been written about similar situations and problems.

Every country wants to be independent. Utah was no exception. And its people had a special reason to wish to be free of persecution and threatened annihilation by the prevailing U.S. culture. (In a similar example, Pakistan (and later Bangladesh) was created to protect Muslims and give them a refuge from the depredations of the larger Hindu society of India).

Utah was treated from the beginning as a colony of the U.S., to be controlled and exploited, just as the U.S. itself had been controlled and exploited by Great Britain. (In fact, Great Britain seems to have tried to help the U.S. persecute the new U.S. "colony" of Utah.) The U.S. had its War of Independence, and Utah did the same, the 1857-1861 "Utah War" fulfilling that parallel purpose and outcome.

Britain practiced "taxation without representation" and generally appointed governors without the approval of the colonists. The U.S. did the same to Utah, especially in the appointment of hostile territorial administrators, many of whom felt it their duty to weaken and punish the Mormons by every means available, fair or foul.

To repeat, every country wants to be independent. The larger and richer countries find that easy, but the smaller and poorer ones have a much harder problem. All wish to have the benefits of the technology and trade with the big countries, but none of the loss of independence such contact can cause. (See the example of Mexico shouting "sovereignty" after the passing of the North American Free Trade Agreement (NAFTA) in 1993 with the United States and Canada.) The choices may either be to be totally isolated and independent (and poorer), or to be more open and dependent and better off economically (although possibly worse off culturally as the larger culture infects and changes that of the smaller country).

Large countries can usually afford to let foreign people buy billions of dollars of their property because even then foreigners will own only a small portion of the total, and regulations can be easily created to control such purchases if they get to a threatening level. On the other hand, a small country could easily be bought out completely and controlled by a larger country, resulting in the "banana republic" syndrome.

So the small countries often struggle to keep the big countries at arm's length. Utah certainly attempted to do this, and because of its strategic location, was able to actually best the U.S. in a military confrontation, a most unusual occurrence in the history of nations. That left economic and legal maneuvering as the only available means for the larger country to attempt to dominate the smaller.

Regardless of the amount of "distance" a small backward country is able to keep between itself and more powerful countries, all still try various internal and external measures to limit the effect of foreigners on their countries. They normally try to control money, trade, property, and people to get the results they want. Some countries make their internal currencies inconvertible so that no free trade can go on between its citizens and the rest of the world. Except for a few small barter deals, only those transactions approved at the highest levels of government can be consummated. Their citizens who may disagree with government policy are kept from being able to circumvent the wishes of the leaders (who may or may not represent the majority view).

The definition of money and its transfer, exchange, and convertibility has much to do with trade, but there are many other regulations one may place on trade. It may be taxed at outrageous levels, made subject to quotas, or simply prevented altogether (except perhaps for a small amount of smuggling). When any trade is allowed, it may be limited to wholesale trade and kept from any retail level direct contact with the natives. A third world country nearly always engages in import restrictions and currency exchange controls.

Property within a country may be kept from foreign control by simply making it illegal for a foreigner to own property there. That may be relaxed somewhat by preventing foreigners from owning a majority interest in property, keeping the final say on all property use in the hands of local citizens. Of course, there are countries that do not even allow their citizens to own property, let alone foreigners.

The flow of people into and out of a country is also an important mechanism of control, since, if foreigners do come in, "where there is a will there is a way," and they may be able to cause undesirable results regardless of all other regulations, perhaps by convincing citizens to act in concert with them to circumvent the regulations, or perhaps even by overthrowing the government. Visa systems may be implemented to control who can come in and who can leave. (While normally the main concern is about foreigners entering the country, if slavery or any form of involuntary servitude is practiced or there is a suspicion of exploitation, then it is important to keep people from leaving the country without permission.)

A country may decide that it must discipline itself, restricting its imports so that it can use its limited foreign exchange to buy technology from outside, especially capital goods which will allow it to create exports that can compete in world trade.

For most backward countries, the first order of business is usually to create "import substitution" industries for the simpler low-technology consumable items so that it can use its own labor and resources to feed, clothe, and house itself while accumulating a surplus that will allow it to import capital goods. In other words, nearly every country wishes to practice a little "mercantilism," that is accumulating money (gold) through trade so that it can acquire crucial items it does not have, as for military defense or economic competition.

Brigham Young used most of the mechanisms described above. In most cases he had little or no legal or force-based means to enforce his preferred regulations, but had to rely almost solely on preaching and "jaw-boning" the saints to get them to do as he wished. We have many cases of Brigham Young having to protect the saints as a whole from the foolishness of many of their own who did not understand their precarious position or how to resist the plans for their control by their enemies.

Brigham Young's "home manufactures" campaign is typical of any backward country. In early times, he restricted trade by trying to keep out nearly all imported consumer goods so that the people would be forced to do "import substitution" manufacturing and keep their scarce gold and currency for capital goods spending. In Utah, some of those capital goods were sugar beet processing equipment (to make sugar) and textile processing equipment (for clothing). Later, he organized import organizations so that the saints could control the costs and prices of the goods they did wish to import, and keep the benefits of economies of scale (and the jobs and profits) for themselves. Brigham Young seemed to be able to exert little direct control over the use of money, but he constantly emphasized the need to not trade with enemies or to build up their presence in the territory. His home manufactures program was a way of keeping all the foreign exchange for capital purchases, and he tried to encourage cooperation to minimize the need to purchase capital goods such as harvesting equipment, etc. In Brigham City they did create and use for a time their own inconvertible scrip "money" to simplify internal transactions and to help control trade and commercial contacts with outsiders. There were some force elements here, because without any convertible money, the residents could only buy what their neighbors produced, even if it was inferior in quality.

On the trade issue, the non-member merchants that had come to Utah, especially with the "Utah War" federal army, were to be boycotted to prevent more like them from coming, to keep the saints from spending all their money on unnecessary consumer goods, and to keep those outsiders from getting money from the saints with which to destroy their freedom and religion.

Some of the early united orders were set up with an exclusivity clause that the members would not trade with non-members. That would help keep out enemies (but might also generate ill-will where none existed before). One apparent purpose of the 1874 united order was to get loan funds from outside to help Utah with economic development. By then the property questions were probably settled, and development funds could be used constructively without fear of loss of control.

On the immigration question, non-members were told they were not welcome to even pass through the state (north to south) and certainly were not welcome to stay. Of course, the danger from Indians was severe (the Mountain Meadow massacre helped make that point), but potentially hostile outsiders were unwelcome anyway. Outside merchants, miners, etc., were not welcome to come there, either to prey on the saints or to entice them to leave for California or otherwise weaken their hold on their mountain fortress and their religion. Hostile federal territorial officer appointees and judges were also not welcome. The institution of polygamy meant that there would be almost no free women in Utah to attract any foreigners or encourage them to stay.

On the property issue, there were some unique factors. For the first 22 years in Utah, there were no property laws which would allow anyone to hold legal title to property. So in one sense there was nothing to control. However, that may have been a blessing to the saints, because if they could not hold legal title, neither could anyone else. The foolish, greedy, or disobedient among them could not break ranks and sell out to hostile outside interests, thus damaging their fellows, as was done in Missouri, where all held title to land they had purchased with the church's help. However, in Missouri, they lost their land anyway, so they could sell it and lose or just lose it. In Utah the damage of selling land would have been far greater.

There was no way that absentee landlords could buy up and control Utah land. If they were not willing to actually come there and live on the land for decades, they had no real chance of controlling it. The saints would not make it easy for such an outsider to live there if he showed hostility. And when land ownership laws were finally enacted, the saints seemed quite able to defend their claims. Perhaps things were a little more settled then, and the saints themselves a little more sophisticated, and better prepared to counter the chicanery of the world. Brigham had called for many of the brethren to study law in preparation for just such encounters.

There was a surge of attempts to dispossess the saints, but most failed. Some persistent attempts at claim jumping were visited by a "committee" to let them know they were not welcome. In one case, a person was killed by accident. It was unintended, but may have showed to others that the Mormons were not to be toyed with.

During the "no-title" period, the religious leaders could have a large effect on the uses to which the land was put and who was to manage it, without having to engage in extended legal wrangling. In fact, as the only source of recognized central authority, they had the duty to make such suggestions and directives. This apparently was the basis for much of the early united order rhetoric.

With no land titles, there were also, of course, no mortgages that might be bought up by outsiders as a means of gaining ownership and control.

There were also generally no legal means of forming corporations to hold property of various types. So there were also no shares of stock to be sold to outsiders wishing to gain control of local industry. By the same logic, there could probably be no bonds secured by property. Probably nothing more than a personal note could be used by an outsider as evidence of any legal claims on the saints.

All this meant that the land was held much as tribal lands are held in other locations. There were local agreements, understandings, and practices that had the effect of law for the local people as to the use of lands, but it could and would be all defended as a whole against any attempted encroachments by outsiders.

One exception to the "no-corporation" regime was the church corporation itself. When there were such things as titles, it held some properties, but was restricted by law to small amounts. This was viewed as a great limitation, since it meant that many grand schemes could not be carried out through direct central control. But when the church charter was revoked and the properties confiscated by the government, perhaps it was a blessing that the ownership was so dispersed. Otherwise, the loss to the church might have been much greater if major industrial properties, held by the church under some grand united order plan, might have been sold off to outsiders, thus giving them control of the economic heart of the territory. As it was, who would have use for mostly religious properties except the Mormons themselves? Keeping and destroying or converting those properties would have been such an act of desecration that even the church's worst enemies could not explain and justify it to the world.

It is an interesting question whether it was better for the saints to have not applied for statehood at all, to have been granted territorial status (as they were), or to have been given statehood at an early date. Becoming a territory at least gave them the proof to show that they were trying to be good citizens. Becoming a state may have risked being a slave state. Even if that could have been prevented, having a comprehensive property system may have contributed to the downfall of the saints because they were so poor that they could easily have been bought out by the east and then ejected or disrupted. Their nebulous "kingdom" status may have been the best over-all strategy, all things considered, and actually gave them the most control.

Often third world countries are controlled by powerful centralized governments. It probably seems necessary even to the citizens that they have a strong and responsive government to react to the maneuvers of outsiders. The threats to these countries are often quite real. In many cases, the leader is a strong man who exercises almost complete control over the country and milks it for all it is worth. Terror and suppression of dissent are common tools.

In Utah's case, there was also a strong central government, centered mostly in Brigham Young, but one quite different from the usual tin-pot dictator. Brigham Young's goal was clearly not to aggrandize himself, but to get the saints through those perilous times and do as much good for them as he could. If they were successful, then they could carry out their larger goal of teaching the world about the restored gospel.

It may be useful to add some other examples here to further illustrate the behavior of third world countries. The author's nine-year stay in Saudi Arabia has had a large influence on this book, and in fact was responsible for the study time and insights that enabled it to be written. The Saudi's have claimed and taken pride in the fact that they have never been under the control of a colonial power, one of the few countries in that part of the world which can make any such claim. After the 1990-91 Gulf War in which Saudi Arabia was protected by the massed forces of several countries, primarily the US, it will be harder to make the non-colonial claim. They may need to make the distinction between being dependent and being subservient. The country may have been of little interest to anyone earlier, more likely a liability than an asset. However, after oil was discovered, the Saudi's were clearly dependent on the west for their technology to exploit it. But here they could argue that they merely were contracting for services, not admitting any political dependency. Even after the war, they might argue that they paid for their protection and so were not subservient, even if dependent. (There is a possibility they will welch on their war payment promises, just to show they were independent.) Their almost incalculable wealth from selling oil to the west has allowed them to appear to be independent, always remembering that any great unreasonableness on their part could result in the takeover of the country.

One policy they have followed is not allowing any outsider to own land in the country. Only Saudi's can hold title. Luckily for them, they seem to have been able to enforce it so far. (They may be positioned to have more leeway as to contiguous territory than did Utah which is clearly part of a large continent. The Saudis are contiguous only to Iraq which was once their friend and ally. But the Gulf War showed that was not to be relied on.) Any use of property by outsiders had to be by lease or other arrangement with a Saudi, usually a member of the large "royal family," the 2000-3000 men who own and control most of the country. This provides a nice income to the rent-seeking class and also keeps them closely linked with their country, the source of all their wealth. This linking of religious leaders, political leaders, and economic ownership gives almost total control to one small group.

The Arabian king is an example of what Brigham Young may have been striving for. The king is the political head, the religious head, and the owner or controller of all the major economic properties in the nation. He calls himself the "Keeper of the Two Holy Mosques" to emphasize his pious religious duties and to divert attention from his nearly total control of all laws and major properties. He has not abused his power to the extent others have and this is laudable in many ways. (His vast wealth has made unnecessary the oppressing of the masses as other dictators have done). The complete forbidding of any other church building or facilities there is a problem, and the suppression of any overt non-Muslim church activities. He usually does not go so far as to persecute individual foreigners for their beliefs, but may interfere with their practices (a nice distinction). Interior groups or those from neighboring countries may be treated more roughly, since the foreigners can just be sent home if they "misbehave," while other discipline must be used on local groups who might foment revolution.

The king has created examples of many laws Brigham Young would probably have liked to use. He has rules to keep foreigners from owning any property and thus gaining any internal control. There are rules to keep out the outside merchants (the multinational corporations) of our day, and to keep them from doing any retail selling. Of course, the Saudi's buy from them on a wholesale basis. The Saudi's love to engage in trading and would want to keep this occupation, and thus keep control, and also employ their local people in their favorite professions.

The Saudi's have many immigration rules. They want tight control of foreigners who enter to avoid any threat to their control. On the other hand, since most of their menial work force are also foreigners (two-thirds of their total work force), and they treat some of them almost as slaves, they want good control over when these people can leave.

Without strong controls on entering the country, Saudi's small and relatively uneducated populace (like Utah in the 1800s) might be at the mercy of more skilled outsiders. Allowing people to become citizens must also be closely guarded to preserve the country for the "real" Saudi's. People cannot become citizens except by birth to Saudis, unless they become Muslims, etc.

Their currency is to some extent convertible, perhaps just to let their foreign workers send home their earnings, but any international transactions of any consequence would be done in U.S. dollars or British pounds or some other major currency.

They have some interesting trade restrictions. They have embargoes and blacklists on any Israeli-produced goods or the goods of any company that does business with the Israelis. This, they seem to believe, helps them reach their political goals, which are probably to get rid of that upsetting example of a democracy, Israel, which is not only a "bad" example to the peoples of the various kingdoms and dictatorships in the region, but also has displaced some of their Arab brethren. Those who can trade internationally are only those trusted members of the "family." Since all trade deals must go through an approved Saudi, those Saudi's can get a percentage of the total with little or no work on their part.

Small countries tend to end up dependent on big ones for defense or become their quasi-colony. They can hassle individuals and even companies in their boundaries as it serves their purpose to placate and impress their citizens and keep the individual foreigners on the defensive, but they may still be vassal states nonetheless, as in the case of Saudi Arabia, and its Gulf War. They may posture to their citizens as being totally independent and restrict the rights of foreign individuals within their country as apparent proof of their independence, but that does not change their vassal status and in fact may increase it. They may have to "pay" more to the outside larger government to make up for the depredations on foreigners at home (done to make their citizens think they are powerful and in control).

The British in their past have had some interesting arrangements somewhat similar to the Saudi's (and the 19th century Mormons). They also had their political, religious, and economic institutions and personnel intertwined. The Church of England was a closely-allied support to the King, and many corporations such as the British East Indies Company enhanced the king's power at home and abroad in his imperialistic adventures. Brigham Young's reaching out for the maximum amount of territory surrounding him was an analogy to the much larger world-wide British expansionism.

The country of Mexico also has some interesting history. For much of that history, Mexico was largely controlled by the Catholic church, with one-half of all property and income owned by the church. The church was very oppressive to the people, while claiming to help. In contrast, Brigham Young was trying to use church ownership and direction to improve the status of the people, to help them to be more efficient, and to create facilities they wouldn't have otherwise, such as a pseudo-corporate form.

The Mexicans today have their *ejidos*, or communal farms, owned by the government and "given" to the masses to operate. However, they are told how much money they will get in loans, what to buy, what to grow, etc., while corrupt bureaucrats skim off their share of the government funds. This is a corrupt version of some of Brigham Young's economic experiments.

The U.S. government's limiting LDS church ownership of property to

$50,000 may have some parallels with the Mexican experience with the Catholic church. The Congress may have used the Mexican struggles against religious tyranny as an excuse to persecute or limit the Utah church. However, the roles were actually reversed. In one case, the Catholic church persecuted the people from greed; the bishops were the richest people in Mexico. In the other case, the eastern government (from greed) persecuted the members of the LDS church and the church itself. The many memorials from the members in Utah, notably the women on the polygamy issue, were proof that the people were not persecuted by the church but upheld it and were upheld by it. The East chose to ignore such statements, finding it better politics to claim that the LDS church was exploiting its people. That may have been the twisted logic it used to disenfranchise the women of Utah.

## CHAPTER 9

# An Historical Overview of The United Order in Utah

I prefer to define the united order as all the cooperative temporal efforts that the saints employed to solve their problems during the 1800's. I believe that is a far more accurate historical meaning than picking any particular form and calling it the "one and only" united order.

The topic of unity was a recurring one from the beginning, but there were times, based on number and intensity of talks given, that were more intense than others. It seems useful to speak of the Utah period and of Brigham Young's united orders in four phases:

### 1. No official program.

The spontaneous helping of each other in a time of obvious, visible great need. There was no need for either rhetorical motivation or any legal organizational means. No unusual doctrines were taught. John Taylor commented on those helping times in Missouri and Illinois as the saints were driven out. JD 17:64-65 JT May 7, 1874 SLC.

### 2. Official program without legal support.

Names used: 1) Consecration, 2) Order of Enoch.

Need is not so visible and immediate, but there is still a terrible long-term need to strengthen the saints for such events as the coming of the army. Saints do not necessarily believe the prophet on this and other major points. Saints are rather ignorant and need much teaching to survive in the moment, let alone prosper enough to ultimately survive in the long term. No useful legal organizations are available, so extra-legal means are created. Religion is used to stir people to action and as an organizational means, a substitute for missing government and business structures and incentives. This is where all the unusual doctrines are taught.

### 3. Official program with legal support (largest of all).

Names used: 1) Order of Enoch, 2) United Order.

The legal means become available in useful forms. The cooperation doctrine is still useful as a motivator, but only legal means need be used. No more need for extreme, questionable doctrines. General goal has essentially been reached of strengthening the saints. End of "gospel" programs for replacement of missing legal mechanisms.

### 4. End of official program, but with some carryover of ideology and traditions.

Goal of keeping saints intact has been reached. Harassment by the federal government is possible, but not extinction. Legal and constitutional means become available for all normal needs, and provide better ways than prior "gospel" methods. No need for either special doctrines or special organizations to defend the saints. Merger with the main society is possible, necessary, and desirable. Some people cling to the past phase.

**Listed below are some of the major events in the development of the united order idea:**

July 24, 1847    Brigham Young predicts Saints will be ready for clash with East in 10 years. News of army coming arrived exactly 10 years later. JD 5:226 BY Sep 13 1857 SLC.

Apr 6, 1852    Brigham Young mentions British government/private combinations as possible model for saints - may have considered East India Company. JD 1:202 BY SLC. This British East Indies idea didn't take full shape until 1874.

Aug 22, 1852    John Taylor gives anti-communism talk. JD 1:23 SLC.

April 1854    The Law of Consecration is a major topic in the April 1854 conference. No particular program was mentioned except generally getting more property into hands of the president for central church purposes. Brigham Young's talk or talks on that direct subject are not printed in the JD; we have only the reactions of others. The talks that were published from that conference are as follows: JD 02:145 JMG APR 02, 1854; JD 02:150 HCK APR 02, 1854; JD 06:322 HCK APR 06, 1854; JD 06:327 BY APR 06, 1854; JD 06:334 OH APR 06, 1854; JD 01:365 JT APR 19, 1854. The fact that John Taylor's talk, including his reaction to Brigham Young's talk, was published in volume 1, before the other talks were published in volumes in 2 and 6, may mean that in fact Brigham Young's talk was not recorded and that John Taylor's talk was the best that could be presented from that potentially important occasion.

April 1854    John Taylor accepts law of consecration as preached by Brigham Young and thus affirms "one-man-power" which in practice means that the president rules in all things. JD 1:375 April 19, 1854.

Sept 10, 1854    Orson Pratt presents concept of total joinder of property, with Brigham Young's apparent assent. JD 2:96 OP Sep 10, 1854 SLC.

June 3, 1855    Brigham Young advocates consecration and centralization of property. Teaches Missouri failure idea, and guilt of saints for not living the united order in Missouri. Possibly related to a frustration that there were no land laws, no business laws, no statehood, etc. JD 2:298.

| 1856-1857 | Reformation and rebaptism movement. Source of some of the "blood atonement" rhetoric. For example, see JD 4:43 BY Sep 21, 1856 SLC. The possibility of the U.S. sending an army to Utah was mentioned at least as early as March 2, 1856 (JD 3:232 JMG Mar 2, 1856 SLC), and its actual movement, although kept secret to the extent possible, was known at least by July 5, 1857 (JD 5:1 BY July 5, 1857 SLC). (Search terms "army" and "troops"). The reformation program may have been instigated to prepare the saints for the coming of the army when there would be an extra need for unity. It could have been unconnected from the threatened military invasion, but chances are that it was related. |

        If one is going to have to fight a battle, one wants to have a well-disciplined army. It would not do to have a large part break ranks and join the opposition or even to waiver and make the opposition think that the will to resist was not strong or that intimidation would work. If all were not ready to stand firm (and have their possessions burned if necessary), then it would be better to be rid of them before the confrontation, lest energy be wasted on controlling that element inside their ranks (like the Tories in the American Revolution). The "blood atonement" talk of executing "sinners" (laggards, rebellious, deviants, subversives) sounds very much like the practice in war time of shooting deserters, to make sure the army held together under stress, the fear of death taking over when the more idealistic patriotism failed. There were times during the revolutionary war when deserters from the American army were publicly shot, an example being during the army's march to Yorktown to meet and attack the British army.

| Mar 1, 1857 | First mention of deeding property to trustee-in-trust as consecration. JD 4:249 HCK SLC. |
| Sep 7-11, 1857 | Mountain Meadow Massacre. ECH 418-422. It might be considered the first (and only) bloodshed in the Utah War. |
| Sep 13, 1857 | John Taylor gives a second anti-communism talk. JD 5:237 SLC. |
| June 26, 1858 | Johnston's army arrives in Salt Lake Valley. ECH 417. |
| Feb 1860 | General Johnston leaves Utah to lead Confederate troops in Civil War. ECH:429. |
| Apr 12, 1861 | Civil war started. Ended April 9, 1865. The Civil War removed the federal army from Utah and greatly weakened the eastern states, especially the southern states which had been so hostile to the saints. |

| | |
|---|---|
| 1861 | Army leaves Utah. ECH 430. |
| Oct 1861 | Transcontinental telegraph completed. ECH 430. |
| July 8, 1862 | Federal "Anti-bigamy" law signed into law by President Abraham Lincoln. ECH 432. Morrill Act, July, 1, 1862. Also limited church organizations to holding $50,000 in real estate in the territories. The $50,000 limit killed many plans for large church-owned-and-controlled economic units. |
| Oct 1862 | California Volunteers arrive, diverted from their plan to fight for the North in the Civil War. CHC 5:16. The 700 troops were less dangerous than the 2,500 to 5,000 who left the prior year, but still caused some problems. |
| 1858-1865 | Brigham Young first discourages Mormon traders, to encourage home manufactures. JD 7:47 BY March 28, 1858. BCG 80. Later suggests that saints get control of trading operations. JD 11:139 BY Oct 9, 1865. BCG 85. |
| Dec 9, 1867 | School of Prophets begun. WW 6:381 Dec 16, 1867 SLC. Ended Aug 3, 1872. Had some functions like later board of united order. Taught business and accounting to brethren. WW 6:378. Started businesses such as banks. WW 7:27 Aug 12, 1871. |
| May 10, 1868 | First use of "Order of Enoch" term. (see "order, enoch" search) JD 12:210 BY SLC. |
| Apr 1869 | Discussions of "One Man Power" in conference, supporting the authority of Brigham Young. JD 13:2 BY Apr 7, 1869 SLC. JD 13:27-28 DHW Apr 7, 1869 SLC. |
| early 1869 | Property laws come into effect. First opportunity for saints to hold title to property. CHC 5:283 BY April 8, 1869. |
| May 1, 1869 | ZCMI organized May 1, 1869 BCG 93. Cooperative movement encouraged in 1869. BCG 110. It moved in 1874 to a more fully integrated form. ZCMI was at first mostly a wholesale operation. ZCMI kept prices down by 20-30%, avoided "scarcity" prices. This is like the united firm of Joseph Smith's day - protecting the saints in Missouri from exploitation. |
| May 10, 1869 | Transcontinental railroad completed. ECH:441. |

| | |
|---|---|
| Oct 3, 1869 | U.S. Vice President Schuyler Colfax visits Salt Lake City and considers war with Mormons. CHC 5:286. Ulysses S. Grant is President. |
| 1870 | Territorial corporation laws passed. BCG 145. |
| 1870 | ZCMI incorporated, 1870. ECH 443. |
| 1871 | U.S. President Grant still talking about war with Utah. WW 7:3, 36. |
| Aug 3, 1872 | School of prophets ended. WW 7:77. Had role similar to later United Order Board. |
| Sep 1872 | Wilford Woodruff goes to California fair. WW 7:81. Great efforts were made to learn ways to improve agriculture and industry in Utah. Treated well by money men of California, but mention of specific deals made. WW 7:84-9. |
| Apr 7, 1873 | Brigham Young calls for up to 5,000 LDS lawyers. Necessary for creating and protecting larger economic units, and for future skirmishes with the federal government. JD 16:9 BY SLC. |
| Feb 20, 1874 | Territorial corporation laws amended Feb 20, 1874. BCG 145. Property tranfers to corporations allowed for stock. April 1874 conference has many united order speeches. This united order called for pooling of labor as well as capital. BCG 146. Note close correlation of organization of ZCMI and United Order to availability of appropriate laws. It appears that calls for "one-man-power" began to fade somewhat after corporations became feasible. The prophet did not need to try as hard to push capital together and hold it in good use with only religious mechanisms. The need for the maximum power of his unique position was partially replaced by adequate corporation laws. |
| Feb 1874 | St. George adopts "gospel" program - copartnership. BCG 157. |
| Apr 6, 1874 | First use of the term "United Order". JD 17:34 OP SLC. |
| Oct 1874 | St. George adopts "legal" program - corporation. BCG 169. |
| July 1875 | Bishops baptized into united order. Wards organized. WW 7:233-4. |
| Aug 9, 1874 | Brigham Young makes first reference to new/old specific revelation on the UO topic. Acknowledges need for better laws to make it work as desired, making trustee-in-trust able to hold property. |

However, says putting property under the direction of the best local men would do just as well. JD 17:154 BY Lehi.

Nov 1, 1875   Baron Rothschild visited SLC and had an interview with Brigham Young.   WW 7:253 & JD 18:199 April 6, 1876 JT SLC. Rothschild's business was lending to governments.  Did he ever lend to Mormons?

June 23, 1876   Brigham Young says members not required to enter united order. JD 18:247-8.  Speaking to Third Ward in SLC which had not joined the order.

Apr 6, 1877   Brigham Young's talk entitled "The Gospel Not Communism." JD 18:353. SLC.  He did not actually use the term communism, but only said that dividing property equally among the people was not his doctrine.

Aug 29, 1877   Brigham Young dies.  John Taylor becomes head of church. ECH 459.

May 1, 1882   John Taylor ends united order doctrine and programs.  CHC 5:498. Also opens up trading to all Mormon merchants, not just ZCMI. BCG 104.

1885   Edmunds Act enforcement (law passed 1882) BCG 291. - Many church leaders put in jail or in hiding for polygamy; no one left to administer united order.  In 1882 pronouncement, was John Taylor deciding that dropping the united order would lessen conflict with gentiles?  Did John Taylor have an incentive to drop the united order, as polygamy was later dropped?  To stop persecution of saints by letting more outsiders exploit them economically?

## Specific organizations, begin/end.

1864-80   Brigham City Cooperative.  BCG 111, 132.

1870-77   Kanab United Order.  BCG 226, 260.

Feb 1874-1877   St. George United Order.  BCG 155, 173.

1874-85   Orderville United Order.  BCG 268, 291.

# OBSERVATIONS

## Prophetic Direction

We do not know the specific stimuli and information Brigham Young was receiving to raise his anxiety level as high as it was concerning organizations and economic and political success, but it seems that historical events proved his earlier concerns to be justified, and that he had a strong prophetic sense of future events.

## Ideology

According to tradition, the ideal united order assumes there is no negative external discipline except counsel of leaders. It ignores the life and death pressures that the Utah saints were actually under. It assumes no one will be lazy or stupid or arrogant or uncreative or unfair or deceitful. It assumes no police are necessary. It assumes that the discipline we give to children will be unnecessary for the adults, and perhaps even unnecessary for children. This is exceptionally idealistic. It creates a society in which there are no defenses against foolishness or selfishness. It would make selfishness seem especially profitable, since there was no immediate penalty for such misbehavior.

The Deming idea of having only one supplier and then working for maximum quality is nice, but any crook on either side looking for short-term benefits could mess up the system. This can make one or the other side, or both sides, vulnerable to exploitation and blackmail by the other, or, perhaps worse, by third parties such as labor unions, who love to let their greed and shortsightedness, their promotion of class warfare, hurt themselves and others.

A friend of mine from the Mormon colonies in northern Mexico told me a interesting story about the wonderful effects of competition: There was only one propane gas delivering company in a Mexican city that used mostly propane for cooking and heating. Gas was delivered by truck to tanks at each home. If a home ran out of gas, it took a week to get a refill. Then another gas company came to the city. Suddenly the response was very quick. In fact, the trucks would usually arrive *before* a tank was empty, and fill it, even giving financial credit by allowing delayed payment if necessary. They even painted some of the old tanks at the homes.

This kind of stimulation and search for new ideas seems to be lacking in most monopoly situations. On the other hand, people have proven that cooperation can be far more economical than competition.

During Brigham Young's time, the brethren never seem to have settled the ideological question. Many leaders still got excited about class warfare, the rich versus the poor, capital versus labor, and the desire for classlessness of society.

Brigham Young eventually said, in effect, but not in the exact words, that the united order was "not communism," but not everyone believed him. Orderville *was* communism, regardless of protestations otherwise. Brigham wished to see some accounting practices that would make it more like a regular business, but the people felt they should not tamper with what they took to be a commandment to use only simple communism.

On the general question of whether wealth was good or bad, there was some disagreement among the early brethren. One spokesman for Orderville said that "Accumulating wealth was not our object, ... our aim was ... equality." BCG 287. Brigham Young would have severely disagreed. He didn't need to have poor, equal, people, he needed rich people who could help the church program along.

In *Building the City of God* it is asserted that

> Finally, it is important that Brigham Young believed strongly in social equality. Ideologically opposed to gradations of wealth and status among his people, he sought instinctively for a scheme that would prevent aggrandizement of a few at the expense of the many.[1]

I strongly disagree with the author's conclusion, apparently more a statement of the author's preference than anything based on historical fact. Brigham Young cared little about equality. He wanted power for the saints, by whatever means. As shown in other chapters, although he seemed to toy with such ideas in the early years, at least in 1856 and thereafter, he consistently decried and resisted the ideological calls for perfect equality. He represented with his own life what he wished others to do - use planning and organization and cooperation to accumulate wealth with which to do good for oneself and for the saints in general.

It appears that as long as we accept the explanation that the united order represents a purely religious commandment, which is applied in an arbitrary fashion, without regard to current reality, I believe we will never understand what was going on in Utah.

**One Man Power**

Probably the most important and enduring idea from the Utah era is that of "One Man Power" which stresses the authority which the prophet has to dictate in all things what the saints should do. It alone would be enough of a doctrine to help the saints save themselves in that or any other crisis; in the future it could be revived again.

The one man power idea may have hit its peak around the 1869-70 timeframe. The east was gaining proximity and influence by the railroad's coming closer, but the saints still could not defend their property because they had no land title laws in effect. The saints had to go through a great "tight spot" on the property retention question. After that, the one man power could fade back a little.

With real, usable laws, and solid property ownership and control by the saints, one man power becomes less important as a means of defending the saints' interests. They finally have the constitutional powers from a reluctant government to take care of themselves individually, and don't need the "army of the Lord" to continually guide and defend them. It also became better to have property dispersed among the members so that the federal agents could not get it so easily. It was harder to justify attacking innocent individuals, as opposed to the "huge and horrible" church, charged with corrupting the people of Utah, and perhaps even the nation.

The property and corporate laws apparently were passed, certainly not for the benefit of the saints, but for that of the gentile corporations, especially the mining interests that wished to operate there. BCG 169.

## Property Concentration

In the beginning of Utah's development, it was good to have more and better organizations. Either no bad reactions from Gentiles were really possible, or the good results clearly outweighed the bad consequences. Later it became different. The saints apparently reached the point where more centralized organizations were counterproductive. The very act of getting stronger and more concentrated through "orders" and exclusive trading apparently had the effect of adding greater pressures to attack Mormon leaders. The gentile merchants were one of the main enemies of the Mormons. They encouraged the use of the polygamy issue as a means to weaken the Mormons and their leaders. We can safely assume that the gentile merchants hated Brigham Young. He was a monopolist and a survivalist himself, being quite prepared to beat the gentile merchants at their own game. He was a better mercantilist than were the merchants. His plan was to spend no money, but only to export and *get* money, to be used for capital upgrades. His consultations with Baron Rothschild presumably had to do with borrowing money for such capital projects.

Brigham Young certainly maximized the state of Mormon centralization and organization. His perseverance may have become perseveration as he neared the end of his life, and sought for the ultimate in organizational power. (The movie entitled "A Bridge Too Far," based on a daring but failed Allied military action against the retreating Germans, comes to mind, where the Allied forces dared too much and lost many troops.) After his death, it became evident that the best way to protect church assets was to have them dispersed to individuals so that the federal agents could not take them as easily.

Five years after Brigham Young's death, John Taylor officially discontinued the united order doctrines and programs, including the central church control of the importing and sale of merchandise.

## The School of The Prophets and the 1874 United Order

The School of the Prophets was organized on December 9, 1867 (before property (1869) and corporate (1870) laws were available), and was disbanded on August 3, 1872. It taught business and accounting to the brethren, and started up businesses such as banks. It had some functions like the later board of the united order. In fact, we should probably consider it an explicit forerunner of the 1874 United Order Board. It was perhaps somewhat similar to the united firm of Joseph Smith's time which acted as a temporary quorum of the twelve and a temporary corporation of the president until the real twelve could return from their missions, and the state laws would allow a corporate form for the church.

## The 1874 United Order

The April conference of 1874 started a great flurry of activity, much of which only lasted 1 or 2 years. Earlier, as in 1869, the "one man power" theme was used as part of a cooperative effort. ZCMI was organized in 1870. The 1874 effort was the "one man power" theme with a major organization to back it up. The 1874 united order could have become almost a complete replacement for all government and business functions. This was getting to the maximum point of organization.

We can probably assume that the higher state of "order" was then both possible and necessary. The war with the world still raged. General Grant had wanted a war with the saints in 1869-70. The coming of the railroad certainly put the easterners closer and allowed them even more influence among the saints. Having a united order was a good idea to keep the easterners from taking over the properties and businesses of the state, or starting their own and pushing out the Mormon businesses and then exploiting their monopoly even more.

Up to 1869-70, Brigham Young had fought the creation of a major merchandising unit, apparently because he assumed it would just bleed out the peoples' money (even more than the gentile merchants were doing), and weaken their resolve to create their own necessities. They had few exports, but would only import. (Wilford Woodruff considered exporting a specialized agricultural product, hops). After 1869, and the coming of the railroad, and 1870, when ZCMI was formed, the Utahns had to combat the forceful merchandising of the easterners, and so had to defensively organize an alternate distribution system to keep the prices down and maintain control of supplies and prevent monopoly.

However, one might wonder whether the 1874 grand organization was too much, too late, and whether it might actually hinder the growth of the church. The united order was still dependent on the territory for a few basic things such as property and business organization laws and perhaps criminal laws. There was a conflict here. By going off even more on their own at this late stage, they might actually threaten the very stability of the new laws that made this separate organization possible, and thus be self-defeating in that sense. It did seem to bring on even greater efforts at government persecution, to kill off what they would see as the competing government structure that was the united order.

The easterners did not have good constitutional or democratic intentions in dealing with the saints. They hoped by doing it their way, the "right" way, the "constitutional" "non-treasonous" way, they could maximize their control of all Utah government and business.

**Rebaptism**

It is worth noting the rebaptism was freely used during the reformation days of 1856-1857, and also during the 1874 united order campaign. Both events seemed to precede, and to be prophetically known to precede, major attacks by the outside world.

**Tithing**

The concept of tithing received several adjustments during the Utah period. Brigham Young often complained that he never received nearly the amount of tithing due the central church - "a tithe on a tithe," one percent, is often all he received. This left the central church with a great lack of resources to carry out its duties. Many of the more complicated programs were invented to overcome this simple problem. For example, the ZCMI corporation at first was to pay tithing on its profits, and only tithe payers could belong (perhaps using the lure of more attractive prices for goods to help encourage people to pay their tithing). BCG 379. This changed as ZCMI become more purely commercial in its operation. The members of the Kanab united order considered themselves exempt from tithing. BCG 238. The Orderville united order paid corporate tithing as did ZCMI, and the members did not pay tithing, but later that was changed to an individual responsibility. BCG 276, 288.

### Combination of Church and State
The use of religious authority to coerce economic results is not generally a good thing. Some aspects of this could be considered "unrighteous dominion," although there was usually a good enough reason.

### Adaptability
Times change, and what made sense for one or two years may quickly became inappropriate. We should not let this united order anomaly, this unusual and difficult time and its unusual solutions, color our ideas of the ideal. There is a tendency in traditions towards foolish nostalgia. Is it always better to be in a military mode, as the Utah saints found themselves? Who could believe that? Looking backward for such a missed "paradise" is not useful, especially one that involves continual conflict. We need to focus our hopes and dreams on a more creative future.

We should be careful not to become like some of the Muslims, among whom it is believed that if Mohammed did something, for whatever reason, they should do that same thing forever. Such unthinking following of precedent will not allow significant progress. They often bestow eternal doctrinal significance on something that was only ad hoc adaptation to circumstance at the time it first occurred. The church today, while encouraging accuracy and stability of doctrine, should not be so conservative as to accept all tradition without adequate examination.

### Organizational Life Cycles
There have been many cases, especially in government, in which an organization finally reaches its full maturity and builds a great structure to house itself. However, this is often the point at which the organization becomes obsolete, and the great structure becomes the mausoleum to house the now "dead" organization. It may continue for a time, but its most important times are over. There seems to be a small element of this in the final united order effort of Brigham Young.

### General Considerations
If there is to be such a thing as the science of theology, there must be allowance for hypotheses, fact finding and theory building. If it is only a process of collecting authoritative statements, it becomes a historical or library project more than a science which seeks answers to new questions or resolution of old ones. Searching for more truth is what has led prophets to receive more authoritative statements from God. Thus, the authoritative statement may be the ultimate goal, but other means are needed

to get access to them.

## Chapter notes

[1] Leonard J. Arrington, *et al, Building the City of God; Community and Cooperation Among the Mormons* (Salt Lake City, Utah: Deseret Book Company, 1976), p. 89.

## CHAPTER 10

# The Original Concept/Impulse: A British Institution

"Where did the united order idea originate?" was a question asked over and over again, even during its active use. Was it by direct, recorded revelation, or was it more a set of inspired reactions to various needs of the time? Note that the previous book, JSUO, made it clear that the united order in Joseph Smith's time was in no way a major societal plan, but merely a temporary business partnership of eleven men assigned the duties of central church business administration before the Corporation of the President could be legally formed.

A quote from an 1852 talk by Brigham Young seems to supply an answer to the "Where did it start?" question. After talking about these topics: the new tabernacle just dedicated, the possibility of the saints becoming as good as the city of Enoch, etc., he mentions a new idea that had just struck him:

> What hinders this people from being as holy as the Church of Enoch? I can tell you the reason in a few words. It is because you will not cultivate the disposition to be so — this comprehends the whole. If my heart is not fully given up to this work, I will give my time, my talents, my hands, and my possessions to it, until my heart consents to be subject; I will make my hands labour in the cause of God until my heart bows in submission to it.
>
> I might here use a just and true comparison which will apply to the Church. The rulers of Great Britain have tried to <u>make every capitalist identify his interest with the Government</u> — that has sustained the kingdom, and is like a powerful network around the whole. Apply this comparison to the kingdom of God on earth.
>
> Brethren, do you wish this heavenly government to stand? There is no government more beautiful, no confederacy more powerful! What shall we do to accomplish this? Imitate the policy of that earthly kingdom, identify our interest with the kingdom of God, so that if our hearts should ever become weaned from loyalty to the sovereign, all our earthly interest is bound up there, and cannot be taken away. We must therefore sustain the kingdom in order to sustain our lives and interests; by so doing, we shall receive the Spirit of the Lord, and ultimately work with all our hearts.
>
> This is a policy which I have not reflected upon until this morning, but before we get through with the Conference, I shall, perhaps, see it entered into, not as the result of any premeditation in the least, but when the condition of our temporal affairs is read from the stand, you will find the Church in considerable indebtedness. If any man is in darkness through the deceitfulness of riches, it is good policy for him to bind up his wealth in this Church, so that he cannot command it again, and he will be apt to cleave to the kingdom. If a man has the purse in his pocket, and he apostatizes, he takes it with him; but if his worldly interest is firmly united to the Kingdom of God, when he arises to go away, he finds the calf is bound, and, like the cow, he is unwilling to forsake it. If his calf is bound up here, he will be inclined to stay; all his interest is here, and very likely the Lord will open his eyes, so that he will properly understand his true situation, and his heart will chime in with the will of his God in a very short time. Were we to dedicate our moral and intellectual influence, and our earthly wealth to the Lord, our hearts would be very likely to applaud our acts. This reasoning is for those who do not feel exactly to subscribe to all that has been said this morning, with regard to dedicating ourselves to the cause of truth. This is what you must do

to obtain an exaltation. The Lord must be first and foremost in our affections, the building up of His kingdom demands our first consideration.

The Lord God Almighty has set up a kingdom that will sway the sceptre of power and authority over all the kingdoms of the world, and will never be destroyed, it is the kingdom that Daniel saw and wrote of. It may be considered treason to say that the kingdom which that Prophet foretold is actually set up; that we cannot help, but we know it is so, and call upon the nations to believe our testimony. The kingdom will continue to increase, to grow, to spread and prosper more and more. Every time its enemies undertake to overthrow it, it will become more extensive and powerful; instead of its decreasing, it will continue to increase, it will spread the more, become more wonderful and conspicuous to the nations, until it fills the whole earth. If such is your wish, identify your own individual interest in it, and tie yourselves thereto by every means in your power. Let every man and every woman do this, and then be willing to make every sacrifice the Lord may require; and when they have bound up their affections, time, and talents, with all they have, to the interest of the kingdom, then have they gained the victory, and their work is complete, so far as they understand. JD 1:202 BY April 6, 1852 SLC.

Brigham Young spent from 1839 to 1841 in Great Britain on a mission and conducting business for the church. ECH 227. He would surely have come in contact with their major business institutions and practices. He does not mention the British East India and other similar institutions by name, but he has described them well enough in his allusions. It should be noted that these were monopolist, mercantilist institutions, mixing both private profitmaking and government and military lawmaking functions. They were quite effective, and Brigham Young was probably impressed by that.

One of Brigham Young's major goals seemed to be creating a reliable legal mechanism by which large amounts of capital could be assembled and put to effective use. He saw the power of the corporate form for business functions at least as soon as the rest of the world, and perhaps was ahead of them in many aspects. However, the territorial legal system did not allow that goal to be met. Eastern hostility kept the saints from using any such effective economic institution until long after they had become commonplace elsewhere. For example, while California was made a state in 1850, Utah was not even allowed to have any land titles until after 1869, and was not granted statehood until 1896.

This inability to organize effectively was surely a great disappointment to Brigham Young. He attempted to devise substitutes using whatever means he had at hand, often using religious mechanisms in place of legal mechanisms.

Some quotes from the *Encyclopaedia Britannica* will illustrate the state of the law of business organizations during Brigham Young's lifetime. It may seem dry material, but without this legal background, much of what Brigham Young was trying to do will be incomprehensible:

EARLY HISTORY OF THE CORPORATION

The corporation is a relatively recent innovation. It has only been since the mid-19th century that incorporated businesses have risen to ascendancy over other modes of ownership. Thus, any attempt to trace the forerunners of the modern corporation should be distinguished from a general history of business or a chronicle of associated activity. Men have embarked on enterprises for profit and have joined together for collective purposes since the dawn of recorded history, but the early enterprises were related to the contemporary corporation only in the sense that new developments always embody some practices from the past. When a group of Athenian or Phoenician merchants pooled their savings to build or charter a trading vessel, their organization was not a corporation but a partnership; ancient societies did not have laws of incorporation that specified the scope and standards of business activity.

The corporate form itself developed in the early Middle Ages with the growth and codification of civil and canon law. Several centuries, however, would pass before business ownership was subsumed under this arrangement. The first corporations were towns, universities, and ecclesiastical orders. They differed from partnerships in that the organization existed independently of any particular membership; but they were not, like modern business corporations, the "property" of their participants. The holdings of a monastery, for example, belonged to the order itself; no individual owned shares in its assets. The same was true of the medieval guilds, which dominated many trades and occupations. As corporate bodies, they were chartered by government, and their business practices were regulated by public statutes; but each guild member was an individual proprietor who ran his own establishment, and, while many guilds had substantial properties, these were the historic accruals of the associations themselves. By the 15th century, the courts of England had agreed on the principle of "limited liability": Si quid universitati debetur, singulis non debetur, nec quod debet universitas, singuli debent ("If something is owed to the group, it is not owed to the individuals nor do the individuals owe what the group owes"). Originally applied to guilds and municipalities, this principle set limits on how much an alderman of the Liverpool Corporation, for example, might be called upon to pay if the city ran into debt or bankruptcy. As applied later on to stockholders in business corporations, it served to encourage investment because the most an individual could lose in the event of the firm's failure would be the actual amount he had originally paid for his shares.

The actual incorporation of business enterprises began in England during the Elizabethan era. This was a period when businessmen were beginning to accumulate substantial surpluses, and overseas exploration presented itself as an investment opportunity. This was also an age that gave overriding regulatory powers to the state, which sought to ensure that business activity was consonant with current mercantilist conceptions of national prosperity. Thus, the first joint-stock companies, while financed with private capital, were created by public charters setting down in detail the activities in which the enterprises might operate. In 1600, Queen Elizabeth I granted to a group of investors beaded by the Earl of Sunderland the right to be "one body corporate," known as the Governor and Company of Merchants of London, trading into the East Indies. The East India Company was bestowed a trading monopoly in its territories and also was given the authority to make and enforce laws in the areas it entered. The East India Company, the Royal African Company, the Hudson's Bay Company, and similar incorporated firms were semipublic enterprises acting as arms of the state, as well as vehicles for private profit. The same principle held with the colonial charters on the American continent. In 1606 the crown vested in a syndicate of "loving and well-disposed Subjects" the right to develop Virginia as a royal domain, including the power to coin money and to maintain a military force. The same was done, in subsequent decades, for the "Governor and Company of the Massachusetts Bay in New England," and for William Penn's "Free Society of Traders" in Pennsylvania.

Much of North America's settlement was initially underwritten as a business venture. But, if British investors accepted the regulations inhering in their charters, American entrepreneurs were apt to regard such rules as repressive and unrealistic. The American Revolution was, in large measure, directed against the tenets of the mercantile system, raising serious questions about the whole idea of a direct tie between business enterprise and public policy. One result of the U.S. War of Independence, therefore, was to establish the premise that a corporation need not show that its activities advance a specific public purpose. Alexander Hamilton, the first secretary of the treasury and an admirer of Adam Smith, took the view that businessmen should be encouraged to explore their own avenues of enterprise. "To cherish and stimulate the activity of the human mind, by multiplying the objects of enterprise, is not among the least considerable of the expedients by which the wealth of a nation may be promoted," he wrote in 1791.

The corporate revolution did not occur overnight. For a long time, both in Europe and in the United States, the corporate form was regarded as a creature of government and monopoly. In the U.S. the new state legislatures granted charters principally to public-service companies intending to build or operate docks, bridges, turnpikes, canals, and waterworks, as well as to banks and insurance companies. Of the 335 companies receiving charters prior to 1800, only 13 were firms engaging in commerce or manufacturing. By 1811, however, New York had adopted a general act of incorporation, setting the precedent that businessmen had only to provide a summary description of their intentions for permission to launch an enterprise. By the 1840s and 1850s, the rest of the states had followed suit. In Great Britain after 1825, the statutes were gradually liberalized so that the former privilege of incorporating joint-stock companies became the right of any group complying with certain minimum conditions, and the principle of limited liability was extended to them. In France and Germany a similar development occurred.

## DEVELOPMENT OF CORPORATE BUSINESS IN THE U.S.

Pools, trusts, and holding companies. In the United States the corporation took its present form in the latter part of the 19th century. The transcontinental railroad lines needed massive infusions of capital and depended on public stock issues. A great spur to incorporation was the Supreme Court case of Santa Clara County v. Southern Pacific Railroad in 1886 when the court ruled for the first time that a corporation should be construed as a "person" and was thus entitled to the protection of the Fourteenth Amendment of the Constitution, which declares: "nor shall any State deprive any person of life, liberty, or property, without due process of law." Under this interpretation, many laws seeking to govern corporate practices were declared to be violations of "due process" and hence unconstitutional.

The 1880s and 1890s witnessed the development of huge companies to serve an emerging national market; the creation of pools, trusts, and holding companies to keep prices high and competition limited; and the appearance of such industrial magnates as John D. Rockefeller, Andrew Carnegie, and James J. Hill. But many large firms remained private holdings. The Carnegie Steel Company, for example, was a partnership not open to public participation, and several of Rockefeller's Standard Oil affiliates were not incorporated. Until almost the turn of the century, corporations continued to be presided over by the generation of men who had originally founded them: the entrepreneurial presence had yet to be replaced by formal organization.

A turn came within a surprisingly brief span of time, as investment banks began to serve as agents for industrial mergers. The half decade from 1899 to 1904 produced United States Steel, United States Rubber, American Can, and International Harvester, along with more than 2,500 other mergers--almost six times as many as had occurred in the preceding four years. By 1904, seven out of every ten of the country's production workers were employed by incorporated businesses. The pattern in the ensuing years was one of growth and expansion by the giant firms. Between 1919 and 1939, for example, the share of net corporate income earned by the 75 percent of the firms at the bottom of the industrial pyramid fell by one-half; even the larger corporations composing the next 20 percent saw their share of the total earnings fall by one-quarter. Between 1916 and 1956, while the nation's population rose by two-thirds, the number of corporations grew almost threefold.[1]

Since Brigham Young seemed to be using the early British corporate form as a model, we should review the history and nature of those institutions:

**East India Company, British**, a British commercial and political organization in India from 1600 to 1873. It was incorporated by royal charter on Dec. 31, 1600, under the name the Governor and Company of Merchants of London trading with the East Indies. Starting as a monopolistic trading body, the company became involved in politics and acted as an agent of British imperialism in India from the mid-18th century.

The company was formed to share in the East Indian spice trade, then a monopoly of Spain and Portugal, which was exposed by the defeat of the Spanish Armada (1588). Until 1612 the company conducted separate voyages, separately subscribed. There were temporary joint stocks until 1657, when a permanent joint stock was raised.

The company met with opposition from the Dutch in the Dutch East Indies (now Indonesia) and the Portuguese. Although the Dutch virtually excluded company members from the East Indies after the massacre of Amboina (1623), the company's defeat of the Portuguese in India (1612) won them trading concessions from the Mughal Empire. The company settled down to a trade in cotton and silk piece goods, indigo, and saltpetre, with spices from South India. It extended its activities to the Persian Gulf, Southeast Asia, and East Asia. After the mid-18th century the cotton-goods trade declined, while tea became an important import from China. This was financed by opium exports, eventually leading to the Opium War (1839-42). The company faced opposition to its monopoly, which led to the establishment of a rival company and the fusion (1708) of the two as the United Company.

The United Company was organized into a court of 24 directors who worked through committees. They were elected annually by the Court of Proprietors, or shareholders. When the company acquired control of Bengal (1757), Indian policy was for a time (1757-73) influenced by shareholders' meetings, where votes could be bought by the purchase of shares. This led to government intervention. The Regulating Act (1773) and Pitt's India Act (1784) established government control of political policy through a Board of Control responsible to Parliament. Thereafter the company gradually lost both commercial and political control. Its commercial monopoly was broken in 1813, and from 1834 it was merely a managing agency for the British government of India. It was deprived of this after the Indian Mutiny (1857), and it ceased to exist as a legal entity in 1873.[2]

Note here that at an early time there were two firms, both presumably British, that consolidated to prevent wasteful competition, using the name United Company. If Brigham Young knew of that history, he might have been impressed by it, and it may even have had an influence on his adopting the similar sounding name "United Order" for his economic projects.

It is interesting that with their own East India Company the French followed the British lead for their colonial administration. That might have served to give the idea further merit in Brigham Young's eyes, if he was aware of it.

**East India Company, French**, French COMPAGNIE DES INDES ORIENTALES, commercial and political organization that directed French colonial activities in India during the 18th century. It was founded in 1664 by JeanBaptiste Colbert, finance minister to Louis XIV. The company lacked working capital and was always virtually under government control. It suffered during wars with the English and Dutch in the late 17th century but revived after 1720 and obtained Mauritius (Ile de France) in 1721 and Mahe in Malabar in 1724. In 1740 the value of its Indian trade was half that of the British East India Company. Its ablest governor, Joseph-Francois Dupleix *(q.v.)*, captured Madras (1746) and thereafter set out to ruin the British company by means of alliances with local Indian powers. This policy collapsed, and Dupleix was recalled (1754). During the Seven Years' War (175663) the French were defeated and Pondicherry captured in 1761; thereafter, it was regularly occupied by the British at the outbreak of each war, to be restored as an open town in 1816. The French East India Company, lacking government support, languished and disappeared during the French Revolution of 1789.[3]

The British East India Company was presumably the pattern for the Hudson's Bay Company. Since, until 1858, that entity included British Oregon in the area it controlled, it was a neighbor of the Utah Mormons. That proximity may have prompted some of Brigham Young's thoughts including his 1852 statement quoted above.

**Hudson's Bay Company,** a corporation that occupies a prominent place in both the economic and the political history of Canada. It was incorporated in England on May 2, 1670, to seek a northwest passage to the Pacific, to occupy the lands adjacent to Hudson Bay, and to carry on any commerce with those lands that might prove profitable.

The territories granted to the Hudson's Bay Company became known as Rupert's Land (after Prince Rupert of the Palatinate, who was a cousin of King Charles II of England and the first governor of the company). The boundaries of Rupert's Land were never clearly defined, but the area was commonly understood to extend from Labrador to the Rocky Mountains and from the headwaters of the Red River to Chesterfield Inlet on Hudson Bay.

The Hudson's Bay Company engaged in the fur trade during its first two centuries of existence. In the 1670s and '80s, the company established a number of posts on the shores of James and Hudson bays. Most of these posts were captured by the French and were in French hands between 1686 and 1713, when they were restored to the company by the Treaty of Utrecht. After the British conquest of Canada (1759-60), increasing competition led the company to build fur-trading posts inland, starting with Cumberland House, in 1774.

By 1783 many of the Hudson's Bay Company's competitors formed the North West Company (q.v.), and for nearly 40 years the two organizations engaged in bitter rivalry. Armed clashes in the early 19th century (see Seven Oaks Massacre) ended only when the British government brought about a union of the two companies in 1821 under the name and charter of the Hudson's Bay Company.

At this time the company was given an exclusive license to trade for 21 years (revived for the same term in 1838) in Rupert's Land, in the Northwest Territories beyond Rupert's Land, and on the Pacific slope. The company took over the fur trade of the Oregon Country (present Oregon, Washington, Idaho, British Columbia, and parts of Montana and Wyoming). Increasing American immigration, starting in 1834 and continuing into the next decade, diminished the company's influence in the southern part of the Oregon Country, and in 1846 the Oregon Country was divided between the United States and Great Britain. The

Hudson's Bay Company continued to control the British part of the old Oregon Country until 1858.

In 1859 the company's monopoly was not renewed, and increasingly independent traders entered the fur trade. In 1870 the company's remaining territories were transferred to Canada in exchange for & 300,000, blocks of territory around its posts, and title to one-twentieth of the lands in the "fertile belt," or habitable portion of western Canada, with mineral rights on all these lands also awarded to the company.

In the 20th century, the Hudson's Bay Company remained the dominant fur-collecting and marketing agency in the world but turned increasingly to retail merchandising. It was governed solely from England until 1931, when a Canadian committee was given exclusive authority in Canada but was held responsible to the governor and committee in England. The company remains one of the chief business firms of Canada.[4]

Some notes on the politics and politicians behind the British corporate form should also be of interest here:

**Fox, Charles James**. A late 18th century Whig leader in the British House of Commons. In 1783 he co-sponsored a bill for ending a system of misgovernment in India that had alarmed and disquieted English statesmen of all parties. [The] bill proposed to change the whole constitution of the East India Company, which effectively controlled British India, by transferring control of the company's territories, revenues, and commerce to seven commissioners who were to be nominated by the British government and removable only upon a vote of either house of Parliament. But vested interests took alarm, and the House of Lords rejected the bill on December 17 after the King had made it known that he would consider as an enemy anyone who voted for it.[5]

**Pitt, William, the Younger**

....

Fox's East India bill had been defeated, but the problems it was designed to solve remained. Britain's increased posessions in India made it necessary for the administration there to be supervised by the government rather than be left in the hands of the commercial East India Company. Pitt, therefore, introduced his own East India bill, which was passed in the summer of 1784. He set up a new government department, the board of control, to supervise the directors of the company. He also ended an inappropriate division of authority in India by making the governor general supreme over the subordinate government of Bombay and Madras. In 1786 a supplementary act increased the authority of the governor general over his own council.[6]

These are all interesting comments on how such large units are governed. The unity of control which was stressed by the British institutions was one of Brigham Young's themes—made necessary because the only authority he really had was his position of prophet. He had to have that control to accomplish all the other tasks he wished to do.

Utah was being treated by the East in much the way that Britain had treated its colonies. There were attempts by outsiders to control all laws, public money, and governmental offices. The goal sought was political and economic power. The means to get it from the Mormons was religious persecution, shown to be successful several times before. Various passions could be inflamed against the Mormons, and used to further other purposes. (See CHC 6 for numerous examples). Utah would be justified in fighting fire with fire and using some of those same techniques against the eastern government under the principle that "turnabout is fair play." Brigham Young's behavior as a monopolist and mercantilist should be seen in the light of resisting those same policies practiced by the East.

## Chapter notes

[1] "Corporation, Business," *Encyclopaedia Britannica*, 15th ed., 30 vols. (Chicago: Encyclopaedia Britannica, Inc., 1981).

[2] "East India Company, British," *Encyc. Brit.*

[3] "East India Company, French," *Encyc. Brit.*

[4] "Hudson's Bay Company," *Encyc. Brit.*

[5] "Fox, Charles James," *Encyc. Brit.*

[6] "Pitt, William, the Younger," *Encyc. Brit.*

## CHAPTER 11

# Brigham Young Rejected
# The Acts "All Things Common" Tradition

It may come as a great surprise to most church members that at least for the last 21 years of his life, from 1856 to 1877, Brigham Young consistently and energetically rejected the property handling traditions stemming from the "all things common" episode in the Book of Acts. There are at least seven specific instances recorded in the *Journal of Discourses*, and all are clear enough to require little commentary. The quotes are instructive on the "all things common" issue, and also raise other important questions which will be addressed in other chapters. There are numerous other quotes which are consistent with the rejection of "all things common."

Some of the traditions that trouble us today predate Brigham Young and also troubled him. In August 17, 1856, he made the following comments:

> Says one, "It was preached thirty years ago, that nothing belongs to us, and, if I have a thousand dollars, to at once give it all to the poor." That is your enthusiasm and ignorance. Were you to make an equal distribution of property to-day, one year would not pass before there would be as great an inequality as now.
>
> How could you ever get a people equal with regard to their possessions? They never can be, no more than they can be in the appearance of their faces.
>
> Are we equal? Yes. Wherein? <u>We are equal in the interest of eternal things</u>, in our God, not aside from Him.
>
> We behold Church property, and not one farthing of it is yours or mine. Of the possessions that are called mine, my individual property, not a dollar's worth is mine; and of all that you seem to possess, not a dollar's worth is yours.
>
> Did you ever organize a tree, gold, silver, or any other kind of metal, or any other natural production? No, you have not yet attained to that power, and it will be ages before you do. Who owns all the elements with which we are commanded and permitted to operate? The Lord, and we are stewards over them. It is not for me to take the Lord's property placed under my charge and wantonly distribute it; I must do with it as He tells me. In my stewardship I am not to be guided by the mere whims of human folly, by those who are more ignorant than I am, not by the lesser power, but by the superior and wiser.
>
> Those who are in favor of an equality in property say that that is the doctrine taught in the New Testament. True, the Savior said to the <u>young man</u>, "Go and sell that thou hast, and give to the poor, and thou shalt have treasure in heaven, and come and follow me," in order to try him and prove whether he had faith or not.
>
> In the days of the Apostles, the <u>brethren sold their possessions</u> and laid them at the Apostles' feet. And where did many of those brethren go to? To naught, to <u>confusion and destruction</u>. Could those Apostles keep the Church together, on those principles? No. <u>Could they build up the kingdom on those principles?</u> <u>No</u>, they never could. Many of those persons were good men, but they were filled with enthusiasm, insomuch that if they owned a little possession, they would place it at the feet of the Apostles.
>
> Will such a course sustain the kingdom? No. Did it, in the days of the Apostles? No. Such a policy would be the ruin of this people, and scatter them to the four winds. We are to

be guided by superior knowledge, by a higher influence and power.

The superior is not to be directed by the inferior, consequently you need not ask me to throw that which the Lord has put into my hands to the four winds. If, by industrious habits and honorable dealings, you obtain thousands or millions, little or much, it is your duty to use all that is put in your possession, as judiciously as you have knowledge, to build up the kingdom of God on the earth. Let this people equalize their means, and it would be one of the greatest injuries that could be done to them. During the past season, those who lived their religion acted upon the principles thereof by extending the hand of charity and benevolence to the poor, freely distributing their flour and other provisions, yet I am fearful that that mode was an injury instead of a real good, although it was designed for good.

Many poor people who receive flour of the brethren, if they have a bushel of wheat will sell it in the stores for that which will do them no good. My object is to accomplish the greatest good to this people. If I can by my wisdom and the wisdom of my brethren, by the wisdom that the Lord gives unto us, get this people into a situation in which they can actually sustain themselves and help their neighbors, it will be one of the greatest temporal blessings that can be conferred upon them. If you wish to place persons in a backsliding condition, make them idle and dilatory in temporal things, even though they may be good Saints in other respects. If the whole of this people can be put in a situation to take care of themselves, individually, and collectively, it will save a great many from apostatizing, and be productive of much good. I have got to wait for the Lord to dictate from day to day, and from time to time, as to what particular course to pursue for the accomplishment of so desirable a result. JD 4:29 BY Aug 17, 1856 SLC.

Brigham Young makes it clear that equality is only necessary in spiritual things. Note that he specifically denies the wisdom of what the early Apostles were trying to do. See the following chapter for a possible explanation which would allow the ancient apostles to be correct, while allowing Brigham Young to be correct as well. Note that his waiting "day to day" for the Lord's instructions precludes any sweeping, ideologically fixed solutions to temporal questions.

His comment in the 1856 quote above about improper interpretation of Christ's comment about the rich young man was amplified in 1870:

> If the poor had all the surplus property of the rich many of them would waste it on the lusts of the flesh, and destroy themselves in using it. For this reason the Lord does not require the rich to give all their substance to the poor. It is true that when the young man came to Jesus to know what he must do to be saved, he told him, finally; "sell all that thou hast and distribute unto the poor, and thou shalt have treasure in heaven, and come, follow me;" and a great many think that he told the young man to give away all that he had, but Jesus did not require any such thing, neither did he say so, but simply, "distribute to the poor." If the poor knew what to do with what they have many, yea very many, in this land would have all that is necessary to make them comfortable. But it is different with the great majority of our friends over the water — they are fettered and bound, and in the prison of poverty, and have not power to extricate themselves from the thraldom and wretchedness they are in, and hence it becomes our duty to lend a helping hand and send for them. JD 13:302 BY Nov. 13, 1870 Ogden.

In 1867 he again decried the false and destructive traditions of "equality" which new people brought with them, and the fault-finding which such people engaged in:

Our brethren and sisters, when they gather here, are apt to find fault, and to say this is not right and that is not right, and this brother or that sister has done wrong, and they do not believe that he or she can be a Latter-day Saint in reality and do such things. The people come here from the east and the west, from the north and the south, with all their <u>traditions</u>, which <u>impede their progress</u> in the truth and are difficult to lay aside. Yet they will pass judgment on the acts of their brethren and sisters. I want to ask who made them the judges of the servants and handmaidens of the Almighty, who, shoulder to shoulder, have borne off this kingdom for more than a third of a century? Thousands upon whom the yoke of Christ has rested so long, and who have borne off the kingdom, are judged and found fault with, by some who probably were baptized last summer or but a short time ago. You know that this is so, you are witnesses to the truth of what I am saying, for you hear it yourselves. Now, who are they who will be one with Christ? If I were to tell the truth just as it is, it might not be congenial to the feelings of some of my hearers, for truth is not always pleasant when it relates to our own dear selves. You take some of those characters to whom I have referred to-day, who want us all to be of one heart and of one mind, and they think we cannot be so unless we all have the same number of houses, farms, carriages, and horses, and the same amount in greenbacks. There are plenty in this Church who entertain such a notion, and I do not say but there are good men who, if they had the power, would dictate in this manner, and in doing so they would exercise all the judgment they are masters of, but let such characters guide and dictate, and they would <u>soon accomplish the overthrow of this Church and people</u>. This is not what the Lord meant when He said: "Be ye of one heart and of one mind." He meant that we must be one in observing His word and in carrying out His counsel, and not to divide our worldly substance so that a temporary equality might be made among the rich and the poor.

You take these very characters who are so anxious for the poor, and what would they tell us? Just what they told us back yonder —— "Sell your feather beds, your gold rings, ear rings, breast pins, necklaces, your silver tea spoons or table spoons, or anything valuable that you have in the world, to help the poor." I recollect once the people wanted to sell their jewellery to help the poor; I told them that would not help them. The people wanted to sell such things so that they might be able to bring into camp three, ten, or a hundred bushels of corn meal. Then they would sit down and eat it up, and they would have nothing with which to buy another hundred bushels of meal, and would be just where they started. My advice was for them to keep their jewellery and valuables, and to set the poor to work —— setting out orchards, splitting rails, digging ditches, making fences, or anything useful, and so enable them to buy meal and flour and the necessaries of life.

A great many good men would say to me —— "Br. Brigham, you have a gold ring on your finger, why not give it to the poor?" Because to do so would make them worse off. Go to work and get a gold ring, then you will have yours and I will have mine. That will adorn your body. Not that I care anything about a gold ring. I do not have a gold ring on my finger perhaps once in a year.

You who are poor and want me to sell that ring, go to work and I will dictate you how to make yourselves comfortable, and how to adorn your bodies and become delightful. But no, in many instances you would say —— "We will not have your counsel, <u>we want your money and your property</u>." <u>This is not what the Lord wants of us</u>.

There was a certain class of men called <u>Socialists, or Communists</u>, organized, I believe, in France. I remember there was a very smart man, by the name of M. Cabot, came over with a company of several hundreds. When they came to America they found the City of <u>Nauvoo</u> deserted and forsaken by the "Mormons," who had been driven away. They set themselves down there where we had built our fine houses, and made our farms and gardens, and made ourselves rich by the labor of our own hands, and <u>they had to send back year by</u>

year to France for money to assist them to sustain themselves. We went there naked and barefoot, and had wisdom enough, under the dictation of the Prophet, to build up a beautiful city and temple by our own economy and industry without owing a cent for it. We came to these mountains naked and barefoot. Are you not speaking figuratively? Yes, I am, for it was only the figure that got got here, for, comparatively, we left ourselves behind. We lived on rawhide as long we could get it, but when it came to the wolf beef it was pretty tough. We lived, however, and built a fort, and built our houses inside the fort. Then we commenced our gardens, we planted our corn, wheat, rye, buckwheat, oats, potatoes, beets, carrots, onions, parsnips, and we planted our peach and apple seeds, and we got grapes and strawberries, and currants from the mountains. The seeds grew and so did the Latter-day Saints, and we are here to-day. JD 12:61 BY June 16, 1867 SLC.

Brigham Young makes it clear that he doesn't think much of the economic effectiveness of the socialist or communist programs.

In another discourse in 1867, Brigham Young revisits the question of the New Testament Apostles' plans. He believes that the Apostles did not know what they were doing, and as a result the early saints were dispersed, a terrible consequence in Brigham Young's frame of reference. He also shows that the current apostles had their doctrinal problems:

The Latter-day Saints believe in the doctrine that was taught by the prophets, by Jesus, and by his Apostles. Much has been said and written concerning the Church that was organized in the days of the incarnation of the Savior, and there has been a great deal of speculation as to the faith of that Church and the doings of its members. To tell what this religion, which we call the gospel of salvation, comprises, would require more than a lifetime. It would take more than our lifetime to learn it, and if it were learned by us we should not have time to tell it. In it is incorporated all the wisdom and knowledge that have ever been imparted to man, and when man has passed through the little space of time called life, he will find that he has only just commenced to learn the principles of this great salvation. In the early days of the Christian Church we understand that there was a good deal of speculation among its members with regard to their belief and practice, and the propagation of these speculative ideas created divisions and schisms. Even in the days of the Apostles there was evidently considerable division, for we read that some were for Paul, some for Apollos, and others for Cephas. The people in those days had their favorites, who taught them peculiar doctrines not generally received and promulgated. The Apostles had the truth, and thought that they were so established in it in their day that they really had the power to unite the Church together in all temporal matters, as Jesus prayed they might be, but they found themselves mistaken. Have we any proof of this? Yes; you recollect reading that the Apostles assembled themselves together to break bread and to administer; and they did administer from house, and from congregation to congregation, the words of life and the ordinances of the gospel. They thought they had power to make the people of one heart and one mind with regard to temporal things, and that they could amalgamate the feelings of the people sufficiently to organize them as one family. And the people sold their possessions and laid the price at the Apostles feet, and they had all things in common. There is no doubt that this is a correct doctrine, and can be practiced to the benefit of a community at large, if believed and understood. But who has got the doctrine; who has eyes to see, ears to hear, and a heart to believe? Who has the authority and the capability to organize such a society? The Apostles thought they had, but when Ananias and Sapphira fell dead because they had lied, not only to man but to the Holy Ghost, in saying they had laid their all at the feet of the

Apostles when they had only laid part there, a great fear fell upon the people, and they dispersed. Have we any history that the people ever assembled in a like capacity afterwards? I think you cannot find it. After the days of the Apostles, when the Council of Nice was called, they then and there determined what they considered to be correct and scriptural and what they would lay aside, but that sure word of prophecy which Jesus had shed forth into the hearts of those who believed on him seemed to he so mixed up and interwoven with darkness and unbelief, that they could not come to understanding and receive the full testimony of Jesus. So the old Christians lived, and so they spent their days down to the days of the Reformation.

If we have eyes to see, we can understand at once, the difficulties that the Apostles had to encounter. If the people had lived according to the gospel that was delivered to them, the Apostles would have had power to accomplish a great deal more than they did, although there can be no doubt but they were mistaken with regard to the time of the winding up scene, thinking it was much nearer than it really was, and they might have made mistakes in other respects. Many of the difficulties they had to encounter, we are not troubled with. We have not only the sure word of prophecy delivered in the days of the Apostles, but we actually have that surer word of prophecy delivered to us through the Prophet Joseph, that in the last days the Lord would gather Israel, build up Zion, and establish His kingdom upon the earth. This is a more sure word of prophecy than was delivered in the days of the Apostles, and is a greater work than they had to perform.

The few hints that I have dropped clearly show, I think, to all who are acquainted with its history, how these schisms and divisions have been introduced into the Christian world. For more than seventeen hundred years the Christian nations have been struggling, striving, praying, and seeking to know and understand the mind and will of God. Why have they not had it? Can you tell me why it is there has not been a succession of the Apostleship from one to another through all these seventeen centuries, by which the people might have been led, guided, and directed, and have received wisdom, knowledge, and understanding to enable them to build up the Kingdom of God, and to give counsel concerning it until the whole earth should be enveloped in the knowledge of God? "O, yes it was the apostacy." Very true, if it had not been for these schisms such might not have been the case. I have taken the liberty of telling the Latter-day Saints in this and other places something with regard to the Apostles in this our day. It is true that we have a greater assurance of the Kingdom and the power of God being upon the earth than was possessed by the Apostles anciently, and yet right here in the Quorum of the Twelve, if you ask one of its members what he believes with regard to the Deity, he will tell you that he believes in those great and holy principles which seem to be exhibited to man for his perfection and enjoyment in time and in eternity. But do you believe in the existence of a personage called God? "No, I do not," says this Apostle. So you see there are schisms in our day. Do you think there was any in the days of the Apostles? Yes, worse than this. They were a great deal more tenacious than we are.

We have another one in the Quorum of the Twelve who believes that infants actually have the spirits of some who have formerly lived on the earth, and that this is their resurrection, which is a doctrine so absurd and foolish that I cannot find language to express my sentiments in relation to it. It is as ridiculous as to say that God —— the Being whom we worship —— is principle without personage. I worship a person. I believe in the resurrection, and I believe the resurrection was exhibited to perfection in the person of the Savior, who rose on the third day after his burial. This is not all. we have another one of these Apostles, right in this Quorum of the Twelve, who, I understand, for fifteen years, has been preaching on the sly in the chimney corner to the brethren and sisters with whom he has had influence, that the Savior was nothing more than a good man, and that his death had nothing to do with your salvation or mine. The question might arise, if the ancient Apostles believed doctrines as absurd as these, why were they not handed down to after generations that they might avoid the dilemma, the vortex, the whirlpool of destruction and folly? We will not say what they did or did not believe and teach, but they did differ one from another, and they would not visit each other. This was not through the perfection of the gospel, but through the weakness of man.

The principles of the gospel are perfect, but are the Apostles who teach it perfect? No, they are not. Now, bringing the two together, what they taught is not for me to say, but it is enough to say this, that through the weaknesses in the lives of the Apostles many were caused to err. Our historians and ministers tell us that the church went into the wilderness, but they were in the wilderness all the time. They had the way marked out to get out of the wilderness and go straightforward into the Kingdom of God, but they took various paths, and the two substantial churches that remain — a remnant from the apostles, that divided, are now called the Holy Catholic Church and the Greek Church. You recollect reading in the Revelations of John what the angel said to John, when he was on the Isle of Patmos, about the Seven Churches. What was the matter with those Churches? They were not living according to the light that had been exhibited. Do the Latter-day Saints live according to the light that has been exhibited to them? No, they do not. Did the ancient saints live according to the revelations given through the Savior and written by the Apostles, and the revelations given through the Apostles, and left on record for the Saints to read? No, they did not. We may say there is some difference between the days of Jesus and the Apostles and these days. Then, Jesus said, "Go ye into all the world and preach the gospel to every creature;" proffer this gospel to all the inhabitants of the earth. That was a day of scattering and dispersion for those who believed in the Savior. When we come to discriminate between the former and the Latter-day Saints we shall find there was a little difference in their callings and duties, and in many points that we may say pertain to our temporal lives. Not in the doctrine of baptism, the laying one of hands for the reception of the Holy Ghost, nor in the gifts of the gospel. There is no difference in these things, but there is a difference in regard to the temporal duties devolving upon us. In those days the command was "Go to the nations of the earth;" in these days it is "Come from the nations of the earth." Do you not see the difference? Read the revelations in the Book of Doctrines and Covenants given through Joseph, and you will find that the burden of the gathering of the House of Israel, the building up of Zion, and the sanctifying of the people, and the preparing for the coming of the Son of Man is upon the elders of this church. JD 12:65 BY June 23, 1867 SLC.

One lesson to us is probably that, if the apostles of both eras were subject to numerous errors of doctrine and practice in temporal matters, perhaps we should be leery of too quickly accepting their sometimes-half-baked economic arguments. Of course, Brigham Young also wished to improve his unconditional power to direct the saints without competition even from the current Twelve. See materials in other chapters on "one man power."

The false tradition of the church-sponsored "free lunch" is one of the most persistent, as demonstrated by another discourse in 1874:

> There is a great deal being said and rumored about what we are teaching the people at the present time with regard to being one in our temporal affairs as we are one in the doctrine that we have embraced for our salvation. I will say to you that erroneous traditions at once begin to present themselves. Why we have received these traditions, those who reflect, read and understand can pass their own decision. You can not find a sect anywhere that strictly

believes in the New Testament. Read over the sayings of the Savior to his disciples, those of the disciples one to another, and of the people, with regard to being one; and then bring up the fact that they believed in this doctrine, and that they taught and practiced it so far that the believers sold their possessions and laid the proceeds at the Apostles feet. Now, what is the tradition on this point? To sell your houses, your farms, your stores, your cattle, and bring the means and lay it down at the feet of the Apostles, and then live, eat, drink and wear until it is all gone, and then what? Do without? Yes, or be beggars. Our traditions lead us to this point, and that throws us into a dilemma, out of which we know not how to extricate ourselves. To the Latter-day Saints, I say, all this is a mistake; these are false ideas, false conclusions. I am here to tell you how things are, and, as far as necessary, to tell you how they were, and then to tell you how they should be, and how they will be. To begin with, we will unitedly labor to sustain the kingdom of God upon the earth. Shall we sell our possessions, have all things in common, live upon the means until it is gone, and then beg through the country? No, no. Sell nothing of our possessions. True, the earth is at present in possession of the great enemy of the Savior, but he does not own a foot of it; he never did, but he has possession of it, and they say that possession is nine points of the law, and it seems to be so. Well, if I have a foot of land that I have dedicated and devoted to my heavenly Father for his kingdom on the earth, I never dispose of that. I have owned a great deal of land, and I now own a great deal of land in the United States, and I have never yet sold a foot of it. I say to the Latter-day Saints, keep your land, dedicate it to God, preserve it in truth, in purity, in holiness; pray that the Spirit of the Lord may brood over it, that whoever walks over that land, may feel the influence of that Spirit; pray that the Spirit of the Lord may cover our possessions, then gather around us the necessaries of life. Dispose of nothing that we should keep, but continue to labor, praying the Lord to bless the soil, the atmosphere and the water. Then we have our crops, our fruit, our flocks and herds to live upon, to improve upon, and then go on and make our clothing, build houses, improve our streets, our cities and all our surroundings and make them beautiful; beautify every place with the workmanship of our own hands. Keep what is necessary, dispose of what we may have to dispose of. To whom? To those who are operating in our mines to develop the resources in our mountains, and to all who have need. By such a course the wasting of our substance, as has been too much the case, will be stopped; and when we labor, let our labor count something for our benefit. We ask concerning the rich, Do we want your gold and your silver? No, we do not. Do we want your houses and lands ? We do not. What do we want? We want obedience to the requirements of wisdom, to direct the labors of every man and every woman in this kingdom to the best possible advantage, that we may feed and clothe ourselves, build our houses and gather around us the comforts of life, without wasting so much time, means, and energy. And instead of saying that I shall give up my carriage for the poor to ride in, we will direct the poor so that every man may have his carriage, if he will be obedient to the requirements of the Almighty. Every family will have all that they can reasonably desire. When we learn and practice fair dealing in all our intercourse and transactions, then confidence, now so far lost, but so much needed, will be restored; and we will be enabled to effectually carry out our operations for the friendly and profitable co-operation of money and labor, now so generally and so injuriously antagonistic. May 3, 1874, JD 17:52-53

Conservation and good management of property were important to Brigham Young, and precluded any wholesale distribution to those with questionable economic wisdom.

The following address by Brigham Young was delivered April 6, 1877 in St. George, and includes a correction to the "equality" teachings of George Q. Cannon:

I think that, as a people, we are nearer alike in the sentiments and feelings of our hearts, than in our words. From the most excellent discourse which we have heard this morning from brother Cannon, I believe that the people might gather the idea that we shall be expected to divide our property equally one with another, and that this will constitute the United Order. I will give you my view, in as few words as possible with regard to this subject, which I will promise you are correct.

The Lord wishes and requires us to develop the ability within us, and to utilize the ability, of these men, women and children called Latter-day Saints.

The most of the inhabitants of the earth are incapable of dictating and devising for themselves. In many instances there is reason for this, for they are opposed to that degree that for the lack of opportunity they are not able to develop the talents and ability that are within them. This is the condition of the people of most of the nations of the earth. All those who come out from the world, espousing the Gospel of Jesus, place themselves in a condition to be taught of him, but instead of teaching them personally, he has raised up his authorized teachers to do this work, and what does he expect of us to do? He requires, absolutely requires, of us to take these people who have named his name through baptism, and teach them how to live, and how to become healthy, wealthy and wise. This is our duty.

Supposing that the property of the whole community were divided to-day equally amongst all, what might we expect? Why a year from to-day we should need another division, for some would waste and squander it away, while others would add to their portion. The skill of building up and establishing the Zion of our God on the earth is to take the people and teach them how to take care of themselves and that which the Lord has entrusted to their care, and to use all that we command to glorify his holy name. This is the work of regenerating, of elevating mankind to the higher plane of the Gospel; in other words, of simply teaching them their duty.

COMMENT: In 1854 Orson Pratt used this same logic to argue for a total joinder of all property to keep everyone always equal—all would have nothing. JD 2:96. Brigham Young here uses the same logic to reach an opposite conclusion. Since Brigham Young apparently didn't criticize Orson Pratt in 1854 as he did George Q. Cannon in 1877, we can probably assume the Brigham Young changed his mind on the topic.

With regard to our property, as I have told you many times, the property which we inherit from our Heavenly Father is our time, and the power to choose in the disposition of the same. This is the real capital that is bequeathed unto us by our Heavenly Father; all the rest is what he may be pleased to add unto us. To direct, to counsel and to advise in the disposition of our time, pertains to our calling as God's servants, according to the wisdom which he has given and will continue to give unto us as we seek it.

Now, if we could take this people, in their present condition, and teach them how to sustain and maintain themselves and a little more, we would add to that which we already have; but to take what we have and divide amongst or give to people, without teaching them how to earn and produce, would be no more nor less than to introduce the means of reducing them to a state of poverty.

I do not wish for one moment to recognize the idea that in order to establish the United Order our property has to be divided equally among the people, to let them do what they please with it. But the idea is to get the people into the same state of unity in all things temporal, that we find ourselves in with regard to things spiritual. Then let those who possess the ability and wisdom direct the labors of those not so endowed, until they too develop the talents within them and in time acquire the same degree of ability.

What do you say to this doctrine? Is it right or wrong? (The congregation answered, "It is right.")

We want to get at a correct understanding respecting all these matters which so materially concern us. What would be the first lesson necessary to teach the people, were we to commence to direct their labors to the great end of becoming of one heart and one mind in the Lord, of establishing Zion and being filled with the power of God? It would be to stop expending and lavishing upon our dear selves all needless adornments and to stop purchasing the importations of Babylon. We can ourselves produce every thing necessary for our consumption, our wear, our convenience and comfort, right here at home. We can produce and manufacture the material necessary to beautify our lands, gardens and orchards; to beautify and furnish our houses, and to adorn the beautiful bodies which we inhabit without sending our means to France, to England and other countries for things which can a little better be made at home among ourselves. The material of which these cushions were made, which adorn the pulpits, were produced here. After it was taken from the sheep, it was manufactured at our Provo factory into the cloth you now see; and the material of which the silk trimmings were made, was raised, spun, and made up by some of our sisters in this Territory. We might exhibit to you handkerchiefs, dress patterns, and shawls, all of silk, made by our sisters out of the raw material produced here through the enterprise and industry of a few. These are only simple specimens of what can be done. Suppose I were to say, "Ladies, how do you like them?" Do you not think they would say, "Pretty well?" We can improve on what has been done, and we want you to do so. Plant out the mulberry tree, and raise the silk, and let your dresses, your shawls, your bonnets and your ribbons, and everything you use to clothe and adorn your bodies, be the workmanship of your own hands. Let the brethren take hold and carry out in every department the same principle of home manufacture until we shall be able to produce the materials, and make up every article necessary to clothe and adorn the body, from the crown of the head to the soles of the feet. Then we shall become a self-sustaining and growing people, and we shall have to do it. All this is in the elements in which we live, and we need the skill to utilize the elements to our growth and wealth, and this is true financiering.

We can now see the growth of the Latter-day Saints, and it is marvelous to us to see the multitude of little towns springing up here and there, and we are under the necessity of saying, Give us more room, for the older settlements are thickening up, and the people are spreading out and filling up new valleys continually. You can see the shoots putting forth and taking root; still the old stock is good, is alive and rapidly increasing.

It has been asked if we intend to settle more valleys. Why certainly we expect to fill the next valley and then the next, and the next, and so on. It has been the cry of late, through the columns of the newspapers, that the "Mormons" are going into Mexico! That is quite right, we calculate to go there. Are we going back to Jackson County? Yes. When? As soon as the way opens up. Are we all going? O no! of course not. The country is not large enough to hold our present numbers. When we do return there, will there be any less remaining in these mountains than we number today? No, there may be a hundred then for every single one that there is now. It is folly in men to suppose that we are going to break up these our hard earned homes to make others in a new country. We intend to hold our own here, and also penetrate the north and the south, the east and the west, there to make others and to raise the ensign of truth. This is the work of God, that marvelous work and a wonder referred to by ancient men of God, who saw it in its incipiency, as a stone cut out of the mountains without hands, but which rolled and gathered strength and magnitude until it filled the whole earth. We will continue to grow, to increase and spread abroad, and the powers of earth and hell combined cannot hinder it. All who are found opposing God and his people will be swept away and their names be forgotten in the earth. As the Prophets Joseph and Hyrum were murdered, and as they massacred our brethren and sisters in Missouri, so they would have served us years and years ago, if they had had the power to do so. But the Lord Almighty has said, Thus far thou shalt go and no farther, and hence we are spared to carry on his work. We are in his hands, the nations of the earth are in his hands; he rules in the midst of the armies of heaven and executes his pleasure on the earth. The hearts of all living are in his hands and he turns them as the rivers of water are turned.

We have no business here other than to build up and establish the Zion of God. It must be done according to the will and law of God, after that pattern and order by which Enoch built up and perfected the former-day Zion, which was taken away to heaven, hence the saying went abroad that Zion had fled. By and by it will come back again, and as Enoch prepared his people to be worthy of translation, so we through our faithfulness must prepare ourselves to meet Zion from above when it shall return to earth, and to abide the brightness and glory of its coming.

My brethren and sisters, I do really delight in hearing our brethren speak on this holy order of heaven. Unity of purpose and action, in carrying out the will of our Father, has been my theme all the day long; but I have continually plead with the Saints not to waste their substance upon the lust of the eye and the flesh, for that is contrary to the will and commandments of God. I wish to say that whoever have faith enough to inherit the celestial kingdom will find that their inheritances will be upon this earth. This earth is our home; by and by it will be sanctified and glorified, and become a fit dwelling place for the sanctified, and they will dwell upon it for ever end ever. I will further say I labor for the earth, I never mean to be satisfied until the whole earth is yielded to Christ and his people. When brother George Q. tells us we should not labor for the earth and the things of this world, he means we should not labor with sinful motives, and to gratify the lusts of the flesh. But if we possessed the treasure of the Gentile world, could we not send our Elders to the ends of the earth, bearing the precious Gospel to all living? Could we not sustain their families during their absence? Could we not build Temple after Temple and otherwise hasten on the work of redemption? Yes. But keep the people in poverty and how are we to accomplish this great work? I say, let us gather and accumulate the things of the earth in the manner indicated by the Lord, and then devote it to God and the building up of his kingdom. What do you say to this doctrine, is it right or wrong? (The congregation said, "It is right.") What little property I have I wish it to be devoted to the building up of Zion, and I suppose I have as much as any other man in the Church. I am always ready to receive and take care of the blessings that God showers upon me, and am always ready and willing to devote the same to the building up of his kingdom.

Many of you may have heard what certain journalists have had to say about Brigham Young being opposed to free schools. I am opposed to free education as much as I am opposed to taking away property from one man and giving it to another who knows not how to take care of it. But when you come to the fact, I will venture to say that I school ten children to every one that those who do who complain so much of me. I now pay the school fees of a number of children who are either orphans or sons and daughters of poor people. But in aiding and blessing the poor I do not believe in allowing my charities to go through the hands of a set of robbers who pocket nine-tenths themselves, and give one-tenth to the poor. Therein is the difference between us; I am for the real act of doing and not saying. Would I encourage free schools by taxation? No! That is not in keeping with the nature of our work; we should be as one family, our hearts and hands united in the bonds of the everlasting covenant; our interests alike, our children receiving equal opportunities in the school-room and the college.

We have to-day, more children between the ages of 5 and 20 years, who can read and write, than any State or Territory of the Union of a corresponding number of inhabitants. This is not exactly sustained by the statistics published of a few of the States, but from what we know of them we believe it to be the fact.

On the whole we have as good school-houses as can be found, and it is our right to have better ones, and to excel in everything that is good.

As to my health I feel many times that I could not live an hour longer, but I mean to live just as long as I can. I know not how soon the messenger will call for me, but I calculate to die in the harness. Amen. JD 18:353-7 BY April 6, 1877 St. George.

Brigham Young apparently did hope to achieve some equality in education, but even when discussing that seemingly harmless topic, he found it necessary to make it clear that he did not mean to imply approval of a more general (and destructive) "equality." If men can be taxed heavily to force and guarantee "equality" (at least of spending for education), they can be taxed enough to nearly destroy them.

In another 1877 discourse, Brigham Young discusses "education equality" and decries the rigid class structures seen in Europe:

Now the object is to improve the minds of the inhabitants of the earth, until we learn what we are here for, and become one before the Lord, that we may rejoice together and be equal. Not to make all poor. No. The whole world is before us. The earth is here, and the fullness thereof is here. It was made for man; and one man was not made to trample his fellowman under his feet, and enjoy all his heart desires, while the thousands suffer. We will take a moral view, a political view, and we see the inequality that exists in the human family. We take the inhabitants of the civilized world, and how many laboring men are there in proportion to the inhabitants About one to every five that are producers and the supposition is that ten hours work by the one to three persons in the twenty-four hours will support the five. It is an unequal condition of mankind. We see servants that labor early and late, and that have not the opportunity of measuring their hours ten in twenty-four. They cannot go to school, nor hardly get clothing to go to meeting in on the Sabbath. I have seen many cases of this kind in Europe, when the young lady would have to take her clothing on a Saturday night and wash it, in order that she might go to meeting on the Sunday with a clean dress on. Who is she laboring for? For those who, many of them, are living in luxury. And, to serve the classes that are living on them, the poor, laboring men and women are toiling, working their lives out to earn that which will keep a little life within them. Is this equality? No! What is going to be done? The Latter-day Saints will never accomplish their mission until this inequality shall cease on the earth. JD 19:46-47 BY June 17, 1877 Farmington.

In summary, Brigham Young was against any forced equality or any forced inequality. In a free society, property ownership is determined by such factors as individual wisdom, experience, economic performance, etc. Having acquired property through one's own merit, hopefully each such person will choose to put that property to good use for the benefit of the furtherance of the gospel.

## CHAPTER 12

# Explanation of "All Things Common" References

The phrase "all things common" appears in three scripture references (Acts 2:44; 4:32; 4 Ne 1:3), and a similar phrase "no poor among them" appears in another (Moses 7:18). From these phrases, and the surrounding historical settings, various commentators have tried to construct an argument for a kind of Christian communism as a gospel principle.

However, this interpretation is sharply at odds with the teachings of the first two prophets of this dispensation. Both Joseph Smith and Brigham Young took exception to that interpretation, and tried in many forceful ways to end any traditions supporting it. (See JSUO and chapter 11 in this book).

How do we reconcile the difference between the traditions we hear today and the strongly contrary views of the first two prophets of this dispensation? Basically, we look again at the circumstances in which those people found themselves, and try to find other more practical reasons for their behavior. This is in contrast to the usual practice of assuming that some purely doctrinal reason was in control, regardless of, or even in spite of, their practical condition.

The following explanations are brief attempts to supply alternate ways of interpreting those puzzling scriptural accounts, beginning with Acts chapters 2, 4, 5, and 8, concerning Ananias and Sapphira, and the people they associated with in Jerusalem, including the apostles.

Acts 8:1 tells us that because of persecution, all the saints except the apostles left Jerusalem shortly after the death and resurrection of Christ. First, they fled to other Judean and Samarian cities, and then on to Cyprus, Antioch, Damascus, and Alexandria.[1] This had essentially been accomplished before the conversion of Saul. The Bible chronology tells us that Saul's conversion occurred in 35 A.D. If we use the date of 33 A.D. as the year of the death and resurrection of Christ, then the large growth spurt of the Church and the exodus from Jerusalem all took place within two years. The Ananias and Sapphira episode occurred somewhere during that time, probably near the beginning of the two-year period.

The persecutions would mean that people would have to flee their homes and lands to avoid imprisonment or death. Selling those possessions where possible would be the most sensible thing to do. The money received could be used to help finance a trip to a new location and the establishment of a new home and occupation. Part of those funds could go to assist those who had no means, perhaps because their belongings had been confiscated or destroyed.

In these circumstances it would probably be important to establish some kind of welfare system. If a person were to turn over all his property to the church, he would then have no property and could logically be classified as "poor." By being a poor person, he could qualify for sharing in the proceeds from other similar donations. Someone such as Joses (Acts 4:36-37) may have set the pattern by donating all his property and then becoming eligible for sharing in the proceeds of other donations.

Apparently, Ananias and Sapphira decided to take advantage of the system by pretending to give all their property and thus become eligible to be maintained by the church. By secretly keeping back a part of the original sales price, they could have two sources of wealth. They thus became some of the first "welfare cheaters" on record. Their behavior would justify a strong action by the Lord so that no one would be tempted to take advantage of the system made possible by the unselfish acts of others.

Although possibly under a higher level of persecution, these Jerusalem saints were somewhat like those latter-day saints who were asked to leave their homes in the eastern United States and migrate to the west as part of the gathering process. They were counseled to do the best they could under the circumstances, that is, to sell their land if they could, or to rent it or simply leave it behind if no other arrangement could be made. D&C 38:37.

Attitudes toward property and its use are likely to be quite different during a time of persecution or forced or required migration. There are many parallels between the Jerusalem saints and the early saints of this dispensation as they were repeatedly displaced and bereft of their possessions. Normal property conservation and administration was simply impossible in these stressful times. A "use it or lose it" or "give it or lose it" philosophy would become reasonable. It might as well be used to help your friends as be left to your enemies. When people are migrating, they give up and share property easily - if they don't use it, they lose it anyway. Nomadic peoples or others in subsistence economies typify some of these practices for very sensible reasons.[2]

In short, these scriptural accounts do nothing to support a socialist system in a settled and stable economy, but are only rational (and therefore moral imperatives) when destructive disarray is the order of the day, and short-term tribal survival techniques are necessary.

The two other scriptural references to communal situations can be explained in a similar way. The reference in the Book of Mormon to a people with "all things common among them," 4 Nephi 1:3, occurred just after the wholesale destruction of cities in the New World. With supplies and facilities gone, people might well have to band together in a tribal subsistence kind of organization in order to survive. As economic conditions improved through hard work and accumulation of supplies and tools, organizational ties could become more casual.

About two hundred years after the gospel-based society originated, the majority of the people rejected the gospel (4 Ne 1:24, 38, 40), and as a consequence, most of the cooperation they had enjoyed was replaced with contention (4 Ne 1:25-49). With only a catch-phrase, "all things common," and a few remarks about the setting to go on, there is little that can be determined about the nature of the society, and we are left almost wholly to speculation.

However, it seems clear enough that the peoples' acceptance of the gospel (4 Ne 1:15, "no contention ..., because of the love of God") was the factor that made possible whatever cooperation there was, rather than the reverse: an economic mechanism does not the gospel bring. In other words, it seems unlikely that the apostasy was a consequence of a change in social structure. It is more likely that the apostasy damaged the social fabric. Even in today's world, the nations that have the most trust and cooperation among their people are the most prosperous ones. The economic "basket cases" are where people continually fight with and deceive each other.

The phrase "no poor among them," Moses 7:18, is often assumed to indicate some kind of communal organization. It comes from a time when the armies of the world were attacking the people of Enoch. The Lord protected the people of Enoch through power given to their leader, but they probably found it necessary to help themselves as well by organizing along military lines for defense. This process could include centralized control of many aspects of life, including the army quartermaster functions of acquisition and sharing of supplies, facilities, and equipment. Having a simple welfare system as we do today would completely fulfill any doctrinal requirement that there be "no poor among you." It is not necessary to go an enormous step further to the centralizing of all economic functions as some seem to conclude.

The common thread running through the New Testament, Book of Mormon, and Pearl of Great Price references to communalism is the hostile, primitive, migratory conditions in which the organizations developed and the survival purpose they served. Brigham Young's united order in Utah and Joseph Smith's in Missouri continued the pattern.

## Chapter notes

[1] New Testament Media Kit, Life of Paul Series Kit, PISI0629, March 1980, Filmstrip #3, "Commitment to Christ," frame #10.

[2] George Dalton, ed., *Tribal and Peasant Economies: Readings in Economic Anthropology* (Garden City, N.Y.: The Natural History Press, 1967), p. 17.

## CHAPTER 13

# United Order Types

There have been many different "united orders" spread over the entire history of the saints in the 1800s and on into today. What was the united order? What is it today? Before 1852 it had no special name, but was just cooperation in all its many useful forms. In 1852 a hint was dropped that some general merger of all the saints' political and economic interests should be attempted, using as a model the British Corporation used in such places as America and India to further British expansion, administration, and trade. In 1854 it became known as consecration. In 1869 it was first called the Order of Enoch. In 1874 it was first called the united order by Brigham Young. All this was the same force, the same program, operating in different times and places under different names to solve similar kinds of problems.

The challenge is in recognizing these many "united orders," in spite of their often unclear or misleading labels. Any cooperative behavior in temporal matters by the saints might be called a "united order." Joseph Smith used the term very loosely and broadly to mean any useful organization. So we should be careful not to get more specific than he did.

We might start with the wagon manufacturing and assembly line in Nauvoo with its 2,000 wagons produced for the trip west. Of course, the trip west itself was a major "united order" in that it combined and coordinated the work of many different groups. These groups included 1) those who planted grain on Indian lands on the way to Utah, 2) those who went to Utah and blazed the trail for others, 3) the Mormon Battalion who went south and on into California and then back to Utah, 4) the people of the main body who moved themselves to Utah and took along the families of some of the preceding groups, 5) the later handcart companies, 6) those who helped the handcart companies directly in getting to Utah, especially the last portion of the trip, 7) those who helped indirectly by supplying the funds for emigration through the Perpetual Emigration Fund and other means, etc., etc., etc. The 1869 business projects included creating banks, manufacturing, trade and agriculture societies, etc. These were superseded by the 1874 united order as superior technical means became available to do so.

All these and hundreds of other examples fulfilled the goal of the "united order" - the temporal union of the saints to accomplish critical tasks. Most historians seem to have ignored all "united orders" except the largest and most complex business arrangement set up in Salt Lake in 1874 using newly available property laws, corporate laws, and railroad transportation facilities.

Calling only the 1874 version the "united order" is missing most of the picture; latching on to that example and bestowing on it special doctrinal status is an arbitrary act. We did finally have a system or at least a concept, which could be interpreted to look like the immense state socialism systems of this century, but that should only appeal to those who already believe that state socialism is a moral imperative. The recent failure of most of those systems should help emphasize that those systems are inherently repressive and should be avoided. Large-scale cooperation is possible and can be beneficial, but a different set of rules must be used.

We should realize that after the main pioneer efforts were completed, the next set of important steps in the saints' temporal development was that of the creation and storage of food, stressing home manufactures and building forts for safety. During that stage, trade with the east was discouraged as too expensive, wasteful, and disadvantageous to the saints. When the railroad arrived, nearly all the previous economic calculations had to be re-done, and many of them turned upside down. Wise trade became a major priority and the "united order" concept had to make an almost complete turn-about to optimize the advantages to the saints.

In other words, at first producer coops or manufacturing coops were promoted at the expense of consumer coops or trading coops. Later, consumer coops were formed to make the best of the trade possibilities. It is obviously more difficult to have one group fostering both producer and consumer coops, since they may be antagonistic to each other. For example, local shoemakers may not appreciate their fellows importing shoes. Many producer coops ceased to operate at the time they came into competition with more desirable eastern goods.

The policy went from avoidance of imports at the beginning to the later control of the import process to keep it efficient and cheap for the saints, much as the original "united firm" of Joseph Smith's day had provided supplies to the Missouri saints at rock bottom prices and avoided possible gouging by outsiders. (Joseph Smith's business unit also helped acquire the Missouri land for the saints to purchase, published scriptures, etc.)

Even during this period of the large 1874 united order organization (or especially by then, as noted by Orson Pratt in the 1879 discourse quoted below), there were numerous "united orders" of all sorts scattered over the Utah area:

> We see a united order established in one place, according to one principle; we go to another part of the land, and we find an order established on a little different principle; and we hear of another, all differing somewhat. And so on until we visit nearly all the settlements of these mountains. And as was stated this forenoon, they differ as do the elders themselves in their views. JD 21:146-147 OP Nov 1, 1879 Logan.

Orson Pratt apparently wanted to see more uniformity, but knew not how to accomplish it. Perhaps he sensed that the steps to achieve his imagined doctrinal purity, the imposing of arbitrary forms, would also bring economic loss.

In *Building the City of God* (BCG) there are separate chapters describing projects in Brigham City, St. George, Richfield, Kanab, and Orderville. Other projects are also described. All were greatly different, the only real commonality being an attempt to use cooperation to improve the quantity and quality of economic results.

It should not be too surprising to find a wide variety of organizations. Businesses today are certainly highly diverse in their organization and methods of operation. One would fully expect that at the beginning, as in the move from Nauvoo west, the Mormon corporate effort would be simple and large scale, involving most of the saints.

Later, after extensive settlement and growth, the "united orders" (temporal business organizations) would proliferate on a grand scale with specialization and differentiation of organizations to fit the product or service to be created or provided.

Putting a religious shell or generalization over all these different creations, both early and late, means the shell must be very general indeed. Shifting metaphors, the basket to hold all these variations must have many compartments. The real summation is simply that the saints cooperated in business projects as seemed best, given all the facts and circumstances, and the businesses changed as did those facts and circumstances, as in any other economically and politically free setting.

As conditions changed, the needs of the saints required that some very large and complex organizations be formed, such as ZCMI to handle the wholesale import trade. These organizations are difficult to create spontaneously, or by a small group, and so it was necessary for central direction to be used.

Besides the small/large, simple/complex, informal/formal categories of "united orders," there were also the urban/rural categories. The groups that were asked to continue the kind of pioneer activities of the original move west, and penetrate the wilds on the periphery of the Utah territory, also found it useful and even necessary to keep the "wagon train" or semi-military mode of cooperation going. Those in more settled areas like Salt Lake City naturally dropped that behavior and went on to the creation of more complex and differentiated activities, such as commercial trading, manufacturing, etc.

Perhaps the most important dichotomy between orders is an ideological one. We might say that there were two basic kinds of orders, the "legal" and the "gospel." The "legal" type used normal business structures such as corporations, partnerships, and associations, kept good individual accounts as to contributions of property and labor, and amounts drawn out, and did voting by shares. The "gospel" type had either no formal legal structure or only the minimum, kept no or very little individual account data, and did voting by membership. The "gospel" version came close to simple "Christian communism." In St. George, there was both a "gospel" version and then a "legal" version.

Orderville is interesting because it was one of the few "gospel" types that was relatively successful and lasted a significant length of time. It was in existence from 1874 to 1885 and passed through many different changes in church and government policy and economic setting. Perhaps its most interesting time was near its end when important questions of ideology and practicality were discussed.

In the following account of Orderville mostly covering 1883 to 1885, we see some wavering back and forth between the "communalism by commandment" and the principles of individualism:

> The hope that unified action might alleviate dire want was regarded, by Brigham Young at least, as justification, along with supposed spiritual benefits, for the adoption of this unique system of social and economic solidarity.
>
> ....
>
> The Order was clearly a short-run solution to a pressing economic problem.
>
> ....
>
> [T]he decision to shift to an unequal wage and partial stewardship system in 1883 [split the

group]. Some thought that the original provision that the labor of all should be subject to common direction and entitled to equal credit (except for the age and sex groups previously mentioned) had led to inefficiency, sluggardliness, and loss of personal freedom. Others thought the original system was the word of God as relayed to Brigham Young, and that any change would be blasphemous. Viewing the procedural disagreement with alarm, <u>Erastus Snow</u>, as resident general church authority in southern Utah, began to emphasize the experimental nature of the Order. He argued that the various enterprises and departments of the Order were not significantly different from ordinary Mormon cooperative stores; that the system of giving equal credit for unequal labor had been unsound; and that <u>the United Order, as practiced, was not a commandment of God but a financial experiment initiated by Brigham Young</u>. He thought resort to simple cooperation might be the better course.

....

A portion of a letter written by one of the directors of the Order on August 18, 1883, shortly after the change was made, gives a particularly revealing comment on the dilemma that faced Order leaders:

> <u>Accumulating wealth was not our object, that was farthest from our minds, our aim was to establish a principle of equality as near that spoken of in the Revelations</u>, as our fallen natures would admit of, striving always to grade upwards towards the mark....
>
> Now <u>this command from God</u>, as we supposed, <u>was our cement</u>; this is what brought us together, what held us together, what comforted us in all our sorrows, what cheered us up when cast down, and in our vicissitudes we felt to rejoice and put on new determinations to endeavor to surmount every obstacle and make every sacrifice necessary to and consequent upon establishing a new order of things.... We verily believed we were in the line of our duty endeavoring to work out a problem and felt that we were sustained by the General Church Authorities <u>until our last quarterly conference</u>, when we were told by Apostle Erastus Snow that <u>our organization was no more (not much more) than Canaan Co-op, Z.C.M.I. or any other co-operative company in the territory, that it was not a commandment of God and never has been</u>, that it was a financial experiment of Brigham Young and that there was nothin[g] binding on the people in that respect.... So you see we are thrown entirely on our own responsibility.... The consequence was many have "drawn out" and have gone and strange to say that no one of our industries have failed yet; but all are moving along as formerly and some of them even more prosperous than formerly.
>
> Finally the Order came to substitute, albeit with considerable hesitancy, a system of limited individual stewardships for the strict common-stock property arrangement under which they had lived for eight years. BCG 283-287.

To confuse things further, in a letter dated June 2, 1884, George Q. Cannon, supposedly speaking for the First Presidency, more or less reversed the counsel of Erastus Snow and suggested they

> return to your old system of giving the people equal credit for labor.
>
> ....
>
> We remain your brethren,
> (signed) George Q. Cannon
> In behalf of the First Presidency. BCG 289-290.

Since John Taylor had already officially discontinued the doctrine of the United Order two years earlier in 1882, and George Q. Cannon had always been the "gospel" united order's outspoken advocate, it makes one wonder what was going on here. Apparently only George Q. Cannon signed the letter, leaving open the possibility that the others did not fully concur, or perhaps were even uninformed. John Taylor apparently wanted the Order to continue, but it is not clear what exact terms he would have preferred. Brigham Young had corrected George Q. Cannon on this exact point of enforced equality at least once before.

As a counselor to Brigham Young, George Q. Cannon was willing to go much further in supporting communalism for communalism's sake than was Brigham Young, who was far more interested in measurable economic results. That surely caused significant confusion in understanding the exact policy Brigham Young was fostering.

George Q. Cannon seemed convinced that working together was always better no matter what the conditions, and he was exciting when groups did their farming together. Efficiency seemed not to be as important to him as did "correct" ideology. As illustrated here, he liked the total Christian communism approach. In contrast, Brigham Young was more concerned that equipment and facilities be used efficiently, suggesting, for example, that farmers share in the purchase and use of reapers and the building and use of granaries. This would help keep valuable funds from being spent on unneeded items. Where bigger organizations were in use, he promoted individual accounts and accountability.

As mentioned in the above quote, Erastus Snow was the man who wished to change the way Orderville worked. It should be noted that during the initiation of the 1874 version of the united order, his was the discourse that went into the most detail on the nature of this new plan. (That discourse appears in the chapter devoted to him in volume 2). From his discourse we may assume that he knew what it was that the brethren were starting, and that in recommending the changes to the Orderville united order, he knew what he was doing. His comments in that discourse seem to indicate that he originally favored the "gospel" version of the united order. He apparently had a shift in his opinions with the accumulation of experience.

The brethren eventually advised that Orderville be reorganized on a more normal basis for holding property and operating businesses. Their past weak accounting practices made them vulnerable to exorbitant claims for money by those leaving the order. The loss of some of their leaders due to the government's persecution of polygamy was also a factor. There was no eternal magic in the system they created. The simple communal system was probably useful at first when poverty prevailed, but soon outlived its usefulness and became a burden.

With the arrival of the railroad in Southern Utah, plus mining and other large industries, the Ordervile organization ceased to have any economic advantage as it competed with goods and services from other locations and companies. In a similar way, Brigham City was greatly weakened when the railroad came, and high quality (or at least more desirable or perhaps stylish) goods from the east made Brigham City products less marketable. Brigham City had a long and interesting history, stretching from 1864 to 1895.

Looking a little bit closer at Orderville, we find that specialization and efficiency were important concerns.  Much of the sameness of clothing and housing occurred because of the mass production methods used.  A descendant of one of the Orderville families recalls that her grandmother only did sewing, and did not have to cook.  She created shirts and overalls for the men.  She continued her specialty after the organization was changed from the communal system to a more individualized system.[1]

Although the Orderville unit was fairly successful in its isolated environment, putting an Orderville system into effect in Salt Lake City would probably have been thought foolishness at the time.  Only we today have latched onto that one small isolated case ("an anomaly within an anomaly") and given it an importance that far outweighs any it had while it existed.  Would not the mainline doctrinal matters be implemented among the largest concentration of saints, as in Salt Lake City?  Just as Christ is not to be found in the desert in the last days, we should not look for him hidden in an obscure mountain valley either.

Matthew 24:26 Wherefore if they shall say unto you, Behold, he is in the desert; go not forth: behold, he is in the secret chambers; believe it not.

In today's world, the need for organized and synchronized cooperation in temporal matters is much different but no less important.  Putting a huge amount of church resources into missionary work and the building of chapels and temples around the world is the first priority, as it should be.  Spreading the gospel is the prime church mission.  There is not much glory in just existing or vegetating in some isolated communal order.

Brigham Young would have loved to put our current level of resources into those areas, but he was largely prevented by the much more pressing need to help the saints survive as an intact group.  We are finally where he would like to have been, and we should use this opportunity to its fullest.  That describes the united order of our day, with its large mission fund, etc., instead of the Perpetual Emigration Fund.

An interesting new element is the donations to world charities as a help in becoming a significant and recognized player in the world arena.  Service is nice, but, with the huge number of people with problems in the world, one needs to choose carefully where to concentrate efforts.  If such service can help tip the scales in getting access to a new country through getting a little public relations value for that service, that is good too, and not to be passed up.  We sometimes praise and honor the anonymous donor, but there are not too many of them in the world.  It is not even a good idea, it seems to me, for the church to try to be anonymous in its good deeds. (The press makes sure that it is non-anonymous in any of its perceived bad deeds). Modesty is OK, but the biggest gift we can give to the world is the gospel itself, so if the service projects can get us in a position to where the real gift can be given, we should not hesitate to let people know about the church goals and activities.

For example, a contribution towards health services for children in a newly independent country of Asia is good service and not bad press, a helpful entry into the counsels of government where the church reward is to be allowed to teach the gospel.

## Chapter notes

[1] Interview August 11, 1992 with Nellie Larsen of Spanish Fork, Utah.

## CHAPTER 14

# Brigham Young's Temporal Philosophy

One might wonder whether it is even possible to discover what Brigham Young's real philosophy was concerning the temporal affairs of the saints. He was not one to present an academic's formal philosophical statement. Can we actually deduce it from his words and acts and put it into terms understandable today? That is the challenge. I have collected a few materials here which at least touch on that topic.

## Review of Actions

The theory presented in this book is that Brigham Young's organizations were always done for the same reason – the safety and strength of the saints. The organizations and the supporting motivational teaching changed as the needs changed, but the reasons and ideology did not. The big united order of 1874 was merely the culmination of a continuum that began with his presidency. He was ordered in his one canonized revelation (D&C 136) to form up the saints into companies and move them west. He did that for the next 30 years.

The early years were easy, doctrinally and motivationally, because everyone could see everyone else's need and the solutions were fairly simple and direct. This period lasted until about 1854 when the saints had a reasonably secure foothold in the mountains of Utah. Their feeling of security was a great danger, however. Brigham Young realized, if no one else did, that they still had many serious threats ahead of them, and that they would likely escape by the skin of their teeth, if at all.

To overcome this complacency, he invented several doctrinal and organizational ideas. His first recorded thought on the topic was that some major joinder of government and private effort should be worked out, using the British model, perhaps such as the British East India Company. Note that BCG, p. 88, mentions the 1844 British Rochdale model used in a consumers' cooperative by Lancashire textile workers. Brigham Young probably preferred the much larger nation-sized or imperialist model of the British East India Company.

The first implementation of this idea in 1854 was a strong emphasis on the consecration doctrine. Brigham Young refashioned it from the Joseph Smith days into a concept and practice very much different, perhaps even the opposite of the earlier form. He specifically rejected and criticized the Joseph Smith model and contrasted it with what he now proclaimed was the correct version of that doctrine.

Later, there was a high point as ZCMI was formed in 1869 to counteract the effects of gentile merchants on the saints, especially with the coming of the railroad.

The most formal version came after the property and corporation laws were such that stable organizations with appropriate property and liability principles could be established. ZCMI was incorporated in 1874. He would have done this kind of thing much sooner if he had had the means. Many of his early efforts were in fact efforts to create substitutes for the missing legal forms.

One excellent history of the united order movements, BCG, claims that Brigham Young strongly desired equality for all. Actually, he seemed to care very little about this topic. Some of his associates were much more concerned than he. He was interested only in "the bottom line" —— what positive addition to the strength and safety of the saints would be contributed by a certain policy or program.

## His Underlying Logic

Brigham Young's 1874 address in Lehi (JD 17:154 Aug 9 1874) may come as close, in one address, as we may ever get to his philosophy. In that address, he makes a number of points: 1) There is no new specific revelation on the united order concept. 2) The saints do not see the big picture, the mission and needs of the church, as the brethren see by the spirit. If the saints understood, they would not seek to minimize their contributions or contain them to tithing, but would contribute according to the need. 3) The exact means of temporal cooperation are not important, but the results are. 4) It is extremely hard to find men who know what to do with large scale productive property such as factories.

It is reported that a general authority recently gave similar instructions to a meeting of area and stake presidents: the saints are to try to be as successful in their temporal efforts as possible so that they can contribute more to the church's programs. That may be an apocryphal report, but, if true, is a good summary of Brigham Young's message. He put much effort into making them rich so that their contributions to the church would give it the means to perform its great mission. As far as equality was concerned, he only wished for an equality of opportunity, as might come from an approximate equality of opportunity in education. He did not wish to see the crushing inequalities of the rigid class system in England, but otherwise, he did not wish to interfere. I believe it has been established as an almost absolute truth that inequality is a requirement of economic progress: any enforced equality is a great damper to economic progress, and all lose.

A quote from a recent news magazine presents clearly the eternal battle as to how a nation's resources are to be used:

> When the economy is perking along nicely, both liberal and conservative economists, whose differing philosophies have long fueled the national economic debate, bring their special brands of gloom to the party. Members of the liberal faith, for decades led by John Kenneth Galbraith, cry that distribution is unfair: ever-bigger slices are going to the rich, ever-smaller slices to the poor, and the widening gap spells economic trouble. From their side, conservative economists voice a different complaint: good times perhaps, but the government's proportion of the national product is forever increasing, denying us the therapy of a free market. The conservative exhortation to every administration, forcefully delivered over many years, by Nobel laureate Milton Friedman, is □ get the government out of the way. Let the rising tide lift all the boats.[1]

The article notes that when the economy is going badly, the "fairness" or redistribution people are more quiet, realizing that one must first have something to distribute before one tries to be "fair" with it.

The above current event commentary on the "perpetual conflict between fairness and growth" can be applied equally well to the Brigham Young era. It seems that many wish to believe that Brigham Young chose the "fair" or redistribution way. In fact, he was much wiser than that, and chose the growth path. He could not afford the stagnation or regression that occurs when there is a wholesale taxing of the strong to allow the "weak" to remain non-contributors.

A rising tide may raise all boats, but there will be no tide at all if a government seawall cuts off the ocean of opportunity, or if the moon is forbidden to show itself (and draw up the tide) lest it shame the weaker stars. (In this metaphorical flight of fancy, by the moon I mean a powerful new economic idea or project, while the weaker stars are those with a compulsion to control others, but add little themselves).

If forced redistribution is destructive, then what about voluntary cooperation as a mechanism of growth (and a possible way to improve genuine fairness)?

## Cooperation and Quality

The saints are certainly not the only ones who know anything about cooperation. Dr. W. Edwards Deming is perhaps the current leading secular prophet of cooperation. His work in helping the Japanese become masters of economic production is legendary. A few quotes from one of the Deming books may help illustrate the practical truths I believe Brigham Young was trying to impart.

In the foreword to the book, *Dr. Deming*, W. Edwards Deming makes the following comments:

> In a well organized system all the components work together to support each other. In a system that is well led and managed, everybody wins. This is what I taught the Japanese top management and engineers beginning in 1950.
> If by bad management the components become competitive, the system is destroyed. Everybody loses. Costs go up, quality declines, the market declines. Unfortunately, this fate awaits the Western world because of the prevailing system of management, which does not understand a system.
> A common example lies in the practice of ranking people, divisions, teams, comparing them, with reward at the top and punishment at the bottom. Jobs and salaries are based on comparisons. Teams naturally become competitive; divisions become competitive. Each tries to outdo the other in some competitive measure. Sales, for example, might be the competitive measure. The result is higher costs, battle over share of market. Everybody loses.[2]

Near the end of the book, the following quotes from Dr. Deming appear:

> What is cooperation? "Some people think that by cooperation I mean taking money out of someone's wallet and giving it to someone else. That's not cooperation!" says Deming. "By cooperation I mean everybody is better off. And I mean *everybody*."
> Cooperation isn't putting a gun to someone's head and saying, do it this way. That's coercion.
> Deming relates a story: "I was stuck on an airplane waiting for several hours to disembark. When we were finally able to get off, the stewardess said, 'Thank you for your cooperation.' That's not cooperation. What choice do prisoners have?" Mandatory

cooperation is a contradiction in terms. Cooperation is win/win as opposed to win/lose.[3]

A simple example of these ideas is given:

### Cooperation Leading to Lower Costs

Let's for the moment consider a hypothetical example. Suppose two full-service gas stations are located on opposite corners of an intersection. In addition to pumping gas, they offer towing and have trained mechanics. In a real sense they are competing against each other, Customers who need to fill up their gas tanks can choose one or the other. They may alternate, but at any given instance they are choosing one to the exclusion of the other.

The gas stations may cooperate. Suppose that Sunday is a very quiet day with little business. As a service to customers, however, the managers of the stations wish to remain open on Sundays. The amount of business doesn't justify two stations being open. One station may easily handle all the business. The stations could cooperate by each opening on alternate Sundays. By their doing so, the customers of both are better served and the costs to the stations are lower.

Each station may have a tow truck. On rare occasions one station may get a call from a customer needing a tow when its truck is out on the road. If the other station's truck isn't being used, why not borrow it and pick up the stranded customer? By sharing unused resources, the stations serve their customers better. Each station increases capacity without increasing costs.

But let's suppose the two stations compete in every way and refuse to cooperate. When one opens on Sunday, the other competes and opens also. One buys a second tow truck and advertises guaranteed availability. To remain "competitive," the other buys a second truck. Now the costs of each have increased. They are aggressively fighting for market share while the market has remained the same. Their revenues are the same while their costs are higher, yet the level of service offered the customer hasn't improved in any meaningful way. Either their profits have to be lower, or their prices for gasoline and other services have to increase.

But let's take our example one step further. The two stations vigorously compete and lower prices, weakening their financial condition. Eventually one wins over the other, who leaves the business. But the winner is also close to bankruptcy and has to build up his financial condition. So he raises prices.

The lesson here is that competition taken to its ultimate conclusion leads not to lower prices but to higher prices.[4]

Can the two service stations act as though they were owned by the same person? Brigham Young advocated something like that. If both are owned by Mormons and the church has a higher mission, and both recognize a charitable or social purpose beyond the comparative economic success of the two stations, they could agree to be as efficient as possible through cooperation, and maximize church contributions. However, they may then begin to act like a monopoly and resist improvements to facilities and service. How does one balance all this? How far can this coordination, this merging of purpose without a formal business merger be carried? Does the "gospel" program of the united order have an answer? If it works with two investors, will it also work with hundreds of investors who may have different views on the corporate goals? Brigham Young apparently never concerned himself much with this problem because there was always plenty of gentile competition and conflict. On the other hand, John Taylor did have to deal with the problems caused by monopolies, and he elected to end them.

For Dr. Deming, the bureaucracy or large organization was a given; it was already in place, and had existed for many decades. He had only to deal with how to manage it and optimize it.

In contrast, Brigham Young's first goal was to create a bureaucracy where none existed before; a second goal was running it. Brigham had to convince everyone that joining together in any kind of large organization was more useful than going it alone. A secondary message was how to behave after the bureaucracy was formed.

Brigham Young probably wished at times that the saints were a little more like the other part of the Israel program, the Jews. They had a much greater ability and propensity to get rich. They were also persecuted for their propensity for economic success and social influence. One might jokingly wonder if the visit by Baron Rothschild in 1875 might have been to give the saints a few pointers on how to become economic Jews.

## 1869 Cooperation

Brigham often spoke of the inability of the saints to understand economics and governing themselves accordingly. The following discourse has Brigham Young in April 1869 General Conference explaining the simplest business principles to his listeners:

> The sisters in our Female Relief Societies have done great good. Can you tell the amount of good that the mothers and daughters in Israel are capable of doing? No, it is impossible. And the good they do will follow them to all eternity. If we get the sisters on our side with regard to trading in stores, with regard to donations, or with regard to improvement, we have gained all that we can ask. What do men care about fashion? You will not find one man in a thousand that cares anything about it. Men have their business before them, and their care and attention is occupied with that. You will find that the farmer, the blacksmith, the carpenter and even the merchant, were it not that he is compelled to appear decently in society, care nothing about fashion. They want the dollars and the dimes. The lawyer cares nothing about fashion, only to gain the feelings of the people and have influence over them, that he can bring them one against another, so that he may get their dimes; that is all he cares about fashion. The doctor cares nothing about fashion. If he can make the people believe that he knows it all, and that they know nothing, he would as soon wear a hat with a brim six inches wide, and the crown an inch and a half high, as he would wear one with the crown six inches high and the brim an inch and a half wide. He cares no more for fashion than that, if he can only get the purses of the people, that is all he cares for. I speak now in general terms, for there are exceptions in every class. It is the ladies who care for fashion. They are looking continually to see how this and that lady are dressed. But if we can enlist their feelings and interests in business matters, then victory is sure. The mothers and daughters in Israel have better judgment, and they do know more than females in the world. They do understand the true principles of comfort, and how to adorn their persons so that they may present an attractive appearance to their husbands, families, friends and neighbours; and if we can make them believe this, I reckon that, by and by, they will begin and make fashions to suit themselves, and will not be under the necessity of sending to Paris or to the East to find out the fashions or to find out whether they shall make their

Grecian bends one-half, two-thirds or one-third as large as in New York; or whether they shall cut a frock so as to show their garters every step or to drag yards on the ground behind them. I think that, after a while, they will consider that they know a little of something as well as other people, and if we can enlist their sympathies and judgments, tastes and abilities with regard to trading, fashion, etc., the battle is won.

The sisters have already done much good, and I wish them to continue and go ahead. Have a Female Relief Society in every ward in the mountains; and have a Co-operative store in every ward, and let the people do their own trading. There are some of the brethren around who have asked me whether they shall trade at the Parent Store or whether they shall send East for their goods. They cannot see and understand things; after a while they will. You take the Lehi Co-operative Store, for instance: Bishop Evans started it there last summer. Suppose he had sent East for his goods in July; if he had had the same luck that others have had, they would have been landed about this time, and some of them by and by, and when they had been operating three months what would they have made? Nothing. But they came down here and bought their goods and took them home, only a thirty miles' drive, and put them on the shelves, and they were soon bought up. They sent to Salt Lake City about once a week to replenish their store, and when five months had passed away they struck a balance sheet and every man that had put in twenty-five dollars — the amount of a share — had, in addition to that amount, a little over twenty-eight dollars to his credit. Have any of our city merchants who have traded from here to New York, made money like this? Not one, and yet the people here have paid one-third more for their goods than the people had to pay in the Co-operative Stores. I understand the brethren in Cache Valley are going to send East for their goods. Well, send for them, and you will get a little knowledge; but you will buy it; however bought wit is pretty good, if you do not pay too dear for it.

Recollect that in trading there is great advantage in turning over your capital often. Suppose the Co-operative Stores were to send to New York for their goods, they might turn over their capital once a year; then instead of making anything they would run under.

I want to impress one thing on the minds of the people, which will be for their advantage if they will hear it. When you start your Co-operative Store in a ward; you will find the men of capital stepping forward, and one says, "I will put in ten thousand dollars;" another says, "I will put in five thousand." But I say to you, bishops, do not let these men take five thousand, or one thousand, but call on the brethren and sisters who are poor and tell them to put in their five dollars or their twenty-five, and let those who have capital stand back and give the poor the advantage of this quick trading. This is what I am after and have been all the time. I have capital, and have offered some to every ward in the country when I have had a chance. I would take shares in such institutions. I am not at all afraid; but nobody would let me take any, except in Provo and in the wholesale store here. I will say to Bishop Woolley, in the 13th ward; do not let these men with capital take all the shares, but let the poor have them. I say the same to the 14th ward and to every ward in the city; and you bishops, tell the man who has five thousand or two thousand to put in, to stand back, he cannot have it. If your capital is doubled every three months, it would make him rich too fast, and he cannot have the privilege; we want the poor brethren and sisters to have the advantage of it. Do you understand this, bishops and people?

The capitalists may say, "What are we to do with our means?" Go and build factories and have one, two, or three thousand spindles going. Send for fifty, a hundred, or a thousand sheep and raise wool. Some of you go to raising flax and build a factory to manufacture it, and do not take every advantage and pocket every dollar that is to be made. You are rich, and I want to turn the stream so as to do good to the whole community.

I am delighted every time I hear a company say, "We do not want your capital, we have plenty." I know what to do with mine. I have been the means, in the hands of God, of starting every woollen, and cotton factory there is in the Territory, and almost every carding machine. We are going to build a large factory at Provo. Some say we have not wool to carry on the business. Yes, we have, and we have plenty of capital. Suppose we send to the States and buy a hundred thousand or five hundred thousand pounds of wool; we are as well able to do it as others; or suppose we send to California or Oregon and buy fifty thousand pounds of wool, and ship it on the railroad and work it up. Will the people wear it? Yes, just as quick as we get the women to tell their husbands to wear home-made instead of broadcloth, they will do it. I would not even wear out the cloth that has been given to me were it not that my wives and daughters want me. If they were to say, "Brother Brigham, wear your home-made, we like to see you in it," I would give away my broadcloth, but to please the dear creatures I wear almost anything. Only let us get the sisters into this mind, and home-made clothing will soon become the fashion throughout the Territory. I had a present sent me the other day of some home-made linen for a coat, and I calculate to wear it this summer. I wear my home-made a great deal, but I have not got it on to-day; if I could only get my wives to say, "Brother Brigham, your home-made is very nice, and we should like to see you wear it," I should certainly wear it.

When the first merchants came here I foresaw all that we have passed through. I knew the foundation was laid for the destruction of this people if they were fostered here, and I know so to-day. We have turned the current, and we are controlling it, and the sisters are helping us. Now, sisters, if you will continue to help us, and will trade with none but Latter-day Saints, just hold up your hands. (The vote was unanimous.) Now, I will tell you why we bother you women, though I acknowledge that if we did not go to see the women they would come and see us; but we are so anxious to see you that we follow you up. But the reason why we are so anxious to have you sisters on our side in regard to these trading matters, is because we know if you will only say whom you will trade with and with whom you will not trade, that we shall follow you.

What I have been saying with regard to these ward co-operative stores doubling their capital once in three months, is for the encouragement of the poor, and to induce them to invest their little means and do something for themselves. Here is the 10th and the 5th and 6th wards, which are looked upon as the poorest wards in the city, though I believe the bishop of the 3rd ward feels that his ward is the poorest in the city; but I will venture to say that if these wards will each establish a store and concentrate their influence, they will double their capital every three months. I know that the 10th ward, which started with 700 dollars, three weeks afterwards had a thousand dollars worth of goods paid for and considerable money in the drawer. Think of that, in that poor little ward, though I will give it the praise of being one of the best wards in the city. It has one of the finest bands of music in the city, and they make one of the best turn-outs when they exhibit themselves.

I have talked long enough. I will turn again to my starting point. Let us have your money to bring home the poor Saints. I feel also to urge upon my brethren and sisters to, observe every word that the Lord speaks. Observe the counsel that leads to life, peace, glory and happiness, but do not observe that which leads to contention, ruin and destruction. Amen. JD 13:34 BY April 8, 1869 SLC.

Brigham Young makes the comment "Recollect that in trading there is great advantage in turning over your capital often." Here is a case where a simple business truth is raised almost to the level of religious doctrine.

Brigham Young dwells at length on this business topic, showing the advantages of a local wholesale outlet versus having each store do its own ordering and long-distance freighting:

There are some of the brethren around who have asked me whether they shall trade at the Parent Store or whether they shall send East for their goods. They cannot see and understand things; after a while they will.

Economies of scale, specialization, and other "obvious" economic and business principles, seem to have been difficult for the saints to understand. Even though the Parent Store prices are surely higher than the prices in the East, having to charge for transportation and administration, that store can still sell items below the costs to small individual stores who choose to do it all themselves. The other advantage is that the small stores need only purchase what they need, like today's efficient "just-in-time inventory systems," and so can turn over their capital very quickly, making a profit on every turn. Even at higher wholesale prices, they can make a greater profit.

## The Greatest Good For the Greatest Number

Brigham Young and others made comments about the political concept of "the greatest good for the greatest number." Although rather vague and imprecise, this idea has some merit as a slogan in mobilizing social forces, but can also represent just one-half of the Three Musketeer's slogan of "One for All," but not necessarily "All for One." Its majoritarian viewpoint may be just what is needed in case of conflict with external forces, when survival is the main goal, but could be confining to minorities in more stable times. If the state decides what is best for all, and then makes everyone conform, many may think that *their* greatest good was kept from them. The voluntary versus forced methods are an important distinction here.

Since those who are able to create and sustain economic growth tend to be in the minority, while ultimately their work can benefit the majority, the calculus and methods of applying this statistical slogan could be extremely difficult to agree upon. Do we have the more informed minority deciding what is best for the majority? Or do we have the peasant masses making these critical social choices? Neither seems particularly attractive.

In practice, the slogan probably tended to mean that Brigham Young, who was in control of nearly all large-scale undertakings, would decide himself what was best for most of the people, and seek to gain support and implement those plans. He wished to have as many opinion leaders as possible follow his lead in these often-altruistic plans.

At least the Utilitarianism theme (as he interpreted it) of growth and improvement for the largest number, is quite some distance away from the leveling and stultifying effects of communism. Looking to the best for the group does not support the equality idea. As shown in economic development studies, a large disparity is one of the requirements to get things going, as long as that disparity relates to and rewards managers and engineers, but not an entrenched feudal system.

Of course, someone might argue that the millennial promises of the communist dogma would lead everyone to the best of all possible worlds, and so would finally be the "greatest good for the greatest number," even if all were equal in poverty for decades (something the early church simply could not afford to trifle with). If there was ever any confusion on that point (John Taylor was never in doubt for a moment), the events of this century, especially the 1980s and 1990s, have discredited such claims to any realistic person.

Some citations where a version of the slogan was used: JD 9:324-5 WW April 8, 1862 SLC (we should grant a bishop's request for something for the public good); JD 11:301-2 BY Feb 3, 1867 SLC (advising a producer's coop be formed to control prices for flour); JD 12:113-4 BY Dec 8, 1867 SLC (Brigham Young says the Constitution embodies this principle); JD 17:58 BY May 7, 1874 SLC; JD 17:74-5 ES May 8, 1874 SLC (advising capitalists to be altruistic in the use of their funds, to "use ... capital and labor to promote the greatest good of the greatest number, and not for my own dear self"); JD 20:66-68 OP Aug 25, 1878 SLC (a man should find the business in which he can do the most good); JD 22:64-5 GGB Jan 30, 1881 SLC ("society is in an immoral state when the good of all is not contemplated, when the greatest good to the greatest number is not the dominant principle"); JD 26:353 JT Feb 20, 1884 SLC ("because you are a good Latter-day Saint, you may not be a good blacksmith, a good carpenter," etc.). Note that much of this rhetoric arises during the major cooperative movements among the saints in the late 1860s and 1870s.

## The Case Against Competition

In a similar vein to Dr. Deming's teachings, arguments about the superiority of cooperation over competition are made in a book called *No Contest, The Case Against Competition.*[5] This book explores extensively the benefits of cooperation and the negative effects of competition. Its discussion and conclusions seem sound enough, except for the occasional implication that government force might be a valid way of lowering competition, the standard socialist argument. (The implication that the lowering of competition in some areas by force will raise the overall level of cooperation in society seems unfounded and unsupported.) With government intervention, you merely move the competition from the market place into the political force channels, where competition for the hearts, minds and votes of legislators, bureaucrats, and citizens becomes the arena for competition. The players and the rules change somewhat, but it is still just another zero-sum competitive game. It then becomes much harder to cooperate creatively.

Complete economic freedom may mean some competition, but it can also mean a very large amount of cooperation. To the extent cooperation is a superior economic tactic, it is likely that those with the freedom to choose will choose cooperation.

It might be noted here that the "competition" fostered by current U.S. Government contracting rules, is so extreme, and so difficult, costly (both to the government and to the companies), and inefficient, that only the largest, most powerful, and most experienced companies can afford to play this expensive game. Large groups of companies are simply excluded, meaning that the number of choices available to the government are often very limited. By this logic, the government both lessens competition and lessens cooperation, achieving the worst of all possible worlds. In contrast, in the commercial world, both competition (the number of choices available) and cooperation are both higher.

In other words, the usual government rules are extremely antagonistic to cooperation, and the government does everything it can to avoid its benefits. However, at the same time, the bulk of the money spent on defense contracts is spent on sole source contracts, meaning there really is no competition. This schizophrenic government behavior is quite confusing. It could not operate without the efficiencies of cooperation, but it fights such cooperation and tries to punish those who would use it.

It appears that Brigham Young sometimes used a little force to get "cooperation" going. This is the potential fault in Brigham Young's program. The application of force to get cooperation going in certain areas can result in lowering the overall level of cooperation and economic creativity. This overall loss may be made up for by (or tolerated because of) the higher output needed in certain survival areas, but one must justify the forced cooperation, not on the basis of general economic theories of efficiency, but on the need for (economically wasteful but) effective self-defense and action on a war-time footing.

The *No Contest* book also appears to be wrong in denigrating the economic growth in the late 1800's and early 1900's (when there were no government controls), while praising the World War II period, where the "cooperation" was forced and controlled, including rationing, price controls, etc.

It is hard to argue with the economic successes of the late 1800's. And it seems wrong to praise the effects of war on making people work more and consume less. Only a tyrant could feel pleasure in using such fear to focus people's efforts on a particular set of outputs, with the obvious and inescapable corollary, that other, more refined or civilized achievements must be foregone. The fact that the people performed well to win a war, does not mean that winning wars is the highest goal of society and the highest form of societal interaction and cooperation.

It is argued by scholars (quoted elsewhere in this book) that the Russian Revolution of 1917 was really an attempt to reproduce the huge growth of the late 1800's, by attempting to adopt (and reap the profits of) the same technology and industry, but do it by force (for the benefit of a small group), not by the free market. It appears that the free market actually demonstrates a much higher overall level of creative cooperation than does any governmentally imposed system, where the "class warfare" (or its democratic analog of interest/pressure groups) becomes institutionalized, and the overall level of cooperation goes down.

There is always the irreducible minimum of "competition" which consists of self-protection against the criminal, dishonest, or merely foolish elements of society. Even with much cooperation occurring, there must always be an allowance for these disruptive elements. In a gospel society, the disruptive elements might be lower than in a non-gospel society, and so allow for a potentially higher level of cooperation and efficiency. But it is not likely that the disruptive elements will disappear, and if safeguards are not kept firmly in place (adding a certain cost to society), then there is a risk of very large losses to these disruptive or criminal elements when they discover "soft targets" for their activities.

In searching for the ideal society, perhaps we can describe the underlying principle, the "bottom line" as follows: if there is no need for competition and coercion to keep people honest, hardworking, and creative, that is a Zion society. The gospel surely should help people in knowing how to cooperate well and productively.

## Brigham Knew These Principles

The principles of cooperation taught by Dr. Deming and Mr. Kahn are the same principles taught by Brigham Young 130 years ago. Brigham Young constantly admonished people to cut expenses by sharing granaries, farm implements, wagons, etc., avoiding waste that could be prevented by cooperation.

He counseled against wasteful duplication of transportation efforts □ no competing teamsters. His goal was to have the saints maximize their income and to maximize the portion that was devoted to further growth, especially the immigration of saints from abroad. He wanted them to be honest, to not take anything from another by fraud or force (and thus damage the efficient social fabric of productivity and incentives) □ no stealing the widows' cow, etc.

He counseled farmers to carefully save and store all their grain and to sell it only to members, and that at a reasonable price. Apparently, there was a strong tendency for the farmers to sell their grain at a low price to outsiders as soon as it was harvested. They thus avoided the effort of storing it, and had cash to spend on frills. Unfortunately, it also meant that when the new immigrants came in the spring, they had to pay exorbitant prices for what little grain was left at the time.

I considered at one time entitling this book, "Brigham Young's United Order: Management Consulting in the Old West" or "Improvising in a Hostile Environment." Other candidates were "modern management concepts in the old west," "teaching modern economic concepts on the old frontier (in a frontier setting)," "saving the church through teaching modern economic and management concepts," "modern concepts in a frontier setting," "expediency in a hostile environment," and "coping with a hostile environment."

These possible titles are perhaps a better reflection of what he did. He was applying Dr. Deming's management ideas in a pioneer setting. He was a precursor, a predecessor of those ideas. He anticipated those ideas. He taught the saints how to run a company, a bureaucracy, a cooperative effort, a "united order." He adapted the Britain, Inc., idea of government/private cooperation, and anticipated Japan, Inc. He worked at collecting and projecting power in a free society. He taught economies of scale and efficiency of cooperation. He noted that the socialists who took over Nauvoo in its built-up state still failed, showing that their philosophy was very weak indeed.

Brigham Young had a much more compelling goal than most managers □ to build up the kingdom, by saving souls and to save souls. Put the kingdom first. Management by objectives has a new meaning in this setting. He had not just the pride of workmanship on a *thing*, but on the quality temporal and spiritual saving of souls. This was not mere commerce or economic success or satisfying ordinary temporal needs, as in business.

Brigham Young was a proactive paradigm changer, with a thirty-year planning horizon. Someone has said that quality and business success are more a function of management style than of specifications.

Brigham Young needed a religious thrust to get unenlightened Mormons to work towards building up the kingdom, which normally means helping others ☐ immigrants, etc. A secular and statistical argument about the superiority of cooperation over competition would be accurate, but might get less conformance. His real point was not some mystical doctrine, but rather just good sense, but people could not seem to grasp and act on the less emotional presentation.

He had to show them that help to themselves as individuals would come from "not going out of business" as a church. They needed to avoid the business failures described by Dr. Deming. But few could see that long-term benefit; most looked to short term profits for self as do bad managers today. One Deming example was of a company that set a goal of 10% revenue growth, while another company set the goal at 8% revenue growth. The first company crumbled, while the second lasted.

Brigham Young's message was "get rich so the church can get more money and do its mission better." That is the same message reported through the grapevine to have been given by one of the Twelve to a meeting of regional representatives in Utah.

Many of his solutions were imposed by enemies and circumstances, and were not the ideal he had hoped to achieve. A tribal subsistence living is the most that his enemies hoped the Mormons could achieve, if, even better, they didn't die in the process.

## Individualism, Cooperation, and Coercion

It should be remembered that there is no inherent benefit in group effort versus individual effort. It depends strictly on the tasks to be done, and the priorities being applied. Fighting wars is usually best done in groups (although there are probably exceptions to this -- remember David and Goliath), but writing music is usually a more solitary activity. The default is normally the individual. Great feats of art and thinking are normally done by individuals. Committees are not famous for anything but discussion. Committees are inherently inefficient in action, although their ability to raise and consider all issues may be useful in those cases when consensus-building is important.

The coordination of individual efforts by a guiding principle is usually much more efficient than a "command" method of coordination, except in particular situations for a limited time.

The communist societies in this century have pretty well shown us how not to do a whole list of things, and what centrally controlled economies are not able to do. Although they have accomplished some amazing tasks, it has often been at an enormous cost in suffering and society-wide crime, often killing all those who object.

The Russian practice in World War II of using KGB barrage battalions to sit behind their front line troops and shoot them if they tried to pull back for any reason, indicates the brutal lengths one must go to get any kind of cooperation from those who prefer not to cooperate. On the other hand, as shown by Book of Mormon fighters and the recent US military clash in the Persian Gulf, there is an awesome power in a soldiery which believes in the rightness and value of the task it is carrying out.

Even in warfare, especially of the modern version, individual initiative is very important. There must be discipline in the control of lethal weapons, such as atomic bombs. Many lives may depend on the quick and creative problem solving of a fighter pilot or of a ground soldier launching an anti-tank rocket. Where there are massed conventional troops, there is likely to be more uniformity and conformity. But in guerilla warfare, much individuality and ingenuity are required. Even in trench warfare, where there may be maximum uniformity and conformity, there may be individual spies and code-breakers working to understand enemy radio transmissions.

There are an infinite number of ways to cooperate effectively, and they can all be discovered if freedom abounds. In contrast, regimentation will usually limit the number of ways found for cooperating, and serendipity and spontaneity will be limited.

We might try to define a positive and a negative form of competition. Positive competition might be trying to outdo someone else at doing good, versus negative competition in which people try to take from each other. Positive competition might be defined as a search for good ideas. For example, brainstorming can be cooperative competition. Negative competition might be defined as power politics, maintaining a balance of power, or fighting, as in labor union tactics which are usually wasteful and destructive.

The main factor or requirement for cooperation seems to be knowledge. Limiting a man's knowledge also limits his action options and freedom. The constitutional founding fathers knew this well. In a degenerate or pathological situation (all too common), a person will give or withhold information for the express purpose of exercising unrighteous dominion over another, or to get gain or personal advantage at another's expense. This is the usual zero-sum game. The optimum situation is that each can see all of the situation, and choose the best course considering all the factors; then there is almost no need to be in a command chain.

Today's information systems allow people to work more that way. The hierarchical structure of organizations was largely for the information processing activities necessary. There were limited eyes and ears, and limited means to communicate relevant data to others. When technology is available to allow everyone to know what everyone else knows, then the minimum command structure will be necessary. Very flat (non-hierarchical) organizations will be possible, as we see in business today. (Government still has not caught on very well.)

## Tolstoy's Spirit of the Army

It may seem strange to consult a Russian general on Brigham Young's relationship with the saints, but Tolstoy's *War and Peace* also seems to contain some eternal practical truths. Tolstoy's lengthy book was a vehicle for him to present his theory of history which tries to account for the interaction of movements of mass opinion in conjunction with the opinions and actions of individual leaders. In Tolstoy's commentary concerning the battle of Borodino between the French and Russian armies near Moscow in 1812, while speaking of Russian Field Marshall Kutuzov, Tolstoy defines something called the spirit of the army:

> By long years of military experience he knew, and with the wisdom of age understood, that it is impossible for one man to direct hundreds of thousands of others struggling with death, and he knew that the result of a battle is decided not by the orders of a commander in chief, nor the place where the troops are stationed, nor by the number of cannon or of slaughtered men, but by that intangible force called the spirit of the army, and he watched this force and guided it in as far as that was in his power.[6]

Concerning the effect of the Field Marshall's announcement of an order for a Russian attack on the French, he makes this comment:

> And by means of that mysterious indefinable bond which maintains throughout an army one and the same temper, known as "the spirit of the army," and which constitutes the chief sinew of war, Kutuzov's words, his order for a battle next day, immediately became known from one end of the army to the other.
>
> It was far from being the same words or the same order that reached the farthest links of that chain. The tales passing from mouth to mouth at different ends of the army did not even resemble what Kutuzov had said, but the sense of his words spread everywhere because what he said was not the outcome of cunning calculations, but of a feeling that lay in the commander in chief's soul as in that of every Russian.
>
> And on learning that tomorrow they were to attack the enemy, and hearing from the highest quarters a confirmation of what they wanted to believe, the exhausted, wavering men felt comforted and inspirited.[7]

The attack could not have happened and did not happen, but that was not very important; maintaining the spirit was more important.

How can any of this apply to the Utah saints? Brigham Young was the general in the battle between the Utah saints and the United States and its government, and had to sense these imponderables and try to cause changes in direction as needed. Brigham Young was surely at least as sensitive to matters of the spirit as was Field Marshall Kutuzov in measuring the ebb and flow of the social and emotional forces affecting the French and Russian individuals involved.

In a similar manner, the technical truth of what was said was not of great importance. What was important was the effect it had on the people, causing them to hear what they needed to hear or wanted to hear. This might well explain some of the strange statements and actions from the Brigham Young era.

From this view, the actual current effect of his statements (not their content) is the main thing to be considered, rather than any theoretical results that might be imagined in another setting. He was not building a structure of theory. He was trying to mold and organize the saints to allow them to remain free and independent, free to practice their religion and to take their place finally as a respected member of a constitutional federation.

The early harassment and delay of Johnston's army, and the later Mormon retreat before the army as it entered the Salt Lake Valley, but with torches ready to burn all their possessions, is like the battle of Borodino and its sequel. In each case the defenders lost a battle, but won the war by astute maneuverings.

(One might wonder why the Mormons did not burn everything in Missouri and Nauvoo to remove any gain from the robbers who wished to steal it. It happened to the Nauvoo temple anyway. Perhaps the answer is similar to Brigham Young's claim that the Mormons were not well organized, integrated and committed at that early time, or not part of a "united order" by Brigham Young's later redefinition of that term. Only later were they ready to carry out such coordinated, convulsive, and desperate acts. In Missouri, some of the saints sold their lands to the Missourians to try to limit their individual losses. No one was allowed to do any such thing in Utah.)

The "all for one and one for all" kind of three musketeers' (and "united order") slogans of the Brigham Young era probably had a similar purpose - to help the saints do what they needed to do, which was to defend themselves and carve out a safe and prosperous place to live.

Incidentally, D&C 19 is an interesting example of using words for their emotional impact, not for the transmission of accurate or logical, understandable information:

5. Wherefore, I revoke not the judgements which I shall pass, but woes shall go forth, weeping, wailing and gnashing of teeth, yea, to those who are found on my left hand.
6. Nevertheless, it is not written that there shall be no end to this torment, but it is written *endless torment.*
7. Again, it is written *eternal damnation;* wherefore it is more express than other scriptures, that it might work upon the hearts of the children of men, altogether for my name's glory.
.....
10. For, behold, the mystery of godliness, how great is it! For, behold, I am endless, and the punishment which is given from my hand is endless punishment, for Endless is my name. Wherefore --
11. Eternal punishment is God's punishment.
12. Endless punishment is God's punishment.

In sum, the scripture tells us nothing at all about eternal torment or damnation except that it is whatever the Lord says or decides it is, which he is not telling us. The words are used explicitly for the purpose "that it may work upon the hearts ... of men." Effect is far more important than accuracy. If the Lord resorts to word games of this sort to get certain results, then perhaps one should not be too harsh in judging his prophets who might do some of the same things or use some of the same techniques.

I hope I will be excused for using various literary excursions into diverse materials to bring other views into this Mormon history discussion. The questions to be answered here are as much emotional as they are historical or doctrinal. Much literature was designed to explore these emotional and philosophical topics and often do so in very engaging and entertaining ways. We are talking about utopian ideas, which tend to deal with what might be the order of heaven and of the appropriateness of independence/inequality and dependence/equality here and hereafter. This is a general topic upon which thousands have expressed their opinions, and we might do well to examine their experiences and viewpoints.

## Another Utopia

Philosophical writers have constructed various stories or parables to illustrate their utopian concepts of individual and societal behavior. Perhaps we can describe a utopia of our own. In it each person would know and understand all the facts and circumstances of the time and situation, would be motivated by the same righteous goals, and thus would tend to reach similar conclusions about the proper course to take in the future. Only minimal coordination, "a word to the wise," would be necessary. This equal understanding and spontaneous cooperation would make possible the fully enlightened unity that is expected of celestial beings.

A really grand utopia, one of the best I have ever heard of, comes from a science fiction novel called *The World of Null-A*.[8] Its name comes from the argument that classical Aristotelian logic, which tends to be either-or in nature, is far too cumbersome a tool to ever deal precisely with actual reality, and also limits our ability to conceive of and live an ideal life. Thus, the book lauds Non-Aristotelian logic, allowing for an infinity of gradations. The phrase is shortened to Null-A for use as a title.

The *World of Null-A* could be taken as a pattern for the celestial kingdom, and would suit it far better than the usual confining equality/tyranny of the socialist paradigm.

In the story, groups of highly intelligent and creative people with a certain disposition are selected to leave earth and live on Venus. There a different society develops. All are able to live independent, almost solitary lives, but are also given access to huge amounts of information. In the test of the society, a marauding band of space pirates/conquerors tries to take over their planet. Since the Venusians seem to have no weapons, no military organization, and are widely scattered, it appears to be a very simple matter to take them over. However, the invaders have a shock coming to them. The people of Venus are highly intelligent, highly motivated, highly moral, and all are kept informed of events. As soon as the first group of soldiers comes to their planet, those in contact with them decide this is bad for their planet and decide to take action.

What we have here is a planet full of informed, decisive generals, not confused low-level troops. At some (calculated) loss of life, the defenders quickly neutralize the invaders and take their weapons. The next wave of invaders would then be forced to face their own weapons, now skillfully manned and aimed against them. They think better of it and decide to look for easier targets elsewhere.

This seems to reflect our expectation about a heaven far better than the anomalous suggestions of Brigham Young and others that heaven is a highly disciplined place where one being controls all property and directs all action. Instead, we have highly intelligent, informed, moral people who may decide to join or not in any particular program or event. If they choose to act in concert, it is because they have considered all the costs and benefits to all concerned, including themselves, and feel that their particular action is appropriate. Their actions might all be different, even though controlled by the same high-level considerations, or, as we might say in more gospel terms, the same spirit. The coordinating factor was their own spontaneous reaction to the situation, the fact pattern at hand, not some central controlling force.

The command and control hierarchy of the usual socialist "utopia" model is based on a few elites having all the information and the rest of the peasants merely obeying their commands. That is hardly what we would wish for in heaven.

Our world today is looking more and more like the *World of Null-A* model. The huge flows of information to each and every person are now a reality. We can receive live, on-the-scene TV coverage of all major events. The electronic town meeting, with a "live" polling process over the phone, could theoretically replace the congress with direct plebiscites on all issues, making unnecessary the voting by representatives. The idea of sending a representative to a central place to act for us may become unnecessary. The changes in our society made possible by instantaneous worldwide continuous news reporting (e.g., CNN) and "electronic town meetings" could make the old republican model out of date. The same process is going on in the private world of business. The flattening of corporate structures and the elimination of the distance between the top and the bottom, the shedding of middle managers is part of this process.

A little more of this counter-hierarchy process, and the whole constitution could change to a new social model more appropriate to heaven and utopia. The main thing that is missing from today's world that is in the *Null-A* model, is the selection out and concentration of those most likely to use the opportunity wisely and benefit most from it; and heaven or the millennium might add that feature. Right now we have a much more diluted "every man's" utopia rather than the ultimate utopia.

The author has a few pet peeves that illustrate the less-than-utopian spirit of cooperation in the world today, the self-inflicted wounds from selfishness. One example is waiting for bags at the airport baggage conveyor after a flight. As one travels around the world, this is an interesting measure of the depth of the counterproductive me-first syndrome. In the worst countries, the people fight to crowd next to the conveyor system, making it so that very few can actually see the passing bags, and even if they can see, they can hardly get through the crush of people to retrieve their bags. If all were to stand back a few feet, as is likely in more civilized areas where higher levels of cooperation are the norm, all could see the bags and retrieve them without hindrance.

The same tendency can be measured at crowded traffic intersections where short-sighted third worlders will usually elect to put what they think is their personal interest first, and, by placing their car as far as possible in the direction they wish to go, create a perfect and durable gridlock for all concerned. In a more civilized (and, therefore, normally more prosperous) country, nearly every driver will instinctively make the choice that keeps traffic flowing freely, even if it involves a tiny apparent "sacrifice" of a few moments of waiting, but ultimately saves time for everyone.

A more sophisticated version of the same test of "enlightened self-interest" occurs in conjunction with the beltway around Washington DC. But here the populace cannot easily observe all the factors operating and so fails the test. During the afternoon rush hour, along the western exits to the Virginia portion of the beltway is where the freeway overload problem occurs. The long-distance north-south traffic completely uses up the capacity of the beltway. If those on the side roads also insist on moving into the fray, then the whole system grinds to a halt and operates at about one-fourth or even one-tenth of its normal capacity. It takes much longer for everyone to reach their destination, including the ones who pushed themselves into the stream. A little restraint by those people from the side roads would be a great gain to all (although the long-distance travelers might benefit more).

Many of society's mechanisms get far more complex (and less obvious) than the cases just mentioned, and even those people with helpful impulses must move with great caution when interfering with these systems.

The opposite of Marxism is not Capitalism, but Christianity. Marxism stands for maximum conflict, minimum cooperation. Class warfare is said to be ideologically justified, but results in huge losses to all. It becomes a self-fulfilling prophecy. One group pushes and the other pushes back. This is like Middle East tribal warfare or the eternally feuding American Hatfields and McCoys. Vengeance goes on forever and all are wounded; an eye for an eye, and all become blind.

## Conflict With the World

On a different topic, the violent conflict with the eastern states, a quotation from the book *Submarine* may be of interest. This book explores some of the methods for maximum stress negotiations between the two rival world powers in the age of potential hair-trigger nuclear warfare. The saints in Utah were usually not on such a tense and compressed time schedule, but the consequences of a small mistake could be just as devastating.

The setting of the book is the commencement of conventional war in Europe between the western and eastern superpowers. The issue is the transport of troops and equipment across the Atlantic from the U.S. to Europe. The U.S. has used its superior technology to slaughter the submarine wolf packs that were attempting to stop that transatlantic reinforcement. Now the eastern power is threatening to use its land-based nuclear armaments to strike the U.S. if the west does not stop its reinforcement process. The east is relying on its submarine-based nuclear missiles, supposedly invulnerable to detection or attack, to allow it to retain the upper hand after its land-based weapons are used or destroyed.

The west in turn answers that the east's submarine-based missiles are as subject to annihilation as were its attack submarines, and sets out to prove it, the idea being that if the eastern power realizes that it will ultimately lose all its defenses anyway, and be at the mercy of an outraged west, it will be deterred from launching its land-based missiles.

In the book, Admiral Rackham, Commander of Submarines in the East Atlantic, presented this (fictional) briefing:

> The Soviet government had demanded cessation of hostilities because of the devastating losses to their submarine fleet during the opening phase of the Atlantic battle, the battle to decide whether trans-Atlantic convoys could reinforce Europe. The Kremlin was demanding the truce. If we refused and continued with trans-Atlantic reinforcements, the Soviets would

commit their ICBMs to the battle. Their SSBNs [Submarine, Strategic Ballistic Missile Nuclear], the vital second strike capability without which no Russian power would remain, were, the Soviets claimed, invulnerable, safe in the depths of the oceans. The West had replied that, just as it had massacred their fleet and patrol submarines in the Atlantic, it could annihilate the Soviet SSBNs, their Delta IIs and their Typhoons, wherever they tried to hide. No way could the USSR then hope to dictate terms to the world, however devastated and desolate.[9]

The U.S. and NATO navies were to persuade the Kremlin that its second-strike capability was at the West's mercy by seeking out and sinking a number of Soviet SSBNs.

If this scenario seems overly complex and dramatic as compared to the position of the saints in Utah, then it only means that the Utah situation has not been sufficiently well portrayed. The saints there were in no less perilous or intricate a situation than were the two world powers at war.

## Using Self-Defense Psychology

In two literary works noted below, the idea is developed of a person becoming part of a group under siege and fighting to defend that group. That idea is interesting in the context of Brigham Young's social organizations. In the two books, the people involved knew little about the greater context in which they existed and operated, and seemed to care little about the political and moral questions that may be involved. Their view was very narrow and limited, but they still played their part.

In a book called *Huey*, the main character, John Vanvorden, could find no adequate explanation for what he and other Americans were doing in the war in Vietnam. After saying he couldn't understand the purpose of the war, he spoke of the camaraderie and esprit de corps that came from spending time in bomb shelters with the other soldiers. Having been reassigned to the 268th Combat Aviation Battalion in Vietnam, John

> did not miss crowding into the bunker with his platoon while rockets and mortars pounded everything topside, but he missed the resultant camaraderie, the esprit de corps that developed in that atmosphere. Platoons did not really hang together here and the spirit in this unit was low. In a lot of ways it had been better at the 155th, and he missed his old friends.[10]

There is a similar story told by a man who had been in the German SS military organization, and later joined the French Foreign Legion as a mercenary. His only morality in life was protecting his buddies and they him, regardless of their nationality or past. Any larger concern with the meaning or rightness of things did not concern him.

Perhaps some of the foot soldiers in Brigham Young's war might have felt similarly. Creating a group and esprit de corps would be important, especially for those who could not or would not respond to the more general strategic setting.

## More Esoteric Considerations

Some religions (or non-religions) teach that there is no existence of any intelligent life forms whatsoever after this life. Others say the individuals on this earth merge with a great single entity after this life. Others say that we retain our individuality, but in a passive state. A few claim that at least some individuals will not only exist after this life, but will have many choices and much power.

What does this have to do with a discussion of social organization here on the earth? As shown elsewhere in this book, the portrayal of heaven is a common device for advocating certain patterns here on the earth, and our view of heaven seems to have a powerful effect on how we conduct ourselves in this life.

This is also true of the life before this, if there was one. The nature of our original source goes to the heart of the metaphysics of the gospel. In the beginning were we uncreated, individual, responsible, choice-making eternal beings as Joseph Smith taught, or were we merely a blob (think of a section of Jello dessert) lopped off from an undifferentiated mass of intelligence and added first to a spirit body and then a physical body? Satan would presumably favor the later theory, the will-less robot. Christ would presumably favor the former concept, with its maximum individuality. We are told Christ is always focused on the one, the individual. That would be pointless if the real goal was reunion with or reabsorption by a larger entity.

Going to the earthly social question, a doctrinally-required merging of individuals with the whole for some "higher" purpose, sounds much like the "Jello" theory of our origin. We seem to have never made a clean break on this question of individuality versus loss of identity into a larger whole; the old required communalism keeps cropping up in rhetoric, and occasionally in action.

This question of group cohesion has real-world significance. The world continues to express fears of a group that acts monolithically. If we form into such a group, or at least teach we should, they may fear that we might also act mindlessly or irresponsibly or in a way that may threaten them in some disregard for law, etc. Many other groups have formed the basis for such power and could not resist [mis]using it. The church would never do that, but perhaps we also need to make sure that we do not even hint that such a call might be justified in normal times. Keeping such a call available on the back burner might be tempting, as an attempt to thereby keep the members at least a little bit prepared to actually do it in a pinch. Only in the ultimate extremity of self-defense could such behavior be justified, and even then it should be clear to all concerned that the action taken was the only wise one.

Other chapters contain Brigham Young's views on poverty, equality, etc., plus some counter-arguments to the theories expressed on other books about Brigham Young's philosophy on these and related topics.

## Chapter notes

[1] Walter Guzzardi, "Unlikely Allies Agree on the Economy: Conservatives and liberals say these are the moves to make." *Time*, July 20, 1992 vol. 140 no. 3 p. 42.

[2] Rafael Aguayo, *Dr. Deming, The American Who Taught the Japanese About Quality* (New

*Brigham Young's Temporal Philosophy*

York: Simon & Schuster Inc., 1991), p. vii.

[3] Ibid., p. 230.

[4] Ibid., p. 224.

[5] Alfie Kohn, *No Contest, The Case Against Competition* (Boston: Houghton Mifflin Company, 1986).

[6] Leo Tolstoy, *War and Peace*, vol. 43 in *Great Books of the Western World*, 55 vols. (Chicago: Encyclopaedia Britannica, Inc., 1952), p.460.

[7] Ibid., p. 461.

[8] A. E. Van Voyt, *The World of Null-A* (New York: Simon & Schuster, 1948)

[9] John Wingate, *Submarine*, (London: Sphere Books, Ltd., 1982), p. 37-39.

[10] Jay and David Groen, *Huey* (New York: Ballantine Books, 1984), pp. 74, 149.

## CHAPTER 15

# Comparing the
# Brigham Young and Joseph Smith United Orders

There is much confusion about the relationship of the united order rhetoric and practice from the two different periods of the Joseph Smith and Brigham Young presidencies. Some writers have concluded that because Brigham Young promoted some "gospel" economic organizations in Utah, that he must have been following the lead of Joseph Smith, without those writers ever bothering to find out what Joseph Smith actually advocated.

In fact, there is very little relationship between the aims and logic behind the two sets of practices, except at the most general level. The two prophets were directed to do what was most helpful for the people in their respective times, but the times and needs were so radically different that the actual programs had little in common. The reader is referred to the predecessor volume in this study set, JSUO, for a detailed examination of the Joseph Smith teachings and practices.

Suffice it to say that the Joseph Smith united order or united firm was nothing more nor less than a temporary quorum of the twelve and a temporary "corporation of the president," operating as a business partnership. Ordinary members had nothing to do with it except as they received benefits from its activities in publishing scriptures, assisting with the land purchases of the migrating saints, providing for supplies at reasonable prices to the saints in Missouri, and assisting the poor.

All "mainline" economic activities were carried out in the normal fashion. Joseph actively fought any claim that the church promoted any kind of socialism, "common stock," or anything like it.

In Brigham Young's case, he did not have the legal means that were available to Joseph Smith in the ordinary pursuits of life, economics, and government, and so had to improvise an entire society outside the normal framework of a constitutional system of laws and practices.

The two prophets did entirely agree that the "all things common" language from the New Testament had nothing to do with the saints of this dispensation. The concept was either entirely wrong, or only applicable to a very narrow set of survival cases.

Although the practical problems the two prophets had to face were vastly different and so required radically different solutions, that does not explain why Brigham Young did not recognize those differences and explain them in an intelligible form. In fact, for a time, he seemed to be insisting that Joseph Smith and the earlier saints had it all wrong, simply because they failed in the sense that they were thrown out of Missouri, and that only the system he was proposing made any doctrinal sense, without really presenting, discussing and exploring Joseph's thoughts on the subject. In contrast, Brigham Young seems strangely quiet about any doctrinal errors relating to the cause of the forced exodus from Nauvoo under his direction.

For one thing, in contrast to Joseph Smith, Brigham Young seemed to have had little interest in historical, philosophical, and academic matters, but was only and always looking forward for the next temporal problem and its practical solution. He was probably only slightly troubled at his lack of information about, or consistency of action with, the prior teachings and programs of Joseph.

In fact, along this vein, there are indicators of a substantial loss of data and experience in the transition from the administrators of Joseph Smith's time to Brigham Young and the rest of the Twelve who carried on afterward. For example, the Twelve discovered for the first time in 1845 (HC 7:412, May 17), and published with fanfare, something that was known to the prior administrators 12 years earlier in 1833 (HC 1:364, June 25). The instructions to Bishop Partridge concerning the Missouri land transactions were ancient and well-worn history, but the Twelve had known nothing of it (see chapter 11 of JSUO).

It should be remembered that not a single one of the original united firm group, the temporary quorum of the twelve, was alive and in the church when the move west from Nauvoo was undertaken. That seems like a staggering loss of "institutional memory," and one might expect it to be crippling to any new organization. However, on balance, in this case, it may have been useful to have few binding precedents, since most of what remained to be done would surely fall outside existing precedents.

With this lack of continuity, there is probably little reason to wonder at the doctrinal drift that seems to have occurred on matters affecting economics. Without contact with the original sources and experiences, these men were left to relearn on their own, and often at great cost, much that was elementary to Joseph Smith when the church was just being organized. Of course, again, the problems and experiences of the two eras and two prophets were so different, that it might have actually been an unnecessary burden and restraint on Brigham Young to have had to work through all the differences in doctrine and policy and their implications.

Joseph's journal was probably not available to Brigham Young on a contemporary basis. Joseph had trouble enough compiling and retaining it himself. Much of what was prepared and intended as formal history was lost through the apostasy or carelessness of his clerical staff. The surviving journal material was not published for the first time until well into the Utah period. Brigham Young certainly read the scriptures, but in some cases seemed to lack information concerning the qualifying circumstances behind the receipt of those modern-day revelations. This is information that could probably only be available to him through Joseph's written record, or through an interview with the man himself, a rather difficult thing to accomplish.

It may be worth noticing that Brigham Young was in Boston for a conference held September 9, 1843, and began a return trip home on October 29. HC 6:11, 39. The Nauvoo discussions on socialism happened in the meantime on September 13 and 14 and October 24. He also missed out on the early events concerning the Kirtland "family," because he did not join the church until more than a year after that event, and did not meet the Prophet until nearly another year had passed. He was abroad during most of the time that the united order was operating. He surely had some contact with the related concepts, but for the really unequivocal refutations of socialism or common stock, he seemed to be elsewhere.

In contrast, he seemed to have had a hand in the "togetherness" times, usually caused by forced migration, such as the movements from Missouri to Illinois. This skewing of experience may account for some of the differences in doctrines taught during the two periods marked by the presidencies of Joseph Smith and Brigham Young.

He was not a member of Joseph Smith's united firm, and probably had little to do with it, since he joined the church just before it started, and before he had any leadership roles in the church, and it had ended before he became concerned with central church administrative matters. Brigham Young was baptized a member April 14, 1832 (ECH 126). He returned to Nauvoo from his mission to England July 1, 1841 (ECH 236). The united firm was organized on April 26, 1832 (D&C 82; HC 1:266-267; JSUO 87) and was disbanded about 1838 (JSUO 188).

There is an interesting area of potential agreement between the two eras on economic matters. In his comments in a Nauvoo discourse against socialism, Joseph Smith recalled the phenomenon of the "the big fish eating up all the little fish" in the 1831 Kirtland setting (HC 6:33 JS Sept 14, 1843 Nauvoo; HC 1:146-7 Feb 1831). His observation appears to be corroborated to some extent by (or is at least consistent with) Israelson's study of Utah towns which had a "united order" mechanism operating, as opposed to those which did not.

In the "united order" towns, the disparity between the economic status of citizens increased: people became more unequal rather than less.[1] This may have been disturbing to the author of the study, but it may actually be a very positive finding. Rather than implying exploitation as was found in Kirtland, this finding would be consistent with Brigham Young's goal of maximizing overall concentrated strength, with less concern about individual equality. Although in the early Utah days, he generally tolerated and even supported some "equality" sermons (for example see JD 2:96), in his later years of life, while still advocating large-scale combination of property for efficiency sake, he specifically stated many times that it was not appropriate to enforce equality among individuals, e.g. JD 18:354.

In the Utah setting, rather than attribute the increased inequality of income to exploitation by the stronger, there is another possibility. It appears from extensive modern studies that the beginning of economic growth in developing countries is always accompanied by an increase in inequality of income: "The first effect of technical progress ... is to increase the inequality of the distribution of income" as skilled engineers and managers begin to appear and to command higher salaries.[2] The long-term positive benefits of growth seem to justify Brigham Young's policies, however inconsistent they may have been with the equality question.

Where Joseph Smith found socialist-style exploitation of the weaker by the stronger in Kirtland, and perhaps some resulting increase in the disparity of income, Israelson found a heightened disparity of income in Utah that may have been based on a different and more positive principle. While the overall wealth of a socialist society usually tends to go down, the overall wealth of a society employing private property and individual freedom and cooperation tends to go up. Both may have a wide disparity in real income levels, but the reasons and overall results are much different.

One interesting question that was not explored and answered by the Israelsen study, was whether the "united order" towns were better off economically than those that did not participate. That was clearly Brigham Young's wish, not some abstract leveling goal. If it is true that he was sensing, reacting to, and anticipating the economic development theories of today, and those theories were applied correctly, we should find that these more organized cities were more successful in economic growth, even while (and partly because) their internal equality diminished. With each person having a smaller percentage of a much bigger pie, everyone's lot can still improve.

Setting up such a question for statistical study would certainly be a challenge. The study that was done on income discrepancy at least could be done on a single group. Trying to compare many groups from much different economic settings would be difficult indeed.

## Chapter notes

[1] L. Dwight Israelsen, "An Economic Analysis of the United Order," *BYU Studies*, Summer 1978, pp. 536-562.

[2] Everett E. Hagen, *The Economics of Development* (Homewood, Ill.: Richard D. Irwin, Inc., 1980), p. 38.

## CHAPTER 16

# Multiple Contemporary Viewpoints

Many in the church today are probably of the opinion that the doctrine of the united order was universally known, understood, and accepted within the church, and that any deviations or failures were merely the result of the weaknesses of men. However, that is not at all consistent with the intellectual history of the period. There were numerous occasions when Brigham Young noted in general terms that differences of opinion existed, and some occasions where he specifically took action to correct those differences if they were too extreme, usually without implying that even those significant differences could be the basis for priesthood disciplining. We might also examine, sift, and compare the discourses of his contemporaries to locate significant differences of opinion which did not receive such explicit treatment.

In an 1856 address, Brigham made a striking statement: "Those who are in favor of an equality in property say that that is the doctrine taught in the New Testament." (JD 4:29 BY Aug 17, 1856, quoted in chapter 11). For our purposes here, the important thing is that Brigham Young recognizes and states that there were differences of opinion about this important matter, that there were various factions on the question, and that it was treated as a political question of the day as well as a religious one. Those differences of opinion included men of importance and not merely the uninformed.

The statement of Brigham Young just quoted is important evidence, a "smoking gun," showing that there was a significant dispute. It gives us reason, then, to look for the differences rather than merely trying to reconcile the many different statements. If we were to assume that all public statements of the brethren were completely coordinated, then we would want to try to reconcile them all, even if they seemed contradictory. With the above quote to begin with, we can be more objective in trying to see how each speaker felt about the important issues; we need not be pre-occupied with trying to reconcile the irreconcilable.

Further, we might conclude from this multiplicity of views that the doctrine was not clearly and unequivocally stated. Had it been more clearly revealed, perhaps in a written revelation all could study and ponder, the various subsidiary questions might well have been detailed and the faithful would have accepted it without much debate. The very fact that there was a significant set of other explanations and views of what was happening, tends to show that it was not a strong and binding doctrinal point. The men who expressed these other views were devout men, such as John Taylor, an apostle who became the next president, George Q. Cannon who was a counselor to Presidents Young and Taylor, Orson Pratt who was an apostle, etc. They could not be uninformed or apostate and also be current leaders in good standing.

More specific evidence of differences of opinion comes from the occasions when Brigham Young explicitly corrected statements made by the brethren in public discourse. The most notable example is Brigham Young's reaction to an (unrecorded) discourse by George Q. Cannon on April 6, 1877 in St. George. In Brigham Young's response, he corrected two misconceptions concerning distributing and accumulating property.

On distributing:

> I think that, as a people, we are nearer alike in the sentiments and feelings of our hearts, than in our words. <u>From the most excellent discourse which we have heard this morning from brother Cannon, I believe that the people might gather the idea that we shall be expected to divide our property equally one with another, and that this will constitute the United Order.</u> I will give you my view, in as few words as possible with regard to this subject, which I will promise you are correct.
> .....
> Supposing that the property of the whole community were divided to-day equally amongst all, what might we expect? Why a year from to-day we should need another division, for some would waste and squander it away, while others would add to their portion.
> .....
> Now, if we could take this people, in their present condition, and teach them how to sustain and maintain themselves and a little more, we would add to that which we already have; but to take what we have and divide amongst or give to people, without teaching them how to earn and produce, would be no more nor less than to introduce the means of reducing them to a state of poverty.
> I do not wish for one moment to recognize the idea that in order to establish the United Order our property has to be divided equally among the people, to let them do what they please with it. But the idea is to get the people into the same state of unity in all things temporal, that we find ourselves in with regard to things spiritual. Then let those who possess the ability and wisdom direct the labors of those not so endowed, until they too develop the talents within them and in time acquire the same degree of ability. JD 18:353 BY April 6, 1877 St. George.

On accumulating:

> My brethren and sisters, I do really delight in hearing our brethren speak on this holy order of heaven. Unity of purpose and action, in carrying out the will of our Father, has been my theme all the day long; but I have continually plead with the Saints not to waste their substance upon the lust of the eye and the flesh, for that is contrary to the will and commandments of God. I wish to say that whoever have faith enough to inherit the celestial kingdom will find that their inheritances will be upon this earth. This earth is our home; by and by it will be sanctified and glorified, and become a fit dwelling place for the sanctified, and they will dwell upon it for ever end ever. I will further say I labor for the earth, I never mean to be satisfied until the whole earth is yielded to Christ and his people. <u>When brother George Q. tells us we should not labor for the earth and the things of this world, he means we should not labor with sinful motives, and to gratify the lusts of the flesh. But if we possessed the treasure of the Gentile world, could we not send our Elders to the ends of the earth, bearing the precious Gospel to all living? Could we not sustain their families during their absence? Could we not build Temple after Temple and otherwise hasten on the work of redemption? Yes.</u> But keep the people in poverty and how are we to accomplish this great work? I say, let us gather and accumulate the things of the earth in the manner indicated by

the Lord, and then devote it to God and the building up of his kingdom. What do you say to this doctrine, is it right or wrong? (The congregation said, "It is right.") What little property I have I wish it to be devoted to the building up of Zion, and I suppose I have as much as any other man in the Church. I am always ready to receive and take care of the blessings that God showers upon me, and am always ready and willing to devote the same to the building up of his kingdom. JD 18:353 BY April 6, 1877 St. George.

Brigham Young clearly implies that George Q. Cannon had argued for an equality of property and had also criticized those who wished to accumulate much of this world's goods and property. (See chapter note 1 for comments on George Q. Cannon). Brigham Young thought distributing property for equality's sake would be destructive, and thought working for money and gain was fine, as long as one used those resources wisely.

On another, much earlier, occasion, Brigham Young applied some gentle correction to comments on a related topic, the nature of the Kingdom of God on earth:

Hence I design to speak a few words concerning the Kingdom of God. Not that I would disagree in the least from the remarks made by brothers Grant and Pratt, or that we differ in our views upon this subject. It is an extensive one, and the usual time never permits a person, in one short discourse, to fully explain such subjects as were presented for our edification this morning. I noticed throughout the remarks of both of the brethren that they did not make sufficient distinction, nor make it plain to the minds of the people, that the Kingdom of God would be different, in a certain sense, from all other kingdoms and empires upon the earth: this was for the want of time. In public speaking a man's mind is often led from one idea to another, branching to the right and to the left upon matters and points that need explanation, and I presume this is more particularly the case upon the subject of the Kingdom than any other. JD 2:309 BY July 8, 1855 SLC.

Again, the original talks are not recorded. The message of interest was and is the correction and clarification given.

Returning to the content of Brigham Young's statement on the question of equality, many today would consider it an ironic reversal to find Brigham Young in the conservative role of defending individual property ownership against the socialists in the church. However, this was not an isolated irony, but his consistent policy position. (See chapter note 2 for comments on historical treatment of the equality question).

As we begin to systematically examine the views of the other leaders who spoke on the subject, we note that they can fairly easily be divided into the left, right, and center categories often used today to discuss political viewpoints. On the left we have Orson Pratt and George Q. Cannon with their strongly socialist and ideological stance on many questions, their love of ideas seeming to make them almost blind to measurable and workable reality. In contrast, we have John Taylor and Orson Hyde, with their highly individualistic, practical and non-ideological viewpoints, who are more interested in results than grand flights of visionary fancy. In the middle we find Brigham Young, who is first of all practical if he is anything, but who also allows ideological "grand vision" elements and motivations to co-exist with the practical. His regular counselors during most of this period (he had five extra ones at times) seemed to have little to say on this important topic, with the exception that Heber C. Kimball often stressed obedience to the directives of the president. (See chapter note 3 for comments on the makeup of the presidency).

It may seem strange to paint Brigham Young as a middle-of-the-roader, but that is what he was. He looked for practical results, and experimented with ideas as motivators to try to get those results. Orson Pratt and George Q. Cannon tended to be far more ideologically motivated than Brigham Young, apparently becoming more enamored with the various ideas themselves than with the positive results those ideas might bring or actually brought. In contrast, John Taylor was always wary of any ideology beyond the simple principles of the gospel. He generally dismissed any doctrinally based reason for action (except that it was a directive from the president and thus had doctrinal significance), and instead looked for the potential practical results of Brigham Young's suggestions. It was he who, as the President of the church following Brigham Young, discontinued all formally denoted "united order" activities, declaring, in effect, that there never had been any revelation requiring any particular method of economic organization, but only a general call to unity of purpose and efficiency.

Apparently, from about 1873 to Brigham Young's death in 1877, George Q. Cannon was a "junior" counselor, one of the five extra counselors called to assist Brigham Young, including two of Brigham's sons. During this time he gave at least two recorded discourses that were noticeably left-leaning, and was corrected on the occasion described above. With the President of the Twelve, John Taylor, being such a non-ideological or rightist person, we might be able to say that Brigham Young thus had a political foot in both camps, and probably sought support from both groups for his programs. Since Brigham Young had something to say about his supernumerary counselor George Q. Cannon (and assisted in the process of adjusting seniority within the Twelve which resulted in advancing John Taylor ahead of two others to become the president of the Quorum of the Twelve), we might be able to compare this very vaguely to a U.S. president choosing his vice president and cabinet to balance the representation of different groups. His visits to local wards to discuss united order topics were similar to grass roots political campaigning "vote for me" trips.

It would take too much space to summarize here all the views of the various speakers; that is done in separate chapters. However, since John Taylor was probably the greatest single counterweight to the communal ideas presented, we might review a few of his ideas here.

In two early talks, in 1852 and 1857, John Taylor made it clear that he would have no patience with any social planning or intervention which in any way looked like socialism or communism. He had obviously done his homework and was very knowledgeable about the topic. It would be interesting to know if his discourses were in direct response against those who proposed radical centralized property control, such as Orson Pratt, an idea ambiguously supported by Brigham Young, at least in 1855.

John Taylor accepted the 1854 announcement of the new version of the consecration doctrine as a valid pronouncement of his president, but he seemed to be quite unconvinced as to its having a separate doctrinal basis.

In 1874, John Taylor explained some "unity" talk by observing the need to put 10,000 men to work during the winter months when they would otherwise be idle. He observed that the saints had spontaneously helped each other in their difficult move to Utah.

Later, after Brigham Young died and John Taylor assumed the office of president, he puzzled over the doctrinal status of the "united order" idea, and finally "de-doctrinalized" it. He recognized that some economically foolish things had been done in the name of doctrinaire religion. He may also have sensed that a merger with the larger society would require giving up the large-scale church-sponsored cooperative efforts.

Perhaps one reason for the differences of opinion was that it was not all that clear to anyone what the real rules should be. In 1874 John Taylor said he did not understand it:

> We have heard a good deal since we have assembled, in relation to what is called the Order of Enoch, the New Order, the United Order, or whatever name we may give to it. It is new and then it is old, for it is everlasting as I understand it. I am asked sometimes -- "Do you understand it?" Yes, I do, no, I do not, yes I do, no, I don't, and both are true; we know that such an order must be introduced, but are not informed in relation to the details, and I guess it is about the same with most of you. We have been talking about an order that is to be introduced and established among the Saints of God for the last forty-two years, but we have very little information given us concerning it, either in the scriptures or in the Book of Mormon. ... I do not know how far Enoch and perhaps some others on this continent went; if we had further records from the Book of Mormon they might throw some light on subjects with which we are not at present very well acquainted. JD 17:47 April 19, 1874 Nephi.

Even Brigham Young has trouble deciding what it is, although he is more confident as to what it isn't:

> You may call it the Order of Enoch, you may call it co-partnership, or just what you please. It is the United Order of the Kingdom of God on the earth; .... We want the time of this people called Latter-day Saints, that we can organize this time systematically, and make this people the richest people on the face of the earth. JD 17:43 April 18, 1874 Nephi City.

> There is a great deal being rumored about what we are teaching the people at the present time with regard to being one in temporal affairs as we are one in the doctrine that we have embraced for our salvation. I will say to you that erroneous traditions at once begin to present themselves. ... [I]n the New Testament ... the believers sold their possessions and laid the proceeds at the Apostles' feet. Now what is the tradition on this point? To sell your houses, your farms, your stores, your cattle, and bring the means and lay it down at the feet of the Apostles, and then live, eat, drink, and wear it until it is all gone, and then what? Do without? Yes, or be beggars. Our traditions lead us to this point, and that throws us into a dilemma, out of which we know not how to extricate ourselves. To the Latter-day Saints, I say, all this is a mistake; these are false ideas, false conclusions. JD 17:52 May 3, 1874. SLC.

Brigham Young might be said to have earlier approved the Ananias teaching indirectly since it was taught in his presence by Orson Pratt. JD 2:98 OP Sep 10, 1854 SLC.

Later in 1874 in the city of Lehi, Brigham Young stated that there had been no new specific revelation on the topic of the United Order, but that existing principles had been used. JD 17:154 BY Aug 9, 1874 Lehi City. Even the doctrinaire Orson Pratt became a little unsure of himself and backtracked a little:

> But I know there are many Latter-day Saints who have formed an erroneous idea or opinion in regard to this common stock fund. Some for want of reflection, may suppose that every man and every woman must have the same fashioned houses to live in, or there would not be an equality; they must have the same amount of furniture or there would not be an equality. ... But this is not the way God manifests himself in all the works of his hands. ... God delights in variety ....
>
> Then again, I do not know that the common stock operation which God commanded us to enter into in Jackson County, MO., will be suitable in the year 1874. I commenced my discourse by showing that what was suitable one year was not always suitable the next. ...
>
> We can not work here as we could in Jackson County, Mo. .... Inquires one, "What is it, what kind of an order is it? Tell us all about it." I would tell you as much as I thought was wisdom, if I understood it myself; but I do not; I have had but very little information about it. JD 17:32-36 OP April 6, 1874 SLC. (See chapter note 4 for comments on Orson Pratt).

There are other indicators that Brigham Young treated the "united order" as an ad hoc process. In 1856 he made the statement "I have got to wait for the Lord to dictate from day to day, and from time to time, as to what particular course to pursue for the accomplishment of so desirable a result" (referring to the temporal salvation of the saints). (JD 4:30 BY Aug 17, 1856 SLC.) This seems to indicate that there was no fixed plan, only daily inquiry into what the best thing to do next might be. This is an incremental approach, not the "grand and eternal design," the complete cure-all, that has been popularized. Does this sound like a total pattern was revealed "all at once" and "once and for all?" No. It was all incremental. The grand vision was there, but was so general as to hardly be more than saying "unity and cooperation are good." Any more detailed program had to be made up as changing circumstances dictated, including examples of complete reversals of policy as conditions changed, as in the case of Mormons being involved in trading operations. There was no detailed plan revealed for the temporal affairs of saints for all time.

In an entry in his journal dated Sunday, April 1, 1877, Wilford Woodruff records, "President Young spoke 12 Minutes. He reproved the 12 for not uniting into the United Order more than they had." WWJ 7:342. Apparently, even as late as 1877, the Twelve remained less than totally convinced of the wisdom of all aspects of the program, or simply could not fathom what it was, perhaps some of them sharing John Taylor's concerns and reservations.

Did the brethren at Brigham Young's time have the same problem we have, of reading the words in the D&C and not really being able to understand what they mean? It is very possible. None of them had had any direct experience with the united firm of Joseph Smith. All their information was hearsay and speculation, much as ours is today.

The brethren seem to have applied the correct principles in situations since Brigham Young's time, even in the face of fact that most surviving available historical evidence and interpretation tends to the contrary. The next generation of leading brethren after Brigham Young seem to have chosen the correct path even though they could not perhaps justify it on apparent historical grounds. That gives me even greater faith that there is inspiration in the church. We need not be subject to an excess of the philosophies of men.

## ENDNOTES

1. George Q. Cannon is reported by some to have been a good economic organizer. The very limited evidence in the *Journal of Discourses* is certainly questionable at this stage (date 1877, his age 50). But since he lived to be 74 (January 11, 1827 - April 12, 1901) he would have had plenty of time to learn the economic lessons Brigham Young was teaching, and been able to foster economic successes. A forthcoming biography of his life based on his journals, sponsored by some of his descendants, may clear up the apparent discrepancy between stated philosophy and effective action.

2. A most interesting question is: Why have we never heard of Brigham Young's actual views on this equality question, even though they were clearly and repeatedly stated? Why are we not aware of this momentous debate? This is a great mystery. What is it about the way our traditions have been created and handed down that has given us only one side of the argument and has obliterated the other?

One possibility is that we are quick to seek a simple authoritative answer on all matters of doctrine, but when we sense conflict or apparent inconsistency, we simply label it a mystery or anomaly and go on. This is possible for us today since we are not asked to apply any of these old teachings.

Another possibility is that we have had those with socialist leanings writing our history for us, and they have tried to make the choices for the rest of us, just as they tried during Brigham Young's time. It is interesting that Brigham Young had to fight socialist tendencies then, even with his own counselors such as George Q. Cannon. It seems clear that the political preferences of many of the historians is leftist. B.H. Roberts evidenced it somewhat in his two histories, as noted in other parts of this book. Another writer produced a few pro-socialist writings before his church history days, while a third had family involved in socialist causes and perhaps absorbed some of those ideas. Works by such writers might logically tend to present and interpret historical comments and experiments as supporting collectivist preferences and assumptions, without exploring alternate possible interpretations.

The selection of matters and views to present can greatly affect the impression of readers. For example, this schism, with Brigham Young on the freedom side, has apparently not been mentioned before. How conscious and willful has the slanting been? In B. H. Robert's case, on several occasions he seems to have taken the obvious meaning of events and documents and put a collectivist spin on it, or expressed surprise and puzzlement when Joseph Smith chose to avoid or resist socialist opportunities.

The joking comment is occasionally made that the church must be true or the missionaries would have destroyed it long ago. A version of this comment might apply equally to historians.

3. A chart of the makeup of the presidency during the Brigham Young period may be helpful:

| 1st C. Heber C. Kimball | Dec 5, 1847 - June 22, 1868 (death) |
| 2nd C. Willard Richards | Dec 5, 1847 - March 11, 1854 (death) |
| | |
| 2nd C. Jedediah M. | 1854 - Dec 1, 1856 (death) |
| 2nd C. Daniel H. Wells | 1856 - (death of Brigham Young) |
| | |
| 1st C. George A. Smith | 1868 - Sep 1, 1875 (death) (1st C. position vacant for a year until 1876) |
| | |
| Sometime before 1873, 5 extra counselors were named (making 7 counselors in all): Lorenzo Snow, Brigham Young, Jun., Albert Carrington, John W. Young, and George Q. Cannon. CHC 5:506. | |
| | |
| 1st C. John W. Young (son of Brigham Young) | Oct 1876 - 1877 (Brigham Young's death) |
| | |
| Brigham Young died | Aug 29, 1877 |
| | |
| John Taylor, President of 12, became presiding officer of the church on Sept 4, 1877. The two previous counselors, Wells and Smith, remain counselors to the twelve, (John Taylor as president) with George Q. Cannon in an administrative committee. CHC 5:522. D. H. Wells was addressed as Counselor, even after death of Brigham Young. (JD 19:367 June 1, 1878 Provo) | |
| | |
| John Taylor became President Oct 10, 1880. | |
| 1st C. George Q. Cannon | |
| 2nd C. Joseph F. Smith | |

Note that two of Brigham Young's sons were also his counselors. Wilford Woodruff has an interesting related note in his journal entry of March 3, 1865 (WWJ 6:215). Heber C. Kimball had just protested the fact that "President Young had ordained his sons alone. He did not have his 2 counselors with him so it is not legal and it will not stand." Apparently at this period 12 years before his death, Brigham Young was trying to add his sons as extra counselors as indicated above. "They have not the same power that his other counsellors have but President Young wished to have his sons lead the church if he died." Another journal entry, dated August 8, 1875, "I Called upon ... President Young at his Office & spent the Evening with him. 60 M. He had buried his oldest Son Joseph A Young to day the funeral at 10 oclok. John Taylor Lorenzo & Joseph Young spoke at the funeral. This death was a hard blow to Presidet Young." (WWJ 7:237) Based on the earlier 1865 quote, the hard blow may have related partly to Brigham Young's succession expectations. These two entries may be evidence that the brethren disagreed on many points, and indicate that Brigham Young wished to have his policies continued as long as possible, but feared they would end with his death (as many policies did), unless he could install his sons in positions of influence.

4. Although Orson Pratt had contacts with Missouri, was apparently a member of Zion's Camp, a member of a Clay County high council, etc., it is not clear to the author exactly what Orson Pratt knew firsthand about the practicalities of the Jackson County experience, and how much he had to rely on the experience of others. He may have been a better missionary than a pioneer, and so was elsewhere much of the time. It would be interesting to more carefully study his life during that period to see if he was part of any cooperative economic activities such as the "Big Farm," etc.

## CHAPTER 17

# The Judgement of History

The united order concept was the subject of much discussion and action during Brigham Young's thirty-year term as President of the Church, but what happened to the concept after his death? John Taylor was his immediate successor, and so bore a heavy burden in deciding what the continuing meaning of the united order concept should be. As discussed elsewhere, John Taylor was one who appeared to reserve some skepticism concerning the united order rhetoric from its very inception, and preferred to discuss economic problems and solutions in more conventional terms. He also may have had more actual business experience than many others.

A year after the death of Brigham Young, we find an interesting presentation being made at a September 21, 1878 priesthood meeting in Ogden. John Taylor mentions both the negative and positive sides of the united order concept for discussion, as though he were troubled himself about making the proper value judgements (for the full text of the discourse, see the chapter on John Taylor):

> I have been desirous to meet with the priesthood of this Stake, and I have invited a number of the presidents of Stakes within this district of country to be present at this meeting, for the consideration of certain questions that have been pressing themselves upon my mind for some time, that I want to lay before the people here.
>
> We have met here in a capacity of the holy priesthood, and all of us profess to be elders in Israel, and to be disposed at least to walk according to the order of God, and to seek to establish the principles of righteousness as far as lies in our power, and to try to build up his kingdom on the earth. That, at least, is our profession, and I believe is the sentiment of the hearts of most of the brethren now assembled. At the same time we have different ideas about many things, particularly things of a temporal nature, so called, We go in a good deal for what is called "free trade and sailor's rights," —— we want to enjoy a large amount of liberty. All these things are very popular and very correct. But in our acts and doings it is necessary that we be governed by certain laws and principles which have been given unto us by the Lord. We all concede to this. But there are some things we seem to be very much confused about, in regard to our temporal matters. During the lifetime of President Young —— several years ago, it seemed as though he was wrought upon to introduce co-operation and the United Order, to quite an extent. He told us at the time that it was the word and the will of God to us. I believed it then; and I believe it now. And yet, at the same time, every kind of idea, feeling and spirit has been manifested. In many places co-operation and the United Order have been started under various forms; in some they have succeeded very well, and in other places people have acted foolishly and covetously, seeking their own personal, individual interests under the pretense of serving God and carrying out his designs. Others have been visionary and have undertaken things which were impracticable, while others have not acted in good faith at all. There has been every kind of feeling among us as a people, that is possible to exist anywhere. And I have thought sometimes in regard to our co-operative institutions, that some of those who are engaged in them and sustained by them are as much opposed to co-operation and United Order as any other class of people we have. At least, I have noticed feelings of that kind. I do not say they are general. But there are certain reflections in relation to these matters that have been pressing upon my mind for some time.

And let me here ask myself a question —— a question not of a personal nature; I have not come here to talk about any personal matters at all, but upon principle and upon some of those principles that we as Latter-day Saints, and as elders in Israel, profess to believe in. The question would be and my text would be to-day, if I wanted to take a text: Shall we sustain co-operation and the United Order, and work with that end in view in all of our operations, or shall we give it up as a bad thing unworthy of our attention? That is where the thing comes to, in my mind. At any rate, we wish to act honestly and honorably in this matter. If we believe that these principles are true, let us be governed by them; if we do not, let us abandon them at once, conclude that we have made a mistake and have no more to do with them. For we, all of us, profess to be at least honest men, and to act conscientiously. If there is anything wrong in these things, let us know the wrong; and if it is not a command of God, and not binding upon us, let us quit it. And then the question naturally arises, Are we prepared to do this? And, on the other hand, if we believe that these are principles that are inculcated by the Lord, then let us be governed by them. In fact, whichever way we decide let us carry out our decisions in good faith, and not have our sign painted on one side in white, and, on the other black or some other color. But let us feel as the prophet Elijah did on a certain occasion, "If the Lord be God, follow him; but if Baal, then follow him." There was a disposition in ancient Israel to have a part of God and a part of the devil or Baal —— an idolatrous god which was worshipped by them. I sometimes think that in some respects we are a good deal like them. Do we believe our religion? Yes. Do we believe in the holy priesthood and that God has restored it to the earth? Yes. Do we believe that God has established his kingdom? Yes. And do we believe that the holy priesthood is under the guidance of the Lord? O, yes; but still we would like a good deal of our own way. If we must introduce something that the Lord has commanded, we would like to put it off just as far as we can, and if we cannot do it any other way we will fight against it, according to circumstances, and how things move and operate. We often wish the Lord would not exact certain things of us; we would rather have our own way. But let us look at things calmly and dispassionately. As I understand it, the Lord has gathered us together to do his will, to observe his laws and keep his commandments. And we have certain obligations devolving upon us in the holy priesthood which God requires at our hands. He requires, for instance, of the Twelve to go, when called upon, to the nations of the earth and preach the Gospel to those nations. If they were not to do it, would they be justified? No, they would not; God would require the blood of the people at their hands. That is the way I figure up these things. I do not know of any half-way house. As one of the Twelve, I do not want to dodge any of these questions, but meet them fairly and squarely. And I think I have done it; and I think the Twelve generally have. They have always been on hand to go anywhere when the Lord has required them to go, whether in sickness or health, in poverty or abounding in means; no matter what their circumstances, or what individualism would have to be sacrificed, the object has ever been to do that will of God. And so it has been with a great many of the seventies, high priests and also with a great many of the elders. Their feelings have been: Let the Lord speak, and here am I ready to do his will and carry out his designs. And this feeling exists today in the hearts of a great many; but there are also a great many who do not feel so, who want to dodge these questions. Here is Brother Eldredge, who is one of the presidents of the seventies; he knows how extremely difficult it is to get men, as we used in former years —— "at the drop of the hat," as it was termed, to go on missions. However, I do not wish to dwell upon that; I merely refer to it in passing along.

COMMENT: According to John Taylor, some of those working in a "united order" and receiving their living from it are opposed to the system. They are certainly the ones who should have the best insight into the good or bad features of the idea. If they are opposed in principle to the system, and are themselves reasonable people, then that could be taken as a major indictment of the system and could be interesting and valuable evidence. Of course, if they are the sort who would complain about any kind of work or system, then we could perhaps ignore their complaints.

If abstract and absolute religious commandments are introduced to govern economics, one might expect it to polarize such practical matters into irrational black and white extremes. To be continually effective, economic organization and activity calls for great flexibility and creativity. Religious absolutisms may bring a "Law of Moses" arbitrary rigidity to the minutia of life.

....

    Now, I know what many of you will say, in speaking of co-operation: "there has been a great many abuses." Yes, I admit it —— numbers of them. "What and under the name of the United Order also?" Yes, any quantity of them. Joseph Smith in his day said it was extremely difficult to introduce these things because of the greed, covetousness, selfishness and wickedness of the people. I wish here to refer to one or two things, connected with this subject I spoke about the Twelve, the seventies, the elders and the high priests; and stated that a great many of them had been out preaching the Gospel, and that some of them felt as though it is hard work. It is, no doubt, very up-hill business for a man to be a Saint if he is not one; and if he has not the principles of the Gospel in his heart, it must be very hard work, I may say an eternal struggle, for him to preach. But if a man has got the pure principles of the Gospel in his heart, it is quite easy for him to expound the truth. Well, now, I will take the words of Jesus: "Except a man can forsake father or mother, wife and children, houses and lands, for my sake, he can not be my disciple." And let me say to you, my brethren, that that Gospel is just as true to-day as it was then, that except a man is prepared to forsake his earthly interests for the sake of the Gospel of the Son of God, he is unworthy of it, and cannot be a true Saint. Now, this is where the hardship comes in and it also accounts for this eternal rubbing and bumping. "How much can't I do, and how little can I do to retain fellowship with the Church; and how much can I act selfishly and yet be counted a disciple of Christ?" Did you never feel as Paul describes it —— the spirit striving against the flesh? I guess you have, and you doubtless know all about it for these are plain matters of fact. This is the position the Gospel has placed us in; and it is a very difficult thing to serve two masters, in fact it is useless for any man to attempt to do it, "for (as the Savior says) either he will hate the one, and love the other; or else he will hold to the one and despise the other. Ye cannot serve God and mammon." And therefore Jesus said: "Take my yoke upon you, and learn of me; for I am meek and lowly of heart, and ye shall find rest unto your souls. For my yoke is easy, and my burden is light."

    But to return to the principles of co-operation and United Order. Supposing a man had come to you elders, when you were out on missions, requesting baptism at your hands, without having repented of his sins, would you have baptized him? No, you would not. But supposing he claimed to believe in the Lord Jesus Christ, but not in baptism; would you receive him into the Church? No, you dare not do such things. But supposing again that he believed in baptism and in the Lord Jesus Christ, and had repented of his sins, but did not believe in the laying on of hands for the reception of the Holy Ghost; would you baptize him? No. And further supposing he had complied with all these requirements, and he had the opportunity to gather to Zion but did not improve the opportunity, would you consider him a very good Saint? No. Now, beside all these, the Lord has given us a law pertaining to tithing; and if he did not comply with that would you consider him a good Saint? No. And we are told to build temples, and the man who would refuse to do this work, you would consider a very poor specimen of a Latter-day Saint. Referring to the United Order, the Lord has given us to understand that whosoever refuses to comply with the requirements of that law, his name shall not be known in the records of the Church, but shall be blotted out; neither shall his children have an inheritance in Zion. Are these the words of the Lord to us? I suppose there are none here to day but would say, Yes. How, then can I or you treat lightly that which God has given us? It is the word of God to me; it is the word of God to you. And if we do not fulfil this requirement what is the result? We are told what the result will be. These things have not taken place now but we have been wandering about from place to place, and the Lord has blessed us in a remarkable degree. And we are gathered together, as I have said, for the purpose of building up Zion, and we are supposed to be the servants of God having engaged to perform this work; and individually, I would say, I do not want to profess to be a Saint, if I am not one, nor if the work we are engaged in is not of the Lord; if the principles we believe in are false, I do not want anything to do with them; on the other hand, if they are true then I want to be governed by them, and so do you. We must carry out the word and will of God, for we cannot afford to ignore it nor any part of it. If faith, repentance and baptism and laying on of hands is right and true and demands our obedience, so does co-operation and the United Order. Some may say, here is such and such a man has been connected with the United Order, and how foolishly he has acted, and others have gone into co-operation and made a failure of it. Yes, that may be all very true, but who is to blame? Shall we stop baptizing people and make no further efforts to establish the kingdom of God upon the earth, because certain ones have acted foolishly and perhaps wickedly! Do the actions of such people render the principles of the Gospel without effect or the doctrines we teach untrue? I think you would not say so. What do we do with such cases? We purge them out, we cut them off according to the laws God has laid down; but we do not stop the operations of the Gospel, such a thought never enters our minds, for we know the work already commenced is onward and upward. Shall we then think of putting an end to these other principles because men have acted foolishly and selfishly and done wrong? No, I think not; I do not think we can choose one principle and reject another to suit ourselves. I think that all of these things, as we have received them, one after another are equally binding upon us, Jesus said, "Man shall not live by bread alone but by every word that proceedeth out from the mouth of God." This is as true to-day as it was when spoken.

 I have seen a disposition among many of the brethren to pull off in every kind of way, and this spirit and tendency is spreading and growing in every part of our Territory. We have co-operative stores started, and we have the eye of God painted over the doors, with the words "Holiness to the Lord" written overhead. Do we act according to that? In a great many instances I am afraid not. But what of that? Shall we depart from these principles? I think not. What was the principle of co-operation intended for? Simply as a stepping stone for the United Order, that is all, that we might be united and operate together in the interest of building up Zion. Well, having started, what do we see? One pulling one way another pulling another way; every one taking his own course. One man says: Such a one takes his own course, and I will take mine. Using the same line of argument, because one man commits a wrong unworthy the calling of a Latter-day Saint, his doing so is to be all excuse for my doing the same thing. As I understand it, I am called to fear God, whether anybody else does it or not; and this is your calling just as much as it is mine. We may indeed shirk it and violate the covenants we have made. The Lord has blessed us with endowments and covenants of which the world know nothing, neither can they know anything about it. And he has given unto us these things that we might be brought into closer union with God, that we might know how to save ourselves, our wives and children, as well as our fathers and progenitors who have gone before us. Having done this, what next? God has revealed certain things to the children of men now as he formerly revealed the Gospel to the children of Israel. But could they stand it? No, they could not. Moses succeeded in leading seventy of the elders of Israel to the presence of God; he would have lead all Israel into his presence, but they would not be led; they turned to idolatry, to evil and corruption, and hence they became disobedient and unmanageably. And when the Lord spake to them they became terrified and said, "Let not God speak unto us lest we die." God wants to bring us near to him, for this purpose he has introduced the Gospel with all its ordinances. Has he been true to us? Yes. And when you elders have been out preaching and baptizing people for the remission of their sins, and when confirming them members of this Church, you have said, Receive ye the Holy Ghost, have they received it? They have, God bearing witness of the truth of your words and of his ministry conferred upon you. JD 21:53-61 JT Sep 21, 1878 Ogden.

John Taylor highlights some of the internal conflicts of the united order endeavors. The "all or nothing" alternatives he mentions are probably the logical product of the anxieties one might feel when the ideology one has been given does not match well with the practical outcomes. "Cognitive dissonance" is a current term for that perceived conflict.

We might wonder when he terminated the united order program (as described below), was it because the people were not willing or able to live a "higher" law, or because he finally decided that "the law" did not make much sense in the current setting, and in fact was never entitled to be placed at the same level of importance as a commandment such as baptism. Perhaps he decided that the opinions of the people who were experiencing the associated problems on a daily basis were entitled to be heard instead of being muffled by an ideological filter. Is the gospel about people striving to do right or is it about dehumanizing and rigid ideological prejudices? The idea of unity was surely a useful one, but when carried to extremes can be damaging.

Finally, probably after much soul searching, John Taylor decided that the United Order program was to be discontinued. In 1882 he answered in the negative his September 21, 1878, question, "Shall we sustain co-operation and the United Order, and work with that end in view in all of our operations, or shall we give it up as a bad thing unworthy of our attention?"

Four years after the united order question was laid before the priesthood group in Ogden, apparently President Taylor reached his final conclusions on the matter. The following excerpt from the CHC seems to signal the complete end of the rhetoric and grandiose plans of the Brigham Young era united order concept:

NOTE
THE LAW OF CONSECRATION AND STEWARDSHIP NEVER ADEQUATELY
ESTABLISHED IN THE CHURCH

President John Taylor in a carefully prepared epistle to the presidents of stakes, high councils, bishops and other authorities of the church, under date of May 1, 1882, reviewing the efforts at cooperation in business and other interests, then contemplated by the church, said of efforts at establishing "United Order" (Consecration and Stewardship):

"Cooperation had been talked about considerably from time to time as being a stepping stone to something that would yet be more fully developed among the people of God, namely, the 'United Order'. *We had no example of the 'United Order' in accordance with the word of God on the subject.* Our cooperation was simply an operation to unite us together in our secular affairs, tending to make us one in temporal things as we were one in spiritual things. * * * Our relations with the world and our own imperfections prevent the establishment of this system [i.e. the system of Consecration and Stewardship spoken of at times as the 'United Order'] at the present time, as was stated by Joseph [Smith] in an early day, it cannot yet be carried out. But cooperation and the 'United Order' [recent attempts at it] are a step in the right direction, and are leading our brethren to reflect upon the necessity of union as one of the fundamental principles of success in temporal things as well as in spiritual things."

The epistle is signed separately by President John Taylor as President of the Church of Jesus Christ of   Latter-day Saints and then by his counselors in the following form:

> [Signed] "John Taylor"
> "President of the Church of Jesus Christ of Latter-day Saints."
> "We concur in the above.
> [Signed] "George Q. Cannon"
> "Joseph F. Smith"
> Counselors in the First Presidency."[1]

The most important content of the epistle is the sentence "We had no example of the 'United Order' in accordance with the Word of God on the subject." It was given textual emphasis in the CHC and apparently was emphasized in the original. This statement clearly puts an end to glorifying and repeating the past economic experiments.

The use of quotation marks around the words "United Order" presumably was in the original. Their use normally implies a questioning of the aptness of the term so enclosed. The phrase "so-called" is often assumed to be implied by the quotation marks. Perhaps this was another way of questioning whether any of the prior economic experiments should be considered to have a continuing scriptural backing or significance.

As has been common ever since, President Taylor felt a need to leave some vague option open for the eventual implementation of some as-yet undefined program attributed to Joseph Smith. This seems to be no more than an attempt to "save face" concerning the past programs which are now to be abandoned in theory as well as practice.

Through the title chosen for the note, the B.H. Roberts history puts a certain interpretation on the epistle, implying that the saints "failed again" to get the united order business correct. Although B. H. Robert's view of these events has been so often taught and accepted as to almost seem unquestionable, nonetheless there is another way of viewing the "united orders" of Joseph Smith and Brigham Young. Viewed in proper context, Joseph Smith's united order was a brilliant success, and not the failure which some have made it out to be. Likewise, Brigham Young's united order was a first-rate success at its main goal of protecting the saints.

There are some difficulties in the text and comments of the above quotation which make one wish to have better data on the full text of the epistle and the context in which it was issued. Notice that the biases of the editor of the CHC have colored the presentation and interpretation of the fragment of the epistle presented. The title given, "THE LAW OF CONSECRATION AND STEWARDSHIP NEVER ADEQUATELY ESTABLISHED IN THE CHURCH," presupposes that there actually was a prior commandment to implement and live some specific temporal order, and that the saints had failed (again) in it. I don't believe that is what John Taylor meant to say. Although he did make a polite reference to some future state of the Saints, I believe he did mean first and foremost to simply end the church-sponsored accumulation and direction of capital.

The use by the editor of the phrase '"United Order" (Consecration and Stewardship)' in his introductory note also seems to imply that the laws of consecration and stewardship can only be in operation under one of the various plans collectively known as the united order. Those two laws of consecration and stewardship can function very well without any Church-prescribed general economic organization.

The editor of the CHC, through his use of editor-supplied titles and comments (some in brackets []), has put his own spin on the meaning of the epistle. I would argue that John Taylor is in fact annulling the doctrine, saying that it never really existed since it was never fully described and understood. He is expunging it from the gospel record. In contrast, the editor is trying to interpret the epistle as saying that the doctrine was and is a good, understood, and continuing one, but the church merely made some practical errors in its implementation.

In analyzing the epistle, I would prefer to focus on the underlined sentence, "We had no example of the 'United Order' in accordance with the word of God on the subject." One could conceivably guess that this sentence implies that President Taylor actually knew what the united order was supposed to be, and that we didn't get it right. However, it is more likely that he did not know what it was supposed to be. He only knew that the revelations did not require anything like what Brigham Young had proposed. In very simple language, I believe he was saying "I don't know if there is one, and if there is one, I don't know what it is, but whatever it is, that wasn't it, and, besides, even if there is such a thing, we are not now required to live it."

This, then, seems to mark the end of the "united order" era. It has not been revived at any time since. Assuming that the Joseph Smith and Brigham Young "orders" were ad hoc organizations created to solve very specific, serious, and relatively short term problems for the saints (both had extra-legal elements), if unique or threatening circumstances arise again, one might predict that the church leaders would do the sensible thing and create a program to solve whatever problem rears its head. There is no reason for it to look like either past solution unless the problem is exactly the same, an unlikely event. Some wisdom might be extracted from the past experience, but otherwise there is no reason to expect the past to control the future.

It should be noted that the saints in Utah, including Brigham Young, had little or no knowledge of Joseph Smith's United Order. For a complete explanation see JSUO. Suffice it for now to say that no one who was a member of that group made it to Utah. Brigham Young himself made disparaging statements about that organization that indicate he had little or no knowledge of it. So by the time John Taylor assumed the presidency, there was probably no accurate firsthand knowledge available. On top of that, John Taylor's contemporaries seem not to have realized that the major battle that Brigham Young was fighting was essentially over. The war with the eastern establishment had been won, although a few skirmishes remained. They may have vaguely sensed that continuing to cooperate in the Brigham Young tradition was no longer appropriate, but could probably not articulate that view. Continuing the aggressive and closed cooperation was becoming counter-productive. The new goals should be to merge with the prevailing society and thus finally win what they would have preferred to have from the very beginning. The conflict scenario was so embedded on both sides that another ten years was required to reach a final accommodation.

The fact that an organization or one of its aspects is changed or terminated does not automatically mean it was a failure in the past. It is normally just an indication that times and needs have changed. Sunday meeting schedules, evening Relief Society meeting schedules, etc., are simple examples of changes to meet new needs. Several important and striking changes have been made in recent times in the highest councils of the church concerning assistants to the Twelve, Seventies, patriarchs, area presidencies; ward budgets and mission payments have been changed; temple ceremonies and name processing practices have been modified, etc. The "united order" items and changes are probably of no greater doctrinal or practical significance than those changes just mentioned.

It is very possible that there were social as well as doctrinal reasons for discontinuing the efforts towards maximal LDS economic cooperation. Any time a large group acts as a block in any society, they arouse the envy and malice of inevitable opponents. Assuming that under Brigham Young's mighty efforts, the Saints had reached a plateau which assured them survival as an entity within the U.S. polity, it was a good time to back away from the confrontational empire-building mode and begin to merge in with the rest of society. This was probably a necessary step toward eventual statehood and general social acceptance of the saints as ordinary Americans. This would allow them to become the leaven which was necessary for later steps in the "rolling forth" process. There were future persecutions of the Saints over such matters as polygamy, etc., but there was never any serious challenge to the very existence of the saints as had occurred so many times before.

We should also consider the problem that surfaced later where any property owned by the Church came under Federal control through an escheat proceeding. The main reaction and solution at that time was to disperse the Church's property to private owners wherever possible. Apparently, decentralizing ownership in anticipation of future Federal raids would have been wise.

In the 1930's, during the Depression days, there were reasons to wonder whether past doctrines on economic cooperation might be called up again. While there were many members who suffered under the circumstances, the Church's very survival was not at stake. The rhetoric of the Brigham Young united orders did not resurface:

> While the security system was being established church leaders seldom spoke of the obvious parallels between it and the united orders established in Mormon communities within the living memory of many of the older saints. The members, however, were quick to notice similarities and to ask authorities if the two systems were related. When Harold B. Lee helped set up the program with Apostle Melvin J. Ballard during the summer of 1936, he noted that the Apostle "was asked everywhere: 'Is this the beginning of the united order?'" Invariably Ballard responded that the program "Is not the beginning of the united order, but it may be that in this movement the Lord may be giving his people an examination to see how far they have come toward a condition where they might live as one." President Heber J. Grant opened the October 1936 conference with an official statement on the early operations of the plan. But though the new welfare system became a dominant theme of the three-day conference, neither President Grant nor other speakers made an explicit connection between it and the united order. The security system was not introduced as a resumption of the traditional mormon compulsion to build the City of God on earth, but rather as an inspired response to calamitous contemporary circumstances. There was almost no suggestion that innovators of the new program had been guided by their understanding of the law of consecration and stewardship taught by Joseph Smith or the united order of Enoch preached by Brigham Young.

COMMENT: The phrase "inspired response to calamitous contemporary circumstances" seems to describe the entire history and explanation for united order efforts. That is all the united order ever was! The "City of God" theme may be equivalent to a theme of "Mormon power." There is no reason in the gospel to build anything of that sort except when actual survival is at stake as in Enoch's day or as in the first 50 years of the church's existence in our time. The saints cannot "leaven" society from inside a walled and exclusive city.

The writer of the prior quote, like many others, still prefers to leave open the possibility of a future complete establishment of a set of temporal rules which have been no more than hinted at in the past:

> Nevertheless, there is evidence that such considerations were in the minds of top church leaders. Describing his initial meeting with President Grant and David O. Mckay of the First Presidency to plan the welfare program, Harold B. Lee remembered his astonishment to learn "that for years there had been before them, as a result of their thinking and planning and as a result of the inspiration of almighty God, the genius of the very plan that is being carried out and was in waiting and in preparation for a time when in their judgement the faith of the Latter-day Saints was such that they were willing to follow the counsel of the men who lead and preside in this church." Apostle and church historian Joseph Fielding Smith told the saints during the October 1936 conference that he looked upon the plan, not as something new, but as "a return to that which is old." J. Reuben Clark, Jr., of the First Presidency added his testimony that the plan "goes back to the principles that were given the church over a hundred years ago, puts us once more on the road leading to the establishment of a Christian rule." BCG 344-5.

The principles of caring for each other and assisting the poor are ancient, and are quite sufficient in themselves to explain the church efforts of the 1930's.

In spite of this continued yearning by some for a new temporal constitution, it seems altogether plausible that there does not exist any such set of rules for the mechanical, technical or temporal union of the properties and income of the saints. In fact, every such set proposed seems only to further disprove the need for or possibility of any such a set of rules. As I believe Brigham Young himself fully recognized at the end of his life, the proper meaning of the unity of the saints is ever changing, and that any attempt to set it in legal concrete is counterproductive. Perhaps we may say that the proper unity of the saints can be achieved and maintained, if and only if, the saints are in tune with the prophet and the spirit. Any needful property arrangements can be taken care of without specific new rules or intervention. In most cases, actual intervention will serve mostly to show that unity of purpose and understanding does *not* exist, and will only serve to further confuse the saints and lessen the spontaneous unity that is the life of the church, whether spiritual or "temporal." If any proposed action of the church begins to look like taxation, conscription, or any other use of institutional force, except when immediate threat to life is involved, it is likely that the proposed action is inappropriate.

In BCG, Arrington seems to be saying that although the brethren maintained a studied effort to not mention the past economic experiments, but only referred in vague terms to general principles of care for the poor taught in the past, they still really wanted to reconfirm the correctness of the "doctrine" that eventually we must become embroiled in a bureaucratic economic leveling operation of some sort. I would prefer to believe that their careful silence concerning the United Order of Brigham Young's day, and their (at least J. Reuben Clark's and David O. McKay's) strongly stated antipathy for anything akin to communism, was really meant to reject the ideas of the past concerning mandatory economic organization and bury them for all time.

It is interesting that the book *Essentials in Church History* (1937) by Joseph Fielding Smith tells us nothing about the united order events of the Brigham Young era. The *Essentials* might be viewed as a brief for the Church and against its antagonists throughout the 19th century. Every significant law suit is mentioned, but no mention at all is made of the united order events and philosophies. That theme certainly can be said to have been of great significance to the saints of Brigham Young's time. Nearly every city and person had some experience with "united orders." The book was written by probably the most knowledgeable church historian the church has ever had, so one must assume that he had a good grasp of the significance of the various aspects of church history.

His leaving out all information concerning the united order may represent a significant judgement on his part. He may have considered it either irrelevant to any audience today or a difficult or embarrassing topic to discuss and so left it out of a brief for the church; let the church's detractors bring it up if it is to be mentioned at all. Even if not an embarrassment, perhaps he considered it something to be buried because it was not a part of the gospel, but only an aberration or special case best forgotten. Whatever his reason for leaving it out, it is probably fair to assume that he did not consider it a positive element of the church and its history. Mentioning it would tend to give strength to the position of the socialist-leaning people within the church and without. That alone might be enough to cause him to avoid giving those episodes and philosophies any free publicity by repeating them in a widely used book.

## Chapter notes

[1] Epistle of John Taylor, pamphlet, pp. 1-11. (CHC 5:498).

CHAPTER 18

# The Mystical Nature of the United Order Tradition

One of the more intriguing or repulsive aspects of the united order tradition, depending on one's viewpoint, is the mystical, mysterious, or magical aspects attributed to it by tradition: in one version, by some magical process, perhaps involving mindless regimentation, one can be cleansed and made better. Is this tradition or myth actually a legitimate part of the gospel?

Before going further, perhaps some dictionary definitions can help focus the discussion:

**Mystical** having a spiritual meaning, existence, reality or comparable value that is neither apparent to the senses nor obvious to the intelligence.

**Mystery** 1. a religious truth revealed by God that man cannot know by reason alone and that once it has been revealed cannot be completely understood.
2. Something that has not been or cannot be explained, that is unknown to all or concealed from some and therefore exciting curiosity or wonder, or is incomprehensible or uncomprehended.[1]

These definitions may help us realize that there is a large mystical element to the united order myth; it is unknown and unknowable, but still somehow important. It seems like a worthwhile goal to take away some of the mystery. This element of mystery appears to be generally destructive, not helpful, to both individuals and society. Its only positive contribution may be that it could bring unthinking obedience, and therefore rapid reaction, in a time of crisis, allowing disaster to be averted.

There are many real mysteries imbedded in the gospel, such as the atonement and resurrection. We are not be able to explain the atonement completely; in fact, most of it is unexplained or unfathomable. However, extending mysticism to such practical matters as economics, items which *can* be understood and articulated by mere humans, is offensive to me, and normally is destructive. The cause and effect relationships of people and organizations is the stuff of which living the golden rule is made. How can one be honest and responsible and helpful to a neighbor if he doesn't know the exact and complete effects of what he does?

This brand of mystical economics suspends scientific attention to cause and effect, and all is replaced with blind faith and ignorance. Is it better to be stupid? It is hard to see any advantage in being stupid and ignorant about economics and government, or how any temporal or spiritual salvation can be earned that way.

The rote laws of the Law of Moses could not exalt anyone. People could live those rules and still have little real understanding of the gospel. Did that almost incomprehensible system of laws make them a better and more enlightened people? Certainly not by itself.

Some versions of the tradition or myth are too much like the religion of Marx, with its powerful and mystical belief in certain axioms of economic dogma and history. After massive trials of hundreds of millions of people for generations, with tens of millions of murders, and persecution of nearly all involved, it finally dawns on many that it is not a good system. Satan seems to have almost unlimited power to muddle the brains of humans with sophistry of this sort.

No one can explain how either system can work, but to even question them may be considered apostate, perhaps with your life being forfeit (blood atonement?) for corrupting or confusing the society. The systems call for blind faith on the part of many, allowing cynical manipulation on the part of others.

These systems can make possible the gaining of power over others by "explaining" or at least pretending to understand these mysteries. This is the basis for priestcraft.

A few simple rules are to solve all problems as if by magic; intelligence and knowledge are not required, and may not be wanted. There are simple explanations for some things and the rest are unexplained or unexplainable.

Anyone who tries to analyze the public statements and the actions and their results will likely be considered dangerous. Stupid people are the best for such experiments; it takes them longer to catch on to how their lives are being manipulated.

Such schemes might work in subsistence farming, standard tribal stuff, where "helping your neighbor" can have a simple and understandable meaning, but certainly is harder to apply elsewhere. Such myths may have contributed to the propensity of Utahns today to be taken in by scams. If causes and effects are unarticulated, and are even said to be unexplainable, and the people accept such vague explanations, then they will be vulnerable to many con artists.

Is it a requirement of the gospel to be vulnerable in that way? Being hospitable and friendly does not also imply the need to be foolish in economic transactions.

As hopefully outlined in this rather long book, Brigham Young, one of the most practical and hardest-headed people ever to live, would certainly have been upset to have any of the world's socialist nonsense attributed to him, or to be said to have accepted or encouraged it.

John Taylor's "I do not believe in any fanaticism" statement was his way of rejecting the philosophical foolishness of the world of his time. As one of the Twelve, he was a check on the flights of social fancy of his associates. As president of the church, he cleaned up any remnants of misunderstandings that may have accumulated.

The false promises of socialism/communism should make one extremely wary of any mystical, utopian plan which involves the use of force to make men "better" and "happier." Clarence B. Carson, in his book *The World in the Grip of an Idea,* presents a magnificent delineation and refutation of the mystical, economic-religious nonsense that so permeates the world today. He begins with a short definition of the idea:

> There are three prongs to the idea which has the world in its grip. The first has already been told: To achieve human felicity on this earth by concerting all efforts to its realization. The second is now before us, and can be stated in this way: To root out, discredit, and discard all aspects of culture which cannot otherwise be altered to divest them of any role in inducing or supporting the individual's pursuit of his own self-interest. The corollary of this

is to develop an ethos which focuses attention on what is supposed to be the common good of humanity.

....

By what instrument is this transformation to be made? This brings us to the third prong of the idea. It is this: Government is the instrument to be used to concert all efforts behind the realization of human felicity and the necessary destruction or alteration of culture.

....

How could the use of force be introduced into the equation? Not by choice but out of necessity. The bent of men to pursue their own self-interest is so ingrained that only government could exorcise it. Force must be used to free men from the hold of selfishness. Hopefully, of course, government would be transformed in the process.

This, then, is the distillation of the idea that holds the world in its grip today. It is not only the idea underlying Soviet Communism or Chinese or Albanian Communism, but also the idea underlying the Fabianism of The British Labour Party, Swedish socialism, American liberalism, German Social Democracy, Canadian interventionism, and the thrust of government into people's lives on a consistent scale everywhere in the world today.[2]

How much like the "united order" does this idea sound? The two ideas are almost identical, if not exact. This should constitute a challenge to any advocate of the united order to present a convincing distinction between the two.

The following scattered quotations from his chapter 37, "Victim of the Idea," should help to show the folly of the mystical promise of Nirvana through organization that has also attached itself to the gospel. I would love to quote the entire book at this point, but that is not possible. However, for one who wishes to understand every facet of this ideological problem, there may be no substitute for reading the entire book.

**Victim of the Idea**

> *There's only one general feeling at Westminster [the British Parliament]. That independence must be stamped out at all costs.... The policymakers in all three parties are in complete agreement on that.*

The thrust of the Idea that has the world in its grip is to take away the independence of the individual. This thrust inheres in the Idea as it is formulated here as well as in the socialist way of looking at conditions which were supposed to be remedied. The formulation of the Idea being used here is that the aim is to concert all human efforts for the common good. The only direct way to achieve this aim is to make the individual into a cog in a vast machine, to make the efforts of each individual coordinate with those of the whole human race. Such a coordination is only possible when individual independence no longer exists or is no longer capable of action.

The animus of the idea runs deeper than this. It is, as has been stated before, to root out the penchant of the individual to pursue his own self-interest. It is a religious, or, at least, quasi-religious, aim at bottom. In the socialist view, man's original sin is the pursuit of self-interest. It is, they think, the source of all the ills of the world. ....

[T]here is an unstated premise in socialism. The premise can be elaborated this way. Man has potentialities for both good and evil. One of his potentialities is for the pursuit of self-interest without regard to the general good. Institutions were devised, such as those protecting private property, which support and license the pursuit of self-interest. These institutions deform man, socialists claim, and Marx held that man would only finally be freed when the individual no longer pursued his own good but rather that of all. The harmony that would result would be a great release from the tension produced by contentions born of each seeking his own.

All efforts to eradicate man's pursuit of self-interest have been to no avail. The greater the effort to erase it, the more determinedly do men pursue their self-interest as they conceive it.

....

There is a reason for this. The denial of the right to pursue self-interest is the denial of the right to life. Our very survival hinges on a lively interest in self.

....

None of this is meant to imply that the individual is alone in his effort to survive, though he may sometimes in some ways be. Ordinarily, though, he may have help from others and render assistance in return. Society is founded on mutual exchange and aid. It is rather to affirm that the individual pursuit of self-interest is as deeply imbedded in his nature as the will to survive, and necessarily so. There is no need to suppose that it is man's only motive, or always his predominant one. Socialists to the contrary notwithstanding, the opposite motive from that of the pursuit of self-interest is the not the pursuit of the common good: it is the pursuit of self-destruction.

Socialism does not succeed, then, in eradicating the individual's penchant for pursuing his self-interest. It can, at most, induce him to conceal it by making hypocritical claims about the motives behind his acts.

....

Socialists use two devices mainly both to take away and undermine the independence of the individual and to instrument him as a cog in the wheel. They are *organization* and *numbers.*

....

Socialists attempt to reduce the individual to a number, to encompass him within a framework of one among many, and to use the weight of number to bring him into line.

....

Independence is essential to individual freedom and responsibility. Freedom without the independence to choose and act is a contradiction in terms, a notion without content. In like manner, the individual cannot logically be held responsible for acts not freely and independently done, not can he assume his responsibilities without a measure of independence. ... Tacitly, socialism promises freedom without responsibility; in fact, it takes away the means -- individual independence -- for exercising either.

....

A case can be make that self-centeredness is the Original Sin, but my candidate is the desire to control others. In any case, it happens that what we may condemn as self-centeredness is largely benign until the self reaches out to take what belongs to someone else or extend its control over them.

....

That is not how the matter stands in socialism. Socialism authorizes, licenses, and gives the stamp of legitimacy to this bent to control others. It bids men to form collectives and use force to bend others to their will. It is virtuous so to do; it is democratic. The bent to control others becomes a virus of the will. The prospect which socialism holds out is dominion over man, to finally have his despised independence obliterated and to have him subservient to organization. The appeal of socialism is to the worst that is in us, the desire to control others and make them subservient to our will. Socialist ideology does not, of course, focus upon these methods; it is an extended apology for the necessity for collective action.

....

To all appearances, the seeking of salvation through organization is by no means an exclusively socialist trait. Socialists are the modern champions of government as the means to cure our ills, but the Idea that has the world in its grip is broader than that. It is the notion of concerting all human efforts, an idea which finds its most explicit expression in socialism but has the world more firmly in its grip by way of the veneration of organization. It is my belief that we can only loosen the grip of the idea when we are ready to put organizations, all organizations, in their place. After all, if organizations are the way, then logic does lie with socialism, for that doctrine follows the premise to its logical conclusion. In order to grasp the impact of organization it is important to understand how organization, as such, tends to confine the individual and sap his independence. That is not to say that organizations should be, or could be, dispensed with but rather contained and limited.

Modern ideological contentions have confused the issue almost beyond hope of unscrambling it. Socialists have focused their attention on business organizations and have ascribed great ills to business activities. Opponents of socialism have focused their attention largely upon the dangers of government and its threat to liberty. Both have tended to ignore, in their polemics, a crucial congruity between industrial organization and governmental organization. Namely, they have ignored how both these have the effect of undermining the independence of the individual.

....

It has sometimes been noticed that businessmen do not oppose socialism very vigorously. ... If businessmen have ever anywhere risen up in determined opposition to socialism, it has escaped the attention of the present writer.

....

Socialism is, to put it metaphorically, the errant child of what Marx called capitalism. The businessman is unlikely to be greatly appalled by the loss of individual independence entailed in socialism, for he was about the business of reducing that independence long before socialists ever came to power.

....

The factory system was a retrogressive development. The failure to recognize this -- though some early socialists did -- has wrought havoc in the world ever since. It was a retrogressive development because those who went into it could no longer manage their own affairs in their work. ... It was retrogressive, above all, because it fastened upon the world the notion that progress is attained by the ever tighter organization of men. The veneration of organization has now become well-nigh universal.

....

In the light of this development, the factory system was a portentious step backward in human arrangements. It fatefully linked the ownership of capital to control over workers.

....

The factory system was a great success, or so it appeared. Goods poured forth from it in such quantity as had never before been seen. ... Was it the factory system itself? That, I think, is what most people have thought, when they have thought about it. Indeed, men have been inflamed in the modern world with what could be accomplished by organizing and controlling men. We cannot grasp the Idea that has the world in its grip until we grasp that. The factory system is the model for the notion that by integrating the undertaking and regimenting men in organizations great wonders can be accomplished.

It is a chimera. The factory system was a historical accident. The initial inventions were made at a time when falling water was the only considerable power system available. Thus, places for housing the machines had to be built adjacent to the water supply. But there was something else of great moment. The principle of separating the ownership of property from control over people was incompletely realized.

....

In any case, the great increase in production was not due to the factory system but to the use of machines and power from falling water or, in time, steam engines. The organization of workers is inessential to production. ... Leonard Read has often made the point that the great weakness of communism is that it utilizes only the intelligence of one or a few men rather than that of the generality of men. The point is well taken, but it applies to the factory system also, and beyond that, to organizations in general.

....

My main point here is that the factory system arose in a particular historical setting in which the subjugation of the generality of men was taken for granted.

....

The factory system did provoke the wrath of men.

....

It was at this juncture that Karl Marx entered upon the scene. Marx claimed that the problem lay in the private ownership of capital, a view that he shared with many other socialists. By grotesque distortion of classical economics, he demonstrated that the worker was being cheated out of his fair share of the product of labor. Indeed, Marx downgraded capital to the point that it is an insignificant factor in production.

....

Marx did something else, without which he would have been just another socialist, despite his polemical skill. He did not reject the factory system or view it as a retrogressive development. He saw it, instead, as a harbinger of a bright tomorrow, as the beginning of the wave of a great and glorious future. Once the workers had seized the factories and were running them, all the problems of the world would be solved. The state would wither away, and men would live with one another in peace and harmony.

Communism is the nineteenth century factory system writ large. It is the factory system taken over by the state and bureaucrats substituted for owners and managers. It is the mill village confiscated by the state, and housing become a prerogative of those who serve and please the government.

....

The struggle between private business and government is not over the necessity, desirability, or even virtuousness of controlling individual man and establishing his dependency on them. On that point, they share a common animus. The struggle is over which shall control him.

....

Socialists do not view private business as a partner of government. It is a contestant with government for control over the individual. Business must be subdued on the way to subduing all individuals.[3]

Like the communism described above, the united order may be just another version of the factory system trying to write itself large in the Mormon psyche. If, as it appears, the united order idea is just another of the factory ideologies, we should want to keep it at a good distance and under tight control. If we are not careful, we may merely have another most-subtle occurrence of the same old ideas of Satan and man about the control of the individual.

In contrast to the several ideologies of the factory, the book *The Third Wave*[4] presents a more heavenly view of man's possibilities on earth, based on extensive new technologies in information processing and manufacturing. We are supposed to be empowered in heaven. These new technological capabilities on earth should help us avoid the individual-crushing ideologies of the past, and through the freedoms individuals can exercise here, and the powers each can command, could help us glimpse the heaven many of us often imagine.

A friend of mine suggests that, implicit in the gospel, there may be a large heavenly reward or spiritual experience promised for making a certain sacrifice of material things. If there were such a promise, the sacrifice might well be worth it. However, I have not seen any such promise in the scriptures or elsewhere. It seems there are a few vague generalizations, mostly referring to heavenly rewards, but with no covenant for any particular reward in this life beyond such things as "health in the navel" and blessings from paying tithing.

The normally devastating results from required collective behavior make it somewhat akin to Abraham being asked to kill his son to show his obedience. The results of carrying out the act would either have wiped out all the more general promises of the future influence of his posterity, or it would have required a great miracle to rectify. Either result is objectionable. In the end, the act was not required, and the potential disaster was averted. Murder and suicide, real or economic, are really not part of the gospel.

Perhaps the economic realm can be viewed the same way as the Abraham story. The willingness to take drastic and destructive economic steps may be of some value as a kind of test of obedience, but the practical devastation of going beyond symbolism makes it highly unlikely to actually be required.

Based on the comments of my friend, the mysticism of the united order appears to be even more embedded in the Mormon society than I feared, and so is all the more worrisome. The expectation of an unspoken and undescribed reward based on an action that is also undescribed in its nature and effect, are together so vague as to be the merest of hints. This is mysticism in my view, and could have damaging effects on society.

A hidden question may be articulated by those who can drag it up from their subconsciousness: "But what if God promises to give us some great spiritual reward or experience or blessing if we will but give up or give away all we have?" In response, the first question to be asked is, has such a promise been given? Where is it described and detailed? Can we act on data we do not have? Even faith has its limits and must have some real data to base itself on.

We might contrast the united order idea with the principle of repentance. Repentance is often said to be the only principle to be taught to this dispensation, and it is clearly spelled out in the scriptures, with numerous examples. The volume of scriptural information leaves little to the realm of mysticism on this most important of doctrines. Heeding the teachings on repentance can have a great effect on a person, changing his life and making him eligible for the assistance of the atonement. In contrast, the united order promise occasionally alluded to, based on some vague principle apparently leading to a total revamping of all society, is supposedly going to be scores of times better than repentance for our understanding, joy, and progression.

It is difficult to accept that conclusion, based on the data we have. Such a radical change ought to require even more scriptural data than we have on repentance.

Supposedly, all things are to be revealed through the mouth of the prophets, and this one has been almost completely skipped.

Any idea that seems to take us out of the mortal bucket of our fallen state, like being translated, might make one very suspicious. The poorly described united order utopia, is sort of like the "perpetual motion machine" of quack scientists, I fear. It simply defies the rules we operate under here -- it is too good to be true, and therefore is false.

The most telling point for me comes back to conflicts concerning the nature of heaven. If we view heaven as the place where ultimate independence is granted along with the power to do enormous things of which we can hardly conceive, how can we square that future with that of a slave here on earth? One would hope that the universe and its levels of beings would be more consistent in principle than that.

If one has been made dependent "for his own good" during his entire mortal life, how would one dare give such a being any independence or powers after this life? He would surely be ill-prepared for it, and would likely do immense damage with any new powers he might have.

Although highly unlikely to work out in practice, it seems theoretically possible to have a society made up of men who would never misuse power given to them. But then we must ask why they would need to have that power assigned to them and why those ruled by them needed to have power taken from them and give to others. (This would require some kind of governmental "taxing and transfer payments" of societal power). Regardless of the strict ethics that might be observed by those involved, postulating such rules for society presupposes that having society divided into the rulers and the ruled is itself crucial for producing the "New Gospel Man" (a concept too chillingly like the "New Soviet Man" of another ideology.) By this logic, independent pastoral nomads such as Abraham would be denied any chance at salvation. Recall that he stayed away from cities for the very reason that he could not live the gospel in such places. Having such a structured society at all is likely to be destructive in and of itself, regardless of the precision with which it is executed. Requiring an army-like organization for all aspects of life is artificial, contrived, and restrictive to individual liberty and growth, and probably bad preparation for heaven. It may be useful to glorify armies when real defense is needed, but carrying that requirement into all aspects of life under the aegis of the gospel is rather difficult to support from the scriptures.

My final summarizing observation on this whole topic of mysticism and the united order, a stark statement of the philosophical problem as I see it, is this: **Many people seem to think that the best way to get close to Christ, and be approved and rewarded by him, is to accept, support, and live Satan's plan!** Or that Satan's plan is really just a better version of Christ's plan! Taking away individual options is the way to salvation!

To me, this nonsense is the great "mystery" embedded in the united order mythology. I simply cannot accept that idea without overwhelming evidence from the scriptures and the prophets, and that evidence is simply not there. Blessings and approval will be given for voluntary and spontaneous help given to the weak and hungry. That is all there is to it. That is the gospel. All else is an unauthorized extension of the scriptures.

Another way to look at the united order myth is to postulate that the people advocating it are really those who want regulation, who want the Law of Moses (carnal, temporal commandments) to save them; they want to be saved by their works only. This "neo-Mosaic" law they seek may the outgrowth of a yearning for a release from the difficult demands of living the gospel in a complex age. They may be seeking to simplify their lives and wish to use the gospel to do it. This retreat from contact with the world is not consistent with our charge to perform missionary work. If they truly wish to help others even more than they do now, (one of the possible reasons for entering into a "united order"), then they are going about it all backwards. The people who need the most help are those outside our own society.

## Chapter notes

[1] *Webster's Third New International Dictionary, Unabridged*, 1976.

[2] Clarence B. Carson, *The World in the Grip of an Idea* (New Rochelle, New York: Arlington House Publishers, 1979), pp. 10-11.

[3] ibid., pp. 465-478.

[4] Alvin Toffler, *The Third Wave* (New York: William Morrow and Company, Inc., 1980).

## CHAPTER 19

# Gini Ratios, Equality, and Developmental Economics

A quote from a recent news magazine presents clearly the eternal battle as to how a nation's resources are to be used:

> When the economy is perking along nicely, both liberal and conservative economists, whose differing philosophies have long fueled the national economic debate, bring their special brands of gloom to the party. Members of the liberal faith, for decades led by John Kenneth Galbraith, cry that distribution is unfair: ever-bigger slices are going to the rich, ever-smaller slices to the poor, and the widening gap spells economic trouble. From their side, conservative economists voice a different complaint: good times perhaps, but the government's proportion of the national product is forever increasing, denying us the therapy of a free market. The conservative exhortation to every administration, forcefully delivered over many years, by Nobel laureate Milton Friedman, is--get the government out of the way. Let the rising tide lift all the boats.
>
> But the disagreement in principle--that perpetual conflict between fairness and growth-- is muted when the economy has been going through a storm. Today, liberal and conservative economists alike are coming to a surprisingly broad consensus on what subterranean deficiencies during the 1980s caused the recession, and what economic policies can help bring both fairness and growth during the 1990s.[1]

The above current event commentary applies equally well to the Brigham Young era. It seems that many wish to believe that Brigham Young chose the "fair" or redistribution way. In fact, he was much wiser than that, and chose the growth path, the same logic used by the welfare plan of today. As implied by Pres. Romney's strong words against the political versions of "welfare" (quoted in chapter 25), the church, in any era, cannot complete its mission if it gets mired in "fair" programs of redistribution.

This policy against forced redistribution has been in effect from the beginning of the organized church in this dispensation. The author of the *Comprehensive History of the Church* (CHC) should not have been so surprised that Joseph Smith was opposed to communal property sharing:

"COMMUNITY OF GOODS" AT KIRTLAND
In Kirtland the experiment of holding all property in common and living as one family -- an experiment already existing before the gospel was preached to that people by Elders Cowdery, Pratt *et al* -- had been continued up to the arrival of the Prophet. It might have been expected that this system of life, having some color of justification both upon New Testament and Book of Mormon authority [Acts 2:41-47; also Acts 4:32-37; Acts 5:1-7. 3 Nephi 26:19, 20. 4 Nephi 1:1-3.], would have appealed to him. On the contrary however he advised against continuance of the experiment, and tactfully brought about the disorganization of "The Family." CHC 1:243.

The statement "It might have been expected that this system of life ... would have appealed to him" probably tells us more about the author of the CHC than it does about Joseph Smith. Many others have presumed to impose their ideological preferences on the lives of the prophets rather than find out what the prophets really taught and felt.

Joseph Smith commented on the phenomenon of the "the big fish eating up all the little fish" in the Kirtland setting. (HC 6:33 JS Sept 14, 1843 Nauvoo; HC 1:146-7 Feb 1831). It may be that he observed that in "The Family," the uncertain property boundaries caused by the "pooling" of property meant that the more aggressive and grasping managed to claim for their own use a larger than average share of the available property. (This may be like the "some are more equal than others" comment made concerning the so-called equality under totalitarian governments.) In a setting where property boundaries and ownership are more clearly delineated, this accumulation by manipulation and exploitation would be harder to do. The charge of exploitation is often made against the rich in any setting, but if they acquired their property by fair means, that is by free trade or purchase, rather than by extortion or deception, then they are entitled to keep it. In communist/socialist countries where property has been wrested or kept from individuals by force, and where private ownership of property is forbidden or severely restricted, obviously those who control the government of the country control all or nearly all property. A man would thus have a large incentive to become a government leader by any means, fair or foul. His chance of gaining huge economic rewards would be far more than where strict private property rules are enforced. Some business leaders in the U.S. are paid large salaries, but none can begin to compete with the billions of dollars plundered by the leaders of totalitarian or highly centralized countries.

In the Summer 1978 issue of *BYU Studies* is an article about the use of Gini ratios to measure the equality-inducing effects of Brigham Young's programs on certain cities in Utah. The Gini ratio is a statistical technique designed to measure differences in economic status among a population. The study expected to find that equality was enhanced by the Brigham Young programs, but instead it found that equality was not enhanced. On the contrary, they resulted in less equality; people became more unequal rather than less.[2] This may seem very strange, and a strong indictment of those programs, a basis for saying that he failed in his goals. However, that is only true if one persists in the idea that equality was a prime goal of Brigham Young. The simple truth is that equality was not a significant goal of Brigham Young, except perhaps in opportunity for education. In chapter 11 it is made exceptionally clear that Brigham Young rejected forced economic equality for all, at least during the last 25 years of his time as prophet.

How can this be? The answer is very simple. Current-day experts in third world economic development have found a clear pattern of difference between successful and unsuccessful developmental countries. The evidence shows that only if the talented engineering and management ranks of society are rewarded well and fully for their labors, can a country ever achieve or sustain a significant growth rate. This means, of course, that there will be very large differences between the poorest and the richest. But the rich will tend to wish to repeat and expand their successes, and will wisely re-invest much of their newly-acquired wealth, to the benefit of the entire country.

In other words, in the Utah setting, rather than attribute the increased inequality of income to exploitation by the stronger, we should consider another possibility. It appears from extensive modern studies that the beginning of economic growth in developing countries is always accompanied by an increase in inequality of income: "The first effect of technical progress ... is to increase the inequality of the distribution of income" as skilled engineers and managers begin to appear and to command higher salaries.[3] The long-term positive benefits of growth seem to justify Brigham Young's policies, however inconsistent they may have been with equality.

As explored at length in chapter 21, Brigham Young preferred to work with rich men than with poor men. They were more responsive and obedient. They had already caught his vision and had gained the skills and resources to help carry it out. He often advised those with less knowledge and skill to put themselves and their property under the direction of those wiser.

Massive recent evidence from the eastern bloc countries shows that every socialist or communist government is doomed to poverty if they actually enforce any of their "equality" ideology. Apparently, Brigham Young sensed this truth early in the game, and adjusted his programs accordingly. Contrary to the conventional wisdom on the subject, Brigham Young's real goal was to maximize the economic differences among the people so that economic growth and overall concentrated strength could be maximized and the saints' survival as a people in the world be made sure. That survival was the overwhelmingly important goal, not some inward-looking ideological "feel-good" goal of all being the same. In spite of his great time commitments to general church business, Brigham Young was himself a very wealthy man through his prodigious management and organizational skills. He wished all to go and do likewise, but few knew how or cared or dared to try.

Recent studies of socialist and Marxist political parties outside the Soviet bloc show that they have not only come to recognize the deficiencies of the totalitarian governments, but also see the weaknesses of their attempts at a "middle ground." Perhaps most remarkable of all is their recognition of the necessity of inequality to foster economic growth. The rather long quote below represents a distillation of much philosophical study and practical experience:

No Third Way:
A Comparative Perspective on the Left
Seymour Martin Lipset

While the attention of the world has been focused on the startling transformation in the communist countries, equally important if less dramatic shifts have been occurring in the non-communist parties of the left. Although less noteworthy, since they do not involve revolutionary economic and political changes, they are as significant ideologically, for they represent a withdrawal from the centralized redistributionist doctrines of the democratic left. Their record confirms the conclusion of the Pierre Mauroy, prime minister of France's first majority Socialist government, who noted in the spring of 1990: "We thought we could find a third way, but it turned out there isn't one." In country after country, socialist and other left parties have taken the ideological road back to capitalism. This movement to the right, well advanced in many countries, stands in contrast to our own traditionally moderate left party, the Democrats, in the last decade. Although opposed to socialism, and operating within the most antistatist society in the industrialized world, the Democrats have moved left, in direct contrast to left-of-center parties elsewhere.

This paper beings with a review of events around the social democratic world and ends by asking why the story of party principles and programmatic shifts is so different between the left in the United States and that in most of the other industrialized countries. How can this conundrum be explained?

## The Comparative Story: The Social Democrats Move Right

Beginning with the German Social Democrats in their Bade Godesberg platform in 1959, and gathering speed in the last decade, most of the overseas left parties have reversed their traditional advocacy of state ownership and domination in favor of market economy, tax reduction, monetarism, and deregulation. Many emphasize that increased productivity, rather than income redistribution policies, is the best way to improve the situation of the economically disadvantaged. Indian political scientist Radhakvishnan Nayar notes unhappily that "few among the Left, in the West at least," question free market beliefs: "The accent of the current debate inside the Western Left is how it can survive within a liberal capitalist system now assumed to be home and dry." Marxist historian Eric Hobsbawn points out: "Today few socialist parties are happy to be reminded of their historic commitment to a society based on public ownership and planning. ... In the 1980s we find, probably for the first time in history, some nominally socialist parties whose leaders compete with Mrs. Thatcher in extolling the supremacy of the market and in increasing social inequality.... [I]n 1990 most socialists ... competed with each other in the rhetoric of the supermarket." The extent of these developments across almost every democratic country is worth exploring in more detail.

### *Australia and New Zealand*

The comparative story may start in Australia, a country whose Labor Party won majorities in a number of states as early as the 1890s. Labor parties have governed the Antipodes, including New Zealand, during the past decade. Coming to office in societies with a strong commitment to extensive welfare state programs and wage increases, these parties faced the dysfunctional effects on economic development of high taxes, government deficits, inflation, and steady growth in wages. Under Prime Minister Robert Hawke and Treasurer Paul Keating, the Labor government in Australia cut interest rates and income taxes, pursued "economic deregulation," and formed a successful accord with the trade unions to limit wage inflation, so that real wages have fallen by at least one percent each year since they took office.

Hawke has gone around the world looking for investment capital, noting that his administration has maintained a policy of reducing the real income of Australian workers. He proclaims the new social democratic gospel that profits, savings, and dividends, rather than high taxes and wages, produce the capital for economic growth. Hawke contends that "if a social democratic government, such as mine, is going ... to do as much for them [the poor outside the productive process] as we possibly can, then we have to have an economy which is growing as strongly as possible and I think in the early days [of the movement] some didn't understand that.... [Y]ou have to be an idiot or just so blind with prejudice not to understand that you've got to have a healthy and growing private sector if you're going to look after the majority of the people."

Complaining about an unjustifiably severe tax structure under his conservative predecessors, Hawke states that to give the private sector "the greatest incentive to invest and employ" it is necessary to get rid of the "appallingly high tax rate, 60 percent of the top bracket, which Labor brought down to 49, and plans to lower further. Beyond changes on the tax side ... we've ... [been] deregulating the economy." On the subject of wage reduction, Hawke argues: "[T]he very reason why we are growing so strongly, why our employment growth rate is twice as fast as the rest of the industrialized world, is precisely because the Australian workers in this country have accepted lower wage levels.... [T]he move in the share of national income away from wages towards profits ... has enabled us to grow.... In September 1990, Hawke and Keating announced a program of privatizing portions of the banking system as well as airlines and telecommunications. A subsequent party conference approved these policies and "officially abandoned its commitment to public ownership in favour of a policy reminiscent of early Thatcherism."

The New Zealand story has been similar. Returning to power in 1984, the Labour party, in office until October 1990, followed the most Thatcherite policy among Western governments, including the original in Britain. In its first year, the new administration "terminated all the exchange controls..., abolished all the price controls, wage controls, interest-rate controls, most of the industrial subsidies, agricultural subsidies, export subsidies and state-corporation subsidies introduced or intensified by the previous conservative government.... It ... cut income tax across the board. This Labour government is also dismantling one of the oldest ... welfare states in the world.... The stated objectives of the policy are to turn New Zealand from an overcontrolled economy with high income tax, into a freer-market economy with low income tax; and to allow each enterprise ... to be exposed to domestic and foreign competition."

An article in a socialist magazine emphasizes that the Labour government continued to follow a free market economic policy. Prime Minister David Lange argued in 1986 that "social democrats must accept the existence of economic inequality because it is the engine which drives the economy." The government removed rent controls and dropped regulations on banking, finance, and transportation. "Almost all supports for agriculture were removed.... Transport was deregulated ... and mergers were regularly approved.... Universality was ended for all social programs; the needy were targeted.... Changes in the tax system ended the tradition of taxation according to ability to pay." Many state enterprises were privatized, including airlines, forestry, oil, coal, and electricity.

Although a declining economy, reflecting world conditions, sharply reduced support for the Labour Party, the government responded by following the Australian model. In midyear 1990 it "struck a deal with the Council of Trade Unions under which it is to limit wage demands to just 2 percent for the coming year, less than half the current rate of inflation." This was reported by the president of the Council of Trade Unions as "an agreement on growth strategy." He said "the agreement safeguarded existing jobs."

These economic changes do not mean the party has dropped its social concerns. *The Economist* comments that Lange "wants to make New Zealand richer so that he can afford to spend more money on what he regards as modern socialist causes": better education, a cleaner environment, and improvement in the situation of a "Maori underclass." He also has "established a Guaranteed Minimum Family Income, set originally at $250 per week for a family with one child." Labour has tried to retain support among the left intelligentsia by opposition to nuclear power and weaponry.

### Southern Europe

Similar stories may be told of other regions. Summing up the situation of the socialists in four southern European countries (Greece, Italy, Portugal, and Spain), Tom Gallagher and Allan Williams note that "in each party by the late 1970s, the Marxist... statutes in the constitutions of the parties [were] being deleted or watered down or simply ignored.... [R]adical economic prescriptions and redistributive policies were absent or else were set out in an opportunistic fashion. However the phrase is defined, none of the governments attempted to implement a specifically socialist economic policy." The four socialist parties, when in office, "all displayed a high degree of economic orthodoxy..., by implication, this means there has been little attempt to secure a substantial shift of resources to the working class, or to restrict the operations of private vs. socially owned capital." In the Portuguese case, when the conservative government replaced the socialists in 1988, the new right-wing prime minister "scolded the PS [Socialist Party] for having been too austere in its economic programme." In Greece, the Panhellenic Socialist Movement (PASOK), which held office from 1981 to 1989, also followed "an austerity programme" from 1984 on, that depressed the income of wage earners while introducing tax "incentives for new investment." A more detailed look at the patterns in Italy, which has had a socialist coalition government and large communist opposition, and Spain, with a socialist majority, is revealing.

In Italy, Bettino Craxi, the leader of a historically minor Socialist Party (PSI), much smaller than the Communist Party (PCI), became head of the coalition government with the Christian Democrats in 1983, and reversed the tradition of statism dating from Mussolini's rule. The public sector had been extended by the Christian Democrats, who emphasized corporatism and communitarianism, in the forty plus governments they headed since the end of the war. In the 1970s, Craxi, seeking a distinctive role for his party, and faced by the massive strength of the church-supported Christian Democrats and the working-class based communists, modified the party's socialist ideology. It "rapidly moved to the center of the spectrum," proclaiming to be "the only 'modern' party in the country and the only... [one] able to represent the rising group who were products of the country's increasingly advanced economic development." These include the "highly successful small businessmen, entrepreneurs and professionals." Craxi's government lasted three years, a record among postwar regimes. It is noteworthy for starting a process of privatization of industry and pressing the unions for major concessions. It cut back on wage increases, regulated strikes, and reformed the welfare state, "gradually increasing the retirement age and adding tougher standards for disability pensions." Rent control was gradually relaxed in order to open the housing market.

The Italian Socialist Party has gained electorally to the point where it now threatens the PCI dominance of the left. For the first time since the war, the PSI secured a higher percentage of the votes than the communists, in the May 1989 local government elections; 19.1 percent compared with 16.9. During the 1970s, the PCI generally gained about one-third of the vote, while the PSI hovered near the 10 percent level.

As the Italian communists declined in votes and membership from their high point in 1976, they sought to modernize their appeal by emphasizing their independence from the Soviet Union, commitment to a multiparty pluralistic system, approval of Italian membership in NATO, and, increasingly, rejection of Marxism. The latter was marked by explicit recognition of the virtues of a market economy, even before Gorbachev came to office in the Soviet Union. In early 1989, Daniel Singer noted that the party had given up "attacking capitalism. It has become a social democratic party, in all but name,... [and] proposes to leave the Communist group in the European Parliament in Strasbourg in favor of the Socialist one."

Achille Occhetto, the PCI secretary, proclaims, "We are not part of an international Communist movement.... There is absolutely nothing left to Communism as a unitary and organic system." The ultimate change was to give up its name, as Secretary Occhetto proposed "to 'refound' the party under a new name" and "to join the Socialist International." In October 1990 the PCI was renamed the Party of the Democratic Left. Occhetto insists: "We want democracy, no longer as a means to achieve socialism, but to achieve democracy as a universal end in itself. If our party were in America, we might call ourselves the Liberal Party." And in commenting favorably about the American political system, he describes it as "a system of alternatives, of weights balanced against counterweights, that allows moral questions to be solved better" than in Italy.

In Spain, Socialist Premier Felipe Gonzalez, elected, to a third term in 1989, converted his party, Marxist in its initial post-Franco phase, to support privatization, the free market, and NATO. Some years ago, he noted in a near Churchillian formulation that a competitive free market economy is marked by greed and corruption, and results in exploitation of the weak, but "*capitalism is the least bad economic system in existence.*" More recently, in 1988, he commented, "My problem is not that there are rich people, but that there are poor people," in seeking to justify an emphasis on economic growth rather than redistribution. Gonzalez's successful efforts to foster growth and reduce inflation have involved policies described as making his government "look somewhat to the right of Mrs. Thatcher's." They include "low wage increases" and "tight money" policies that have led to conflicts with the unions. Following his narrow electoral victory in October 1989, Gonzalez reemphasized the need to "pursue policies attractive to Spanish business executives and foreign investors," to continue the country's high economic growth rate. These hit the intended target. In reviewing the factors underlying the Socialist triumph of the polls, Alan Riding, a *New York Times* correspondent, quotes a leading industrialist: "The new right supports the Socialists. They... are completely committed to the market economy."

*France*

The same wave of ideological and programmatic moderation is cresting north of the Alps and Pyrenees. In France, socialists have "come to realize that the creation of wealth must be given priority over the re-distribution of wealth to the less well-off."

The French Socialists (PS), under Francois Mitterrand, sought in 1981 to implement their historic commitments to nationalization and income redistribution, but witnessed these changes producing economic reverses "and by the spring of 1983 they had effectively reversed almost every priority of their original plan." Minister Jacques Delors acknowledged: "The Socialists are in the process of making the adjustment that the Barre government [the conservative administration they attacked and defeated in 1981] did not dare to do, politically or in terms of the social classes." Nationalization turned out to be an economic disaster. Faced with the need to compete on the international market, "the government adopted a program of controlled austerity. Wages were deindexed, which meant that their real value fell and profits absorbed all of the positive gains from productivity."

Mitterrand won reelection in 1988. His new prime minister, Michel Rocard, the leader of the social democratic forces in the party, resembles Craxi and Gonzalez in his approach to politics and economics. He, too, argues that road to social and economic justice is paved with increased investment enhanced by tax cuts. He and his finance minister, Pierre Beregovoy, have emphasized the need for wage restraint, while putting off income redistribution.

In the 1980s the Socialists moved away from their historic hostility to business as they came to acknowledge that entrepreneurship is the power behind increased productivity, behavior minimally present in state-owned industry: "Once the Socialists have understood that the goose of capitalism did not automatically lay the golden egg, they began to revise their ideas of the importance of enterprise, the entrepreneur and profit." Jean-Pierre

Chevenement, as minister of industry and research, noted the need to give "industry the respect it has always been begrudged in our country."

During the 1988 election, Mitterrand and Rocard took the unusual step of arguing that it would be bad for the country if one party, their own, had a majority in Parliament as well as the presidency. The president said, "It is not healthy for just one party to govern." In effect, they argued that middle-of-the-road centrist government is preferable to control by an ideological tendency. Rocard in fact publicly promised an "opening to the centre." Not surprising is the survey finding that as of the start of the 1990s, "61 percent of the French public see no difference between left and right."

### Germany and Austria

The Social Democrats of Germany and Austria rejected Marxism in favor of populist, rather than class, allegiance sooner than most of their continental brethren. As noted earlier, the German party set the path for the other affiliates of the International in its 1959 Bad Godesberg program. A recent history of Germany notes: "The program represented a fundamental shift in philosophical direction for the party, from primary emphasis on Marxism and Marxist solutions for problems of social and economic life, to primary emphasis on recognizing the achievements of liberal capitalism.... It therefore rejected the goal of state ownership of the means of production." As political scientist Russell Dalton emphasizes, "Karl Marx would have been surprised to read this Godesberg program and learn that free economic competition was one of the essential conditions of a social democratic economic policy." Speaking in 1976, Social Democratic Chancellor Helmut Schmidt noted his party's interests in extending profits: "The profits of enterprises today are the investments of tomorrow, and the investments of tomorrow are the employment of the day after." The Social Democrats (SPD), when heading the government from 1969 to 1982, did not press for structural or other major changes. Proposed "reforms such as vacations from work for educational purposes, the building of investment funds in the workers' hands -- as a contrasting program to nationalization -- ... were largely dropped from the [Schmidt] government's agenda." To control the national debt, the cabinet in the early 1980s publicly considered major cuts in social services for the lowest strata and in unemployment insurance, programs adopted by their Christian Democrat successors.

After leaving office, the SPD sought to evaluate its basic commitments. In 1984, a party commission established to analyze the future of the welfare state noted that Social Democrats could "defend the welfare state successfully against its conservative and liberal critics only if they call publicly for its comprehensive reform." It concluded that "the economy simply will not support a social policy that aims solely at increasing the relative share of the social budget in the national income." Just to maintain existing social services will require "a substantial increase in taxes," which the commission doubted would be "either possible or desirable."

During the 1980s, the SPD lost electoral support to the Greens. In reaction, at a national conference in December 1989, it adopted the Berlin Programme "described as Bad Godesberg plus feminism and environmentalism." It notes that within "the democratically established setting, the market and competition are indispensable. The incalculable variety of economic decision-making is effectively coordinated through the market.... Competition benefits consumers and their free purchasing choice. The market is an instrument for attaining a balance between supply and demand." Oskar Lafontaine, vice-president and the party's candidate for chancellor in the 1990 election, whose major following is among the "new middle class," seeks to deemphasize government intervention in the economic process. He states categorically: "Either you abolish the system, or you stick to the rules of the game."

These policies have won the SPD support among some "modern entrepreneurs," most notably Daimler-Benz (Mercedes) board president Edward Reuter, who is a dues-paying party member.

The Austrian party has held office either alone or in coalition with its major rival since World War II. The country has more public ownership than any other Western society as a result of the nationalization of all German-owned property at the end of the war. But the nationalized firms have operated like private companies with respect to investment decisions, collective bargaining, and dividends. The government has not attempted economic planning. Regardless of electoral outcomes, business, unions, and government have adhered to a corporatist alliance policy designed to maintain economic stability, avoid strikes, and foster growth. The party-linked unions have "accepted lowish wage settlements and so helped keep costs down." The party in government "pursues politics that focus on growth rather than redistribution." From the mid-1980s on, as the country faced increasing economic difficulties and large budget deficits, the Socialist-led administration under Franz Vranitzky carried out a policy of gradual denationalization and deregulation. State-owned banks and industries have either been sold to private companies, both domestic and foreign, or their shares have been floated on Austrian and foreign stock exchanges. These include energy, railway, mining, steel, plastics, and other businesses. Socialist Finance Minister Ferdinand Lacina has reduced income taxes and is pressing to reform the pension system to allow private schemes.

Both German-speaking parties continue to adhere to the Bad Godesberg orientation. They have accepted the monetarist tight money policies of the Bundesbank (which Austria follows since the schilling is tied to the mark). Given the existence of three parties, which makes it almost impossible to project majority governments, the Social Democrats do not differ much in domestic policy terms from their major Christian Democratic and People's Party rivals. Essentially the national politics of the two countries are characterized by competition between the center-left and the center-right. In Germany, the Socialists have been more critical of the close American connection and more supportive of environmental reforms than their major opponents.[4]

Apparently, the closest thing there is to a "third way" is the practice of burdening "free" enterprises with the maximum levels of taxation and regulation they can bear without contraction or collapsing. The result of a government's search for this "optimal" line is minimal growth and change, minimal research and development, and stagnation. Major elements of technology and the economy are frozen at a fixed stage and time. Progress is prevented and "rust belts" are created of ancient and obsolete factories. Some say this is good and call it a "postindustrial" period.

This rigid focus on a single economic goal and method was one of the great errors of Soviet communism. It created an economy that was frozen in the distant past. Eventually it became totally obsolete and collapsed as irrelevant, it was so far behind the advances in other countries having more freedom to change.

In trying to understand Brigham Young, the lessons of history should be helpful. He could not change by decree the laws of economics, human nature, and human relations any more than the other leaders of countries who probably wished that they could. The Lord apparently did intervene with major miracles in many past dispensations, but has been more sparing in our day. The fact that nearly all current cultures have reached similar conclusions concerning economics after much expensive experimentation should be significant to us in our own search for economic/religious truth.

## Chapter notes

[1] Walter Guzzardi, "Unlikely Allies Agree on the Economy: Conservatives and Liberals say these are the moves to make," *Time Magazine*, July 20, 1992 vol. 140 no. 3 p. 42.

[2] L. Dwight Israelsen, "An Economic Analysis of the United Order," *BYU Studies*, Summer 1978, pp. 536-562.

[3] Everett E. Hagen, *The Economics of Development* (Homewood, Ill.: Richard D. Irwin, Inc., 1980), p. 38.

[4] David Chirot, ed., *The Crisis of Leninism and the Decline of the Left: The Revolutions of 1989* (Seattle: University of Washington Press, 1991), p. 183-190.

## CHAPTER 20

# Poverty and Inequality - Reason and Cure

Brigham Young had some strong feelings on the topic of the cause and cure for poverty. Many of the saints suffered from poverty because of their many travels to get to Utah, their losses on the way, and the lack of preparation and education for their new labors in the west. His general view was that the poor continued in their condition because they were uneducated and unwise. To solve their problems, they needed training and direction, not handouts, first, because there were few "handouts" to be had, and, second, because the region needed to develop the basis for long-term growth and economic development. Giving the poor material goods, as in any kind of leveling process, would only cause loss to the community of needed capital, and would encourage slothfulness among the poor.

He spoke on the topic often. A discourse dated January 17, 1858, given while the federal army was on its way to Utah, includes the statement that "The great majority of men and women do not know how to take care of themselves."

JUDGEMENT ACCORDING TO WORKS —— TEMPORAL NATURE OF DIVINE
REVELATIONS —— TEMPORAL RESOURCES AND DUTIES OF THE SAINTS ETC.
A discourse by President BRIGHAM YOUNG, delivered in the
Tabernacle, Great Salt Lake City,
January 17, 1858.
REPORTED BY G. D. WATT.

We have heard much in regard to the knowledge and understanding of this people, —— also of the nations of the earth; and it is very true that the best of us have only commenced to learn true principles. We are but children in the kingdom of God. We understand, in a great measure, the knowledge that is in the world: we have been brought up in the wisdom the world professes, and that we understand. But the things of God are so directly in opposition to the vain imaginations of the inhabitants of the earth, that it is hard for people to learn them. They remove our erroneous traditions from us. At the same time, all the morality, and good works, and good thoughts and words that tend to good, that are in the world, are of the Lord. Honest hearts, the world over, desire to know the right way. They have sought for it, and still seek it. There have been people upon the earth all the time who sought diligently with all their hearts to know the ways of the Lord. Those individuals have produced good, inasmuch as they had the ability. And to believe that there has been no virtue, no truth, no good upen [upon] the earth for centuries, until the Lord revealed the Priesthood through Joseph the Prophet, I should say is wrong. There has been more or less virtue and righteousness upen [upon] the earth at all times, from the days of Adam until now. That we all believe. Men who have lived without the Priesthood will be judged according to their works, as well as those who have had the privilege of it. That is our doctrine. That is what the Lord has told us, through his servants, from the beginning. No matter where they have lived, or to what nation they have belonged, all people will be judged according to the works or deeds done in the body.

Honest hearts produce honest actions —— holy desires produce corresponding outward works. That is what we understand and believe; yet the traditions of the fathers are so diverse from the holy Priesthood, that it is hard for people to learn even the smaller things pertaining to the kingdom of God —— one of the smallest items pertaining to life. If we should have ability to sustain ourselves here on the earth, we certainly should have to live; for if we have not the ability to live, we certainly should pass behind the vail. In that case, we could not be capable of doing good in our present organization. As you have often been told, and as we believe, good men and good women ought to live the longest on the earth and set good examples, teach good doctrines, and produce righteousness.

Individuals or a community that have not the ability to preserve themselves in this life have no power to perform works to be judged by; consequently, there is no judgment passed upon them for deeds done in this probation. The duty of a good people is to know how to preserve themselves in this life. The first revelation given to Adam was of a temporal nature. Most of the revelations he received pertained to his life here. That was also the case in the revelations to Noah. We have but very few of the instructions the Lord gave to Enoch concerning his city; but, doubtless, most of the revelations he received pertained to a temporal nature and condition. And certainly the revelations Noah received, so far as in our possession, almost exclusively pertained to this life. The same principle was carried out in the days of Moses, and in the days of his fathers, Abraham, Isaac, and Jacob. We may say that eight or nine-tenths of the doctrines and principles set forth in the revelations given to those men were of a temporal nature.

As soon as Moses was called upon to go and deliver Israel, the revelations the Lord gave to him were of a temporal nature, pertaining to the temporal life of the children of Israel —— instructing Moses how to deliver them from bondage and lead them from the servile state in which they then were. He taught them in the same manner while they were travelling through the wilderness; and so it continued down to the days of the judges, and then to Saul, whom the Lord permitted them to make a king, and then through the teachings of the Prophets. The greatest recorded digression from that course was when the Saviour came. He repeatedly alluded to a spiritual kingdom, in his sayings to his brethren. The people had become so corrupt that it was all useless to then endeavour to establish a literal kingdom of God on the earth. The children of Abraham had wandered so far from the true doctrine, the Priesthood, the principles, and ordinances that the Lord had revealed, that the Saviour had not opportunity to more than drop a hint, as it were, about a temporal kingdom. Yet the idea of a temporal kingdom was so indelibly riveted upon the minds of his disciples, that they supposed he alluded to it, and that when the Saviour should make his appearance, he would actually establish a literal kingdom on this earth and reign over it. The institutions and traditions which had been handed down pertained to a temporal kingdom, and they could not see that the corruptions and wickedness of the people were so great that he could not teach or suggest anything that they could understand pertaining to a temporal kingdom; therefore he alluded to a spiritual kingdom —— the kingdom of God that should be set up in the heart. And those principles taught to the people and received by them would gather them together in the latter days, when he could prepare and organize a literal kingdom on the earth.

The first revelations given to Joseph were of a temporal character, pertaining to a literal kingdom on the earth. And most of the revelations he received in the early part of his ministry pertained to what the few around him should do in this or in that case —— when and how they should perform their duties; at the same time calling upon them to preach the Gospel and diffuse the Spirit and principles of the kingdom of God, that their eyes might be open to see and gather the people together —— that they might begin and organize a literal, temporal organization on the earth. All that has been done, and has been done by the wisdom of God. The wisdom revealed through Joseph was the wisdom of our Father in heaven, —— it was not of himself.

*Poverty and Inequality - Reason and Cure*

The revelations to us teach us to first cleanse our hearts —— to purify ourselves, in order to have our eyes sufficiently opened to see the kingdom of God; for, without the spiritual birth referred to in the New Testament, we cannot see the kingdom of God. The revelations to Joseph were —— Go forth, my servants, preach the Gospel by the power of the Holy Ghost, and open the eyes of the people, that they may see the kingdom of God, and not look into eternity to see the Father seated upon his throne and the angels around him, nor seek to know what he is doing there. The people need teaching by the power of the Holy Ghost sent down from heaven, that their eyes may be open to see that the Lord is commencing a literal Kingdom upon the earth. When they can discern that, then they have the opportunity to be born of water, to enter into this kingdom. Nearly all the teachings to us pertain to this life; and if we have not ability to preserve our lives in our present existence, what can we do here to promote the kingdom of God on the earth; or to prepare the earth or the people for the coming of the Son of Man? Nothing. Consequently our labour is chiefly a temporal labour.

Brother Taylor has enquired how we are to be clothed another year? We have either to obtain new clothes or to wear those we have now. Some one may say, "My clothes will not last another year." Perhaps they will, if you will take good care of them.

When we first came here, the people were told, and many saw and believed it as much then as they can now, that the Lord in his providence led the people into these mountains to separate them from the Gentile world, in order that he might establish his kingdom —— his laws, and commence his Zion in the mountains, where his people could have but little connection with the world. They were taught that when they first came here; and now the prospect is very fair for separating us from the rest of the world, and most of the people can see it. They were taught then as much as they are taught now, that it was necessary to go to and provide for ourselves. Do any of the brethren who came here ten years ago last July remember that you were instructed that every facility that we could need was here in the elements? —— that the gold, the silver, and the iron were in these mountains? —— that the wool, the flax, the silk, the cotton, and everything necessary to sustain man were in the elements around us? "What, is silk here?" Yes, in as great abundance as in any part of the earth; and the finest broadcloth is here, and everything to make life desirable is here.

It is for the people to go to and develop the resources surrounding us. Sugar, starch, and glue are the chief ingredients in the sustenance of man. The saccharine matter is in everything that grows here: it is in the vegetables and in the animals. We have as good beef as there is in the world, furnishing gluten —— a substance that acts its part in sustaining man. We can raise as good potatoes and wheat as can be raised in any other part of the earth; also other products affording starch, and all the necessary variety and quality of articles of food. We can make sugar from the beet; but we are now cultivating the Chinese sugar-cane, which produces as good a sweet as any we have imported. We have the materials for feeding the body. And as to clothing, we can produce as good wool here as they can in any part of the world; but we must have the sheep to enable us to do so. And we must sow flax and plant cotton for the manufacture of linen and cotton cloth; but the elements are here from which they all will grow.

Import silkworms and mulberry trees, and you will find that this is as good a country and climate in which to raise silk as any on the face of the earth. Do some understand this? Yes, there are persons here from the Eastern States who have raised silkworms and manufactured silk; and here are scores and hundreds of silk manufacturers from the old country. Why, then, do we not have silk? Because no man takes steps to organize certain elements into the silk. All this was told you in the beginning, and why did not men understand?

<u>You may take the Latter-day Saints, as a whole, and they have but very little good, sound, worldly sense.</u> Look over this congregation, and then go through the Territory, and you can find thousands that, during the first four years of our settlement here, flooded these

valleys with waggons and cattle, and every facility for raising what we needed. We drove in the sheep, brought the flax-seed, and this, that, and the other useful articles. But what did we see? Men, women, and children run to California to get gold. They were then told what I can now prove. "Go to California, if you will; we will not curse you — we will not injure nor destroy you, but we will pity you. If you must go for gold, and that is your god, go, and I will promise you one thing: Every man that stays here and pays attention to his business will be able, within ten years, to buy out four of those who leave for the gold-mines." Since then some of those persons have come cringing back, and thinking, "O dear, I declare I wish the brethren could not know that I had been away! I want to appear as though I had not gone to California, and to be full of good works and faith." Poor, ignorant, pusillanimous creatures! They come whining back and want to be considered in full fellowship, after leaving this place to which our God has led us, and after having used their means to feast and build up the Gentiles.

Brother Heber and I told the company that went to San Bernardino with Amasa Lyman, that they would never reach here again without help from this people, and we are now sending all the teams we can raise from the southern settlements to bring them back. Why? Because they cannot stay there, and they are not able to remove. They were told at the start that they would have to renounce their religion, or else come whining back to these valleys. You may take all who have unadvisedly gone from this Territory, (and hundreds and thousands have so gone,) and I believe that I alone am able to buy the whole of them, though when I came here I had but very little property, except what I owed for. I also believe that brother Kimball and many others who have listened to what is taught now own more property than the whole of those characters. They could not believe that I knew enough to instruct them in temporal affairs. Do they now believe that I do? They are obliged to admit it, though some think, "Really, I do not know whether it is so or not." What are those persons good for now?

Obedience is one of the plainest, most every-day and home principles that you ever thought or knew anything about. In the first place, learn that you have a father, and then learn strict obedience to that parent. Is not that a plain, domestic, home principle? How long will it take the men and women here to learn it? You have learned, from year to year, scores, if not hundreds of principles of the Gospel taught; and one of the first principles to be learned by the Saints is to be of one heart and mind, to obey your leaders, to obey the Lord. If you have leaders who do not teach you the words of life and salvation who do not give you the words of the Lord, why not have faith sufficient to remove them out of the way and have better men? If this people are righteous and have any leaders that are not capable of dictating you, why not stretch your faith to the heavens for God to remove them and give you men that are capable of leading you?

Could I make a brother in the Church believe, after passing through the troubles in Missouri, after again being driven from our homes in Nauvoo, Illinois, and after being led to this secret retreat and sustained all the time by the matchless power of our God, that the love of riches would have so blunted the minds of many as to cause them to run to California after gold? Why not have stayed here, where we could have improved this Territory three times as much as we have? We could have extended our settlements still farther on the right and on the left. But no; they must run and leave us. And many of those that have tarried have but a little more confidence, when they have improved upon and learned the lesson taught by those who have left.

The great majority of men and women do not know how to take care of themselves. Let me refer the whole of you to a circumstance in winter quarters. We left Nauvoo in February, 1846, made our own roads through Iowa, except some 40 or 50 miles, built bridges, cut down timber, turned out 500 men to go to Mexico, came this side of the Missouri river, and there wintered. How did you live there? Do you know how you got anything to eat? Brethren came to me, saying, "We must go to Missouri. Can we not take our families and go to Missouri and get work?" Do you know, to this day, how you lived? I will tell you, and then you will remember it. I had not five dollars in money to start with; but I went to work and built a mill, which I knew we should want only for a few months, that cost 3,600 dollars. I gave notice that I would employ every man and pay him for his labour. If I had a sixpence, I turned it into 25 cents; and a half-bushel of potatoes I turned into half-a-bushel of wheat. How did I do that? By faith. I went to brother Neff, who had just come in the place, and asked him for and received 2,600 dollars, though he did not know where the money was going. He kept the mill another year, and it died on his hands. I say, God bless him for ever! for it was the money he brought from Pennsylvania that preserved thousands of men, women, and children from starving. I handled and dictated it, and everything went off smoothly and prosperously.

Can you sustain yourselves? Yes. How can you clothe and feed yourselves? Keep Gentiles out of here, and not permit any more supplies to come from them; and then you will raise sheep and take care of them and their wool; then you will raise cotton and flax, and dress the lint. We have women who know how to manufacture flax into thread and the finest cloth in this house. Why do you not make linen? "Because we can turn a calf on to the range, and after awhile sell it for 20 or 30 dollars and buy store goods." That course is temporal ruination to this people. It is a far greater injury than benefit for us to purchase imported goods. Shut down the gate and make your own hats, bonnets, and every other article of wearing apparel. We have the furs and all necessary facilities for making every article we need. We can also make our dye stuffs, so soon as we can get a greater variety of seed. For ten years we have advertised the brethren to bring indigo seed; and I have not obtained any, only a little that brother William Willes brought from the East Indies. I have also wished them to bring madder seed, for you can raise it where you can raise corn. Do we know enough to raise indigo and cotton? Yes, when the gate is shut down.

I told the brethren, yesterday, that I was not afraid of men's apostatizing when war and trouble are on hand, for then they will stick together. It is in calm weather, when the old ship of Zion is sailing with a gentle breeze, and when all is quiet on deck, that some of the brethren want to go out in the whaling-boats to have a scrape and a swim; and some get drowned, others drifted away, and others again get back to the ship. Let us stick to the old ship, and she will carry us safely into the harbour. You need not be concerned. I want the brethren to raise flax.

I want some man, who has got the requisite spirit and nerve, to prepare a quarter-of-an-acre as they prepare ground for flax in Ireland, and then sow about a bushel-and-a-half or two bushels of seed, and let it grow as thick as a horse's mane; if necessary, brace it up while growing; pull it at the period when the lint will be the silkiest, and prepare it for the women to exercise their skill in, making fine thread. A bushel of flax-seed to the acre produces a coarse lint, suitable for making ropes and coarse cloth.

Brother Taylor remarked that about 60 out of every 75 lambs had died in this Territory. Yes, you may say that, out of every 75 lambs about 90 have died. Where were our sheep in 1848-49? I then had 100 sheep, and I would now have 40,000 if they had been taken care of as they ought; but instead of that, I have bought about 550 since; and now I have 400 or 500.

Sheep are driven into the Territory, and then they decrease. What is the difficulty? It is, "Hurrah for the gold! hurrah for the stores! hurrah for the merchants! hurrah for hell! —— let us have a portion of hell here."

Elders who have been to St. Louis and had credit for a cent should not have brought a thousand or two thousand dollars' worth of goods here and fooled them away, having fooled them out of merchants who still remain fools.

Shut down the gate, and stop bringing ribbons and foolery here. I wish the ribbons and like articles were all sunk in the bottom of the sea, rather than have them brought here. Do you know enough to clothe yourselves? Yes, when you are driven to it. It makes me think of what we passed through in Missouri, when Joseph was preaching the Consecration law for surplus property. Would any man listen to that law? No, not a man. "Will you pay Tithing?" "I cannot any way in the world, for I have not as much property as I want."

When the army came and took away the guns, killed our cattle, fired our houses, took possession of our fields, and compelled the brethren, at the point of the bayonet, to sign away their property to pay the expenses of the war, one fellow said, "By —— ,see these men, how keen and fine they look! Old Joe has been trying for years to make them consecrate their property, but he could not persuade them to do it. We can make them consecrate."

The brethren felt well: but suppose they had been required to sign deed of trust to the kingdom of God on the earth, would they have done it? No; they would have suffered themselves to be damned before they would have done it. Can you not see the ignorance of the people in those things? And to this day you can see men come here penniless, and hear them say, "We had plenty of money where we came from." Then why did you not gather when you had money? "We wanted to make more, to bring a great amount into the kingdom." Thus men come here penniless, and feel well about it. Enquire into the matter, and you will often learn that last year they had several thousand dollars, but it has gone into the hands of the Gentiles.

Suppose a poor Elder, while on mission, should borrow ten dollars of such a person, that person will come here and be ready to apostatize, unless that money is paid; but if the devils get it, "Oh, it is all right." Such feelings are in the hearts of some men and women now before me. With them it is, If my enemies get my property, all well; but I don't want the kingdom of God to have it." Ask them whether they want the kingdom of God to have their property, and they will reply, "O yes; ourselves and they we have are in the kingdom of God:" but touch a dollar of theirs, and they will squirm.

We are trying to become Saints, and by-and-by we will actually become Saints. When men are Saints, they will bring their thousands and lay them at the feet of the bishops, Apostles, and Prophets, saying, "Here is my money; it is now where it should be." But now what do you see? If an Elder has borrowed a little money, or been helped in any manner, he must be chased home and made to pay the uttermost farthing, or there is dissatisfaction. Fortunately that is not the case with all. A portion of the principle of darkness is in the hearts of the people; but it is fast going out, and they are coming to a knowledge of the truth.

One of the first and plainest principles to be believed and practised is to put ourselves and all we have into the kingdom of God, and then be dictated by the Lord and his servants. Is there any danger? Some say ready to say, "Yes, we are afraid to trust ourselves and our means here and there."

Brother Taylor has just said that the religions of the day were hatched in hell. The eggs were laid in hell, hatched on its borders, and then kicked on to the earth. They may be called cockatrices, for they sting wherever they go. Go to their meetings in the Christian world, and mingle in their society, and you will hear them remark, "Our ministers dictate our souls' salvation;" and they are perfectly composed and resigned to trust their whole future destiny to their priests, though they durst not trust them with one single dollar beyond their salaries and a few presents. They can trust their eternal welfare in the hands of their priests, but hardly dare trust them with so much as a bushel of potatoes. Is that principle here? Yes, more or less.

Can we feed and clothe ourselves? Yes, we can, as well as any people on the earth. We have a goodly share of the genius, talent, and ability of the world; it is combined in the Elders of this Church and in their families. And if the Gentiles wish to see a few tricks, we have "Mormons" that can perform them. We have the meanest devils on the earth in our midst, and we intend to keep them, for we have use for them; and if the Devil does not look sharp, we will cheat him out of them at the last, for they will reform and go to heaven with us.

We have already showed the invading army a few tricks; and I told Captain Van Vliet that if they persisted in making war upon us, I should share in their supplies. The boys would ride among the enemy's tents and one of their captains ran into Colonel Alexander's tent one night, saying, "Why, Colonel, I'll be damned if the Mormons won't be riding into your tent, if you don't look out."

We have the smartest women in the world, the best cooks, the best mothers; and they know how to dress themselves the neatest of any others. We are the smartest people in the world. But look out, pertaining to taking care of and sustaining ourselves, that the children of this world are not smarter than the children of light. I say that they shall not be; for we will beat them in every good thing, the Lord and the brethren being our helpers. The Lord bless you! Amen. JD 6:169 BY Jan 17, 1858 SLC.

He focused more specifically on the poor and their needs in a May 25, 1862 discourse and commented on many related points:

ENDLESS VARIETY OF ORGANIZATIONS. — BLESSINGS THAT
AWAIT THE FAITHFUL.
Remarks made by President BRIGHAM YOUNG, Tabernacle,
Great Salt Lake City, May 25, 1862.
REPORTED BY G. D. WATT

Our mortal existence is a school of experience. Could we improve every hour of our time in the best possible way until we attain a ripe old age, there will be still much to learn pertaining to this world, pertaining to our natural lives, to the organization of our bodies and spirits, to the object and design of our existence, and the will of Heaven concerning us.

Some of our speakers, in their public addresses, express themselves as seeing great reason to be thankful for the improvements we are making in self-government, and our rapid advancement towards the fountains of knowledge. Others have a long experience to relate of constant trials, tribulations, difficulties, and disappointments which they have now to pass through, and gloomy forebodings of more in the future; they dwell upon how we are tried with each other, and become dissatisfied with each other and with ourselves, &c. Now, this is all good, and if properly received is for our mutual edification and advancement, giving us much to reflect upon, and lessons to learn from the experience of each other. But should our lives be extended to a thousand years, still we may live and learn. Every vicissitude we pass through is necessary for experience and example, and for preparation to enjoy that reward which is for the faithful. Others consider it a lamentable fact that we live to send abroad and preach the Gospel, and gather the people, and then they will apostatize. We only understand in part why we required to pass through those various incidents of life. There is not a single condition of life that is entirely unnecessary; there is not one hour's experience but what is beneficial to all those who make it their study; and aim to improve upon the experience they gain. What becomes a trial to one person is not noticed by another. Among these two thousand persons I am now addressing there cannot be found two that are organized alike, yet we all belong to the one great human family, have sprung from one source, and are organized to inherit eternal life. There are no two faces alike, no two persons tempered alike; we have come from different nations of the world, and have been raised in different climates, educated and traditioned in different and, in many instances, in opposite directions, hence we are tried with each other, and large drafts are made upon our patience, forbearance, charity, and good will —— in short, upon all the higher and godlike qualities of our nature —— for we are required by our holy religion to be one in our faith, feelings, and sentiments pertaining to things of time and eternity, and in all our earthly pursuits and works to keep in view the building up of the kingdom of God in the last days. Our work is to bring forth Zion, and produce the Kingdom of God in its perfection and beauty upon the earth.

The impulses of our different natures present an almost endless variety of pursuit, manner, and expression, yet all this under a wise and judicious direction will accomplish the great end of our existence and calling as ministers of the Most High. "Br. Brigham teaches that it is essentially necessary to improve every moment of our time in some useful and profitable labour, and by frugality and honest care obtain property by cultivating the earth, raising useful animals, &c., and thus make ourselves wealthy and independent, surrounding ourselves with everything to please the eye, gratify the taste, and gladden the heart." Now, both you and I are aware that there are persons in our midst who do not understand this kind of religion; but we hail them as good brethren. When they address us they are full of faith that the time will come when the earth and its fulness will be given to the Saints of the Most High, yet, should the Lord hand out a small portion of it now, they cannot endure it.

We believe the earth is to be renovated, purified, glorified, celestialized, and prepared for the habitation of the Saints, who will possess not only the silver and gold now held by the wicked nations of the world, but every good thing, for "The young lions do lack, and suffer hunger: but they that seek the Lord shall not want any good thing." This "any good thing" will embrace horses, chariots, houses and lands, gardens and orchards, promenades and places for recreation, and everything to amuse and delight the heart of man. We are now beginning to get these things together and devote them to God, but, as I have remarked, some of this people cannot endure this kind of blessings. It is written, "The earth is the Lord's, and the fulness thereof; the world, and they that dwell therein." Again, "And one cried unto another, and said Holy, holy, holy, is the Lord of hosts: his glory is the fulness of the whole earth." He will give this fulness to the Saints. But the actions of some of this people speak in language like the following: "If you give me any of this riches and glory, Lord, I will apostatize; if you fill my lap with gold, I will cease serving you, and go to the Devil."

The revelation that Br. James Cummings read is true. The people, at the time that revelation was given, were slow to remember the Lord in the day of their prosperity, and were covetous. I was not there, but was acquainted with many who were. I knew them before they went there, and I know they were covetous and filled with greediness. I know, if the Lord had blessed them with the good things of this earth, which he had prepared for the Saints at that day, not any of them would have stood. It would have been as Joseph said to me in Kirtland, "Brother Brigham, if I was to reveal to this people what the Lord has revealed to me, there is not a man or a woman would stay with me." In the day of prosperity now the people are slow to follow the Lord. If he were now to bless this people with gold and silver, houses and lands, with everything to make them wealthy and comfortable here in Deseret or Utah, a great many would turn away from him to worship their idols.

"But," says one, "this will not do for us; if we are the children of God we must be poor, we must see sorrow and affliction, and pass through much tribulation." I have no fear but that every child of God will receive all the suffering he can bear while passing to his exaltation. Those who have suffered from sore eyes, I am satisfied, are contented not to suffer another moment with that dreadful malady, should they live on the earth a thousand years. The sisters who have been afflicted with sick headache never want to suffer from it another moment. Do you wish to have any more toothache? No, you think that you have suffered enough from that ache, and never wish to have it again while you live. So we may say of fevers, pains, aches, and diseases of every kind to which the human body is subject. I might inquire of the Nauvoo Saints whether they ever want to endure another chill and fever while they live. I am satisfied there is not one of them that would wish to pass through another day of their Nauvoo experience in sickness. Again, I ask the brethren who have come from the different nations of the earth, who have there suffered hunger, nakedness, cold, and oppression, are you satisfied with what you have suffered, without passing through the same in this land? I think you are. I have seen the time that I had not food to satisfy the craving of my nature, and I have suffered enough in this line of suffering. I know what it is to be <u>hungry</u>, and need not suffer hunger again to give me that kind of experience. I know what it is to be in <u>poverty</u>, and to be <u>destitute</u> of the raiment necessary to keep any body warm. Many of you have also had this kind of experience, and <u>we do not wish to pass through it again</u>. Many of us know what it is to be in the midst of false brethren, which is the most hateful thing of all. Are you satisfied with what you have suffered from tattlers and busy bodies? Yes. Do you wish any person to bear false witness against you, to take away your liberty, and turn you out from your houses and possessions, and thirst for your life? Do you wish to see the Prophets and servants of God imprisoned, bound in chains, and sacrificed in blood? When you are brought face to face with suffering, you see nothing in it that is desirable, then <u>why cultivate a morbid desire for suffering? You will find all you can bear</u>, though you surround yourselves with all the comforts and conveniences of life, and enjoy them as gifts from the Lord, acknowledging his hand, offering unto him constantly the incense of a grateful heart. Leave this kingdom, and I will promise you more suffering than the tongue of man can utter, until you are consumed soul and body —— until you are wasted away —— the body in the death pronounced upon it, and the spirit in the awful sufferings and torments attending the second death. Then stick firmly to the kingdom, and be satisfied with the pains, aches, and afflictions you have already suffered.

The time has come for us to begin to glorify our Father in Heaven with the earth and its fulness, and <u>let</u> the gold and the silver, and the fruits of the earth, and <u>all precious things produced by the industry of man praise God</u>, and let all men acknowledge his name, honour his character, bow to his divinity, glory in his supremacy, and admire the wonders of his providence over the earth and its fulness. The time has come for us to put forth our best efforts to bring forth the Zion of God and gather all things in one, even in Christ Jesus.

<u>There is a great variety of talent among this people, but as a people they know but little as to the uses of the world in which they live</u>, and the design of God in its creation. There is not one in a million of mankind that is filled with that intelligence that an intelligent being should be filled with, but they pass from this stage of action, are no more, and are apparently forgotten. This is decidedly the case with the world outside, and very much so with many of this people who have been gathered out from the world. <u>Here they have to think and do a little for themselves</u>, which gives them a course of useful experience. This is not so much so <u>with the outside world, for the great masses of the people neither think nor act for themselves</u>, but are acted upon, and act accordingly; and <u>think as they are thought for</u>; it is, as with the Priest so with the people. I see too much of this gross ignorance among this chosen people of God.

I will now portray a little of the feelings and conduct of the <u>labouring classes</u>. When a man can only earn a dollar a-day, and has no way of increasing his finances only by his labour, he is obliged to be frugal, if he is honest, and he manages to keep a wife and a few children comparatively comfortable. By-and-bye the times improve and wages rise so that he can earn ten dollars per week instead of six. "Now, wife, we will allow a little more for the bread, and more for the meat, and more for the tea, the coffee, sugar, fruit, spices, &c. We must buy our daughter a pair of fine shoes, and our little boy must have a whistle, and the baby a doll, and you shall have a new bonnet by-and-bye, and I must have a pair of fine boots, and a new coat and other things in keeping, for you know, wife, I am now getting ten dollars per week, and by-and-bye I may yet double or treble that amount." In this way they manage to live out all their means. This is a peculiarity in the majority of the old country people, and you can see the same thing here. You say you would rather hear something else than this. I would rather hear this. I am as far ahead in the Gospel and power of God as any of you, I know as much about it as any man in the Church, yet I need to know more. I think it is necessary, however, that you should learn to live to-day, and to-morrow, this year, and next year, and learn to honour your lives continually. We must prepare for that which is coming, and be ready to receive that which the Lord has in store for us.

I know how you live. Do we see poverty here? We do. How many are there who declare that they cannot pay their emigration expenses, and cannot give anything to bring their friends? You could, if you had a disposition to try. Use just enough of your earnings to make your bodies and your families happy and comfortable, and save the residue. I probably support more than any ten men in the Territory or in this State. I feed and clothe multitudes of men. women and children — and I like the man that gets me in debt to him. I consider that such a man has calculation and management, and is preparing himself to be useful, and to have something in his hands to use and to devote to noble purposes. But I pay men nine, ten, twelve, and twenty-five dollars per week, and when the year comes to a close they are owing me hundreds of dollars, when, if they had managed properly, there would have been a large credit in their favour. There is a class of men here who do not know but what they will apostatize by-and-bye, and they do not wish anybody in debt to them, nor do they wish to owe anybody. You had better be about square, the whole of you that wish to apostatize and go off, for you cannot leave the country with your debts unpaid. The better way is to keep in the faith, and pay your debts. When some men are doing well they will become anxious for a change, and they want to raise stock, or possess a farm in Weber or Cache Valley; they go and stay year after year until they are reduced to poverty in consequence of their inexperience in that class of industry, and by-and-bye they come back deploring their lack of sense in not knowing when they were well off. I have such persons here to deal with, and I have to keep along with my brethren at this slow rate of progression, until we know how to gather the heavens and the earth.

If there was impatience in heaven they would be impatient with the slothfulness of the Latter-day Saints. The heavens are waiting to be gracious, and are ready to shed forth all the blessings heaven and earth can bestow on the Saints, as soon as we can receive them and make use of them to the glory of God. If we do not first learn the little things, we cannot learn the greater things. "He that is faithful in that which is least, is faithful also in much; and he that is unjust in the least, is unjust also in much. If therefore ye have not been faithful in the unrighteous mammon who will commit to your trust the true riches? And if you have not been faithful in that which is another man's, who shall give you that which is your own?"

Every moment of human life should be devoted to doing good somewhere and in some way. We are all dependent upon a Being greater than ourselves, and we owe, our talent, time, and every pulse of our nature to the Supreme of the Universe. We have nothing of our own, and ought to devote ourselves to usefulness; we ought to learn to be economical, which, coupled with industry, will make us wealthy. And while we are handling the things of this world, let us not neglect to become rich in faith, in humility, and to learn the ways of God, and be constantly and actively devoted to his service and the building up of his kingdom upon the earth, or the riches of this world will do us no good.

I heard it said to a young lad, "I will give you a dollar and a half a-day and board you." After a little reflection the young lad said, "If you will pay me three dollars a-day, I think I will work for you a spell." The principle of the thing flashed before me, like a flash of light, that such a course would be ruinous to this people. I could see, under such circumstances, that the lad could not live here two years before he would not know how to secure himself a pair of pantaloons; he might receive great wages, and yet be in the depths of poverty; he might be paid more than he earned, and still be needy. "I am getting three dollars a-day," says a brother. What next? He must have as fine a pair of boots as any man wears in this community, and he will have them. When I was a boy a young man in our neighbourhood went into a hat shop to buy a five dollar beaver. He said to Mr. Merill. "Have you any five dollar hats?" "No, but I have some very nice three dollar hats." The young gent did not want such a hat; he would not wear such a hat, but said, "I want a five dollar hat?" "Can you make me a a five dollar hat?" "Yes." "When shall I call for it?" "In two weeks." Merill took a three dollar hat that fitted the young man, marked it, and put it by. In too [two] weeks the young man called for his hat, when the hatter reached down the same hat the young man had tried on before, saying, "that is a five dollar hat." "Ah, that is the hat I want; what is the price?" "Five dollars." He paid five dollars for a three dollar hat, and was perfectly satisfied. That is the case with hundreds of my brethren; they do not know the difference between a three dollar and a five dollar hat. I do not wish to tantalise any one's feelings, though I know that I often use extreme cases in comparison.

We have had to feed, clothe, and find house room, fire-wood, &c., for quite a number of people in this community. The first place we set apart and devoted to the poor, was a house built by Enoch Reese, in the 13th Ward; we bought that place, and the Bishop prepared it for the poor to live in. We appointed Dr. Doremus to take care of that house. Could we get any one to occupy it? No, but "if you will build us a house close by the Temple block we will live there, otherwise we will live with our neighbours where we can, and be at liberty to go where we please; we will not have your charity unless ye dictate." Is this not about so, Bishops? (Voices, "Yes.") Unless a Bishop will suffer himself to be dictated by those who need his aid, they will not have his charity. This, I know, is the extreme in such cases.

**What causes poverty among this people? It is the want of discretion, calculation, sound judgment.** I am paying men more or less by the day, and where do you see those who get the least wages? Seated back in the barber's chair three or four times a week. Next at a store to get a box of blacking to put upon fifteen dollar boots, if they can get them. They must have four or five dollar handkerchiefs, as fine things for their wives and children, and as much in quantity as any other man has. At the end of the year there are two or three hundred dollars on the debit side of their accounts. This is not good policy in them. Suppose that they want to go on a mission to California after gold, or to apostatize and go away, they have debits upon them that will perplex them. Other poor men want a yoke of cattle, and must have the best yoke that can be had; they want the best waggon that can be bought; and there goes two hundred dollars more. Then they must hire a man to drive the team, and the hired man goes to the kanyon with the model team and waggon, and returns home with one of the wheels on the geering, and a pole under the axletree. "Well, where is the wood?" "Oh, it is yet in the kanyon." "Where is the new axe I bought?" "I forgot it, it is up in the kanyon, I expect." It costs him ten dollars to get the waggon repaired, he pays his teamster a dollar and fifty cents a day, has lost a new axe, and has no wood.

With us the Bible is the first book, the Book of Mormon comes next, then the revelations in the book of Doctrine and Covenants, then the teachings of the living oracles, yet you will find, in the end, that the living oracles of God have to take all things of heaven and earth, above and beneath, and bring them together and devote them to God, and sanctify and purify them and prepare them to enter into the kingdom of heaven. Gold and silver, houses and lands, and everything possessed by the Saints will be purified and cleansed by the power of God, and prepared to enter into the new Jerusalem when the earth is sanctified. We have to learn to handle all things which pertains to the heavens and earth in a way to glorify God, and devote all to the building up of his kingdom, or we cannot magnify our Holy Priesthood and calling.

Some go away because they are poor, some because there is no revelation, some because they have too much revelation, and others because they have gathered gold and silver and enriched themselves by filching from the Saints. I say to all such, go, but first pay your debts, and then steal nothing.

May God bless the righteous. Amen. JD 9:292-298 BY May 25, 1862 SLC.

In the above quotation, Brigham Young comments that there is no need to be poor, but lack of wisdom means many are poor and would apostatize if they had more. Some even think it is REQUIRED that they be poor to receive salvation. This "morbid desire for suffering" is counterproductive; they should seek to be economically successful and to help others. Brigham Young sees no value in self-imposed poverty.

In a June 16, 1867 discourse, Brigham noted that there was a grasping element among the poor. He felt it was better to let them earn their own luxuries than to give them free assistance:

Our brethren and sisters, when they gather here, are apt to <u>find fault</u>, and to say this is not right and that is not right, and this brother or that sister has done wrong, and they do not believe that he or she can be a Latter-day Saint in reality and do such things. The people come here from the east and the west, from the north and the south, with all their <u>traditions,</u> which impede their progress in the truth and are difficult to lay aside. Yet they will pass judgment on the acts of their brethren and sisters. I want to ask who made them the judges of the servants and handmaidens of the Almighty, who, shoulder to shoulder, have borne off this kingdom for more than a third of a century? <u>Thousands upon whom the yoke of Christ has rested so long, and who have borne off the kingdom, are judged and found fault with, by some who probably were baptized last summer or but a short time ago.</u> You know that this is so, you are witnesses to the truth of what I am saying, for you hear it yourselves. Now, who are they who will be one with Christ? If I were to tell the truth just as it is, it might not be congenial to the feelings of some of my hearers, for truth is not always pleasant when it relates to our own dear selves. You take some of those characters to whom I have referred to-day, <u>who want us all to be of one heart and of one mind, and they think we cannot be so unless we all have the same number of houses, farms, carriages, and horses, and the same amount in greenbacks.</u> There are plenty in this Church who entertain such a notion, and I do not say but there are good men who, if they had the power, would dictate in this manner, and in doing so they would exercise all the judgment they are masters of, but let such characters guide and dictate, and they would soon accomplish the overthrow of this Church and people. This is not what the Lord meant when He said: "Be ye of one heart and of one mind." He meant that we must be one in observing His word and in carrying out His counsel, and not to divide our worldly substance so that a temporary equality might be made among the rich and the poor.

You take these very characters who are so anxious for the poor, and what would they tell us? Just what they told us back yonder — "Sell your feather beds, your gold rings, ear rings, breast pins, necklaces, your silver tea spoons or table spoons, or anything valuable that you have in the world, to help the poor." I recollect once the people wanted to sell their jewellery to help the poor; I told them that would not help them. The people wanted to sell such things so that they might be able to bring into camp three, ten, or a hundred bushels of corn meal. Then they would sit down and eat it up, and they would have nothing with which to buy another hundred bushels of meal, and would be just where they started. My advice was for them to keep their jewellery and valuables, and to set the poor to work — setting out orchards, splitting rails, digging ditches, making fences, or anything useful, and so enable them to buy meal and flour and the necessaries of life.

A great many good men would say to me —— "Br. Brigham, you have a gold ring on your finger, why not give it to the poor?" Because to do so would make them worse off. Go to work and get a gold ring, then you will have yours and I will have mine. That will adorn your body. Not that I care anything about a gold ring. I do not have a gold ring on my finger perhaps once in a year.

You who are poor and want me to sell that ring, go to work and I will dictate you how to make yourselves comfortable, and how to adorn your bodies and become delightful. But no, in many instances you would say —— "We will not have your counsel, we want your money and your property." This is not what the Lord wants of us. JD 12:61 BY June 16, 1867 SLC.

In the following April 6, 1877 discourse, Brigham Young repeats his long-held opinion that "The most of the inhabitants of the earth are incapable of dictating and devising for themselves," and also repeats his conviction that any leveling would be destructive, contrary to George Q. Cannons apparent earlier remarks:

DISCOURSE BY PRESIDENT BRIGHAM YOUNG,
DELIVERED AT THE SEMI-ANNUAL CONFERENCE, HELD IN THE TEMPLE,
AT ST. GEORGE, FRIDAY MORNING, APRIL 6, 1877.
(Reported by Geo. F. Gibbs.)
THE UNITED ORDER —— THE DUTY OF THE PRIESTHOOD —— THE GOSPEL
NOT COMMUNISM —— TEACHING THE PEOPLE HOW TO LIVE —— INDEPENDENCE
OF BABYLON —— THE SAINTS WILL CONTINUE TO SPREAD —— UNITY
OF PURPOSE AND ACTION, WILL BRING AGAIN ZION —— FREE SCHOOLS
CRITICISED —— EDUCATIONAL STATUS OF OUR CHILDREN.

I would like to say a great deal during this Conference to the Latter-day Saints, but I shall be able to talk but little, and therefore when I do speak I wish you to listen, and this I believe all of you will do.

I think that, as a people, we are nearer alike in the sentiments and feelings of our hearts, than in our words. From the most excellent discourse which we have heard this morning from brother Cannon, I believe that the people might gather the idea that we shall be expected to divide our property equally one with another, and that this will constitute the United Order. I will give you my view, in as few words as possible with regard to this subject, which I will promise you are correct.

The Lord wishes and requires us to develop the ability within us, and to utilize the ability, of these men, women and children called Latter-day Saints.

The most of the inhabitants of the earth are incapable of dictating and devising for themselves. In many instances there is reason for this, for they are opposed to that degree that for the lack of opportunity they are not able to develop the talents and ability that are within them. This is the condition of the people of most of the nations of the earth. All those who come out from the world, espousing the Gospel of Jesus, place themselves in a condition to be taught of him, but instead of teaching them personally, he has raised up his authorized teachers to do this work, and what does he expect of us to do? He requires, absolutely requires, of us to take these people who have named his name through baptism, and teach them how to live, and how to become healthy, wealthy and wise. This is our duty.

Supposing that the property of the whole community were divided to-day equally amongst all, what might we expect? Why a year from to-day we should need another division, for some would waste and squander it away, while others would add to their portion. The skill of building up and establishing the Zion of our God on the earth is to take the people and teach them how to take care of themselves and that which the Lord has entrusted to their care, and to use all that we command to glorify his holy name. This is the work of regenerating, of elevating mankind to the higher plane of the Gospel; in other words, of simply teaching them their duty.

With regard to our property, as I have told you many times, the property which we inherit from our Heavenly Father is our time, and the power to choose in the disposition of the same. This is the real capital that is bequeathed unto us by our Heavenly Father; all the rest is what he may be pleased to add unto us. To direct, to counsel and to advise in the disposition of our time, pertains to our calling as God's servants, according to the wisdom which he has given and will continue to give unto us as we seek it.

Now, if we could take this people, in their present condition, and teach them how to sustain and maintain themselves and a little more, we would add to that which we already have; but to take what we have and divide amongst or give to people, without teaching them how to earn and produce, would be no more nor less than to introduce the means of reducing them to a state of poverty.

I do not wish for one moment to recognize the idea that in order to establish the United Order our property has to be divided equally among the people, to let them do what they please with it. But the idea is to get the people into the same state of unity in all things temporal, that we find ourselves in with regard to things spiritual. Then let those who possess the ability and wisdom direct the labors of those not so endowed, until they too develop the talents within them and in time acquire the same degree of ability.

What do you say to this doctrine? Is it right or wrong? (The congregation answered, "It is right.")

We want to get at a correct understanding respecting all these matters which so materially concern us. What would be the first lesson necessary to teach the people, were we to commence to direct their labors to the great end of becoming of one heart and one mind in the Lord, of establishing Zion and being filled with the power of God? It would be to stop expending and lavishing upon our dear selves all needless adornments and to stop purchasing the importations of Babylon. We can ourselves produce every thing necessary for our consumption, our wear, our convenience and comfort, right here at home. We can produce and manufacture the material necessary to beautify our lands, gardens and orchards; to beautify and furnish our houses, and to adorn the beautiful bodies which we inhabit without sending our means to France, to England and other countries for things which can a little better be made at home among ourselves. The material of which these cushions were made, which adorn the pulpits, were produced here. After it was taken from the sheep, it was manufactured at our Provo factory into the cloth you now see; and the material of which the silk trimmings were made, was raised, spun, and made up by some of our sisters in this Territory. We might exhibit to you handkerchiefs, dress patterns, and shawls, all of silk, made by our sisters out of the raw material produced here through the enterprise and industry of a few. These are only simple specimens of what can be done. Suppose I were to say, "Ladies, how do you like them?" Do you not think they would say, "Pretty well?" We can improve on what has been done, and we want you to do so. Plant out the mulberry tree, and raise the silk, and let your dresses, your shawls, your bonnets and your ribbons, and everything you use to clothe and adorn your bodies, be the workmanship of your own hands. Let the brethren take hold and carry out in every department the same principle of home manufacture until we shall be able to produce the materials, and make up every article necessary to clothe and adorn the body, from the crown of the head to the soles of the feet. Then we shall become a self-sustaining and growing people, and we shall have to do it. All

*Poverty and Inequality - Reason and Cure*

this is in the elements in which we live, and we need the skill to utilize the elements to our growth and wealth, and this is true financiering.

We can now see the growth of the Latter-day Saints, and it is marvelous to us to see the multitude of little towns springing up here and there, and we are under the necessity of saying, Give us more room, for the older settlements are thickening up, and the people are spreading out and filling up new valleys continually. You can see the shoots putting forth and taking root; still the old stock is good, is alive and rapidly increasing.

It has been asked if we intend to settle more valleys. Why certainly we expect to fill the next valley and then the next, and the next, and so on. It has been the cry of late, through the columns of the newspapers, that the "Mormons" are going into Mexico! That is quite right, we calculate to go there. Are we going back to Jackson County? Yes. When? As soon as the way opens up. Are we all going? O no! of course not. The country is not large enough to hold our present numbers. When we do return there, will there be any less remaining in these mountains than we number today? No, there may be a hundred then for every single one that there is now. It is folly in men to suppose that we are going to break up these our hard earned homes to make others in a new country. We intend to hold our own here, and also penetrate the north and the south, the east and the west, there to make others and to raise the ensign of truth. This is the work of God, that marvelous work and a wonder referred to by ancient men of God, who saw it in its incipiency, as a stone cut out of the mountains without hands, but which rolled and gathered strength and magnitude until it filled the whole earth. We will continue to grow, to increase and spread abroad, and the powers of earth and hell combined cannot hinder it. All who are found opposing God and his people will be swept away and their names be forgotten in the earth. As the Prophets Joseph and Hyrum were murdered, and as they massacred our brethren and sisters in Missouri, so they would have served us years and years ago, if they had had the power to do so. But the Lord Almighty has said, Thus far thou shalt go and no farther, and hence we are spared to carry on his work. We are in his hands, the nations of the earth are in his hands; he rules in the midst of the armies of heaven and executes his pleasure on the earth. The hearts of all living are in his hands and he turns them as the rivers of water are turned.

We have no business here other than to build up and establish the Zion of God. It must be done according to the will and law of God, after that pattern and order by which Enoch built up and perfected the former-day Zion, which was taken away to heaven, hence the saying went abroad that Zion had fled. By and by it will come back again, and as Enoch prepared his people to be worthy of translation, so we through our faithfulness must prepare ourselves to meet Zion from above when it shall return to earth, and to abide the brightness and glory of its coming.

My brethren and sisters, I do really delight in hearing our brethren speak on this holy order of heaven. Unity of purpose and action, in carrying out the will of our Father, has been my theme all the day long; but I have continually plead with the Saints not to waste their substance upon the lust of the eye and the flesh, for that is contrary to the will and commandments of God. I wish to say that whoever have faith enough to inherit the celestial kingdom will find that their inheritances will be upon this earth. This earth is our home; by and by it will be sanctified and glorified, and become a fit dwelling place for the sanctified, and they will dwell upon it for ever end ever. I will further say I labor for the earth, I never mean to be satisfied until the whole earth is yielded to Christ and his people. When brother George Q. tells us we should not labor for the earth and the things of this world, he means we should not labor with sinful motives, and to gratify the lusts of the flesh. But if we possessed the treasure of the Gentile world, could we not send our Elders to the ends of the earth, bearing the precious Gospel to all living? Could we not sustain their families during their absence? Could we not build Temple after Temple and otherwise hasten on the work of redemption? Yes. But keep the people in poverty and how are we to accomplish this great work? I say, let us gather and accumulate the things of the earth in the manner indicated by the Lord, and then devote it to God and the building up of his kingdom. What do you say to this doctrine, is it right or wrong? (The congregation said, "It is right.") What little property I have I wish it to be devoted to the building up of Zion, and I suppose I have as much as any other man in the Church. I am always ready to receive and take care of the blessings that God showers upon me, and am always ready and willing to devote the same to the building up of his kingdom.

Many of you may have heard what certain journalists have had to say about Brigham Young being opposed to free schools. <u>I am opposed to free education as much as I am opposed to taking away property from one man and giving it to another who knows not how to take care of it.</u> But when you come to the fact, I will venture to say that I school ten children to every one that those do who complain so much of me. I now pay the school fees of a number of children who are either orphans or sons and daughters of poor people. But in aiding and blessing the poor I do not believe in allowing my charities to go through the hands of a set of robbers who pocket nine-tenths themselves, and give one-tenth to the poor. Therein is the difference between us; I am for the real act of doing and not saying. Would I encourage free schools by taxation? No! That is not in keeping with the nature of our work; we should be as one family, our hearts and hands united in the bonds of the everlasting covenant; our interests alike, our children receiving equal opportunities in the school-room and the college.

We have to-day, more children between the ages of 5 and 20 years, who can read and write, than any State or Territory of the Union of a corresponding number of inhabitants. This is not exactly sustained by the statistics published of a few of the States, but from what we know of them we believe it to be the fact.

On the whole we have as good school-houses as can be found, and it is our right to have better ones, and to excel in everything that is good.

As to my health I feel many times that I could not live an hour longer, but I mean to live just as long as I can. I know not how soon the messenger will call for me, but I calculate to die in the harness. Amen. JD 18:353, 356 BY April 6, 1877 St. George.

Brigham also asks that the people save more of what they earn. Obviously, economic growth requires significant savings. His comments about not being taxed by government for "free" services to the poor indicates he wished to maintain control of his resources and their use.

Note that, as discussed in a December 8, 1867 discourse of Brigham Young, there was a fast day on one Thursday a month, held for the purpose of supplying the most basic needs of the poor. It appears that this practice was either re-emphasized or re-instituted at this time. The organization of ward Relief Societies was also encouraged at this time:

Now, Bishops, you have smart women for wives, many of you; <u>let them organize Female Relief Societies in the various wards.</u> We have many talented women among us, and we wish their help in this matter. Some may think this is a trifling thing, but it is not; and you will find that the sisters will be the mainspring of the movement. Give them the benefit of your wisdom and experience, give them your influence, guide and direct them wisely and well, and they will find rooms for the poor, and obtain the means for supporting them ten times quicker than even the Bishop could. If he should go or send to a man for a donation, and if the person thus visited should happen to be cross or out of temper for some cause, the likelihood is that while in that state of feeling he would refuse to give anything, and so a variety of causes would operate to render the mission an unsuccessful one. But let a sister appeal for the relief of suffering and poverty, and she is almost sure to be successful, especially if she appeals to those of her own sex. If you take this course you will relieve the wants of the poor a great deal better than they are now dealt by. We recommend these Female Relief Societies to be organized immediately.

Another thing I wish to say. You know that the first Thursday in each month we hold as a fast day. How many here know the origin of this day? Before tithing was paid, the poor were supported by donations. They came to Joseph and wanted help, in Kirtland, and he said there should he a fast day, which was decided upon. It was to be held once a month, as it is now, and all that would have been eaten that day, of flour, or meat, or butter, or fruit, or anything else, was to he carried to the fast meeting and put into the hands of a person selected for the purpose of taking care of it and distributing it among the poor. If we were to do this now faithfully, do you think the poor would lack for flour, or butter, or cheese, or meat, or sugar, or anything they needed to eat? No, there would be more than could be used by all the poor among us. It is economy in us to take this course, and do better by our poor brethren and sisters than they have hitherto been done by. Let this be published in our newspapers. Let it be sent forth to the people, that on the first Thursday of each month, the fast day, all that would be eaten by husbands and wives and children and servants should be put in the hands of the Bishop for the sustenance of the poor. I am willing to do my share as well as the rest, and if there are no poor in my ward, I am willing to divide with those wards where there are poor. If the sisters will look out for rooms for those sisters who need to be taken care of, and see them provided for, you will find that we will possess more comfort and more peace in our hearts, and our spirits will be buoyant and light, full of joy and peace. The Bishops should, through their teachers, see that every family in their wards, who is able, should donate what they would naturally consume on the fast day to the poor. JD 12:115 BY Dec 8, 1867 SLC.

It appears that the payment of tithing did represent a step upward in dependability and magnitude of donations.

Brigham Young was concerned to avoid classes such as in Europe where some are trapped in a servant condition and cannot escape. The specific evil of using social force to maintain classes as is done in Europe is certainly objectionable, but taking steps to use force to prevent classes can be just as unfair.

Now the object is to improve the minds of the inhabitants of the earth, until we learn what we are here for, and become one before the Lord, that we may rejoice together and be equal. Not to make all poor. No. The whole world is before us. The earth is here, and the fullness thereof is here. It was made for man; and one man was not made to trample his fellowman under his feet, and enjoy all his heart desires, while the thousands suffer. We will take a moral view, a political view, and we see the inequality that exists in the human family. We take the inhabitants of the civilized world, and how many laboring men are there in proportion to the inhabitants About one to every five that are producers and the supposition is that ten hours work by the one to three persons in the twenty-four hours will support the five. It is an unequal condition of mankind. We see servants that labor early and late, and that have not the opportunity of measuring their hours ten in twenty-four. They cannot go to school, nor hardly get clothing to go to meeting in on the Sabbath. I have seen many cases of this kind in Europe, when the young lady would have to take her clothing on a Saturday night and wash it, in order that she might go to meeting on the Sunday with a clean dress on. Who is she laboring for? For those who, many of them, are living in luxury. And, to serve the classes that are living on them, the poor, laboring men and women are toiling, working their lives out to earn that which will keep a little life within them. Is this equality? No! What is going to be done? The Latter-day Saints will never accomplish their mission until this inequality shall cease on the earth.

We say but very little about politics. If we have laws, we should have good laws, and we should get good men to adjudicate those laws. And if we are at variance with our neighbor, and are in want of better judgment than we have to settle our difficulties, let us call three or twelve men, and leave it to them to decide between us. Adopt this course, and it will save an immense amount of time, and set the lawyer to raising his own potatoes and wheat, instead of gulling the people. The non-producer must live on the products of those who labor. There is no other way. If we all labor a few hours a day, we could then spend the remainder of our time in rest and the improvement of our minds. This would give an opportunity to the children to be educated in the learning of the day, and to possess all the wisdom of man.

But we are to revolutionize the world. Do you think these Latter-day Saints can do it? I do not know. It is the work of the Almighty; and if he sends forth his Spirit to teach the people true principles, we have a right, a moral right, a religious right, to tell the truth to the people without interruption; and men have no business to raise their anger against this people, when we are merely telling the truth to the inhabitants of the earth, and instructing them how they can better their condition. JD 19:46-47 May 27, 1877 Ogden.

Brigham Young's solution to the problem of social classes was to merely to make education available:

Now that I am upon free schools I say, put a community in possession of knowledge by means of which they can obtain what they need by the labor of their bodies and their brains, then, instead of being paupers they will be free, independent and happy, and these distinctions of classes will cease, and there will be but one class, one grade, one great family. JD 16:20 BY April 7, 1873 SLC.

In the following October 8, 1874 discourse, George Q. Cannon confirms some of Brigham Young's ideas about productivity of people and property. However, he exhibited some ambiguity on the question of equality. It is not possible to have it both ways: One cannot actively take steps to prevent any classes from forming while also saying that nothing will be taken from the wealthy. As noted earlier in this chapter, George Q. Cannon and Brigham Young did not see eye to eye on all issues.

The people feel very well so far as I have had opportunity to observe. We have explained the articles of association to them; they have been gratified at the explanations which have been made. Many, have reasoned upon it like this — "if I put all I have got in to the United Order, and I begin to draw days' wages only out of the Order, I have got a large family, how can I sustain them upon my day's wages? It takes the product of my property managed with care and economy, in addition to my own labor, to enable me to live, and if I put all my property into the Order, how am I to live? This has been the inquiry more frequently made than another. It is not the intention, in establishing the United Order, to destroy the productiveness of property; it is not the intention to take property from men who have it and give it to those who have none. There are two extremes to be avoided, one is the disposition of the rich to aggrandize themselves at the expense of the poor. That is what we are trying, in this United Order, to put a stop to, so that we may, prevent the growth of class distinctions, the increase of wealth in a certain class, and that class have interests diverse from and frequently adverse to the rest of the community. That is one extreme. The other is this idea to which I have referred, the anxiety of poor people to get possession of the accumulations of the rich, and to have them divided among them, and a general levelling take place. There is no such idea connected with this order, such a thing could not stand vary long; and let me say to you who find fault with this United Order, ask yourselves when you ever saw anything connected with this Church or its doctrines that was unnatural, that was not consistent with good common sense? Do you think that we can teach and practice anything that will repress people, that will destroy individual effort, that will take away from enterprise its incentive? No, there is nothing connected with this system of this character, and it is upon this point that men and women are so much deluded by the false and slanderous reports which are circulated. There never was a day since our organization as a people, according to my ideas and my reading of our early history and my subsequent experience, when there were so many falsehoods in circulation about any principle as there have been about this United Order. There is far too much ignorance among us, and men take advantage of this to deceive the people by their falsehoods. It is the intention to preserve that which we have. If a man is a man of business let him have a chance to show his business capacity, not stop him, not take his property from him and give it to somebody who never had anything. The intention is to use the skill of the business man in elevating those who are not business men, to bring up the poor from their level to the broad upper level, not to pull down the upper level to the plane of the lower. That is not the design, but it is that we shall work for each other's good; and where men have property let them take means to preserve it, not to destroy it. It is not the intention for boards of directors to use arbitrary power over men and property.

There are many cases where if a man were to put all that he has into the Order, it would be found that he already manages that property better than the board of directors could. Under such circumstances it would be better to say: "Here, you have managed this property economically, you have done well with it, we could not do so well with it if we took it. There is no object to be gained by our taking it from you; you continue to use and manage it as a stewardship, and keep up its productiveness." This will have to be done doubtless in many instances. JD 17:240-1 GQC Oct 8, 1874 SLC.

# CHAPTER 21

# Rich Men and the United Order

Brigham Young, as a builder, putting efficiency far before equality, wanted men who could create wealth, not redistribute it, and he had no desire to drain off anything from them except what would specifically build up the kingdom in visible terms. A small portion would normally need to go the really poor, but that was to be kept to a minimum, not become a major drain on society, or a goal in itself to expand transfer payments to the poor.

It is interesting that Brigham Young preferred to work with rich men, those who had useful economic knowledge and skills, as mentioned in this April 7, 1873 discourse:

> I have a few things to lay before the Conference, one of which is-and I think my brethren will agree with me that this is wise and practicable —— for from one to five thousand of our young and middle-aged men to turn their attention to the study of law. I would not speak lightly in the least of law, we are sustained by it; but what is called the practice of law is not always the administration of justice, and would not be so considered in many courts. How many lawyers are there who spend their time from morning till night in thinking and planning how they can get up a lawsuit against this or that man, and get his property into their possession? Men of this class are land sharks, and they are no better than highway robbers, for their practice is to deceive and take advantage of all they can. I do not say that this is the law, but this is the practice of some of its professors. The effort of such lawyers, if they are paid well, is to clear and turn loose on society the thief, perjurer and murderer. They say to the dishonest and those who are disposed to do evil, "Go and lay claim to your neighbor's property, or to that which is not your own, or commit some other act of injustice, and pay us, and we will clear you and make your claim appear just in the eye of the law;" and officers and judges too often join in the unrighteous crusades for the lawyers to wrong the just. I have been in courts and have heard lawyers quote laws that had been repealed for years, and the judge was so ignorant that he did not know it, and the lawyer would make him give a decision according to laws which no longer existed. Now, I request our brethren to go and study law, so that when they meet any of this kind of lawyers they will be able to thwart their vile plans. I do not by any means say these things of all lawyers for we have good and just men who are lawyers, and we would like to have a great many more. You go to one of the pettifogging class of lawyers, and get him to write a deed for you, and he will do it so that it can be picked to pieces by other lawyers. Employ such a man to write a deed, bond, mortgage or any instrument of writing, and his study will be to do it so that it will confound itself. This is the way that such men make business for their class. We want from one to five thousand of our brethren to go and study law.
>
> If I could get my own feelings answered I would have law in our school books, and have our youth study law at school. Then lead their minds to study the decisions and counsels of the just and the wise, and not forever be studying how to get the advantage of their neighbor. This is wisdom.
>
> My mind is so led upon the subject brother Pratt has been speaking upon with regard to the orders that God has revealed that I can hardly let it alone when I am talking to the people. He said there are many rich men who are willing to do any thing that the Lord requires of

them. I believe this, and there is quite a number of poor men, likewise, who would like to do anything if they could only know that it was the will of the Lord. I am about to make an application of my remarks with regard to the willingness of men. But in this I shall except brother Pratt, for the simple reason that I do not know a man who is more willing to do what he is told than he is. If he is told to teach mathematics, he is willing to do it; if he is told to make books, preach the Gospel, work in a garden or tend cattle, he is willing to do it, and I know of no man more willing to do anything and everything required of him than he is. But I want to say to our willing, kind, good brethren that, so far as obeying the orders which God has revealed, I can bring the rich into line quicker than I can get many poor men who are not worth a dollar, and who do not know how to raise a breakfast to-morrow morning. I have tried both, and know. Who is there among us who came here rich? It was alluded to by brother Pratt. Look over our rich men, where are they? Who is there among the Latter-day Saints that is wealthy? When I came to this valley I was a thousand dollars in debt. I left every thing. I think I got about three hundred dollars, a span of horses, and a little carriage, for all my property I left in Nauvoo. But I bought cattle, horses and wagons, and traded and borrowed and got the poor here by scores myself; and I have paid for these teams since I have been here.

When I got here I was in debt only about a thousand dollars for myself and family to a merchant in Winter Quarters, but I was in debt for others, and I have paid the last dime that I know anything about. When I reached here I could not pay one-tenth —— I could not pay my surplus —— I could not give my all —— for I had nothing.

Here is Horace S. Eldredge, he is one of our wealthy men. What did he have when he came here? Nothing that I know of, except just enough to get here with his family. William Jennings has been called a millionaire. What was he worth when he came here? He had comparatively little. Now he is one of our wealthy men. William H. Hooper is another of our wealthy men. He is worth hundreds of thousands of dollars. How much had he to pay as surplus when he came here. He could pay no surplus, for he was worth nothing; but he is now wealthy. If he had gone to California I believe he would have been poor to-day.

There is any amount, of property, and gold and silver in the earth and on the earth, and the Lord gives to this one and that one —— the wicked as well as the righteous —— to see what they will do with it, but it all belongs to him. He has handed over a goodly portion to this people, and, through our faith, patience and industry, we have made us good, comfortable homes here, and there are many who are tolerably well off, and if they were in many parts of the world they would be called wealthy. But it is not ours, and all we have to do is to try and find out what the Lord wants us to do with what we have in our possession, and then go and do it. If we step beyond this, or to the right or to the left, we step into an illegitimate train of business. Our legitimate business is to do what the Lord wants us to do with that which he bestows upon us, and dispose of it just as he dictates, whether it is to give all, one-tenth, or the surplus. I was present at the time the revelation came for the brethren to give their surplus property in to the hands of the Bishops for the building up of Zion, but I never knew a man yet who had a dollar of surplus property. No matter how much one might have he wanted all he had for himself, for his children, his grand-children, and so forth.

If we are disposed to enter into covenant one with another, and have an agreement made according to the laws of our land, and we are disposed to put our property into the hands of trustees, and work as we are directed —— eat, drink, sleep, ride, walk, talk, study, school our children, our middle-aged and our aged, and learn the arts and sciences, the laws of the Priesthood, the laws of life, anatomy, physic and anything and everything useful upon the earth, the Lord has not the least objection in the world, and would be perfectly willing for us to do it, and I should like, right well, for us to try it. I know how to start such a society, right in this city, and how to make its members rich. I would go to now, and buy out the poorest ward in this city, and then commence with men and women who have not a dollar in the world. Bring them here from England, or any part of the earth, set them down in this ward and put them to work, and in five years we would begin to enter other wards, and we would buy this house and that house, and the next house, and <u>we would add ward to ward until we owned the whole city, every dollar's worth of property there is in it. We could do this, and let the rich go to California to get gold, and we would buy their property</u>. Would you like to know how to do this? I can tell you in a very few words — never want a thing you can not get, live within your means, manufacture that which you wear, and raise that which you eat. Raise every calf and lamb; raise the chickens, and have your eggs, make your butter and cheese, and always have a little to spare. The first year we raise a crop, and we have more than we want. We buy nothing, we sell a little. The next year we raise more; we buy nothing, and we sell more. In this way we could pile up the gold and silver and in twenty years a hundred families working like this could buy out their neighbors. I see men who earn four, five, ten or fifteen dollars a day and spend every dime of it. Such men spend their means foolishly, they waste it instead of taking care of it. They do not know what to do with it, and they seem to fear that it will burn their pockets, and they get rid of it. If you get a dollar, sovereign, half-eagle or eagle, and are afraid it will burn your pockets, put it into a safe. It will not burn anything there, and you will not be forced to spend, spend, spend as you do now. See our boys here, why if my boys, by the time they are twenty, have not a horse and carriage to drive of their own, they think they are very badly used, and say, "Well, I do not think father thinks much of me." A great many things might be said on this subject that I do not want to say.

Brethren, we want you to turn in and <u>study the laws of the Territory of Utah, of this city and other cities, and then the statutes of the United States, and the Constitution of the United States. Then read the decisions of the Supreme Court.</u> I do not mean the self-styled "United States Supreme Court for the Territory of Utah;" but the United States Supreme Court that sits at Washington — the seat of government. Read up their decisions, and the decisions of the English judges and the laws of England and of other countries, and learn what they know, <u>and then if you draw up a will, deed, mortgage or contract</u>, do not study to deceive the man who pays you for this, but <u>make out a writing or instrument as strong and firm as the hills, that no man can tear to pieces, and do your business honestly and uprightly, in the fear of God and with the love of truth in your heart</u>. The lawyer that will take this course will live and swim, while the poor, miserable, dishonest schemers will sink and go down. We live by law, and I only condemn those among the lawyers who are eternally seeking to take advantage of their neighbors. JD 16:9 BY April 7, 1873 SLC.

Here Brigham Young is encouraging people to become lawyers and to practice their trade accurately and honestly. This is not the anti-rich rhetoric of a socialist. He is a capitalist through and through.

Notice that instead of making the united order idea a strict commandment, here it is more of a challenge to excel in economic matters by using all the timeworn principles for economic success.

In a June 4, 1864 discourse, Brigham Young thought the rich were as entitled to revelation as the poor:

We say to the brethren, at this time, seek not after gold, nor after silver, nor after any of the precious metals that are hid up in the earth, for as yet they would do you no good if you possessed them. But suppose we had a few thousand millions of gold and silver, would it follow that we should be destroyed, because we possessed this wealth? Not in the least; if we are destroyed through the possession of wealth, it will be because we destroy ourselves. If we possessed hundreds of millions of coin, and devoted that means to building up the kingdom of God and doing good to His creatures, with an eye single to His glory, we would be as much blessed and as much entitled to salvation as the poor beggar that begs from door to door; **the faithful rich man is as much entitled to the revelations of Jesus Christ as is the faithful poor man.**

Whether we are poor or rich, if we neglect our prayers and our sacrament meetings, we neglect the spirit of the Lord, and a spirit of darkness comes over us. If we lust for gold, for the riches of the world, and spare no pains to obtain and retain them, and feel "these are mine," then the spirit of anti-Christ comes upon us. This is the danger the Latter-day Saints are in, consequently it is better for us to live in the absence of what is called the riches of this world, than to possess them and with them inherit the spirit of anti-Christ and be lost.

We had better labor to produce and treasure up the golden wheat, the fine flour, the pure wine, the oil of the olive, and every product for food and clothing that is adapted to our climate. JD 10:300 BY June 4, 1864 SLC.

In an October 10, 1875 discourse, Joseph F. Smith agreed that being rich is not a bad thing:

There is a circumstance recorded in the Scriptures, that has been brought forcibly to my mind while listening to the remarks of the Elders who have spoken to us during Conference. A young man came to Jesus and asked what good thing he should do that he might have eternal life. Jesus said unto him — "Keep the commandments." The young man asked which of them. Then Jesus enumerated to him some of the commandments that he was to keep — he should not murder, nor commit adultery, nor steal, nor bear false witness, but he should honor his father and mother, and love his neighbor as himself, &c. Said the young man — "All these I have kept from my youth up, what lack I yet?" Jesus said — "If thou wilt be perfect, go and sell that thou hast and give to the poor, and thou shalt have treasure in heaven, and come and follow me." And we are told that he turned away sorrowful, because be had great possessions. He would not hearken to, or obey the law of God in this matter. Not that Jesus required of the young man to go and sell all that he possessed and give it away; that is not the principle involved. The great principle involved is that which the Elders of Israel are endeavoring to enforce upon the minds of the Latter-day Saints to-day. When the young man turned away in sorrow, Jesus said to his disciples — "How hardly shall they that have riches enter into the kingdom of God!"

Is this because the rich man is rich? No. May not the rich man, who has the light of God in his heart, who possesses the principle and spirit of truth, and who understands the principle of God's government and law in the world, enter into the kingdom of heaven as easily, and be as acceptable there as the poor man may? Precisely. God is not a respecter of persons. The rich man may enter into the kingdom of heaven as freely as the poor, if he will bring his heart and affections into subjection to the law of God and to the principle of truth; if he will place his affections upon God, his heart upon the truth, and his soul upon the accomplishment of God's purposes, and not fix his affections and his hopes upon the things of the world. Here is the difficulty, and this was the difficulty with the young man. He had great possessions, and he preferred to rely upon his wealth rather than forsake all and follow Christ. If he had possessed the spirit of truth in his heart to have known the will of God, and to have loved the Lord with all his heart and his neighbor as himself, he would have said to the Lord — " Yea, Lord, I will do as you require, I will go and sell all that I have and give it to the poor." If he had had it in his heart to do this, that alone might have been sufficient, and the demand would probably have stopped there, for undoubtedly the Lord did not deem it essential for him to go and give his riches away, or to sell his possessions and give the proceeds away, in order that he might be perfect, for that, in a measure, would have been **improvident**. Yet, if it had required all this to test him and to prove him, to see whether he loved the Lord with all his heart, mind, and strength, and his neighbor as himself, then he ought to have been willing to do it, and if he had been he would have lacked nothing, and would have received the gift of eternal life, which is the greatest gift of God, and which can be received on no other principle than the one mentioned by Jesus to the young man. If you will read the sixth lecture on faith in the Book of Doctrine and Covenants you will learn that no man can obtain the gift of eternal life unless he is willing to sacrifice all earthly things in order to obtain it. We cannot do this so long as our affections are fixed upon the world. JD 18:134 JFS Oct 10, 1875 SLC.

Just as Joseph F. Smith points out here that we must not misunderstand the Savior's directive to the young man to require improvidence, recall that Brigham Young did not accept that the young man was being asked to destroy and disburse all his wealth before he could be acceptable to Christ. See chapter 11.

Even Orson Pratt, perhaps the most outspoken advocate of absolute equality, in an April 6, 1856 discourse, wanted rich men (presumably both members and non-members) to come to Utah to build it up. One cannot reasonably expect rich men to come if they can expect to have their riches taken from them by some stratagem, religious or otherwise. One must respect all property laws, or the rich will flee or stay away.

Where can you find a people or nation, that scarcely begin to have the liberty and privileges which the Latter-day Saints enjoy here in these mountain? They cannot be found. What wretchedness, tyranny, oppression, and every other evil that can be named, are already falling upon the nations of the earth! Pestilence, plague, the want of confidence in officers, rulers, governors, kings, and emperors, is every where manifest; and, in fact, there is, at the present time, scarcely any confidence between man and man; business men have lost confidence in their neighbors with whom they transact business; and why? Because of fraud and bankruptcy. In a moment, when all is supposed to be favorable, when it is believed that debtors are handling their millions, a sudden rumor breaks upon the unhappy creditor, like the roaring thunder of heaven, proclaiming that their debtors have become bankrupt. Confidence is gone, it has taken the wings of the morning and flown away from the nations, and found a resting-place within these peaceful vales.

Will confidence again be restored, while the wicked rule? No; it will grow weaker and weaker. Officers will not have confidence in one another; the people will not have confidence in their rulers; and rulers will not have confidence in the people. Why? Because rulers have oppressed the people; they have trampled upon their rights; they have governed with partiality and injustice; consequently, they know that the people, if they had the power, would revolutionize their governments and overthrow their power; therefore, they have no confidence in the people, and the people have no confidence in them, neither in one another.

Merchants and the great men of the earth have but little confidence in each other; hence, their business transactions are continually being broken up. Many become bankrupt with millions in their pockets, which is calculated to destroy confidence.

What is to be done? I will tell you what will be done. The day is near, even at our doors, when the wise and thoughtful among the great men, rich men, and heavy capitalists, will look to these mountains and to the inhabitants of these peaceful vales for safety, not only for themselves, but for their abundance of riches. They will come, bringing their riches with them, to secure their own safety, for there will be so (no?) safety but among the people of God; and they will say, "Behold they are united, they are strong, they are at peace, they can be depended upon, they are not bankrupts, they will not cheat their creditors while they have millions in their pockets. We will go up there, and we will deposit our riches in their midst for security, and there also we will dwell, for there is no safety abroad for us."

Latter-day Saints, do you think, when you hear me relating these things, that I am in earnest and mean what I say, as a reality; or do you think that it is merely a wild fancy that passes through the imagination, like a dream of the night?

Do you suppose that these things are mere chimeras of the brain, or like castles in the air that vanish away with the bidding? No; you know them to be facts, predicted years ago.

I am declaring to you realities, as they do and will exist, and as they will come to pass, as sure as the Lord God lives, and rules, and reigns in the heavens. Where can the people look for confidence and safety, if not in the kingdom of God which is built up in the last days, and which, according to the Prophets, shall never be thrown down, and never perish? JD 3:302 OP April 6, 1856 SLC.

Brigham Young says below, in an April 17, 1853 discourse, that the Lord (not the church) may allow or cause a man to lose his riches, as occurred in Missouri and Nauvoo. But the church had no part in it, and instead tried to keep everyone's property intact. On the other hand, Brigham Young prospered and became a rich man everywhere he landed. He was profitable to himself and many others and to the church. His was the example for all to follow.

This people commenced with nothing. Joseph Smith, the honored instrument in the hands of God to lay the foundation of this work, commenced with nothing; he had neither the wisdom nor the riches of this world. And it is proven to our satisfaction, that when rich men have come into this Church, the Lord has been determined to take their riches from them and make them poor; that all His Saints may learn to obtain that which they possess by faith.

How many times has He made us poor? Thousands of dollars worth of property in houses and lands, which the Lord gave me, are now in the East, in the hands of our enemies. I never said they were mine, they were the Lord's, and I was one of His stewards. When I went to Kirtland, I had not a coat in the world, for previous to this I had given away everything I possessed, that I might be free to go forth and proclaim the plan of salvation to the inhabitants of the earth. Neither had I a shoe to my feet, and I had to borrow a pair of pants and a pair of boots. I staid there five years, and accumulated five thousand dollars. How do you think I accomplished this? Why, the Lord Almighty gave me those means. I have often had that done for me that has caused me to marvel. I know, as well as I know I am standing before you to-day, that I have had money put into my trunk and into my pocket without the instrumentality of any man. This I know to a certainty. Ask an apostate, if they can, in truth, bear testimony to such a thing. They cannot do it. Enough about that. JD 2:128 BY April 17, 1853 SLC.

The socialist group that came to Nauvoo after the Saints left had every possible advantage from pre-existing property, and still failed. That is definitely not a part of the church program.

Of course, being rich was only useful to Brigham Young if those resources are used for righteous gospel purposes. As he noted in an October 6, 1863 discourse, many do not use their wealth in that way:

> I want neither gold nor silver, but I want to build the Temple and finish the new Tabernacle, send the Gospel to the nations, and gather home the poor. "Do we not need gold for this?" Yes. "Then would it not benefit us to dig some out of the ground for this purpose?" The world is full of gold, and we would do better to get some of that in a lawful way, which is already made into coin, for it is easier handled than the gold dust, and better cleansed from particles of sand and other foreign substances. If we possessed true knowledge and power with God, we should know how to get gold in great abundance. The world is full of it, and they do not need but a little of it. We want riches but we do not want them in the shape of gold. Many of us know exactly what we do want, and a great many do not know. I want to build that Temple; I want to supply the wants of the poor, and I try my best according to what judgment and influence I possess, to put every poor person in a way to make their own living.
>
> We all wish to posess [possess] true riches; how shall we possess them? God has given to us our present existence, and endowed us with vast variety of tastes, sensations and passions for pleasure and for pain, according to the manner in which we use and apply them; he also gives us houses and lands, gold and silver, and an abundance of the comforts and necessaries of life. Are we seeking to honor God with all these precious gifts, or are we trying to establish interests separate and apart from God and His Kingdom, and thus waste the ability and substance the Lord has given us with riotous living and wanton prodigality? But few rich men have come into this Church who have not sought diligently to put their means into the hands of the devil. There are persons with us now who might have given their scores of thousands of pounds to this Church to spread the Gospel, build the Temple, and gather the poor Saints, but no, they have sought and do and will seek diligently to place their means into the hands of the wicked, or situate it so that they may get it. I wish you to understand, however, that a man giving his means to build up the kingdom of God is no proof to me that he is true in heart. I have long since learned, that a person may give a gift with an impure design.
>
> The Lord gives us possessions, and he requires of us one-tenth of the increase which we make by the putting to good use the means he has placed in our hands. I am sorry to see a disposition manifested in some to go to distant parts to trade and build up themselves and make money, while the ability which God has given them is not concentrated in building up His kingdom, in gathering the house of Israel, in redeeming and building up Zion, in renovating the earth to make it like the garden of Eden, in overcoming sin in themselves, and in spreading righteousness throughout the land. We find what we have always found and shall continue to find, until the Lord Almighty separates the sheep from the goats and when that will be I do not know. JD 10:268 BY Oct 6, 1863 SLC.

Brigham Young often complained, as in an April 9, 1871 discourse, that not one-hundredth part (one percent) had been paid as tithing, instead of the 10 percent requested. One must assume that some of his economic plans were designed to get the church's fair share by some other means such as corporate withholding as in ZCMI and Orderville.

> I want to say a little now with regard to tithing. Some of this people think they pay their tithing. I expect they do; but I can make the same comparison that Jesus did when in Jerusalem. Here came the Scribes, Pharisees, Sadducees, &c., and put their substance in the

Lord's storehouse; and there came along a poor widow with nothing, to all appearance. She had not clothing to make her comfortable, but she had two mites, which she had saved probably by her labor, and she placed them in the storehouse of the Lord. Jesus lifted himself up, and, seeing what they were doing, said, "Of a truth I say unto you that this poor widow hath cast in more than they all; for all these have of their abundance cast in unto the offerings of God; but she of her penury hath cast in all her living that she had." Now, there are a few of just this same kind of characters here who do pay their tithing. But do we rich men pay ours? Not by considerable. I can inform the Elders of Israel and everybody else that since we have been raising grain in these valleys the deposits paid in on tithing have not amounted to one-hundredth part of all that has been raised, whereas one-tenth was due the storehouse of the Lord. You may say, "Brother Brigham, have you paid in yours?" No, I have not. There is a number of the brethren who have paid in considerable, but I expect I have paid more tithing than any other man in this Church. I expect I have done more for the poor than any other man in the Church; yet I have hardly commenced to pay my tithing. How is it with you? I know how it is. There are a few poor who pay their tithing, and who are pretty strict; but take the masses of the people, and they have not paid one-twentieth of their tithing. Do you believe it? I know it. If I were to reason over this and attempt to show the Latter-day Saints the inconsistency of their course in the matter, I would plant my feet on this ground: We are not our own, we are bought with a price, we are the Lord's; our time, our talents, our gold and silver, our wheat and fine flour, our wine and our oil, our cattle, and all there is on this earth that we have in our possession is the Lord's and he requires one-tenth of this for the building up of his kingdom. Whether we have much or little, one-tenth should be paid in for tithing. What for? I can tell you what for in a hundred instances, but I will only tell you just a few, and will commence with the poor. You count me out fifty, a hundred, five hundred, or a thousand of the poorest men and women you can find in this community; with the means that I have in my possession, I will take these ten, fifty, hundred, five hundred, or a thousand people, and put them to labor; but only enough to benefit their health and to make their food and sleep sweet unto them, and in ten years I will make that community wealthy. In ten years I will put six, a hundred, or a thousand individuals, whom we have to support now by donations, in a position not only to support themselves, but they shall be wealthy, shall ride in their carriages, have fine houses to live in, orchards to go to, flocks and herds and everything to make them comfortable. But it is not every man that can do this. The Bishops cannot do it; not that I would speak lightly of the wisdom of our Bishops, but we have hardly a Bishop in the Church who knows A with regard to the duties of his office. Still we have good men, but our hearts are somewhere else, and we are not studying the kingdom, the welfare of the human family, nor what our office calls upon us to perform. We do not seek after the poor and have every man and woman put to usury. This ought to be, for our time is the Lord's. All we want is to direct this time and use it profitably. There is abundance of labor before us. We have the earth to subdue, and to make it like the Garden of Eden. Do you believe it? I know it. But how do we live? Very much like the rest of the world. We are ready to run over all creation. Just as I have said to some of the brethren, and to some that I have known in the world; they get their eye on a dime; they see it roll away and they go after it. By and by they stub their toe against an eagle; soon they come to another one, a doubloon or a slug, and they will stub their toe against it, and down they go; but they are up again, for their eye is on that dime, and, in their eagerness to obtain it, they stumble over the eagles they might pick up if they had wisdom to do it. Is this so? O yes, they who have eyes to see can see. Take things calm and easy, pick up everything, let nothing go to waste.

You, sisters, know I have sometimes told you what my office is. Does it make you ashamed of me when you hear some of the brethren say, "Well, I do not believe that Brother

Brigham has anything to do with my farm or household matters, or with temporal things; I do not think the First Presidency has anything to do with my temporal affairs." O, yes, we have; and to come right down to the point, it is my privilege, if I were capable, to teach every woman in this Church and kingdom how to keep house, and how to sweep house, cook meat, wash dishes, make bread without any waste, &c. I may go to a house and what do I see? Perhaps the bottom or top of the bread is burnt to a coal. Why did you not do different? "O, these are accidents." Yes, because we never think of the business on our hands. Mother gets up and it is: "O, Sally, where is the dish cloth, I want it in a minute?" "Susan, where in the world have you put that broom?" or, "Where is the iron holder?" and Susan knows nothing about either dish cloth or broom, and says, "We have no iron holder except some waste paper." If I had nothing but a piece of an old newspaper folded for a holder I would have it where I could put my hand on it in a moment, in the dark if I wanted it. And so with the dishcloth, the broom, the chairs, tables, sofas, and everything about the house, so that if you had to get up in the night you could lay your hand on whatever you wanted instantly. Have a place for everything and everything in its place. JD 14:87 BY April 9, 1871 SLC.

One might conclude that Brigham Young should be called the foreman of the church, directing all the labors and investments of the whole.

George Q. Cannon was usually more doctrinaire on class and equality issues than Brigham Young. He seemed to be far more concerned with the "fairness" question than about the actual accomplishments and strengths of the saints as a whole. Brigham Young did not indulge in any of this "socialism for its own sake" logic. As mentioned in an October 8, 1872 discourse quoted below, George Q. Cannon seemed to prefer to avoid having any rich men around to be an embarrassment to his egalitarian ideas. Brigham Young corrected him at times on his excess zeal for equality.

But I have said that this is <u>only a stepping stone to something beyond that is more perfect</u>, and that will result in the diffusion of the blessings of God to a greater extent among us. In <u>other lands</u> you see the people divided into <u>classes</u>. You see <u>beggars</u> in the street, and men and women who are short of food, dwelling in hovels and in the poorest of tenements. At the same time, others revel in <u>luxury</u>, they have everything they need, and more than they need to satisfy all, their wants. Every philanthropist who contemplates this, does so with sadness, and measure after measure has been devised to remedy this state of things. Our community is not a prey to these evils. <u>Beggary and want are unknown in this Territory; at the same time we have no very rich men among us.</u> Like other new communities we are more on an equality than we would be if we were older, and if we were to become an old community under the system which prevailed before co-operation was established, then it is very probable that some of the <u>class distinctions</u> to be seen in other communities would be seen in ours. <u>It is to avoid this that God has revealed that which I have alluded to, and his design is to bring to pass a better condition of affairs, be (by?) making men equal in earthly things</u>. He has <u>given</u> this earth to <u>all his children</u>; and he has given to us air, light, water and soil; he has given to us the animals that are upon the earth, and all the elements by which it is surrounded. They are <u>not given to one or to some, to the exclusion of others; not to one class</u>, or to one nation to the exclusion of other classes or other nations. But he has given them to his children in all nations alike. Man, however, abuses the agency that God has given him, and he transgresses his laws by oppressing his fellow-men. There is <u>selfishness in the rich, and there is covetousness in the poor</u>. There is a <u>clashing of interests</u>, and there is not that feeling among men which we are told the Gospel should bring —— a feeling to love our neighbor as we love ourselves. This does not exist on the earth now, it is reserved for God to restore it. We pray that God's will may be done on earth as it is in heaven, and when it shall, then the order which exists in heaven will be practiced and enjoyed by men on the earth. I do not expect, when we get to heaven, that we shall see some riding in their chariots, enjoying every luxury, and crowned with crowns of glory, while the rest are in poverty.

I have spoken longer than I intended, but there are some few thoughts on my mind to which I will allude in this connection before I sit down, and that is, brethren and sisters, that we should, to the extent of our ability, foster these institutions that have been established among us. We should do all that we can to sustain ourselves — sustain our own factories, do all in our power to maintain these things that we have established, and seek with all our energy to foster them. We have factories here that can make as good cloth as any of their size, probably, in the nation. They ought to be stained (sustained?) by us. Brother Erastus Snow related an incident a day or two ago in relation to their operations at St. George. They received quite a quantity of cloth from the factory of President Young. He told the store-keeper at St. George not to say anything about where it was manufactured. At the same time they received a consignment of eastern manufactured goods. They were put side by side on the shelves of the store and sold to the people. There were very few — some two or three persons — who knew that any of these goods were manufactured in the Territory. They sold very readily to the people, who said they were the best goods they had bought. They wore them, and they wore well. Several lots were received from the President's factory, and sold in the same way, the people remaining in ignorance a good while as to the place of their manufacture, and imagining that they were brought from the east. There is an idea prevailing among many of us that something manufactured abroad is better than that manufactured at home. President George A. Smith, Elder Woodruff and myself, on our recent visit to California, examined the Oregon and California goods. We went through a woollen factory there, where very excellent goods were made. We saw some blankets and some other things which were manufactured there, which can not be surpassed. I recollected that I had heard parties here, who had purchased Oregon cloth, praise it very highly; but in examining that class of goods in California, I found that the cloth manufactured in this Territory compared very favorably with it, and had they been put side by side, bolt by bolt, it would have been very difficult to tell which was Utah and which was Oregon manufacture. Indeed if there was any preference I was inclined to give it to our own cloth. JD 15:209 GQC Oct 8, 1872 SLC.

As shown in the November 20, 1870 discourse below, George A. Smith wanted to have it both ways, to avoid extremes and have the best of both worlds: be rich to do the Lord's work, but be poor to be humble. He did not suggest that the church would do any redistribution, but that the blessings would come as the saints were prepared for them and the Lord granted them. Still, putting any religious upper limit on what a man is allowed to do economically must have some negative effect on motivation and creativeness.

I do not expect to be permitted to address you again for some months. I expect to travel and visit the brethren in the southern country during the winter; shall probably visit some thirty-three settlements in our Dixie, and be absent several months. I wish to bear my testimony to the principles of the Gospel which have been revealed. I know these things are true. I don't come here believing them simply, I know they are true, and that God has revealed them and I also know that all the plans, powers and schemes of the wicked can never overthrow them. Distress may be brought upon individuals; and the fact is, that many of us, who have seemed to move along prosperously, and have surrounded ourselves in an incredibly short space of time with many of the comforts of life may cling too close to them and be unwilling to surrender them; and it may be necessary that we and the Lord should know by actual experiment whether we worship the things of this world more than we do the things of a better. It may be necessary for us to ask ourselves the question, and consider it thoroughly and carefully: "Do we love the Lord Jesus Christ, and his laws and the principles of his Gospel more than we love a piece of land, a little orchard, a garden, field, store, vineyard, ranch, or a herd of cattle, &c. How is it? Ask these questions, and if we do, it is time for us to repent, and we had better begin and make sacrifices. We had better contribute for the Temple, to help the poor and needy, &c. I remember, very well, reading of a man who came to the Savior, and said, "Good master, what must I do to inherit eternal life?" After the Savior had answered him he said, "All these things have I kept from my youth up." The Savior replied, "Yet lackest thou one thing, <u>go and sell all that thou hast and give to the poor and come and follow me</u>." And we are told that he went away sorrowful. Why? Because he had great possessions and could not part with them. Are we getting into that track? The Savior once remarked that it was very hard for a rich man to get into heaven. I do not pretend to quote these passages exactly, you are familiar with them. But we are told that it is a very hard matter for a rich man to get into heaven. That is the substance of it. <u>Don't let us get so rich that we can't go there; and don't let us get so poor that we can't contribute our mite to help to roll on the work of God</u>. I remember reading in the Proverbs of an individual who prayed the Lord not to make him either rich or poor. He didn't want to be rich for fear he should get proud and forget the Lord; and if he became poor he was afraid he might steal and take the name of the Lord in vain. We don't want to go to either <u>extreme</u>. The time is coming, and is not far hence, when the Latter-day Saints will get so much knowledge of the things of God that they will be able to bear wealth and control it, and use it to the glory of God; and when that time comes, to use a familiar expression, "the Lord will open the windows of heaven and pour out a blessing upon them that there will not be room to receive it." JD 13:298 GAS Nov 20, 1870 SLC.

In summary, perhaps we may say that Brigham Young was for equality of schooling and opportunity, but certainly not for equality of result. In some of today's interest group politics, especially those involving race, the spokesmen for those groups claim to want equality of economic result, almost regardless of economic skill and inputs to the process. This would not fit with Brigham Young's philosophy.

## CHAPTER 22

# Treasure and Heart

The expression "For where your treasure is, there will you heart be also" (Matthew 6:21; Luke 12:34; 3 Ne. 13:21) is familiar to most people. It is an observation that anyone might make about people's feelings and behavior. However, during Brigham Young's day, this harmless observation was given new meaning when it was used as the basis for social engineering. As a means of focusing peoples' labor and other activities, their property was moved into new relationships, the idea being that their heart (and their labor and cooperation) would then be applied according to the preference and counsel of their church leaders. The goal was a good one, that is, the maximum growth of the church in size and power, but the means were unusual, incorporating an element of force.

The logic was used in at least two areas or with two meanings, one for earthly property or "treasure," and one for heavenly expectations, a different kind of "treasure." The saints' possible future lives in heaven were at times redescribed to try to change their daily behavior here, especially their willingness to be obedient to every word of the prophet on temporal matters.

This was not exactly socialism or communism; they did not normally abolish individual property ownership altogether, but pooled that property and used that change to focus people's attention on the desired economic result.

One practical reason for that approach was the reality that there really was no other means of handling an investment process. They had little money that could be separated from their real estate or animals and put into a larger organization. And there were no limited liability business forms protected by law. Common law partnerships were inherently unstable with a large and constantly changing group of participants. It was even questionable whether a simple contract could be enforced in the way intended, with the saints not having control of their own legal system, but instead having it controlled by a hostile force. Many transactions were at the barter or tribal gift-trading level, or had nothing to hold a temporal organization together except the force of individual religious commitment.

Four quotes from the period of 1855 to 1881, two by Brigham Young and two by George Q. Cannon, are presented below with the "treasure and heart" concept in context. There are 13 other references to "treasure and heart" together, but they are less focused on joint economic activities. The first quote finds Brigham Young promoting his unclear first version of the "structured consecration" idea that received more detailed definition in later years:

> Hence they see the mountains and do not know how they are made, the grass, but do not know upon what principle it grows; the cattle come and go, but they do not know their first origin. Mankind spread abroad, upon the earth, but do not know how they came here, and are not familiar with the workings of the power that sustains them. This the people ought to find out in the first place, and then they will know that the earth is the Lord's, and the fulness

thereof, and that there is an eternity of matter yet to be organized. When the Saints find out the truth as it is, they will learn that they have nothing to consecrate in reality, that they have nothing to give to the Lord, because they hold nothing but what already belongs to Him. We seem to possess much, and if we are faithful and endure to the end will be crowned, and then the Lord will say, "It is enough, you have proved yourselves faithful." Comparatively speaking, He will talk with them as a father does with his children. To one son he says, "Go and improve that farm, though I do not deed it to you;" to another he says, "Take that farm"' and to a third, "Take this'" and all upon the same conditions, "and I will see what you will do with these my farms." They think the farms are already theirs, but they are mistaken, for the father did not deed the farms to them. The eldest son fences, plows, and improves it, builds a house and a good barn upon it, plants an orchard, raises cattle, and makes the possession much more valuable than when the father put it into his hands. "Now, John," says his father, "you have proved yourself a wise and faithful steward, I will now give you a deed of this property which I have owned so long, that it may be your property." He says to William, "How is it with your farm?" "Well, father, it is much the same as when you gave it to me to improve; I have not done much; I raised a little wheat and corn." "Where is your house, William,?" "O I was not sure that the land was mine, and I did not build one." "Why did you not build a barn?" "Well, I did not know that I was going to possess it, so I did not put myself to that trouble; as for an orchard, I was not going to set one out for you to give to some other of the boys." "You are an unfaithful steward, and you can go now and get you a farm, and I will take this that you might have improved, and possessed for an everlasting inheritance, and give it to John, for he has been faithful." The parable delivered by Jesus Christ is a fit illustration of this principle, wherein he likens the kingdom of heaven to a man travelling into a far country, who called his own servants, and delivered unto them his goods; "and unto one he gave five talents, to another two; and to another one," &c. The one who received the one talent hid it up; he was unfaithful and unprofitable, and so his master took away from him the one talent, and gave to him that had ten. So it is with the Lord in all things. If men are faithful, the time will come when they will possess the power and the knowledge to obtain, organize, bring into existence, and own. "What, of themselves, independent of their Creator?" No. But they and their Creator will always be one, they will always be of one heart and of one mind, working and operating together; for `whatsoever the Father doeth so doeth the son, and so they continue throughout all their operations to all eternity. John will be counted worthy to receive his inheritance, but William will be disinherited, and that which he seemed to have will be taken from him, and given to the faithful steward. What have we that is really our own to consecrate? Nothing at all. What is our duty? It is our duty to improve upon every blessing the Lord gives to us. If He gives us land, improve it; if He give us the privilege of building houses, improve it; if He gives us wives and children, try and teach them the ways of the Lord, and exalt them above the dark, degraded, and sunken state of mankind, &c.; if He give us the privilege of gathering together, let us sanctify ourselves. In His providence He has called the Latter-day Saints from the world, has gathered them from other nations, and given them a place upon the earth. Is this a blessing? Yes, one of the greatest the people can enjoy, to be free from the wickedness of the wicked, from the calamities and clamor of the world. By this blessing we can show to our father in Heaven that we are faithful stewards; and more, it is a blessing to have the privilege of handing back to Him that which He has put in our possession, and not say it is ours, until He shall say it from the heavens. Then it is plain that what I seem to have I do not in reality own, and I will hand it back to the Lord when He calls for it; it belongs to Him, and it is His all the time. I do not own it, I never did. He has called upon the people to consecrate their property, to see whether they could understand so simple a thing as this. When they bow down to worship the Lord, they acknowledge that the earth is His, and the cattle upon a thousand hills; and tell the Lord there is no sacrifice they are not willing to make for the sake of the religion of Jesus Christ. The people were crying this continually among the churches when the Book of Mormon came forth, and the Lord spoke through Joseph, revealing the law of consecration, to see whether they were willing to do as they said in their prayers. In their weekly meetings they have told how the Lord has blessed them and forgiven their sins, what glorious visions they have had, and have declared that the Lord was present, and that they had angels to visit them, and they felt so good that they would give all for Christ. Said the Lord to Joseph, "See if they will give their farms to me." What was the result? They would not do it, though it was one of the plainest things in the world. No revelation that was ever given is more easy of comprehension than that on the law of consecration, which the Christians had acknowledged all their days, and we are all Christians by birth, and all believed that we owned nothing, but that all belonged to the Giver of all good. We believe in God the Father, and in His Son Jesus Christ, the Savior of the world, and we believe that he was actually going to possess the earth, and reign with his people on the earth; that all is his, and for ever will be. Yet, when the Lord spoke to Joseph, instructing him to counsel the people to consecrate their possessions, and deed them over to the Church in a covenant that cannot be broken, would the people listen to it? No, but they began to find out that they were mistaken, and had only acknowledged with their mouths that the things which they possessed were the Lord's. When the Latter-day Saints arise to speak, or bear testimony in their meetings, they tell us about the Lord's owning the earth, and being the maker of it, and I have thought, sometimes, that we could pick up a class that would acknowledge this principle, both out of doors and in. Not like a man who spoke to me last summer, as I was riding in my carriage; he shook hands with me, and kept a firm hold of the carriage with his other hand, and said, "Brother Brigham, how do you do? I am going to consecrate all my property, could you not buy me a farm?" I got my hand out of his, and the other off from the wheel, and he went reeling with drunkenness, and I told him I did not want anything to do with such men.

Another says, "Brother Brigham, I want to consecrate all I have, but you must build me a house for it, or get me my wood." This class will acknowledge that all is the Lord's, both out door and in. I wish to see the people acknowledge the principle of consecration in their works, as well as in their prayers. Do I, as an individual, want to see the people deed all they have to the Church? It does not concern me individually; I would not give the ashes of a rye straw for a personal deed of all the Latter-day Saints possess. Yet they are trying to acknowledge that all is the Lord's, and will say, "Let brother Brigham come and get what he wants, but I do not believe in giving up this property, it is mine, and I may want to trade this, that, or the other article." I do not want one red cent from you, but the Lord would be glad to see the people practise out of doors what they hypocritically profess before Him in doors. They say they are the Lord's, and when their children are taken sick, or their wives, fathers, mothers, or husbands are taken sick, O, how humble they then are, and they will send for the Elders to pray for them, and acknowledge that all is the Lord's, and say, "We give ourselves and all we have to thee." The Lord makes them well by His power, through the ordinances of His house, but will they consecrate? No. They say, "It is mine, and I will have it myself." There is the treasure, and the heart is with it, and what will be the end thereof? That which they seem to have will be given to those who are faithful, and they will receive nothing at all. They will not get an inheritance upon the earth, and cannot be crowned as kings and rulers in kingdom of God; but if they are saved at all it will be as servants, to do the drudgery of those who are faithful, and who live the religion out doors which they say they have in their hearts. If the people knew themselves, if they understood their own feelings and reasonings, and the spirits operate upon them, and of what spirit they are, there would be no need of thus talking to them. JD 2:306 BY June 3, 1855 SLC.

In the following November 1869 discourse by Brigham Young, he speaks of the benefits of united action in temporal matters:

> We find a great many trying to be Saints and endeavoring to understand how they may be of the most benefit in building up the kingdom of God on the earth. My brother Joseph says it is an easy matter to be a Saint. So I say. And taking another view of it, again, it is a hard matter. This is true. It is not an easy thing to serve God and mammon. If the Saints comprehend what they have to do in order to establish Zion, and go to work with ready hands and willing hearts to accomplish the labor, they will find it a comparatively easy matter; but unless there is a unity of action on the part of those who are engaged in the work it is not very easily performed. When there is a great work to be accomplished, and there are but few hands to perform it, the burden weighs very heavily on those who are engaged in it. If we have a farm of six hundred acres to fence, and there is only one man engaged in getting the poles and lumber from the kanyon, we find it a slow and tardy work; but if we have a hundred men engaged it is much easier and pleasanter; if a thousand, still more so. So it is in regard to establishing the kingdom of God in the hearts of the children of men. It is not a very hard matter to prevail on a person to put his treasure where his heart is. Our difficulty is in not understanding the principles of the kingdom of heaven sufficiently to enter into it with our whole hearts. JD 13:151 BY Nov 14, 1869 SLC.

Here Brigham Young seems to merely be saying that people do not know where their treasure really is or ought to be, and so make choices that are suboptimal for their real interest or treasure. Implied here is the need to change their focus by any means available that way work; if high means do not appeal to them or they cannot understand them, then use lower means to get the same result.

It is interesting that in the statement "It is not an easy thing to serve God and mammon," Brigham Young appears to be saying that serving both at once is the task that must be done. He is not saying that it is a conflict to be avoided or that we should ignore mammon altogether, as George Q. Cannon or others taught.

In the following October 1874 quote by George Q. Cannon is perhaps the strongest case where the principle of "treasure and heart" was used in a direct way to focus and control the energies and property of the saints:

> I afterwards visited a little settlement of the name of Hebron, where there are about thirty families. The Bishop, George H. Crosby, said they had brick and lumber on hand to build several residences, but they hesitated about building as they had some thought of carrying out the suggestions which President Young made to the people, or to some of them, to enter into a family arrangement, and they thought that, probably it would be well to use their material and build a suitable building. It was afterwards suggested that they build a dining-room and a commodious kitchen, etc., and that they live in their own residences during this coming summer and try the effect of eating together. This they may do. They had found that it would be far more convenient for them, in their labor, to be together during the summer season at least and, the weather being fine, they could walk from their houses to the dining room and eat their meals, and then the men go to their labor and the women and children separate again. In that settlement they have labored during this past season in the United Order, and they told me they had raised double the amount of crops they ever raised before; and all their labors are proportionately advanced, and this is the testimony of a good

many settlements. There are some complaints as a matter of course. I heard some about tools being misused, about wagons not being greased, about animals not being fed, harness not being cared for; but these results are due to a great extent to want of system.

Another objection that we found and that has resulted badly in some instances, is that men have put in a portion of their property only and kept out a portion; of course, the portions that is kept out absorbs nearly all their attention, while that which is put into the Order does not receive that share of attention which it should have, and when they were called upon to labor they had other interests which called them off, and they excused themselves or sent their boys to attend to it. In some wards and settlements they have been crippled in consequence of this. But recent instructions which have been given by the First Presidency, that no one should be admitted into the Order, unless he enters with all he has, (except in case of debt, then the board of directors to exercise their discretion about that,) will have a good effect throughout the entire South. It will concentrate the labors of the people in one direction, and where a man's treasure is there will his heart be also; and if all a man's property is in the United Order if he be a Latter-day Saint, he will labor with fidelity for the furtherance of the objects which the Order has in view.

There is one thing which has been demonstratrd [demonstrated] by this season's labor, namely, that better results can be produced by a combination of labor, as proposed in the United Order, than by individual effort to the same extent. I was much gratified at finding that this was the universal testimony of all with whom I conversed on the subject. JD 17:239 GQC Oct 8, 1874 SLC.

In the last quote, dated June 1882, George Q. Cannon is on one of his favorite topics of maintaining classlessness at all costs, even if the saints needed to all stay poor to do it.

I do not wish to convey the idea that plural marriage can be universal. In the very nature of things as I have often said, it is impossible; the equality of the sexes would prevent this, were men ever so desirous to make it so. Take our own Territory: the males outnumber the females; it cannot therefore be a practice without limit among us.

No one need be afraid of the extensive spread of this system even if the Edmunds' law were not in operation. Besides all this, it should be borne in mind, that God did not give this revelation and commandment to us to urge upon the world for its practice.

The greatest foe we have to contend with is ignorance. We are not known. We are lied about most extensively, and every avenue is blocked against us. Popular journals are afraid of injuring their circulation by speaking the truth concerning us. The publishers are affected by the same influences as the politicians — the pulpit and this popular clamor cause men to be afraid. If we could be known as we really are — not in Salt Lake alone, for this city is not a fair sample of Utah; if it were possible for the people generally, who reiterate these popular cries against us, to travel through our settlements north and south, and see our people, there would be a very different public feeling in regard to us. But we have been inundated by falsehood, we are nearly covered by its waves, and people who know nothing about us are so startled at this idea of polygamy, as it is called, that they are prepared to believe anything that may be said about us. We have this to contend against. In the end, however, we shall be abundantly successful, for a people possessing the qualities that the people of Utah do, can and will live — a people who are united, a people who are honest, a people who are frugal, a people who are temperate, a people who are orderly in their lives and who are virtuous, truly virtuous, can withstand a tremendous amount of pressure. There is only one way in which this people can be checked and that is by extirpation. Otherwise, the qualities they possess are bound to live in the struggle. The doctrine of "the survival of the fittest," applies to us, and insures us a long, a prosperous, and uninterrupted and a glorious career. We can live in spite of commissioners, in spite of governors, in spite of acts of persecution; we can live and still flourish, and still grow and still increase; and we shall do it. I am not at all afraid as to the result. Of course legislation of the Edmunds' kind can pinch us; it can be made excessively disagreeable to us. It may test us in ways that may be new to us; but sincerely I say to you, my brethren and sisters, that I dread other things that exist in our midst more than I do hostile legislation.

I dread the increase of luxury; I dread the increase of class distinctions which I see growing up. The disintegrating influences of wealth are far more to be dreaded than any outside pressure of this character. All that is being done in this direction is to hoop us up, as the cooper hoops up barrels. This has been the case already. During the last five or six months I have had letters from all parts of our Territory, and they uniformly bespeak a determination to cling together.

But watch the effect of wealth; look at its effects. Communities get wealthy and they begin to think about their wealth. Where their treasure is there is their heart also. Especially is this the case if they are divided into classes. Then the rich are in a position to be tempted and tried far more than they would be if they were on the same plane with their fellows. If we are nearly alike temporally we feel alike. In this has consisted much of our strength in the past. We were not divided into classes, with interests diverse one from the other. The sacrifices we had to make fell pretty equally upon all, and there was no temptation offered one class because of its greater wealth, to compromise with principle, or to question the policy of standing up unflinchingly for principle, or to feel different from the bulk of the community.

The increase of wealth, therefore, and the consequent increase of fashions are more to be dreaded than hostile legislation. Let a wife follow all the fashions of the day, and then let her children do the same, and a man must have a deep pocket to sustain such a family. Give him two of more wives and their children of this kind, and how long can he keep up? Introduce fashions among us, and make women fashionable, and make their daughters fashionable, and what is called "the problem" will not be long in being solved. If a man then had more than one wife he would need a large income to sustain them. Some women might be shrewd enough to understand this, and if not wanting their husbands to have another wife, might take pains to consume all the income. JD 24:46 GQC June 25, 1882 SLC.

As shown elsewhere, Brigham Young did not agree with George Q. Cannon on this push for equality and classlessness, finding no advantage for the church to all be equal in poverty.

## CHAPTER 23

# Tithing and the United Order

The principle and practice of tithing played an interesting relationship to the united order ventures, probably just the opposite of what one might expect from the traditions. In Brigham Young's view, tithing was the "greater" law, not the "lesser" law, especially in terms of the resources it could supply for the central church's use. He often complained about the small amount of resources (and the even smaller amount of cash) that the saints actually contributed, claiming that he did not get "the tithing on the tithing," or barely one percent of the total income of the saints, instead of the one-tenth the scriptures allocated to the central authority.

Following are four samples of Brigham Young's comments on the tithing. In the first example, Brigham Young speaks in April 1852 of the need for payment of tithing and in the same breath makes his first recorded suggestion that a larger organization is needed, thus implying that the tithing system is not working and needs to be supplemented:

> I do not feel like preaching a discourse upon any particular subject; but of urging the necessity of the brethren and sisters absolutely coming to this determination this morning, and dedicating themselves and all they have to the Lord from this time henceforth. <u>Can we come to this conclusion, to firmly, faithfully, and unitedly enter into a covenant with ourselves, saying, I am for the Lord and none else</u>; from this time henceforth, I will do the will of my Father who is in the heavens, who has called me to minister the fulness of the Gospel, and to share the glory that is prepared for the righteous I will be like clay in the hands of the potter, that He may mould [mold] and fashion me as seemeth Him good; and if He will make known to me His will, mine shall bow to it, my affections shall be placed upon eternal things, and shall not rest upon the fading, transitory objects of time and sense? Can we make this covenant with ourselves this morning. Not only to say we dedicate this house and ourselves, our flocks, herds, families, and possessions, to the Lord, but actually perform the work, dedicating our affections to His service. If our affections are won [one] and wholly dedicated to His cause, we have then obtained the victory.
>
> Perhaps we may find one here and there who will say, "I cannot do this, I may say it with my lips, but to feel it in my heart, the case is hard; I am poor and needy, and desire to go to the gold mines to obtain something to help myself, by speculating upon the Gentiles, and thus get me a good farm and team, with which to get out of this thraldom and difficulty; my mind is so perplexed, I cannot say my affections are fully dedicated to the Lord my God." What is to be done in such a case? I know what I would do, for I have experience in these matters —— I would call upon the Bishop, and make known to him my distress. <u>There are many who in these words complain, and say they are so poor they cannot pay their tithing</u>; say they, "I have only got three horses and two yoke of cattle and about fifty sheep; I want one horse to ride, and the others to haul wood, I therefore do not know how I can possibly pay my tithing." While on the other hand, <u>others who have only got half a dozen chickens can willingly pay their tithing. You may say, "It is easier for them to pay tithing than for those who possess so much, for they are so very poor, it does not infringe upon other matters.</u>" Now if I had but one cow, and felt thus, I would give her away forthwith. If you

have only six horses and ten yoke of cattle, or only one cow, and you are too poor to pay your tithing, give the whole into the public works. I speak thus to those who are inclined to love the substance of this world better than the Lord. If you have gold and silver, let it not come between you and your duty. I will tell you what to do in order to gain your exaltation, the which you cannot obtain except you take this course. If your affections are placed upon anything so as to hinder you in the least from dedicating them to the Lord, make a dedication of that thing in the first place, that the dedication of the whole may be complete.

What hinders this people from being as holy as the Church of Enoch? I can tell you the reason in a few words. It is because you will not cultivate the disposition to be so — this comprehends the whole. If my heart is not fully given up to this work, I will give my time, my talents, my hands, and my possessions to it, until my heart consents to be subject; I will make my hands labour in the cause of God until my heart bows in submission to it.

I might here use a just and true comparison which will apply to the Church. The rulers of Great Britain have tried to make every capitalist identify his interest with the Government — that has sustained the kingdom, and is like a powerful network around the whole. Apply this comparison to the kingdom of God on earth. JD 1:202 BY April 6, 1852 SLC.

Another of the early requests for more tithing was given in November 1852 by Heber C. Kimball, counselor to the Prophet:

Now let us go to work, every one of us, and pull together, and put means into the hands of the Trustee-in-trust, pay up our tithing, and then if we have a surplus which we do not want to put out to usury now, put it in the hands of the Trustee-in-trust. Go to work, not only next spring, but now make preparations, and let us build a temple.
....
It is necessary to unite and cultivate the hearts of this people together, more than any thing else. The subject of building a temple alone will not do it, or your means; but to bring this to a focus, your hearts must be where your treasure is. If you place your treasure in the temple, your hearts must be there, they are wherever you place your treasure. The Scripture says so, and so say I. I am a servant of God, a man of truth, and President Young is my brother, my leader, and governor, and shall be forever and ever, and you cannot unhorse me if you try, and we will unhorse the whole of you if you do not do right. Shall we go to work, and build a temple, and a wall around it? JD 1:357 HCK Nov 14, 1852 SLC.

Notice that apparently already there was back tithing owing, now needed for the central purpose of building a temple. The other standard themes are there also, about the need for combining treasure and the need to heed the prophet's directives.

Brigham Young's complaint about only getting the "tithing on the tithing" is contained in the following January 1861 quote:

Some complain and say that they are taxed by tithing. We ask no tithing of any man. In this we are as independent as the Lord is. I say, Do not pay another dollar in tithing unless you want to. And to those who say that tithing should defray all classes of public expenditure, I will say, If you will put into my hands one-twentieth instead of one-tenth, I will pay every dollar of expenses for territorial, county, and city purposes. But do I, as Trustee-in-Trust, receive one-fiftieth, or one-hundredth? No. I do not get the tithing on the tithing that is due, and which it is my province to dictate. Are you afraid that I will make a bad use of it? I have plenty of money for my private use. You may wish to know how I get it. I believe I will tell you how I get some of it. A great many of these Elders of Israel, soon after courting these young ladies, and old ladies, and middle-aged ladies, and having them sealed to them, want to have a bill of divorce. I have told them, from the beginning, that sealing men and women for time and all eternity is one of the ordinances of the house of God, and that I never wanted a farthing for sealing them, nor for officiating in any of the ordinances of God's house; but when you ask for a bill of divorce; I intend that you shall pay for it. That keeps me in spending money, besides enabling me to give hundreds of dollar's to the poor, and buy butter, eggs, and little notions for women and children, and otherwise use it where it does good. JD 8:345 BY Jan 20, 1861 SLC.

In April 1871, ten years later, Brigham is still saying that not one percent of the community's gross income is ever turned over to the church as tithing:

I want to say a little now with regard to tithing. Some of this people think they pay their tithing. I expect they do; but I can make the same comparison that Jesus did when in Jerusalem. Here came the Scribes, Pharisees, Sadducees, &c., and put their substance in the Lord's storehouse; and there came along a poor widow with nothing, to all appearance. She had not clothing to make her comfortable, but she had two mites, which she had saved probably by her labor, and she placed them in the storehouse of the Lord. Jesus lifted himself up, and, seeing what they were doing, said, "Of a truth I say unto you that this poor widow hath cast in more than they all; for all these have of their abundance cast in unto the offerings of God; but she of her penury hath cast in all her living that she had." Now, there are a few of just this same kind of characters here who do pay their tithing. But do we rich men pay ours? Not by considerable. I can inform the Elders of Israel and everybody else that since we have been raising grain in these valleys the deposits paid in on tithing have not amounted to one-hundredth part of all that has been raised, whereas one-tenth was due the storehouse of the Lord. You may say, "Brother Brigham, have you paid in yours?" No, I have not. There is a number of the brethren who have paid in considerable, but I expect I have paid more tithing than any other man in this Church. I expect I have done more for the poor than any other man in the Church; yet I have hardly commenced to pay my tithing. How is it with you? I know how it is. There are a few poor who pay their tithing, and who are pretty strict; but take the masses of the people, and they have not paid one-twentieth of their tithing. Do you believe it? I know it. If I were to reason over this and attempt to show the Latter-day Saints the inconsistency of their course in the matter, I would plant my feet on this ground: We are not our own, we are bought with a price, we are the Lord's; our time, our talents, our gold and silver, our wheat and fine flour, our wine and our oil, our cattle, and all there is on this earth that we have in our possession is the Lord's and he requires one-tenth of this for the building up of his kingdom. Whether we have much or little, one-tenth should be paid in for tithing. What for? I can tell you what for in a hundred instances, but I will only tell you just a few, and will commence with the poor. You count me out fifty, a hundred, five hundred, or a thousand of the poorest men and women you can find in this community; with the means that I have in my possession, I will take these ten, fifty, hundred, five hundred, or a thousand people, and put them to labor; but only enough to benefit their health and to make their food and sleep sweet unto them, and in ten years I will make that community wealthy. In ten years I will put six, a hundred, or a thousand individuals, whom we have to support now by donations, in a position not only to support themselves, but they shall be wealthy, shall ride in their carriages, have fine houses to live in, orchards to go to, flocks and herds and everything to make them comfortable. But it is not every man that can do this. The Bishops cannot do it; not that I would speak lightly of the wisdom of our Bishops, but we have hardly a Bishop in the Church who knows A with regard to the duties of his office. Still we have good men, but our hearts are somewhere else, and we are not studying the kingdom, the welfare of the human family, nor what our office calls upon us to perform. We do not seek after the poor and have every man and woman put to usury. This ought to be, for our time is the Lord's. All we want is to direct this time and use it profitably. There is abundance of labor before us. We have the earth to subdue, and to make it like the Garden of Eden. Do you believe it? I know it. But how do we live? Very much like the rest of the world. We are ready to run over all creation. Just as I have said to some of the brethren, and to some that I have known in the world; they get their eye on a dime; they see it roll away and they go after it. By and by they stub their toe against an eagle; soon they come to another one, a doubloon or a slug, and they will stub their toe against it, and down they go; but they are up again, for their eye is on that dime, and, in their eagerness to obtain it, they stumble over the eagles they might pick up if they had wisdom to do it. Is this so? O yes, they who have eyes to see can see. Take things calm and easy, pick up everything, let nothing go to waste.

You, sisters, know I have sometimes told you what my office is. Does it make you ashamed of me when you hear some of the brethren say, "Well, I do not believe that Brother Brigham has anything to do with my farm or household matters, or with temporal things; I do not think the First Presidency has anything to do with my temporal affairs." O, yes, we have; and to come right down to the point, it is my privilege, if I were capable, to teach every woman in this Church and kingdom how to keep house, and how to sweep house, cook meat, wash dishes, make bread without any waste, &c. I may go to a house and what do I see? Perhaps the bottom or top of the bread is burnt to a coal. Why did you not do different? "O, these are accidents." Yes, because we never think of the business on our hands. Mother gets up and it is: "O, Sally, where is the dish cloth, I want it in a minute?" "Susan, where in the world have you put that broom?" or, "Where is the iron holder?" and Susan knows nothing about either dish cloth or broom, and says, "We have no iron holder except some waste paper." If I had nothing but a piece of an old newspaper folded for a holder I would have it where I could put my hand on it in a moment, in the dark if I wanted it. And so with the dishcloth, the broom, the chairs, tables, sofas, and everything about the house, so that if you had to get up in the night you could lay your hand on whatever you wanted instantly. Have a place for everything and everything in its place. JD 14:87 April 9, 1871 SLC.

It should be easy to see that if the tithing problem was really that bad for the twenty years covered by these statements, and much evidence indicates that it was (recall the plea by Lorenzo Snow for the people to start paying tithing again), then one might have to reconsider whether the "higher law" tradition is really based on any facts, or whether just the opposite is true, that a "lower" law had to be invented to get the saints through a time when they would not do their duty and pay an honest tithing.

A repeat of a quote contained in JSUO may be applicable here as well:

A comment from a period shortly after Brigham Young's time gives rise to an interesting question concerning the "displacing" tradition:

The Lord revealed to his people in the incipiency of his work a law which was more perfect than the law of tithing. It comprehended large things, greater power, and a more speedy accomplishment of the purposes of the Lord. But the people were unprepared to live by it, and the Lord, out of mercy to the people, suspended the more perfect law, and gave the law of tithing, in order that there might be means in the storehouse of the Lord for the carrying out of the purposes he had in view; for the gathering of the poor, for the spreading of the gospel to the nations of the earth, for the maintenance of those who were required to give their constant attention, day in and day out, to the work of the Lord, and for whom it was necessary to make some provision. Without this law these things could not be done, neither could temples be built and maintained, nor the poor fed and clothed. Therefore the law of tithing is necessary for the church, so much so that the Lord has laid great stress upon it. Joseph F. Smith, *Gospel Doctrine* (Salt Lake City, Utah: Deseret Book, 1977) p. 225. (April Conference Report, 1900, p. 47).

One might wonder at the need for the "higher" law mentioned in this passage, since within the same passage, it appears that every legitimate temporal need of the church is shown to be accomplished by tithing. Today, the church is making every effort to make tithing meet all of its needs for funds, and to avoid numerous other requests for contributions.

The only time, it seems, that tithing would not be sufficient is when people do not pay it. Then some substitutes may be invented, as apparently was done during Brigham Young's day, and has also been done in this century with building programs, etc., in which typically the few who did pay tithing also got to pay another large amount for buildings. Perhaps we can say that even now we are not fully living the law of tithing, but that we have apparently come a long way from the times of Brigham Young. I assume that the records of the church would show that more than one percent of church member income is paid in as tithing today.

An obligation closely related to tithing was the repayment of the travel expenses paid out through the Perpetual Emigration Fund. Many took advantage of that service and then never repaid the part they received. The central church was left to make up the difference.

In short, the central church never did have enough resources to carry out its duties properly, and apparently one of the purposes of the latest and greatest united order plan was to help remedy that situation. When ZCMI was first formed, its basic document or charter obligated it to pay tithing on its income. Since it was to handle most of the imported goods the saints purchased, its income, and therefore its tithing, could potentially be rather large.

Besides ZCMI, Orderville also paid corporate tithing, and others may have done so also. Those in the Kanab united order considered themselves exempt from the law of tithing. After all, they were living the "higher" law were they not? This attitude could represent a blow to the central church's income.

Tithing was thus in some cases paid as a corporate responsibility, not an individual responsibility. It was handled much as our withholding taxes are today, probably for the same reason or fear: if the money were not taken at its source, much of it would never be paid in voluntarily. Or we might compare it to a mortgage payment: if it is not paid, the house (or company) could be taken over. Or a dividend payment: if it is not paid, the shareholders could complain.

Would Brigham Young have been willing to accept tithing only, and forego the other more complicated economic plans to get central church resources? Very possibly. But, of course, there were other reasons to organize, such as for defense, to control imports, efficiency, provide jobs for new emigrants, etc.

There was, of course, a logical limit to the "tithing as a tax" idea. Tithing is supposed to be a voluntary contribution, so any serious attempt to collect it by legal action would fail. Some plans called for mortgaging property to borrow economic development funds from outsiders. But many lenders to governments count on the force of the taxing power to extract money to repay the debt. Tithing would probably not be sufficiently enforceable to satisfy such lenders.

Note that since so much of the tithing was paid in kind, the church had some interesting logistical and accounting problems. It did not make sense to move large amounts of cattle and grain all to one central place for storage, especially the cattle that needed to graze. Therefore, the tithing cattle and tithing grain were kept in distributed locations. This may have made ownership and accounting a bit tricky to keep straight. A man might give cattle to the church and then keep tending them.

The movement south before the coming of the federal army including moving the tithing cattle and grain. At that point, they probably wished that even more grain had been kept in distributed locations.

It is possible that the program of having corporate businesses pay tithing may have had a long-term negative effect. Lorenzo Snow told the people of St. George to pay their tithing and they would be blessed. It is possible that part of the saints' habits of non-payment of tithing may have come from that history of corporate payment of tithing which tended to de-emphasize the individual responsibility to pay.

There is one last question that might be raised here. At various times in the history of the gospel, there has been more than one way to "pay" tithing. For example, in the earliest days of the church, Joseph Smith and Oliver Cowdery proposed to devote ten percent of their income to the benefit of the poor, the choices and administration to be done by themselves. (HC 2:174-5, Nov. 29, 1834). In a similar way, some of the saints in Brigham Young's time may have in fact distributed up to ten percent of their income in assisting those around them. However, Brigham Young seemed to be focussing exclusively on the resources being channeled to the central church where he would have full control of them. By implication, he may have been redefining the nature of tithing and saying now that individually administered tithing was no longer acceptable. He may have felt that individually administered tithing, if there was any, was going to purposes that he disagreed with or at least had not specifically approved. Or he may have meant to say that individually administered tithing simply didn't count any more in his new definition of tithing, where only resources given to the central church would be counted.

## CHAPTER 24

# The United Order and Communism

In this chapter I wish to review and explore what connections there are between Brigham Young's united order and communist/socialist ideas, policies, and structures.

Various people have *claimed* or *implied* that Christian communism or even Marxist communism is or should be a part of the gospel -- "Communism as a Commandment" -- while others have *worried* that it might be true. Apparently, if communism could be shown to be a commandment, that would make many left-wing church members happy today (and even more outside the church, especially those in breakoff groups). The point of this book is to demonstrate that no such thing has happened or is likely to happen.

As detailed in *Joseph Smith's United Order*, Joseph Smith was always against socialism, communism, and "common stock" ideology and practice, and, to counteract the misinformation of his enemies, took great pains to make his views known. The Brigham Young period is more ambiguous and confusing, but when examined in detail and in context, still offers little support to those with a "church as a socialist institution" preference. The most direct anti-communism statements come from Brigham Young's repeated denunciations of the New Testament "all things common" references (See separate chapter on the topic). Brigham Young was always more interested in effective economics than in the social effects of excessive humiliation, altruism, and inherent waste of the socialist political line.

The following section of the chapter contains all references in the *Journal of Discourses* concerning "communism."

## Communism in the *Journal of Discourses*

John Taylor was certainly the best informed and most outspoken person on the topic of communism. Of the 22 references to communism in the *Journal of Discourses*, contained in 15 discourses, John Taylor is responsible for 14 of the references in 8 of the discourses.

It seems clear enough that he wanted there to be no confusion in the church about its relationship to communism. Some of his associates were much less informed and much less precise in their use of related concepts and language.

He started off early, in August 1852, just after the first hint had been dropped by Brigham Young of a possible new organizational mode. If anyone were to propose that there had been a divine direction to employ communism, John Taylor would apparently be the first to disagree:

> I was speaking, a while ago, about the people there [in France] being divided into three classes. One of them you may call infidel, under the head of Socialism, Fourierism, and several other isms. Communism is a specimen of the same thing, and they call it religion! These are generally known under the head of what is called Rouges, or Red Republicans. There is one class that think it is necessary to sustain religions as a national policy, to subdue

the minds of the people, and make them easier to govern. The third class is in the minority a long way; it is those who are actually sincere in their religion. JD 1:23 JT Aug 22, 1852 SLC.

In September of 1857 John Taylor made it clear that in his mind, anything more ideological than "baptism for the remission of sins" was carrying things too far:

Among the number of social movements in our day, there is that of Robert Dale Owen, who thought he could ameliorate the condition of mankind by a sort of communism, having a fellowship of goods among them —— a sort of common stock principle. Everything pertaining to this speculation, however, has flatted out; and in all his schemes and movements, whether in England or in this country, they have signally failed.

It is so also with Fourierism —— a species of French philosophy, established by one Fourier, a Frenchman, and advocated by Greeley of the New York Tribune. They had tried it in France, and then came over to this country; and not far from New York a society of this kind was established. They had a good deal of property, and I am informed they established something of the nature of what is called the free love principle; but within twelve months back, while I was residing in New York, everything they had was sold under the hammer.

Mr. Cabet commenced lecturing in France, and had very extensive societies there. About the time we left Nauvoo to come to this land, Mr. Cabet, with a company of his men, came there. This is a species of communism; they are called "Communists," believing, with Mr. Owen, in a community of goods. They published a newspaper in Nauvoo, and one or more in France. I baptized one of their editors while in Paris on my mission-a man who is now in this valley, by the name of Bertrand.

Mr. Krolokoski, who was also an editor of the same paper with Mr. Bertrand, came to me to have conversation about the first principles of the Gospel. After a long conversation, he said, "Mr. Taylor, do you propose no other plan to ameliorate the condition of mankind than that of baptism for the remission of sins?"

I replied —— " This is all I propose about the matter."

"Well," he said, "I wish you every success; but I am afraid you will not succeed."

Said I, "Mr. Krolokoski, you sent, some time ago, Mr. Cabet to Nauvoo. He was considered your leader —— the most talented man you had. He went to Nauvoo when it was deserted —— when, houses and lands were at a mere nominal value: he went there with his community at the time we left. Rich farms were deserted, and thousands of us had left our houses and furniture in them, and there was everything that was calculated to promote the happiness of human beings there. Never could a person go to a place under more happy circumstances. Mr. Cabet, to try his experiment, had also the selection in France of whom he pleased. He and his company went to Nauvoo, and what is the result? You have seen the published account in the papers. We were banished from civilized society into the valleys of the Rocky Mountains to seek for that protection among savages which Christian civilization denied us —— among the peau rouges, or red skins, as they call them. There our people have built houses, enclosed lands, cultivated gardens, built school-houses, opened farms, and have organized a government and are prospering in all the blessings and immunities of civilized life. Not only this, but they have sent thousands and thousands of dollars over to Europe to assist the suffering poor to go to America, where they might find an asylum. You, on the other hand, that went to our empty houses and farms —— you, I say, went there under most favourable circumstances. Now, what is the results I read in all of your reports from there, published in your own paper in Paris, a continued cry for help. The cry is to you for money, money: 'We want money to help us to carry out our designs.' The society that I represent comes with the fear of God —— the worship of the great Eloheim: they offer the simple plan ordained of God —— viz., repentance, baptism for the remission of sins, and the laying-on of hands for the gift of the Holy Ghost. Our people have not been seeking the influence of the world, nor the power of government, but they have obtained both; whilst you, with your philosophy independent of God, have been seeking to build up a system of communism and a government which is, according to your own accounts, the way to introduce the millennial reign. <u>Now, which is the best —— our religion, or your philosophy?</u>"

"Well," said he, "I cannot say anything."

He could not, because these were facts that he was familiar with.

What has become of that society? There are very few of them left. They have had dissensions, bickerings, trouble, and desertions, until they are nearly dwindled to nothing.

I might enumerate many societies of a similar nature, commenced in different parts of the world and at various times. The results, however, would be proved to be the same: they commenced in the wisdom of man, and ended as speculative bubbles. Truth, based on eternal principles, alone can stand the test.

If Owen, Fourier, Cabet, and other philosophers have failed, —— if all the varied schemes of communism have failed, —— if human philosophy is found to be at fault, and all its plans incompetent, and we have not failed, it shows there is something associated with this people and with "Mormonism" that there is not with them.

Now the question is, What is this principle? —— why is there a difference?

The first account I ever heard of this Gospel was simply preaching what are termed the first principles of the Gospel of Christ. There was nothing very ostentatious about it —— nothing very grand —— no great pomp or parade. The Elders were in many instances uneducated: they had no particular advantages among men; but they had received certain principles, certain doctrines, that were plain and easy to comprehend —— things that were childlike and simple, and that recommended themselves to every intelligent, unbiassed mind.

What was it we first learned in relation to this Gospel? Was it something very profound and philosophical, that some sage either in this or some other country had discovered —— the plan of some politician or statesman?

Verily no; it was no such thing. What was it? It was a proclamation made, declaring that a holy angel from heaven had appeared —— that he had revealed himself unto a young man that was born in the backwoods of America —— a farmer's son, without any particular educational advantages; that this angel, having appeared unto him, had revealed unto him an ancient record that gave an account of the aboriginal inhabitants of this country; that in this record there was an account of Prophets having existed on this continent in former days, of Jesus having appeared, and of angels having administered unto them, —— an account of their having been in possession of the Gospel, having the same doctrines, the same blessing, the same privileges and powers that were associated with the Gospel on the Asiatic continent; and that this record agreed with the Bible in doctrines, ordinances, teachings, and blessings.

And furthermore, these men referred us to the Bible, and showed us that this book was spoken of—— that it was to come forth —— that it was the "stick of Joseph," and that it was to be one with the "stick of Judah," —— one in prophecy, one in revelation, one in unfolding the purposes of God, and one in bringing to pass the great events that were to transpire in the last days.

We heard of these things, and to many of us they seemed foolish. We heard the cry of "False prophet and I heard from a priest, after hearing this Gospel preached by Parley P. Pratt, some twenty years ago, was the cry of "Delusion!", I was immediately informed that "Joe Smith was a money-digger," that he tried to deceive people by walking on planks laid under the water, and that he was a wicked and corrupt man, a deceiver, and one of the biggest fools in creation, and so forth. I heard every kind of story; and the priests have kept up the same things, pretty much, to the present day.

I remember, when I first had an Elder introduced to me, I said to him, "I do not know what to think about you 'Mormons.' I do not believe any kind of fanaticism: I profess to be acquainted with the Bible; and, sir." said I, "in any conversation we may have, I wish you, to confine yourself to the Bible; for I tell you I shall not listen to anything in opposition to that word."

From the report which I had heard of "Mormonism," I thought it was anything but a religious system. I was told about the French prophets —— I was told about Matthias, Johanna Southcote, and of all the follies that had existed for centuries; and then they put "Mormonism" at the end of them all.

In my researches, I examined things very carefully and critically. I wrote down six of the first sermons I heard preached by Parley P. Pratt, in order that I might compare them with the Bible, and I could not find any difference. I could easily controvert any other doctrine, but I could not overturn one principle of "Mormonism."

I have travelled to preach these doctrines in most of the United States and in the Canadas; I have preached them in England, in Scotland, in Wales, in the Isles of Man and the Jersey, in France, Germany, in the principal cities of America and Europe, and to many prominent men in the world; and I have not yet found a man that could controvert one principle of "Mormonism" upon scriptural grounds. If there is a man, I have yet to find him.

The first proclamation by the Elders was, that the ancient Gospel had been restored. We had had Methodism, Presbyterianism, Dunkerism, Shakerism, Catholicism, Quakerism, and every other ism that you could think of; but there was none that had the ancient Gospel, —— no, not one.

I was, however, well acquainted with theology. I consider that if ever I lost any time in my life, it was while studying the Christian theology. Sectarian theology is the greatest tomfoolery in the world.

....

Again: You know that you are in the kingdom of God; for God, among other things, has revealed this to you. And while the Communists, Fourierites, and others have sought to bring about a reign of righteousness without revelation, God has revealed unto you a kingdom that shall abide for ever, by the principles of eternal truth and by the revelations of God. You know that you are associated with this kingdom: you feel it; and no man can deprive you of this feeling, nor rob you of that Spirit.

Satan has had the dominion over the world for centuries, and no nation or people has acknowledged God or bowed to his sceptre. They have anointed their kings, they have hewn down and trampled upon the rights of man, and their hands reek with blood. In this condition they have had priests to come and anoint them kings! But they are wholesale murderers and robbers. JD 5:237 JT Sep 13, 1857 SLC.

In an October 10, 1875, address, John Taylor reiterates his conviction that the simple gospel contains all the rules about the association of men that are necessary for reaching the only real "utopia" of the reign of Christ on earth, or at least the preparation of a people for his coming:

The Gospel that we talk of, although it may be a personal thing, yet at the same time is as high as the heavens, wide as the universe and deep as hell. It permeates through all time, and extends to all people, both living and dead. We talk sometimes about the Church of God, and why? We talk about the kingdom of God, and why? Because, before there could be a kingdom of God, there must be a Church of God, and hence the first principles of the Gospel were needed to be preached to all nations, as they were formerly when the Lord Jesus Christ and others made their appearance on the earth.  And why so?  Because of the impossibility of introducing the law of God among a people who would not be subject to and be guided by the spirit of revelation.  Hence the world have generally made great mistakes upon these points.  They have started various projects to try to unite and cement the people together without God; but they could not do it.  Fourierism, Communism — another branch of the same thing — and many other principles of the same kind have been introduced to try and cement the human family together.  And then we have had peace societies, based upon the same principles; but all these things have failed, and they will fail, because, however philanthropic, humanitarian, benevolent, or cosmopolitan our ideas, it is impossible to produce a true and correct union without the Spirit of the living God, and that Spirit can only be imparted through the ordinances of the Gospel; and hence Jesus told his disciples to go and preach the Gospel to every creature, baptizing them in the name of the Father, Son, and Holy Ghost, and said he — "Lo, I am with you always, even to the end."  It was by this cementing, uniting spirit, that true sympathetic, fraternal relations could be introduced and enjoyed.  JD 18:137 JT Oct 10, 1875.

He presents the powerful insight that external techniques, organizations or programs, and economic or ideological dogmas can never "cement the human family together." Only individuals accepting and living the gospel and viewing and relating to their fellows using the golden rule, ten commandments, etc., can bring about that temporal unity.  The external manipulations are in fact in conflict with the gospel principles of valuing the individual, allowing freedom and agency, using only righteous influences of unfeigned love, instruction, and persuasion.

What follows, in a June 1867 discourse, appears to be the only time in the Journal of Discourses that Brigham Young used the term "communist" or any of its variants. In this single case, he recognizes the economic weakness of the communist philosophy, and the destruction that would come to the saints if they indulged in it:

There was a certain class of men called Socialists, or Communists, organized, I believe, in France.  I remember there was a very smart man, by the name of M. Cabot, came over with a company of several hundreds.  When they came to America they found the City of Nauvoo deserted and forsaken by the "Mormons," who had been driven away.  They set themselves down there where we had built our fine houses, and made our farms and gardens, and made ourselves rich by the labor of our own hands, and they had to send back year by year to France for money to assist them to sustain themselves.  We went there naked and barefoot, and had wisdom enough, under the dictation of the Prophet, to build up a beautiful city and temple by our own economy and industry without owing a cent for it.  We came to these mountains naked and barefoot.  Are you not speaking figuratively?  Yes, I am, for it was only the figure that got here, for, comparatively, we left ourselves behind.  We lived on rawhide as long we could get it, but when it came to the wolf beef it was pretty tough.  We lived, however, and built a fort, and built our houses inside the fort.  Then we commenced our gardens, we planted our corn, wheat, rye, buckwheat, oats, potatoes, beets, carrots, onions, parsnips, and we planted our peach and apple seeds, and we got grapes and strawberries, and currants from the mountains.  The seeds grew and so did the Latter-day Saints, and we are here to-day.  JD 12:61 BY June 16, 1867 SLC.

On June 23, 1874 Brigham Young spoke in the Third Ward Meeting House in Salt

Lake City. He strongly encouraged the ward to join the united order movement, but made it less than mandatory:

I will now say to my brethren and sisters, the Lord, in the first place, commenced to bring the people together upon the ground of union and oneness; but they could not bear this. You can read, on page 161, of the Book of Doctrine and Covenants, a revelation given to the Colesville Branch. <u>Lemon Copley had a tract of land that was to be given to the Saints</u>, and they were to build up a stake of Zion until there was another place prepared for the centre stake; <u>but he apostatized and the people went away</u>. Before this the Lord revealed to Joseph, that the people would gather out from Babylon, and establish the kingdom of God upon the principles of heaven. They went up to Jackson County, Mo., with this in their faith, and with the express understanding that when they got there, everything was to be laid at the feet of the Bishop, not at the feet of the Apostles, as they did anciently. Then, you know, they sold all they had, and brought their substance and laid it at the feet of the Apostles. The revelation given through Joseph was <u>to lay all at the feet of the Bishop, who was to distribute it among the people, according to the revelation given for that purpose, for their benefit. But they could not bear this, consequently they were driven from Jackson County</u>, and assembled again, some in Caldwell, and some in Davies County, and finally they were driven from the State. This was in the fall of 1838. I recollect, in Far West, Joseph, talking upon these matters, said —— "The people cannot bear the revelations that the Lord has for them. There were a great many revelations if the people could bear them." I think it was the eighth day of July, 1831, <u>Joseph had a revelation that the people should consecrate their surplus property for the building of the Temple there in Far West</u>, for the support of the Priesthood, for the paying of the debts of the Presidency, etc., which I could give an account of, for I was present when it came. Joseph was doing business in Kirtland, and it seemed as though all creation was upon him, to hamper him in every way, and they drove him from his business, and it left him so that some of his debts had to be settled afterwards; and I am thankful to say that they were settled up; still further, we have sent East to New York, to Ohio, and to every place where I had any idea that Joseph had ever done business, and inquired if there was a man left to whom Joseph Smith, jun., the Prophet, owed a dollar, or a sixpence. If there was we would pay it. But I have not been able to find one. I have advertised this through every neighborhood and place where he formerly lived, consequently I had a right to conclude that all his debts were settled.

We will now pass on. You know the history with regard to our leaving Nauvoo. Now I have it in my mind to ask the question of the Latter-day Saints —— Are they in earnest? Do they mean what they say, when they say they believe that brother Brigham Young is the legal successor of Joseph Smith, the Prophet? We believe in Joseph the Prophet; he sealed his testimony with his blood, consequently we can, with impunity, believe on him a little better than if he were living. When he was living, his testimony was not in force upon the people as it is now. But is brother Brigham the legal successor of brother Joseph? This people, called Latter-day Saints, by their acts, by their voting, say they believe he is. Well, we will admit the fact. I have a little to say, then, and shall come back to former days with regard to the duties of the individual who leads the kingdom of God on the earth.

In all ages of the world that we have any knowledge of, when there was a people on the earth whom God acknowledged as his people, he has invariably dictated them in spiritual and in temporal things. This question was agitated year after year in the days of Joseph. The first two Bishops in the Church —— Edward Partridge was the first —— I was well acquainted with him, and Newel K. Whitney was the second —— <u>questioned the propriety of Joseph having anything to do with temporal things</u>. Joseph would argue the case with them a little, and tell them how things were, and bring up Scripture to show them that it could not be otherwise —— that it was impossible for the Lord to dictate people unless he dictated them in temporal affairs. The very first act after believing is a temporal act. After I hear the Gospel preached and believe it, I go down into the waters of baptism, which is a temporal act: it is an act that pertains to my will and my body, I will that my body shall go down into the water and be immersed for the remission of my sins, consequently I have to go to the Elder who taught me the Gospel, the spiritual portion of the kingdom, and apply to him to administer this temporal ordinance, and he has to do it; having taught the doctrine he officiates in the act, and you will find it through life, every circumstance, in every case the man that dictates the spiritual kingdom of God, must dictate the temporal affairs, it can not be otherwise. I say this to you, because the idea in the minds of a few of the people is —— "Brigham ought not to meddle with temporal affairs." They said so to Joseph, and they said so much about it, that I went into the Temple at Kirtland, and challenged the men who were querying on this, to prove or bring up one instance where God did not manifest his will concerning temporal things whenever he made known his will to the children of men for establishing his kingdom on the earth. They always came to the floor; they had to do it, there was nothing else for them; it prostrated every person. There were William E. McLellin, John F. Boynton, and Lyman Johnson, who belonged to the Twelve, Frederic G. Williams, second counselor to Joseph, and two-thirds of the High Council all talking about this, and I went into the Temple and just <u>challenged them to show wherein the Lord ever conferred upon any man in the world the power to dictate in spiritual affairs, that he did not in temporal affairs? They could not do it</u>. I told them they could not draw the line between the spiritual and the temporal. All things were created first spiritual, and then temporal. Everything in the spirit world was presented as we see it now, and this temporal earth was presented there. We were in the spirit world, and we came here into this time, which is in eternity, nothing in the world only a change of time and seasons allotted to a change of being that makes it time to us. It is in eternity, and we are just as much in eternity now, as we shall be millions of years hence. But it is time measured to finite beings, and it is changeable, and we call it temporal, while the fact is it is all spiritual in the first place, then temporal, then spiritual, and made immortal, consequently you can not divide them. I say this for those to reflect upon who think that there is a difference between temporal and spiritual things. I do not say, for I do not know, that there any such here.

Now we come to our present condition. You know the past. These children who were born in his city or Territory, know what they can remember, and many of them arc [are] old enough to have many reflections and can see and understand a great many things; but the older ones know that this people have drifted just as far as they can without a reformation. Every spiritual mind knows this. I will now say to my brethren and sisters, that while we were in <u>Winter Quarters,</u> the Lord gave to me a <u>revelation</u> just as much as he ever gave one to anybody. He opened my mind, and <u>showed me the organization of the kingdom of God in a family capacity</u>. I talked it to my brethren; I would throw out a few words here, and a few words there, to my first counselor, to my second counselor and the Twelve Apostles, but with the exception of one or two of the Twelve, it would not touch a man. They believed it would come, O yes, but it would be <u>by and by</u>. Says I, "<u>Why not now?</u>" If I had been worth millions when we came into this valley and built what we now call the "Old Fort," I would have given it if the people had been prepared to then receive the kingdom of God according to <u>the pattern given to Enoch</u>. But I could not touch them. One would say, "I am for California," another one, "I am for gold," and I am for this and I am for that; and some used their influence in trying to persuade others to go to California. They said —— "You can't stay here, you can't raise anything here, it is too cold, too frosty, these mountains are not fit to live in, this is not the place for white people, let us go to California and get some gold," etc.

Now I am going to tell a dream that I had, which I think is as applicable, to the people to-day —— the 21st day of June, 1874, as when I had it. There were so many going to California, and going this way and that way, and they did not know what they wanted, and said I —— "stay here, we can raise our food here, I know it is a good stock country, a good sheep country, and as good a country for raising silk as there is in the world, and we shall raise some of the best of wheat. There stands a man —— Burr Frost, and there is Truman O. Angell, who were present at the time. Said I, "We can raise all we want here, do not go away, do not be discouraged." That was when the pioneers came; the next year, it was California, California, California, California. "No," said I, "stay here." After much thought and reflection, and a good deal of praying and anxiety as to whether the people would be saved after all our trouble in being driven into the wilderness, I had a dream one night, the second year after we came in here. Captain Brown had gone up to the Weber, and bought a little place belonging to Miles Goodyear. Miles Goodyear had a few goats, and I had a few sheep that I had driven into the Valley, and I wanted to get a few goats to put along with the sheep. I had seen Captain Brown and spoken to him about the goats, and he said I could have them. Just at that time I had this dream, which I will now relate. I thought I had started and gone past the Hot Springs, which is about four miles north of this city. I was going after my goats. When I had gone round the point of the mountain by the Hot Springs, and had got about half a mile on the rise of ground beyond the Spring, whom should I meet but brother Joseph Smith. He had a wagon with no bed on, with bottom boards, and tents and camp equipage piled on. Somebody sat on the wagon driving the team. Behind the team I saw a great flock of sheep. I heard their bleating, and saw some goats among them. I looked at them and thought —— "This is curious, brother Joseph has been up to Captain Brown's and got my goats." There were men driving the sheep, and some of the sheep I should think were three and a half feet high, with large, fine, beautiful white fleeces, and they looked so lovely and pure; others were of moderate size, and pure and white; and in fact there were sheep of all sizes, with fleeces clean, pure and white. Then I saw some that were dark and spotted, of all colors and sizes and kinds, and their fleeces were dirty, and they looked inferior; some of these were a pretty good size, but not as large as some of the large fine clean sheep, and altogether there was a multitude of them of all sizes and kinds, and goats of all colors, sizes and kinds mixed among them. Joseph stopped the wagon, and the sheep kept rushing up until there was an immense herd. I looked in Joseph's eye, and laughed, just as I had many a time when he was alive, about some trifling thing or other, and said I —— "Joseph, you have got the darndest flock of sheep I ever saw in my life; what are you going to do with them, what on earth are they for?" Joseph looked cunningly out of his eyes, just as he used to at times, and said he —— "They are all good in their places." When I awoke in the morning I did not find any fault with those who wanted to go to California; I said, "If they want to go let them go, and we will do all we can to save them; I have no more fault to find, the sheep and the goats will run together, but Joseph says, "they are all good in their places."

This will apply precisely to what we are doing at the present time. We are trying to unite the people together in the order that the Lord revealed to Enoch, which will be observed and sustained in the latter days in redeeming and building up Zion; this is the very order that will do it, and nothing short of it. We are trying to organize the Latter-day Saints into this order; but I want to tell you, my brethren and sisters, that I have not come here to say that you have got to join this order or we will cut you off the Church, or you must join this order or we will consider you apostates; no such thing, oh no, the Saints are not prepared to see everything at once. They have got to learn little by little, and to receive a little here and a little there. Since we commenced to organize at St. George, I have not had a feeling in my heart but to say to those who can not see this order —— Try and live your religion; get the Spirit of the Lord and keep it; humble yourselves before the Lord and get his Spirit; ask the Father in the name of Jesus to open your minds and let you see things as they are, and you will delight in it. And I say to all those who wish to receive the Order, come along and we will organize you, and we will do the very best we can for you. It is true that some who are in the Order talk very foolishly to those who do not feel to come into it; they throw out some very unbecoming expressions. This is entirely wrong. It is not called for, it is not needed, and it will not do the least good in the world. We must manifest and show to our brethren a purer life than we have heretofore. I will say to you, who want to be organized in this Order, we will not take one red cent from you, but the Lord will add to you riches and honor, if you will take counsel. As we have said from the beginning, we do not want a man's farm, we do not want his gold and his silver, and nothing in the world but just his time. We want to dictate the time of the Latter-day Saints, to show them that we can come into the Order of God, and that we will be that people that the Lord has said with regard to temporal things. Speaking of the Latter-day Saints, the Lord has said —— "I will make you the richest people on the earth," and he can do it just as well as not, if we have a mind to let him. It is the time of the people we want to dictate.

I will branch off to another thread of the subject. Here is a brother who says, "Why, yes, you may have some of my property, or even take it all; but I want to be a man for myself; I do not want to be dictated; I want to preserve my own freedom; I do not want to be a slave" What an idea! It is from the enemy, and because a person has not the Spirit of the Lord to see how things are. There is not a man of us but what is willing to acknowledge at once that God demands strict obedience to his requirements. Bnt [But] in rendering that strict obedience, are we made slaves? No, it is the only way on the face of the earth for you and me to become free, and we shall become the slaves of our own passions, and of the wicked one, and servants to the devil, if we take any other course, and we shall be eventually cast into hell with the devils. Now to say that I do not enjoy the volition of my own will just as much when I pray as I would to swear, is a false principle, it is false ground to take. You take the man who swears, and he has no more freedom, and acts no more on his own will than the man who prays; and the man who yields strict obedience to the requirements of Heaven, acts upon the volition of his own will and exercises his freedom just as much as when he was a slave to passion; and I think it is much better and more honorable for us, whether children or adults, youthful, middle-aged or old, it is better to live by and better to die by, to have our hearts pure, and to yield strict obedience to the principles of life which the Lord has revealed, than be a slave to sin and wickedness. All that the Lord requires of us is strict obedience to the laws of life. All the sacrifice that the Lord asks of his people is strict obedience to our own covenants that we have made with our God, and that is to serve him with an undivided heart.

I say this because I want youo [you] to understand our position. I am the director and counselor to this people for building up the kingdom of God on the earth. I am the one who will tell what shall be done, and how it shall be done, and any may who deviates or says that there is any design in connection with the United Order other than to put the people in a condition and situation to be better and freer, and in which they will enjoy more of the blessings of heaven and earth than they can out of it, does not tell the truth. You all know that it takes intelligence to enjoy. Persons in good-health enjoy their food. Why? Because they have sensibility and nervous feeling. Take that away and they would be like that stovepipe. Cut a hole in that, and put therein a nice beef steak, plum pudding, or a sweet cake, and would the stovepipe enjoy it? No. Why? Because it has no sensibility. We enjoy because we have sensibility. Promote this sensibility, seek to get more and more knowledge, more wisdom, and more understanding, and to know the things of God. He is the author of life and of all joy and comfort; he is the author of all intelligence and of all good to us; then become satisfied to obey him, and seek to get more and more of his nature, and learn more and more of him. This will give us greater sensibility, and we shall know how to enjoy, and how to endure. I say, if you want to enjoy exquisitely, become a Latter-day Saint, and then live the doctrine of Jesus Christ. The man or woman who will do this will enjoy and endure most; and if they will be humble and faithful they will enjoy the glory and the excellency of the power of God, and be prepared to live with Gods and with angels.

We want to build up the kingdom of God on the earth. I do not know but I am spending more time than I should, but I must say some things more. This Third Ward is not organized. I do not know when it will be. We asked your Bishop, and he did not feel exactly prepared to enter into the Order. We know the reason why. Will he be prepared? Yes. I want to prophesy tbat [that] he and his Ward will be prepared by and by, and I hope my prophecy will be fulfilled. He does not see things as quickly as I do. I will tell you what my position has always been. Before I embraced the Gospel, I understood pretty well what the different sects preached, but I was called an infidel because I could not embrace their dogmas. I could not believe all of Methodism; I could not believe all of the Baptists' doctrines; there were some things they preached I could believe, and some I could not. I could not fully agree with the Presbyterians in their doctrines, nor with the Quakers, nor the Catholics, although they all have some truth. As far as their teachings were in accordance with the Bible, I could believe them, and no further. I was acquainted with the creeds of nearly all the various sects of dissenters in America, for I had made it my business to inquire into the principles in which they believed. I was religiously inclined in my youth, but I could not believe in their dogmas, for they did not commend themselves to my understanding, though a child I had attended their camp meetings, and had seen what they called the power of God. I had seen men and women fall, and be as speechless and breathless as that stove before me. I had seen scientists hold the lightest feather they could procure at the nostrils and mouths of females to see if a particle of air passed to or from the lungs, and not a particle was discernable. When a child I saw all this, but I could not believe in their dogmas. I could not say the people were not sincere in their faith and acts, but it was all a mystery to me. I was not old enough, and did not understand enough to decide. In the days of Joseph, when the revelation came to him and Sidney Rigdon, while translating that portion of the New Testament contained in the 29th verse of the third chapter of John, in reference to the different degrees of glory, I was not prepared to say that I believed it, and I had to wait. What did I do? I handed this over to the Lord in my feelings, and said I, "I will wait until the spirit of God manifests to me, for or against." I did not judge the matter, I did not argue against it, not in the least. I never argued the least against anything Joseph proposed, but if I could not see or understand it, I handed it over to the Lord. This is my counsel to you, my brethren and sisters, and if I were sure my prophecy would be fulfilled, I certainly would prophesy that all here, who profess to be Latter-day Saints, will come into the holy Order and rejoice in it. And if you do not feel to came into the Order, assist those who do, and do not say anything against them. You who come into the Order, do not lisp anything against those who do not; if you feel right you will not have the least feeling against them. Come along, for, as I have said, if I do not find more than fifty men in the kingdom of God who will go with me to organize the Church and kingdom of God more perfectly, I shall go ahead. What for? More knowledge, wisdom, and perfection in the management and control of our temporal affairs. This is what I calculate to do, and I am going to do. Ask me if I am going into the Order with all that I have? Yes, as I told them in a meeting not long go, I am going in with hat, coat, vest, pants, shirt, boots, and all I have. And if the question is asked, If your family do not go into the Order, what are you going to do with your property? I am going to seal it up to the kingdom of God, for I do not mean that the enemies of the kingdom shall have a penny if I can help it. I want it to go to the kingdom of God, I want it appropriated for the salvation of the human family, to build Temples, to sustain the families of the Elders who go abroad to preach; I want it to be used for the good of the poor and for the establishing of truth and righteousness on the earth. That is all it is for; I have no pleasure in it, I have no delight in it, it is nothing to me; I want everything that the Lord places in my possession, my time, my talents, every ability I have, every penny that he has committed to me to be used to his glory, and for the building up of his kingdom on the earth. I have nothing but what he has committed to me. What do you say to that, Jacob? Is that right? It is exactly. There is not a man here who has got his sight, hearing, taste and smell, but he is indebted to the Lord for them. The Lord gave us everything we possess, whatever ability or talents we have; our Tabernacles and all we enjoy, are the gifts of the Lord, and all should be devoted to the promotion of his kingdom on the earth, and I mean that mine shall be, the Lord being my helper.

I do not want to say to this Ward, you must come into the Order, or we shall not fellowship you, for we shall fellowship you if you do not. A short time ago, I said to those of this Ward who intended to be organized, go to the Eighth Ward and organize with them, but it was a misunderstanding, that I had dismissed Bro. Weiler from being Bishop here; and if anybody else understood so, I think they are mistaken. He is your Bishop still, and I charge him now in God's name, not to trifle with the sacred things of the kingdom of God, or to throw cold water on them; if he does he will be left dark, and finally apostatize. I say to you Bishop and to the brethren and sisters, be faithful, live so that the Spirit of the Lord will abide within you, then you can judge for yourselves. I have often said to the Latter-day Saints —— "Live so that you will know whether I teach you truth or not." Suppose you are careless and unconcerned, and give way to the spirit of the world, and I am led, likewise, to preach the things of this world and to accept things that are not of God, how easy it would be for me to lead you astray! But I say to you, live so that you will know for yourselves whether I tell the truth or not. That is the way we want all Saints to live. Will you do it? Yes, I hope you will, every one of you. I say to the Bishop, here, go along and do not contend against the things of God. You and your counselors are disposed to argue in regard to the United Order. There should be no argument in this case; the Spirit of the Lord is the only thing that can enlighten our minds, and give us a knowledge of the things of God. No earthly argument, no earthly reasoning can open the minds of intelligent beings and show them heavenly things; that can only be done by the spirit of revelation. I testify this to the Latter-day Saints, and I feel to say God bless you, peace be with you. I have not come here to scold you, or anybody else. I am sometimes very rough in my language to the people, and I give them a rough scolding, but I do not wish any evil to the individual, it is to his wrong acts. If a person does wrong I am for exposing that, and chastening the perpetrator if he persists in it. I want wrong doers to refrain. Now, I say, brother Jacob, teach the things of God. Do not have a doubt about this any more than about baptism, nor say a word against it. How many are there in this Church who are now wavering and shaking because they have spoken against the ordinances of heaven, and especially against that ordinance which God has revealed for the exaltation of the children of men in celestial marriage? Hold that as sacred as your own soul: if you cannot see the beauty and glory of it, and feel it in your own hearts, say nothing against it. This earth was placed in the hands of Adam and his sons, and he is the Lord of the earth; the male portion of the human family are the lords of the earth, and they are full of wickedness, evil and destruction, and especially in their acts towards the female sex. But God will hold them accountable. The fact is, let the pure principles of the kingdom of God be taught to men and women, and far more of the latter than of the former will receive and obey them. What shall we do with them? They want exaltation, they want to be in the great family of heaven, they do not want to be cast off, then they must be taken into the families of those who prove themselves worthy to be exalted with the Gods. Who is it that can not see the beauty and the excellency of celestial marriage, and having our children sealed to us? What should we do without this? Were it not for what is revealed concerning the sealing ordinances, children born out of the covenant could not be sealed to their parents ; children born in the covenant are entitled to the Spirit of the Lord and all the blessings of the kingdom. I know that our children, universally, have the Spirit of the Lord, and when they get old enough to judge right from wrong, if they turn from the good and promote evil in their hearts, then will be the time they sin.

Now, I say to you, brother Jacob, teach the things of God, and do not trifle with this; do not argue about this at all; if you do not see and understand, stand still and see the salvation of God. Labor and help those who wish to go forward, and the Lord will bless you in it. He will open your minds and give you light and understanding, and you will be far happier than the wicked. How blessed are you when you are for God and none else! Then you are ready for whatever he reveals. How sweet you can sleep! Your dreams are pleasant and delightful, and the days, weeks, months and years pass away easily and joyfully, you are so happy.

I pray God to bless you, Amen. JD 18:235 BY June 23, 1874 Third Ward Meeting House, SLC.

In this Third Ward talk, Brigham Young says that no property will be taken and no force used to make them join (so it is not communism.) However, it is still not without any economic ideology. His ideas are still distinct from pure economic freedom. He does want all their time to be controlled and directed. Some might find that more intrusive than taking their property. There may be no real philosophical difference, since men create or enhance property by spending their time on it.

Brigham Young's telling the third ward that he would not use (excessive) force on them, is interesting. Why should he even have to make such a statement if there were not a certain level of coercion employed (or implied) in the past and present?

In this talk, as in the one following, Brigham Young again claims (incorrectly) that the failure to live the law he is espousing is what caused the expulsion from Missouri. He apparently laid that "guilt trip" on the saints on several different occasions, presumably because it had the desired psychological effect on them of frightening and shaming them. However, there appears to be no basis for his claim, except for its current effects on the listeners.

In another discourse, dated August 15, 1876, delivered in Logan, Brigham Young repeats his story of the curse that befell the saints in Missouri. He also discusses property questions, seeming to first say that only time and obedience is required, then alluding to the taking of property:

You Elders of Israel, do you not see the necessity of an advance? Do you not see that we have traveled just as far as we can, without adopting the revelation the Lord gave at Independence, Jackson County, namely, that "the property of the Saints should be laid at the feet of the Bishops, etc., and unless this was done a curse would befall them?" They refused to do it, and the consequence was, they were driven from their homes. Unless we obey these first revelations, the people will decline in their faith, and they will leave the faith of the holy Gospel. Do the Elders sense this? Yes, a great many of them do —— also a great many of the sisters. Were it not for the faith and prayers of the faithful ones, this Church would have been given into the hands of our enemies. It is the faith of the Priesthood, who cling to the commandments of the Lord, that holds the people where they are. Supposing you were in a state to say, We will do what is required of us: It would be enough for me to say, It is your duty to finish that house (the Tabernacle) without delay, and it would be done, every man doing his part cheerfully. But, instead of that being the case, we might apply to brother John for his team: says brother John, "It is very hard of you to ask for my team. I have only the one span, and I don't see that I can let you have it." Brother John keeps his team; but if he could have had faith sufficient to obey the request, the Lord would have blessed him with two teams. But because he keeps it, that is his all, and very probably, will remain his all. Again, say the Priesthood, "I want your house." "Take it." "Your garden." "Take it." Says one —— "Do you feel so, brother Brigham?" Precisely so, I want to entertain no other feeling. I have nothing but what, if the Lord requires, it must go freely. He can take nothing more than is already his. I say, take it, I will trust in him for more. This is the only safe ground to walk upon. It is the only way by which we can secure eternal life. Jesus says, " Strait is the gate, and narrow is the way, which leads to life eternal," but which the New Translation made, that leads to "the lives," and few there be who find it. But wide is the gate and broad is the way that leads to destruction and many there be who go in thereat. JD 18:216 BY Aug 15, 1876 Logan.

In an April 6, 1877 address in St. George, Brigham Young corrected George Q. Cannon on the question of being required to divide property equally:

DISCOURSE BY PRESIDENT BRIGHAM YOUNG,
DELIVERED AT THE SEMI-ANNUAL CONFERENCE, HELD IN THE TEMPLE,
AT ST. GEORGE, FRIDAY MORNING, APRIL 6, 1877.
(Reported by Geo. F. Gibbs.)
THE UNITED ORDER —— THE DUTY OF THE PRIESTHOOD —— THE GOSPEL
NOT COMMUNISM —— TEACHING THE PEOPLE HOW TO LIVE —— INDEPENDENCE
OF BABYLON —— THE SAINTS WILL CONTINUE TO SPREAD —— UNITY
OF PURPOSE AND ACTION, WILL BRING AGAIN ZION —— FREE SCHOOLS
CRITICISED —— EDUCATIONAL STATUS OF OUR CHILDREN.

I would like to say a great deal during this Conference to the Latter-day Saints, but I shall be able to talk but little, and therefore when I do speak I wish you to listen, and this I believe all of you will do.

I think that, as a people, we are nearer alike in the sentiments and feelings of our hearts, than in our words. From the most excellent discourse which we have heard this morning from brother Cannon, I believe that the people might gather the idea that we shall be expected to divide our property equally one with another, and that this will constitute the United Order. I will give you my view, in as few words as possible with regard to this subject, which I will promise you are correct.

The Lord wishes and requires us to develop the ability within us, and to utilize the ability, of these men, women and children called Latter-day Saints.

The most of the inhabitants of the earth are incapable of dictating and devising for themselves. In many instances there is reason for this, for they are opposed to that degree that for the lack of opportunity they are not able to develop the talents and ability that are within them. This is the condition of the people of most of the nations of the earth. All those who come out from the world, espousing the Gospel of Jesus, place themselves in a condition to be taught of him, but instead of teaching them personally, he has raised up his authorized teachers to do this work, and what does he expect of us to do? He requires, absolutely requires, of us to take these people who have named his name through baptism, and teach them how to live, and how to become healthy, wealthy and wise. This is our duty.

Supposing that the property of the whole community were divided to-day equally amongst all, what might we expect? Why a year from to-day we should need another division, for some would waste and squander it away, while others would add to their portion. The skill of building up and establishing the Zion of our God on the earth is to take the people and teach them how to take care of themselves and that which the Lord has entrusted to their care, and to use all that we command to glorify his holy name. This is the work of regenerating, of elevating mankind to the higher plane of the Gospel; in other words, of simply teaching them their duty.

With regard to our property, as I have told you many times, the property which we inherit from our Heavenly Father is our time, and the power to choose in the disposition of the same. This is the real capital that is bequeathed unto us by our Heavenly Father; all the rest is what he may be pleased to add unto us. To direct, to counsel and to advise in the disposition of our time, pertains to our calling as God's servants, according to the wisdom which he has given and will continue to give unto us as we seek it.

Now, if we could take this people, in their present condition, and teach them how to sustain and maintain themselves and a little more, we would add to that which we already have; but to take what we have and divide amongst or give to people, without teaching them how to earn and produce, would be no more nor less than to introduce the means of reducing them to a state of poverty.

I do not wish for one moment to recognize the idea that in order to establish the United Order our property has to be divided equally among the people, to let them do what they please with it. But the idea is to get the people into the same state of unity in all things temporal, that we find ourselves in with regard to things spiritual. Then let those who possess the ability and wisdom direct the labors of those not so endowed, until they too develop the talents within them and in time acquire the same degree of ability. JD 18:353 BY April 6, 1877 St. George.

Brigham Young does not use the word "communism," but the headnotes summarize his meaning as precluding principles of communism being associated with the united order. His idea of letting the more experienced direct the labors of those with less knowledge seems like a sensible one. However, if one's time is taken by any forceful means, it is hardly any less an affront than taking one's property. In fact, involuntary servitude would be worse. Willing men are far more productive than unwilling men, so it is good economics to have a free system.

This being 1877, the year of Brigham Young's death (in August), it is surprising that this question of "is the united order communism" still needs to be discussed, and assurances given that it is not.

Lorenzo Snow, in an address dated April 21, 1878, in Ogden, declared that "The United Order is not French Communism:"

A great deal might be said in regard to the principles of the United Order, that I do not feel to talk about this afternoon, but I do feel to urge on those brethren who have the means and are in circumstances, to search out the mind and will of God in regard to these matters, and let us try to build up Zion. Zion is the pure in heart. Zion cannot be built up except on the principles of union required by the celestial law. Is high time for us to enter into these things. It is more pleasant and agreeable for the Latter-day Saints to enter into this work and build up Zion, than to build up ourselves and have this great competition which is destroying us. Now let things go on in our midst in our Gentile fashion, and you would see an aristocracy growing amongst us, whose language to the poor would be, "we do not require your company; we are going to have things very fine; we are quite busy now, please call some other time." You would have <u>classes</u> established here, some <u>very poor</u> and some <u>very rich</u>. Now, the Lord is not going to have anything of that kind. There has to be an <u>equality</u>; and we have to observe these principles that are designed to give every one the privilege of gathering around him the comforts and conveniences of life. The Lord, in his economy in spiritual things, has fixed that every man, according to his perseverance and faithfulness, will receive exaltation and glory in the eternal worlds —— a fulness of the Priesthood, and a fulness of the glory of God. This is the economy of God's system by which men and women can be exalted spiritually. The same with regard to the temporal affairs. We should establish the <u>principles of the United Order</u>, that give every man a chance to <u>receive these temporal blessings</u>. I do not say that it would be proper to give a man just baptized the fulness of the Priesthood at once. Neither would it be right to <u>give</u> a man who has just come from the old country <u>the home and possessions</u> of him who has been here and labored and toiled for years to accumulate them. It would not be right for the possessor to step out of his house, and let the one who has never labored and toiled go in and take his place; but this man who has got the blessings of God around him, should be willing to sacrifice a portion of his surplus means to <u>establish some industry</u>, that this poor man can work and obtain a good remuneration for his labor, that he can see comfort and convenience before him, by persevering as he has done who has been thus blessed. This is the spirit and aim of the United Order, and that we should endeavor to establish. We should <u>employ our surplus means in a manner that the poor can have employment</u> and see before them a competence and the conveniences of life, so that they may not be dependent upon their neighbors. Where is the man who wants to be dependent upon his neighbors or the Tithing Office? No! He is a man, and is the image of God, and wants to gather the means around him, by his own, individual exertions. Blessed of God, are we, who have surplus means, and we should be willing to employ those means whereby such individuals may have, as before mentioned. <u>The United Order is not *French Communism*</u>. It is not required of those who possess the means of living to expend those means among those who know nothing about taking care of and preserving them. But let no man be oppressed and placed in circumstances where he cannot reach forth and help himself.

Well, I wanted to say a few things by way of suggestion to the brethren. May God bless his people in Ogden. Take the Book of <u>Doctrine and Covenants</u>, trace the subject of the <u>United Order</u>, and you will find it <u>explained fully</u>. And there need not be any difficulty in regard to what is required at our hands.

May we so live as to be worthy of a standing in the presence of God. Amen. JD 19:349-350 LS April 21, 1878 Ogden.

Since Marx was associated with French Communism, we may assume Lorenzo Snow was referring to Marx's ideas.

It is interesting that as late as 1878, Lorenzo Snow felt it useful or necessary to say that "The United Order is not French Communism." The general unity theme had been discussed almost continually for over twenty years, and it still was not clear to everyone that it was not communism. Communism included the idea of taking of property by force, or, the same thing, preventing anyone from acquiring it individually. The various united order schemes usually contained various elements of force, such as threatening one's salvation or church membership if all was not conveyed or all labor was not directed a certain way. Even if one had a good goal (nearly all promoters of such ideas claim to have good goals), is it justified to use force to get someone to do something good? If they were adequately informed they would probably do it anyway, but there is always a risk they will choose otherwise. The path of education and persuasion is often a slow and frustrating one, but it is the gospel way.

No one can fault Lorenzo Snow's economic logic of using savings to create productive employment for newcomers (or anyone in their society). However, this horrible fear of an aristocracy seems greatly overblown. How many Vanderbilts were there in Salt Lake City anyway? It sounds like the speaker has implicitly accepted the Marxist/Communist premise that ghastly class warfare is a dire and imminent threat and can only be prevented by making sure no one is too successful - employing force, in other words, to accomplish a "therapeutic" leveling. Brigham Young never accepted that principle, as far as the *Journal of Discourses* goes, but many of his associates apparently did.

In other words, his protestations that the united order was not French communism, seems merely to mean that in fact the united order does partake of the principles of French Communism, but just in a lesser or "nicer" way. His talk about equality implies a leveling and that implies force of some sort. Force, propaganda, misinformation, and intimidation are some of the techniques often used in such settings. We certainly have a mild form here, hardly Stalin's killing of millions to get control, but there is a slight similarity of methods used to extract "surplus" from the peasants to build up specific economic sectors on a forced-march basis.

If the D&C explained the united order fully, we should certainly have saved the many tons of ink spilled on that topic. In fact, the D&C says almost nothing about the economic and organizational problems the saints are grappling with here.

In an address dated July 7, 1878, one year after Brigham Young's death, George Q. Cannon spoke of general economic and political conditions and mentioned the existence of communist influence in the land:

> I consider our condition to-day in these mountains the best condition that we can occupy. When I travel through the States and converse with gentlemen who are familiar with the affairs of the nation through its length and breadth, I never arise from such conversation without feeling impressed more than ever with the excellence of this circumstances which surround us. It is true we have a desert land, that it is a land requiring excessive toil to make it fruitful and habitable for those who live in it. The grass does not clothe our hills spontaneously; our territory is not favored with the rains of heaven to make it green with verdure: our fields would be barren indeed, if it were not for the labor of irrigation and the constant efforts of the husbandman. In this respect our country differs very much from every other place east of us. In travelling through the broad prairies of Illinois, with the continuous fields of grain; and through Iowa and Nebraska, so far as <u>Nebraska</u> is settled, and contrasting the <u>ease</u> with which those lands are cultivated, compared with the <u>toil</u> required in this <u>mountain region</u>, I could not help thinking that if we were permitted to live in so goodly a land, under favorable circumstances, we would soon convert it into an Eden. But in the providences of the Almighty we were driven out and led to this land, and the Lord has showed unto us, and is showing to the inhabitants of the earth, that when a people will do that which He requires of them, that he is abundantly able to sustain them and make their labors successful. He has done this in leading us to this country, and iu [in] sustaining us since we came here. Our condition in many respects is far superior to those who live in those favored localities to which I have referred. We have a healthy land; we have a land that the Lord has blessed and made fruitful as the result of our labors. It is a land in which <u>men</u>

cannot, from the very nature of things, monopolize large bodies of land to the exclusion of their poorer neighbors. This is an advantage to the people of this country. The nature of our surroundings compels us to occupy small holdings and the result is our land is better cultivated, there is a more widespread ownership of the soil than you will find in any part of these United States; that is, there are more men holding land and owning and occupying it, in this country, in proportion to the entire population, than you can find elsewhere. The result is a condition of <u>independence</u> you cannot find elsewhere. At the present time, in the <u>western States</u> especially, men are greatly concerned about the element known as <u>Communism</u>, which has taken possession of the minds of a numerous class of the people. The <u>working classes</u> are becoming very dissatisfied, and men are trembling for fear of what will come upon the nation. One of the strongest arguments that was made in favor of keeping up the United States army up to its present numbers was, that there would probably be riots in large cities and in populous centres, which would require the presence of the military acting as police to quell. And had it not been for this evil the army would have been cut down. But a good many men were anxious to have it increased, deeming it necessary for the preservation of life and property. When we reflect upon this it shows how changed have become the affairs of our nation, when it is deemed necessary to appeal to military power to maintain good order in the Repnblic [Republic]. There can be no surer sign of the decay of a republic than when human life and property and liberty cannot be sustained by the masses of the people, and the military power, the ranks of which are filled with hired soldiers, has to be appealed to sustain good order in the midst of the people. Let such a state of thing continue and there would soon be an end of true republicanism.

In this respect we also have our difficulties. The business of furnishing employment for our poor people, so that our streets shall not be filled with idle men and boys, has no doubt pressed, and will continue to press itself upon the minds of the leading men of this Territory. But in comparison with the magnitude of this question elsewhere, it seems to sink into insignificance here. It is a matter of small moment, comparatively speaking, in this Territory; because the great bulk of the people have employment, and can easily furnish themselves with employment. However, this is a matter that should receive attention and from those, too, who care for the people and have their welfare at heart. No doubt everything will be done that should be to preserve good government throughout this Territory, and throughout all these valleys which are inhabited by the Latter-day Saints. The fact is, the time will come, concerning which there has been so much said in the past, when it will devolve upon the people of these mountains to maintain good government, to uphold constitutional rights; and we are receiving the training necessary to fit and prepare us for that great and glorious destiny. I have no doubt that the day will come, and come speedily, when <u>Utah</u> will be looked to, as <u>an example of good government</u>, and that the condition of affairs in this Territory will be pointed to as an example for other communities and other societies to imitate with advantage to themselves and the country at large. There is every inducement therefore for us, as Latter-day Saints, to <u>continue to persevere in the direction in which we are going</u>.

I have no doubt many of you would be surprised if you knew the interest that is being taken, outside of our Territory, in our affairs. When the news of the <u>death of President Young</u> reached the east, there was, I might say, a general expectation that <u>rival claimants to the power</u> he wielded would arise, that dissensions would ensue and that the work of <u>disintegration</u> would commence and the speedy overthrow of the system soon follow. I suppose I have beeu [been] spoken to hundreds of times upon this point and men seem surprised that this has not been the result. Many have said to me, "Your affairs seem to go on prosperously, notwithstanding the death of your great leader." Yes. "Well, we scarcely expected this would be the case; we have heard so much said through the newspapers concerning the probability of dissensions in your midst and quarrels over the leadership, that we were expecting you would have trouble." I have told them invariably that President Young had all his life-time acknowledged that the qualities and powers he possessed he owed to what the world call "Mormonism;" that he was not the creator of "Mormonism," but he himself was the product of it, and that this would continue to increase, no matter how many leaders might die or pass away. The results which have followed the decease of President Young have given to thinking men a higher idea of the strength and power of this system. It assumes a different position in their minds. The idea now begins to prevail that it is not entirely dependent upon the life or the ability of auy [any] single individual; and I think the death of President Young has had the effect also to cause men to pause, and to look upon the work a little differently. He was the target at which every arrow was aimed he was the object of every plot and scheme; every combination for evil had for its object, his destruction or his embarrassment. His withdrawal from the scene spoiled these combinations, and brought these plots to naught. To this I attribute the quiet of the past season. Although I have often been at Washington for the past 20 years, and have spent a considerable portion of my time there for a number of years past, I have never seen less of the disposition on the part of public men to take adverse measures against the people of Utah Territory than there has been this season. The feeling has been to let us alone for the present; and although there were emissaries sent down from here who labored very diligently to stir up feeling and to secure action against the people of Utah, their efforts scarcely created a ripple upon the surface of political affairs, and they attracted no attention outside of the committees, to whom they addressed themselves. Though it is unpleasant upon some accounts to have men there who are circulating all manner of falsehood about the people of Utah to gain their ends, they have their uses. They create discussion. They stir one up, and their presence and opposition furnish opportunities to talk to committees and members about Utah affairs, which otherwise the Delegate would not have. Such discussions made things lively in the committee rooms, but outside of the committees there was not a feeling that I could discover particularly hostile to Utah. This is a remarkable condition of affairs; ond [and] I attribute it in part to the effect that the death of President Young has had upon the public mind throughout the entire country. JD 20:33-34-35 GQC July 7, 1878 SLC.

His comment about communism in the western states is an interesting one. It may relate to then-current events in California. An article dated 1879 entitled "Communism in California" (see text quoted below) discusses the March 1879 results of an 1878 constitutional convention in California. The proposed new constitution contained provisions which gave the legislature powers to interfere with property and citizenship which it had not previously held, and enacted some specific provisions favoring consumers and attacking large corporations. The terms were suggested by a powerful minority calling themselves Communists. Some examples are allowing graduated income tax, setting an 8-hour work day, making lobbying illegal, requiring courts to determine cases quickly, restricting tolls by railroad, telegraph, and gas companies, preventing Chinese from becoming citizens, and restricting the sale of corporate stocks.

This type of constitution sounds more like those of third world countries controlled by dictators. Those constitutions are more like party platforms, or a program of legislation than a general constitution in the American sense. The American constitution is a general set of principles and procedures, with restrictions on, and the allocation of, government authority.

By his use of the term "working classes," he seems to see the world somewhat in Marxist terms -- class warfare, etc. He makes one wonder whether or not he is actually excited by the threatened uprising. He mentions the topics of good government and employment for poor people without mentioning the united order which dealt with the same subject matter. Perhaps he has changed his views and values from his earlier enthusiasm for leveling.

His mention of the plots against Brigham Young and the calm that ensued when those plots came to naught because of his death, seems a little like the polygamy sequence of events, wherein a great political and legal momentum was built up, but before any really serious damage could be done, the polygamy issue was taken from the church's enemies by the discontinuance of the principle, leaving those enemies high and dry, and with no major club with which to beat the saints, but having raised a lot of dust internationally so that the saints got more free publicity than they could ever have paid for.

In an address dated February 6, 1881 in Salt Lake City, John Nicholson observed that "this Church is ... the highest phase of communism and individualism combined:"

> Let us, then, who belong to this great Church —— the Church of Jesus Christ of Latter-day Saints —— prize that which God has given to us for our instruction and edification, and let us not treat them as things that are of no moment. We live in a great day, the greatest of all ages, the greatest of all dispensations. It is a great privilege to be associated with so noble a work as that with which, we are connected, and I believe that the time will soon come when the Church will go forth clear, purified by the agencies which God will bring to bear upon it for that purpose. I expect to see the time come when the hypocrite in Zion shall tremble, being afraid because of the power of God that shall be in the midst of the people who will be living as they should live. I expect to see the day when there shall be less worshiping of the god of this world, which wins the hearts of many people from the worship of the true and living God. There is a sin which God has denounced in every age; it is the sin of idolatry. In ancient times, the people were less cultured than they are now, they bowed themselves down before blocks of wood and stone, and golden calves, and worshiped at such shrines, prostrating the powers that God had given them before that which was a dumb and unintelligent. But there are different forms of idolatry. Whatever a person uses his powers most to accomplish is that which he worships. If a man exercise the gifts that God has given him exclusively in pursuing the object of self-aggrandizement —— the building up of self, to all intents and purposes that individual is all idolater before the shrine of mammon. God is a jealous God, and He wills not that any of His people should have any other God than Him. Let the poor and the meek be lifted up in their hearts and rejoice before God for He hath them in remembrance, and let those who truckle to position and to wealth beware, for the Lord will not suffer it long. Let the hand of fellowship be extended to him who is cast down, that he may be comforted. Surround him with a halo of love and friendship, and let him know that he is not forgotten, and the Lord will remember those who act this brotherly part. I am reminded sometimes of the weakness of humanity, when called to the scenes of death which sometimes visit us. We are called to the funeral of some man, some Elder in Israel, or some sister or friends who has departed this life; and, O, how we love to dwell upon their good qualities, to speak of their goodness and to cast the vail of undiscerning charity over their faults. We should not wait until our brethren and sisters are seized with the chill hand

of death, and their bodies are about to be laid it, the cold tomb, to recognize the good points in their characters. We should manifest a little of that appreciation while we are surrounded by them. This course would be much more consistent. Let us cultivate the spirit of the living God, which leads to righteousness. Every sentiment of our hearts that leads to good is planted there by the living God, and that which leads to evil is placed there by the adversary of our souls. There are but two sources, one of light and one of darkness. The Holy Ghost, the Spirit of God, is given to us to cultivate in our hearts as a well of water springing up to everlasting life. It can be so cultivated in a human being that it can be listened to as a voice of a familiar friend, in every time of difficulty and trial. Its voice is known and distinguished as a voice of friendship, for that spirit is the friend of every Saint who cultivates its acquaintance. It is a searcher, a deep searcher, of the motives by which men and women are inspired. If we merely have an outward semblance of righteousness and our motives within are not of the godlike character they should be, that spirit will depart from us, leaving us in greater darkness than before we possessed the Holy Spirit. This Church is a brotherhood or it is nothing. It is an unity; it is the highest phase of communism and individualism combined. It cultivates man to perfection as a social and individual being. It meets the legitimate wants and aspirations of every class of humanity.

I pray that the power of God may increase in the midst of the people from the head to the feet, throughout the whole of the body religious, and that we may be successful in uprooting evils that are manifested in our midst as a community or as individuals. God has revealed the laws and principles for the purification of His Church. They are contained in His statute books — in the Book of Mormon, in the Doctrine and Covenants, containing the revelations of Jesus Christ, and in this Bible. The Lord tells us we are to deal with all things according to the laws of His Church. We know what these things are; they are contained in these books to which I refer. Then I say that he law of God and the power of God will ultimately correct every evil existing in the Church of Christ, for it must ultimately become pure, and those who will not purify themselves will, sooner or later, be cast off from the body-religious, as to that kind of material to be used in the building up of the glorious kingdom of our Heavenly Father. JD 22:25-26 JN Feb 6, 1881 SLC.

This "highest phase of communism" is rather a shocking statement if taken literally. Is the gospel the highest form of communism, the "withering away of the state," the end of class warfare, etc? Did he really mean to refer to Marxist doctrines in using the word "communism?" I think not. The thrust of his comments is that the gospel provides helps and guides to the individual and his place in an uplifting society or community. The twisted, atheistic views of Marx were surely not on his mind when he made that statement, but just the reverse. Man can be perfected in all ways by the proper understanding and living of the gospel, wherein each helps and supports the other in a community. This is not communism, but cooperation and community. There is no forceful dispossession of property and freedom, etc.

In the following discourse, dated April 4, 1881, Erastus Snow describes the liberty-supporting influence of the gospel, and decries any group or concept that would weaken that liberty. These thoughts on liberty certainly do not support any coercive system of economics as being consistent with the gospel. Perhaps we may surmise that the apparently coercive elements proposed in conjunction with earlier church programs stemmed from external pressures and the resulting desperation and not from anything inherent in the gospel. As an outspoken advocate of some the earlier programs, perhaps Erastus Snow has modified his own views somewhat.

The Gospel as understood and expounded by the Savior and his ancient Apostles, is a perfect law of <u>liberty</u>. Everything pertaining to the spirit of the Gospel, as taught and expounded and practiced by the Savior and His Disciples, tended to liberty. All the <u>revelations</u> which God ever gave to man from the beginning of the world <u>tended to liberty</u>. The government which our heavenly Father has exercised, or attempted to exercise is over His children on the earth or in the heavens, has not in the least tended to restrain or abridge them in their liberty, but rather to enlarge it, to extend it, to insure, to preserve and maintain it. The Gospel of Christ, and all of the revelations of God to man have sought to mark <u>the line of distinction between liberty and license,</u> between correct principles of government and anarchy or oppression and slavery. Oppression and slavery are the result of sin and wickedness, violations of the principles of the everlasting Gospel either by the rulers or ruled or both, and generally both. True freedom of mind and body and true liberty even the enjoyment of human rights is founded and maintained, and rests upon human integrity and virtue and the observance of those principles of truth on which all true happiness and true freedom is founded. Sin was never righteousness, nor can be; license was never liberty nor can be; misery was never happiness, nor can be; and yet because of the blindness and ignorance of some people, they never appear to be happy only when they are perfectly miserable. And there are some people too who think they are always in slavery and bondage unless they are trying to get themselves into trouble; and they think there is no true liberty only in acting like the devil. <u>The Nihilists of Russia, the Socialists of France and their sympathizers in America, including the "Liberals" of Utah, are panting for liberty; they are restive under the restraint of order and law; they are opposed to government, and like the French Socialists and Communists, they would destroy Jehovah himself and behead the king and burn up Parliament and assassinate every representative of power and government; and when they had reduced the country and themselves to anarchy, they would look upon their condition as the acme of freedom and human liberty.</u> The world to-day is drifting in this direction, including our own liberal America.

If we take a retrospective view of the dealings of God with his people who he recognized, and who acknowledged his laws, and among whom he raised up Prophets, and with whom he established his covenants, we will find that they have been <u>the freest of all peoples</u> which have existed on the earth. The students of the Bible and the Book of Mormon know this to be the case. They know that the first king who ruled over ancient Israel, was chosen at their own earnest solicitations, when they began to apostatize from God, and to despise His counsels. They know that Samuel the Seer, who judged them in righteousness, and who taught them faithfully the ways of the Lord, earnestly remonstrated with them when they <u>clamored for a king</u> to go out and in before them and lead them to battle, that they might be as other nations who were around them. Samuel foretold the results —— that <u>such a course tended to bondage;</u> that they were but forging the links of the chain that would bind them and deprive them of freedom. He labored long and arduously to dissuade them from it; but they would not listen to him. And yet they were not willing to consent for anybody else to make them a king but that same Samuel; and when he had prayed to the Lord, the Lord told him to "hearken to the voice of the people in all that they say unto thee; for they have not rejected thee but they have rejected me, that I should not reign over them." Samuel did as the Lord commanded him, and Israel was ruled over by a king of their own choosing. But the heavens were displeased with them for so doing, and you who are conversant with Bible history are familiar with the troubles and sorrows which befell Israel in consequence of this departure from the ways of God. And those who read the Book of Mormon find the same spirit breathed throughout that book. <u>The people, in the days when they were willing to</u>

listen to the voice of Prophets and inspired men, were the freest and best of all people; but when they began to apostatize and harden their hearts against the words of the Lord and the counsel imparted to them by His servants, they began to drift with sin and oppression and bondage. Anarchy —— shall I say, is the worst of all governments? No: Anarchy is the absence of all government; it is the antipodes of order; it is the acme of confusion; it is the result of unbridled license, the antipodes of true liberty. The Apostle Paul says truly: "For there is no power but of God: the powers that be are ordained of God." At first this is a startling statement. Even the monopoly of the one-manpower as in Russia, or the monopoly of the aristocracy as in other parts of Europe, or the imbecility and sometimes stupidity of a republic like our own, is far better than no government at all. And for this reason, says the Apostle Paul, "The powers are ordained of God," not that they are always the best forms of government for the people, or that they afford liberty and freedom to man kind, but that any and all forms of government are better than none at all, having a tendency as they do to restrain the passions of human nature and to curb them, and to establish and maintain order to a greater or less degree. One monopoly is better than many: and the oppression of a **king** is tolerable, but the oppression of a **mob**, where every man is a law to himself and his own right arm, is his power to enforce his own will, is the worst form of government. The efforts of extremists clamoring for human freedom are all tending in this direction; and those who clamor for human rights are, as a general thing, the first to trample them under foot -I mean those who are the most loud-mouthed; their ideas of freedom are all on their tongue; they conceive of no freedom only when they wield the sword, or dictate terms to others. The Gospel of the Son of God extends to the world that perfect law of liberty. Founded on truth, and a proper appreciation of those principles which tend to the largest possible happiness to humanity. it restrains mankind, not in the enjoyment of freedom and liberty, but from efforts to deprive their fellows of it. In other words, the power which God has sought to exercise, and which he has recommended and sanctioned, is only to seize the arm which is raised to fell his fellow, and to stop the loud tongue of the raging maniac, which would destroy the peace of his fellow-man, and who would seek to build himself up on the ruin of others. There is no system of government ever instituted among men which is so well calculated to give and maintain human freedom, and at the same time to restrain the vices and excesses of fallen humanity, as the government of the Gospel sought to be established by the Savior and His Apostles. We heard quoted this forenoon the words of God spoken through the Prophet Joseph, and which are and always will be in force among this people, to the effect that the powers of the Priesthood are inseparably connected with the powers of heaven, and cannot be exercised in any degree of unrighteousness; that the power of that man departs from him when he attempts in the least degree to exercise an unrighteous dominion over his fellow-man-or any power or dominion except that power of truth and of persuasion founded upon it. JD 22:149 ES April 4, 1881 SLC.

His idea of it being better to support existing governments is a plausible generalization, especially where that government may be based on such an uplifting document as the US Constitution. Tribal warfare (the "many monopolies" or the rule by mobs) is a miserable alternative. However, as he would probably recognize, there are numerous exceptions to the general rule. The church had much experience with lawless mobs sponsored by legitimate governments. There at least the existence of the Constitution had the small good influence of making the criminals resort to subterfuge since they could not accomplish their evil designs completely under the law of the land. The law was being honored in the breach, etc. The hypocrite at least recognizes the higher law while breaking it.

The communists certainly promised to be as bad as any historical experience. In that sense we might say he predicted the outcome of the Russian Revolution of 1917.

It is interesting that Erastus Snow links the "Liberals" of Utah with the "Nihilists of Russia" and the "Socialists of France." It would be interesting to have more information on this Utah group and their activities, especially on any possible influence on the views and traditions of the members of the church.

Erastus Snow would probably have agreed that the genocidal madness of Hitler and Stalin put them beyond the pale of those governments that should be sustained. Genghis Khan was another mass murderer whose jurisdiction might be difficult to sustain. The peace of Rome was often a brutal one. The followers of Mohammed caused both destruction and enlightenment. The tradeoffs can be close at times between order and its costs.

With his apparent support for existing governments, one might wonder how he would judge the American revolution against a foreign tyrant king. But there the choice was not between an oppressive king and a mob, but between an oppressive king and a much grander concept of freedom and government than had ever before been conceived of and implemented.

It is interesting that Erastus Snow links the "Liberals" of Utah with the "Nihilists of Russia" and the "Socialists of France." It would be interesting to have more information on this group and their activities, especially on any possible influences on the views and traditions of the members of the church.

In a discourse dated July 3, 1881, John Taylor again condemns communism for its atheism, even diabolism, and its plots and attempts to overthrow governments, destroy freedom and stamp out all competing viewpoints and ideologies. The gospel's spirit of tolerance is inimical to the fanatical and violent communists:

> I am sorry to see this murderous influence prevailing throughout the world, and perhaps this may be a fitting occasion to refer to some of these matters. The manifestations of turbulence and uneasiness which prevail among the nations of the earth are truly lamentable. Well, have I anything to do with them? Nothing; but I cannot help but know that they exist. These feelings which tend to do away with all right, rule, and government, and correct principles are not from God, or many of them are not. <u>This feeling of communism and nihilism, aimed at the overthrow of rulers and men in position and authority</u>, arises from a spirit of diabolism, which is contrary to every principle of the Gospel of the Son of God. But then do not the Scriptures say that these things shall occur? Yes. Do not the scriptures say the men shall grow worse and worse, deceiving and being deceived? Yes. Do not the scriptures tell us that thrones shall be cast down and empires destroyed and the rule and government of the earth be trodden under foot? Yes. But I cannot help but sympathize with those who suffer from their influences; while these afflictions are the result of wickedness and corruption, yet we cannot shut our eyes to the fact that those who engage in these pernicious practices are exceedingly low, brutal, wicked and degraded. I would say "my soul come not thou into their secret; unto their assembly, mine honor, be not thou united."
>
> I have traveled abroad myself quite extensively among the nations of the earth. Did I ever interfere with them? No, not in the least particular. Did I see things that were wrong? Yes, but it was not for me to right them. That was not my mission. I had no command of the

kind. My mission was to preach the Gospel of salvation to the nations of the earth, and I have traveled hundreds of thousands of miles to do this, without purse or scrip, trusting in God. And so have many of my friends traveled. We did not hurt anybody, did we? For instance, now, right in our own city, we have Methodists, Presbyterians, Baptists, Catholics, Episcopalians, and all kinds of isms. Do we interfere with them? We do not. Would you interrupt them in their worship? I know of no such thing, good Latter-day Saints will not do it. Would I malign or persecute them? No, I would not. If we told the truth about some of them it would be quite bad enough without stating falsehoods, and if other men cannot afford to treat them properly and to give the fullest and broadest liberty to all who come within our reach; liberty to do right, not liberty to oppress, not liberty to trample on correct principals not liberty to rob men of their property or religion. Men who would do this are villains which we want nothing to do with; but all honorable men, all men who do right and maintain the laws and the Constitution of the United States, we are their friends and will sustain them to the last. These are my thoughts in relation to that matter. JD 22:142 JT July 3, 1881 SLC.

John Taylor's October 9, 1881, discourse, quoted below, in which he mentions communism, is similar to his earlier discourse of July 3, 1881. He condemns the potential destructiveness of communism:

As I before said, we have not time to enter into all these matters. You have had a good deal of needful instruction. Let us profit by it and honor our God. And I say God bless all men who love the truth, whether here or anywhere else; God bless all men who maintain human rights and freedom; and God confound the opposers of these principles everywhere. These are my principles and feelings. We want nothing like communism, or nihilism, or any of the outrageous infamies that are beginning to vex and perplex the nations. Yet these things will roll on until it will be a vexation to hear the reports thereof, and unless this nation speedily turns round God's hand will be upon them; unless they speedily adhere to the principles of equal rights and freedom, He will be after them. Now, you can set that down if you like, and see whether it will come to pass or not. I say, then God bless every lover of right, whether among this people or anywhere else, and God bless the rulers of this land who rule in righteousness, and God remove those who do not. (Amen). And let us honor our God and our religion and adhere to the principles of truth. God will stand by us, and the glory of God will rest upon us, and no power this side of hell can hurt us if we be followers of that which is good. JD 22:296 JT Oct 9, 1881 SLC.

In the following April 9, 1882, discourse, John Taylor asserts that the saints expect to maintain their rights in a legal, peaceful and constitutional manner, without stooping to the use of secret combinations, as do the communists and other groups:

We have peacefully, legally and honorably possessed our lands in these valleys of the mountains, and we have purchased and paid for them; we do not revel in any ill-gotten gain. They are ours. We have complied with all the requisitions of law pertaining thereto, and we expect to possess and inhabit them. We covet no man's silver or gold, or apparel, or wife, or servants, or flocks, or herds, or horses, or carriages, or lands, or possessions. But we expect to maintain our own rights. If we are crowded upon by unprincipled men or inimical legislation, we shall not take the course pursued by the lawless, the dissolute and the unprincipled; we shall not have recourse to the dynamite of the Russian Nihilists, the secret plans and machinations of the communists, the boycotting and threats of the Fenians, the force and disorder of the Jayhawkers, the regulators or the Molly Maguires, nor any other secret or illegal combination; but we still expect to possess and maintain our rights; but to obtain them in a legal, peaceful and constitutional manner. As American citizens, we shall contend for all our liberties, rights and immunities, guaranteed to us by the Constitution; and no matter what action may be taken by mobocratic influence, by excited and unreasonable men, or by inimical legislation, we shall contend inch by inch for our freedom and rights, as well as the freedom and rights of all American citizens and of all mankind. As a people or community, we can abide our time, but I will say to you Latter-day Saints, that there is nothing of which you have been despoiled by oppressive acts or mobocratic rule, but that you will again possess, or your children after you. Your rights in Ohio, your rights in Jackson, Clay, Caldwell and Davis counties in Missouri, will yet be restored to you. Your possessions, of which you have been fraudulently despoiled in Missouri and Illinois, you will again possess, and that without force, or fraud or violence. The Lord has a way of His own in regulating such matters. We are told the wicked shall slay the wicked. He has a way of His own of "emptying the earth of the inhabitants thereof." A terrible day of reckoning is approaching the nation of the earth; the Lord is coming out of His hiding place to vex the inhabitants thereof; and the destroyer of the Gentiles, as prophesied of, is already on his way. Already the monarchs of the earth are trembling from conspiracies among their own people; already has one Czar of Russia been destroyed and another holds his life by a very uncertain tenure through the perpetual threats and machinations of an infuriated populace; already have the Emperor of Germany, the King of Italy, the Queen of England, the King of Spain, the Sultan of Turkey, and many others of the honorable and noble rulers of the earth had their lives jeopardized by the attacks of regicides; already have two of the Presidents of this Republic been laid low by the hands of the assassin; and the spirit of insubordination, misrule, lynching, and mobocracy of every kind is beginning to ride rampant through the land; already combinations are being entered into which are very ominous for the future prosperity, welfare and happiness of this great Republic. The volcanic fires of disordered and anarchical elements are beginning to manifest themselves and exhibit the internal forces that are at work among the turbulent and unthinking masses of the people. Congress will soon have something else to do than to proscribe and persecute an innocent, law-abiding and patriotic people. Of all bodies in the world, they can least afford to remove the bulwarks that bind society together in this nation, to recklessly trample upon human freedom and rights, and to rend and destroy that great Palladium of human rights —— the Constitution of the United States. Ere long they will need all its protecting influence to save this nation from misrule, anarchy and mobocratic influence. They can ill afford to be the foremost in tampering with human rights and human freedom, or in tearing down the bulwarks of safety and protection which that sacred instrument has guaranteed. It is lamentable to see the various disordered and disorganized elements seeking to overthrow the greatest and best government in existence on the earth. Congress can ill afford to set a pattern of violation of that Constitution which it has sworn to support. The internal fires of revolution are already smouldering in this nation, and they need but a spark to set them in a flame. Already are agencies at work in the land calculated to subvert and overthrow every principle of rule and government; already is corruption of every kind prevailing in high places and permeating all society; already are we, as a nation, departing from our God, and corrupting ourselves with malfeasance, dishonor, and a lack of public integrity and good faith; already are licentiousness and debauchery corrupting, undermining and destroying society, already are we interfering with the laws of nature and stopping the functions of life, and have become the slayers of our own offspring, and employ human butchers in the shape of physicians to assist in this diabolical and murderous work. The sins of this nation, the licentiousness, the debauchery, the murders are entering into the ears of the Lord of Sabbaoth, and I tell you now, from the tops of these mountains, as a humble servant of the living God, that unless these crimes and infamies are stopped, this nation will be overthrown, and its glory, power, dominion and wealth will fade away like the dews of a summer morning. I also say to other nations of the earth, that unless they repent of their crimes, their iniquities and abominations, their thrones will be overturned, their kingdoms and governments overthrown, and their lands made desolate. This is not only my saying, but it is the saying of those ancient prophets which they themselves profess to believe; for God will speedily have a controversy with the nations of the earth, and, as I stated before, the destroyer of the Gentiles is on his way to overthrow governments, to destroy dynasties, to lay waste thrones, kingdoms and empires, to spread abroad anarchy and desolation, and to cause war, famine and bloodshed to overspread the earth.

Besides the preaching of the Gospel, we have another mission, namely, the perpetuation of the free agency of man and the maintenance of liberty, freedom, and the rights of man. There are certain principles that belong to humanity outside of the Constitution, outside of the laws, outside of all the enactments and plans of man, among which is the right to live; God gave us the right and not man; no government gave it to us, and no government has a right to take it away from us. We have a right to liberty — that was a right that God gave to all men; and if there has been oppression, fraud or tyranny in the earth, it has been the result of the wickedness and corruptions of men and has always been opposed to God and the principles of truth, righteousness, virtue, and all principles that are calculated to elevate mankind. The Declaration of Independence states that men are in possession of certain inalienable rights, among which are life, liberty and the pursuit of happiness. This belongs to us; it belongs to all humanity. I wish, and the worst wish I have for the United States, is, that they could have liberality enough to give to all men equal rights, and, while they profess to have delivered the black slaves, that they strike off the fetters of the white men of the South, who have been ground under the heel of sectional injustice, and let them feel that we are all brothers in one great nation, and deliver all people from tyranny and oppression of every kind, and proclaim, as they did at the first, liberty throughout the land and to all people. That is the worst wish I have for them. And when I see them take another course I feel sorry for it. I would like if I had time to talk a little upon constitutional rights; I would like a little to discuss the unconstitutionality of that Edmunds bill; but it was ably done by many senators of the United States, and by others in the House of Representatives. Very ably done; and I honor the men who maintain such sentiments. It is true that most of them apologized and said that they were as much opposed to polygamy as anybody. Well, that is a matter of their own; they have a right to their opinions as much as I have a right to my opinion. Would I deprive them of that right? No, I would not. I preach the Gospel to the world. What is it? Force, tyranny and oppression? No: it is all free grace and it is all free will. Is anybody coerced? Did anybody coerce you, Latter-day Saints? Are any of you forced to continue Latter-day Saints if you do not want to? If you think you are, you are all absolved to-day. We know of no such principle as coercion; it is a matter of choice. The principle that I spoke of before — that is, men receive the Holy Ghost within themselves, is the cementing, binding, uniting power that exists among the Latter-day Saints. What right have I to expect that members of the House of Representatives or the people of the United States should advocate polygamy? They would not understand it. Nor would it be reasonable for us to expect it at their hands; but what I admired in those Senators and Members was their fealty to the government, to the Constitution and the maintenance of the freedom and the inalienable rights of man, of every color, creed and profession. JD 23:61 JT April 9, 1882 SLC.

It is an interesting irony that in their mountain stronghold, the saints were protected from the corrupt administrators of the constitution, so that they, the Mormons, could proceed in accordance with the constitution.

George Q. Cannon was always the avid proponent of consecration and central control of property, and continues even at the late date of 1883, in a discourse dated August 12. He has doubts about communism, but is not willing to condemn it with the vehemence of John Taylor:

This being the case, is it any wonder that God makes requirements of us, and expects a perfection on our part that is not looked for nor expected of the rest of the world? We were told this morning — and the truth cannot be too often repeated in our hearing that God, our Eternal Father, has placed all these possessions and blessings — that is, the possessions of the earth and the blessings connected with the earth — that He has placed them in our hands merely as stewards, and that we hold them subject to Him, in other words, in trust for Him, and that, if He calls upon us to use them in any given direction He may indicate, it is our duty as His children, occupying the relationship that we do to Him, and with the hopes in our breasts that we have, to hold them entirely subject to Him. There is not another people upon the face of the earth that I know anything about who are taught such ideas and doctrines as these. I do not think that any other denomination of people, either religious or secular, have such doctrines as we have heard this morning taught to them respecting their duties and their obligations to God. Of course you will very frequently hear in sectarian churches, many things connected with this subject; that it is the duty of the rich to help the poor and to be benevolent and to hold all things in a way that will please God; but to bring this down to what we would call, practical consecration, to practically consecrate their wealth, and hold it as though they would have to practically consecrate it at any time, is a doctrine that I do not think is taught in any other church, or so-called church, nor is it believed in by any other people. There are, it is true, <u>people who indulge in very wild vagaries about property, such as communists and others, but they have no **system** of religion, they do not believe in God</u>, they do not believe in the principles that He teaches and which we accept. They would not carry them out on any such basis.

Let me ask you, my brethren and sisters, is it not appropriate that we should be required to make — I was going to say sacrifice. Well, that is a word that is so commonly used, that I suppose I could not use any other that would convey the idea to your minds clear enough. I will use it, therefore. Is it not appropriate to make sacrifices of this character, considering who we are and what we are? If we are expecting to reach a glory and an exaltation such as we think about and talk about and pray for, it seems to me that there should be something to be done on our part commensurate with the expectations and hopes and desires that we entertain, and I do not know myself any better test that can be brought to bear upon human beings than this test to which allusion has been made this morning, the test of holding ourselves — that is our individual persons, with our time and the ability that God has given unto us, our wives, our children, and the possessions that God has placed in our hands to control — to hold all these subject to His dictation and to His approval.

"Now," says one, "I am quite willing for that; I would be quite willing to receive all that doctrine and to believe it if God himself were to come and make the requirement of me. I am quite willing that God should dictate to me about my wives and children; and if He wants me to use my talents and give up my life or to yield up my property — I am quite willing to do all these things if He will come and tell me himself, or if He will send an angel to tell me. But I look upon my brethren who preside over this Church, and I see that they are mortal men, and I see that they do many things that mortal men do, and I have not quite confidence enough in them to dispose of my property as they may dictate. They are mortal, they are like I am, and I do not know whether they will do the right thing or not. I have some doubts about that. I have not got confidence in their management as business men. I do not know but I have better business qualities myself than they have, and I can manage my own affairs to better advantage than they can. I am not willing therefore, to do as my fellow men dictate." JD 24:272 GQC Aug 12, 1883 Logan.

Apparently, George Q. Cannon is not really against communism; he seems always to have been attracted to their property ideas, especially if they were ever actually able to carry out their ideas in practice instead of just talking about it, or ending in failure as they usually did. However, he is put off by their lack of religion in the process. He might charge them merely with "a lack of system," his favorite excuse and prescription for Mormon failures in communal property experiments.

It should be remembered that by letter of May 1, 1882, more than one year before this discourse of George Q. Cannon, John Taylor officially terminated the united order program of Brigham Young. Elder Cannon seems to be resisting that change in direction.

In an address dated October 19, 1884, John Taylor again states both his desire to protect his rights and to do it in a peaceful and constitutional way. We might observe that the means and the ends are closely bound together. One can hardly sustain the Constitution by ignoring its processes and using violence and subversion to gain individual ends.

I remember some little time ago a gentleman named Mr. Pierpont (who was Attorney-General under President Grant) called upon me. I was pleased to see him, and am pleased to see all honorable gentlemen. I invited him to dinner, and we had quite a chat. But here let me introduce another affair. At the time when the <u>Edmunds law</u> was passed I was living in what is known as the Gardo House. I had most of my wives living with me there, and after looking carefully over the Edmunds law I thought to myself, why Congress is growing very wild; this Government is getting very, very foolish; they are <u>trampling upon Constitutional rights</u>. No matter, I said, I will obey this law. I had comfortable places for my family elsewhere, and <u>I requested my wives to go to their own homes</u>, and live there, and they did so in order that I at least might fulfill that part of the law; for foolish or not foolish, my idea was to fulfill as far as practicable the requirements of the law, and not place myself and my family or my friends in jeopardy, through any foolishness of mine. <u>It was expected</u> by many of those corrupt men —— I do not say in speaking of these that all are corrupt —— that when these laws were passed <u>we should turn our wives out</u> and deal with them as they do with their women under such circumstances —— make strumpets of them. There is no such feeling as that in my bosom, nor in the bosoms of this people. We have made eternal covenants with our wives, and we will abide by our wives, and God will sustain us in protecting the rights of innocence, and in fulfilling those eternal obligations which we have entered into. But <u>we can once in a while yield a little to the follies and weaknesses of men, when no principle of truth is involved</u>. Under these circumstances I had a sister of mine who was keeping house for me when Mr. Pierpont came there to dine with me. I said: "Mr. Pierpont, permit me to introduce you to my <u>sister. It is not lawful for us to have wives here</u>." (Laughter.) After talking further with him upon the subject I said, "Now, Mr. Pierpont, you are well acquainted with all these legal affairs. Although I have yielded in this matter in order that I might not be an <u>obstructionist</u>, and do not wish to act as a Fenian, or a Nihilist, or a <u>Communist</u>, or a Kuklux, or a Regulator, or a Plug Ugly, or a Molly Maguire, <u>yet, sir, we</u>

shall stand up for our rights and protect ourselves in every proper way, legally and constitutionally, and dispute inch by inch every step that is taken to deprive us of our rights and liberties." And we will do this in the way that I speak of. We are doing it to-day; and as you have heard it expressed on other occasions, it looks very much like as though the time was drawing near when this country will tumble to pieces; for if the people of this nation are so blind and infatuated as to trample under foot the Constitution and other safeguards provided for the liberties of man, we do not propose to assist them in their suicidal and traitorous enterprises; for we have been told by Joseph Smith that when the people of this nation would trample upon the Constitution, the Elders of this Church would rally round the flag and defend it. And it may come to that; we may be nearer to it than some of us think, for the people are not very zealous in the protection of human rights. And when legislators, governors and judges unite in seeking to tear down the temple of liberty and destroy the bulwarks of human freedom, it will be seen by all lovers of liberty, that they are playing a hazardous game and endangering the perpetuity of human rights. For it will not take long for the unthinking to follow their lead, and they may let loose an element that they never bind again. We seem to be standing on a precipice and the tumultuous passions of men are agitated by political and party strife; the elements of discord are seething and raging as if portending a coming storm; and no man seems competent to take the helm and guide the ship of State through the fearful breakers that threaten on every hand. These are dangerous things, but it becomes our duty as good citizens to obey the law as far as practicable, and be governed by correct principles.

I had some papers read over at the General Conference, giving my views in relation to some of these matters. They have been published, but I will have one or two extracts read for your information.

President Cannon then read as follows:

The distinction being made between Polygamy and Prostitution:   JD 25:349 JT Oct 19, 1884 Ogden.

John Taylor was certainly consistent in his message about communism and other ideologies of its ilk. In an address dated February 1, 1885, he again described his determination to avoid any ideology except the simplicity of the gospel, even when provoked by such outrageous action as the government's unconstitutional *ex post facto* criminalization of plural marriage.

> The history of these things is quite familiar to you as Latter-day Saints, and you do not think it anything strange. Some or our young people think that the present proceedings are very remarkable. But many of us, grey-headed folks, have seen plenty of such proceedings, and have had many experiences of this kind; they are nothing new to us at all. And did we ever expect them to get better? We have not so understood it. We are told in the Scriptures, and we have kept teaching it all the while, that "the wicked would grow worse and worse, deceiving and being deceived." That is doctrine which I have believed in for the last 50 years and I have had a good deal of testimony and practical confirmation on that point. We expect that these things will transpire. We have been told about secret organizations, that should exist, and they are beginning to permeate these United States, and are laying the foundation for disruption, disintegration and destruction. It is not necessary that Congress and the Judiciary should set examples of tyranny and violation of Constitutional law, and attack the fundamental principles of free government and the rights of man; for there is plenty of that kind of spirit abroad; yet men who profess to be the conservators of the peace and the maintainers of law join in these nefarious, unholy, tyrannical and oppressive measures.

There are any number who are ready to follow in their footsteps, and the whole nation to-day is standing on a <u>volcano</u>; but they do not seem to comprehend it. Well, are we surprised? I am not. It is strictly in accordance with my faith: it is strictly in accordance with the Old Testament Scriptures; and it is strictly in accordance with the Book of Mormon; it is strictly in accordance with the revelations given to us by Joseph Smith, and all these events that have been predicted will most assuredly transpire. But I suppose it is necessary that "judgment should first begin at the house of God," and if it does, "where will the wicked and the ungodly appear," when it comes upon them? We are told that <u>the wicked shall slay the wicked. We need not trouble ourselves about the affairs of the nations. The Lord will manipulate them in His own way</u>. I feel full of sympathy for the nation in which we live, and for other nations, in consequence of the troubles with which they are beset and which are now threatening them; yet they do not seem to comprehend the position. I know a little of some of the things that will transpire among them, and I feel sorry. Do you feel sorry for yourself? Not at all, not at all. Do you feel sorry for your people? Not at all, not at all. The Lord God has revealed unto us great and eternal principles which reach beyond this earth into the eternal heavens, and which have put us in possession of light an truth and intelligence, and promises and blessings that the world are ignorant of and do not and cannot comprehend. I feel every day to bless the name of the God of Israel, an feel like shouting, "Hosanna! Hosanna!! Hosanna!!! to the God of Israel, Amen and Amen," Who will rule among the nations of the earth, and manipulate things according to the counsel of His own will. These are my feelings in regard to these matters. But then I feel interested in the welfare of my brethren and sisters, and when I see their <u>rights</u> interfered with and <u>trampled ruthlessly under foot</u>, I feel that there is something at work that ought not to be, and yet that is quite necessary to teach us some of the <u>principles of human nature</u>, that we may be able to discern between the good, the virtuous, the upright and the holy; and the impure, the foolish, the vindictive, the corrupt, the lascivious, and those who are trampling under foot the laws and principles of eternal truth. God has revealed unto us certain principles pertaining to the <u>future</u> which men may take objection to. He has revealed unto us certain principles pertaining to the perpetuity of man and of woman; pertaining to the sacred rights and obligations which existed from the beginning; and He has told us to obey these laws. The nation tells us, "If you do we will persecute you and prescribe you." Which shall we obey? I would like to obey and place myself in subjection to every law of man. What then? Am I to disobey the law of God? Has any man a right to control my conscience, or your conscience, or to tell me I shall believe this or believe the other, or reject this or reject the other? No man has a right to do it. These principles are sacred, and the forefathers of this nation felt so and so proclaimed it in the Constitution of the United States, and said "<u>Congress shall make no law respecting an establishment of religion, or prohibiting the free exercise thereof.</u>" Now, <u>I believe they have violated that</u>, and have violated their oaths, those that have engaged in these things and passed that law, and those that are seeking to carry it out. Congress and the President of the United States and the Judiciary, and all administrators of the law are as much bound by that instrument as I am and as you are, and have sworn to maintain it inviolate. It is for them to settle these matters between themselves and their God. That is my faith in relation to this matter. Yet by their action they are interfering with my rights, my liberty and my religion, and with those sacred principles that bind me to my God, to my family, to my wives and my children; and shall I be recreant to all these noble principles that ought to guide and govern men? *No, Never*! No, NEVER! NO, NEVER! I can endure more than I have done, and all that God will enable me to endure, I can die for the truth; but <u>I cannot</u> as an honorable man <u>disobey my God at their behest</u>, forsake my wives and my children, and trample these holy and eternal obligations under foot, that God has given me to keep, and which reach into the eternities that are to come. I won't do it, so help me, God. (Here the speaker vigorously struck the book on the desk, and the large audience responded with a loud "Amen.") The Constitution expressly says that no law shall be passed <u>impairing the obligation of contracts</u>. But we have entered into covenants and contracts in our most sacred places, and that, too, in many instances, <u>before there was any law prohibiting the same</u>, and yet the attempt is now being made to give the <u>Edmunds law</u> an *ex post facto* application and to punish us for these contracts which were not criminal, even from the standpoint of our enemies, at the time they were formed. I myself <u>married my wives long before there was any law upon the subject</u>, and many of you did the same, yet by an *ex post facto* application of laws since enacted the attempt is now made to punish us as criminal. I have never broken any law of these United States, and I presume that some of you, whom our enemies now seek to criminate and drag into court as violators of law, can say the same. Under the present system of things in this Territory, <u>harlotry and adultery</u> are vindicated <u>sustained</u> unblushingly protected, and honorable and virtuous wedlock is trampled upon, condemned and punished. Well, what will you do? <u>I will obey every Constitutional law so far as God gives me ability.</u> What else will you do? I will meet these men as far as I can without violating principle, and I have done it. When this infamous Edmunds law was passed, I saw that there were features in that which were contrary to law, violative of the Constitution, contrary to justice and the rights and the freedom of men. But I said to myself I will let that law take its course; I will place myself in accordance with it, so far as I can. Did I do it? I did. I remember talking to Mr. Pierrepont, who was Attorney General under President Grant's administration. He with his son called upon me. They dined with me, and perhaps I can explain my views on this subject by repeating our conversation as well as any other way. I have a sister keeping my house for me —— the Gardo House. When Mr. Pierrepont came in, I said:

"Mr. Pierrepont, permit me to introduce you to my sister, who is my house-keeper. It is <u>not lawful for us to have wives now</u>. And when the Edmunds law was passed I looked carefully over the document, and saw that <u>if I was to continue to live in the same house with my wives that I should render myself liable to that law</u>. I did not wish —— although I considered the law infamous —— to be an obstructionist, or act the part of a Fenian, or of a Nihilist, or of a Kuklux, or communist, or Molly Maguire, or any of those secret societies that are set on foot to produce the disintegration of society and disturb the relations that ought to exist between man and man, between man and woman, or man and his God. I desired to place myself in obedience or in as close conformity as practicable to the law, and thought I would wait and see what the result would be; and that if the nation can stand these things I can or we can. These are my feelings. Men and nations and legislators often act foolishly, and do things that are unwise, and it is not proper that a nation should be condemned for the unwise actions of some few men. Therefore I have sought to place myself in accord with that law. I said to my wives: "We are living in this building together. We were quite comfortably situated, and we might so have continued, but I said to them that under the circumstances it will be better for me or for you to leave this place; you can take your choice. They had their homes down here which they now inhabit; which were quite comfortable. So I said to them, you can go there and I will stay here, or you can stay at the Gardo House and I will go there or somewhere else; for I wish to conform to this Edmunds law as much as I can."

I am always desirous to let everything have its perfect working. We talk sometimes about patience having its perfect work. If we have laws passed against us I like to see them have a fair opportunity to develop and see what the result will be. These were my feelings then, and they are my feeling to-day.

Well, do you think, then, that <u>the people have been outraged</u>? I most certainly do. The usage has been in all legal trials among all civilized nations to <u>presume</u> that all men are <u>innocent</u> until proven guilty; but we now have <u>test oaths</u> introduced, which is another violation of the Constitution and by which an attempt is being made to hold all men guilty until they prove themselves innocent. Again: there is a usage which has existed among the civilized nations, and in this nation also, that a man must be tried by a jury of his peers, selected from the vicinage, but the juries selected for our courts are composed to-day of our bitter persecutors and our most relentless enemies, and in many instances selected form the lowest and most debased men who can be found or picked up from the gutters. We also have another class of courts improvised for the occasion in the shape of "U. S. Commissioners' courts," which are operated and run after the order of the ancient notorious "Star Chamber." Such institutions provoke the contempt of all honorable men, and the parties assuming such offices place themselves in a position to be despised of their fellows. I might enumerate many other outrages, but time will not permit on this occasion. No man's liberties are safe under such administration. What will be the result? The result will be that those that sow the wind will reap the whirlwind. When men begin to tear down the barriers and tamper with the fundamental principles and institutions of our country, they are playing a very dangerous game, and are severing the bonds which hold society together, and the beginning of these irregularities is like the letting out of water. The next step that followed the Edmunds Act was the introduction of a test oath. The legislation already provided was not good enough for some of our officials here and another portion of the Constitution must be broken to introduce a test oath without any authority. I think this was introduced by our Governor. Then comes another class of men called Commissioners, rather a new idea in American Government. Yet it was thought necessary that extraordinary operations should be entered into in relation to the Mormons. Why? Because it is necessary that they should be dealt with differently from anybody else.

Now, I have seen some of my brethren shot to pieces in cold blood and under the protection of the State Government, and the promise of the Governor made to myself and Dr. John M. Bernhisel, who is sometime ago dead. In Missouri a great deal of that thing was done. In Georgia lately, and in Tennessee acts of the same kind have been perpetrated. Now, I want to know if anybody can tell me —— here is a large congregation, and many thousands of you acquainted with our history —— I want to know if any one of you can tell me of any individual that was ever punished according to law for killing a Mormon. Speak it out, if you know it. I do not know of any such thing. Brother Snow says there is not an instance on record. Well, I would rather be on the side of the Mormons in that case than on the side of those who are their persecutors and murderers, for they have got something to atone for yet, which we have not under those circumstances. We have got through with our part of it. The other is not through with yet. There are eternal principles of justice and equity that exist in the bosom of God, and He, in His own time, will manipulate these things according to the counsel of His own will; and with what measure men mete, as sure as God lives, it will be measured to them again, pressed down and running over. JD 26:153 JT Feb 1, 1885 SLC.

His comments on the "principles of human nature" brings to mind the many earlier arguments that by taking away everyone's property and causing them all to work together, the people would somehow miraculously become more refined, spiritual, selfless, etc. I expect that John Taylor does not believe that dogma. The gospel and the constitution both contemplate a great amount of individuality and freedom, the maximum possible. To claim that the gospel requires a monastic, propertyless, worker-bee humiliation and subjugation of individuals is very far from the spirit of the gospel. The mass producing of "gods" who are automatons might fit into Satan's plan, but individuality and character are the key ingredients of the smaller number of quality beings the Lord's plan is designed to produce.

## Communism in California

A few comments in the Journal of Discourses refers to communism in the United States. John Taylor's July 3, 1881 discourse quoted above is one example. More specifically, in a July 7, 1878 discourse quoted above, George Q. Cannon mentioned the western states as a location where communism was having an influence during the 1870's. The following essay from the time describes the California phenomenon in some detail:

EDWIN L. GODKIN: Communism in California

*In 1878 a constitutional convention was called in California to remedy a number of problems that were unsettling the state. The issues causing public discontent were many: a confused system of land tenure and uncertain property titles going back to days of Mexican rule; the influx of Chinese immigrants; railroad monopoly and consequent high shipping rates; domination of the state legislature by the powerful railroad interests. The new constitution was completed in March 1879 and submitted for ratification. Because it incorporated compromise rather than radical solutions of several issues, it was attacked by many who would have preferred either a more extreme or a more moderate approach. One such attack came from Edwin L. Godkin, editor of the Nation, who characterized the California constitution as a foolish and unfortunate departure from traditional American constitution making.*

Source: *Nation*, April 3, 1879: "A New Kind of State Constitution."

The Convention which has recently completed its work in California has reported a new constitution, which will be voted upon the first Wednesday of May next. The work of the Convention deserves more than ordinary attention, because it is the result of movement new in American politics. Hitherto, constitutional conventions have generally been in the hands of a very conservative class and usually have been controlled by lawyers. In California, the anti-Chinese party, combined with the Communists under Kearney, have exercised such an influence in politics during the past year or two that a powerful minority of the Convention was led by statesmen of the Kearney order. Antecedently, therefore, it might be expected that the new instrument would be somewhat unlike those drawn up for American states hitherto, and such is most certainly the fact.

A state constitution may be regarded as the most complete expression by an American community of its fundamental and permanent ideas of law and government. The constitutions of the Revolutionary and pre-Revolutionary period may be said, in a general way, to have consisted of three parts: first, provisions relating to the formal organization of the government; second, a definition of the powers of the three branches of the government; third, a few positive provisions for the protection of the person and property of the citizen, including habeas corpus, trial by jury, etc. These provisions, however, were not at all new but drawn directly from the same source from which the common law of the various states came - the English statute book.

Indeed, with regard to them, it would not be unfair to say, considering the supposed revolutionary origin of American constitutional law, that what is most remarkable about them is not their novelty but their antiquity, the great body of them having been taken from English statutes passed in the reigns of Charles II and James II, while some of the most important of them go back to the time of John. These safeguards of life, liberty, and the pursuit of happiness had already proved their value to so many generations of Englishmen and Americans that it was by no figure of speech that they were generally termed then, as they have ever since been, a common birthright.

In the hundred years which have elapsed since the Revolution, the spirit of constitution making in the various states has undergone several marked changes, which have attracted more or less attention and criticism. The first serious change, of course, was that which swept through all the states thirty years ago, and introduced universal suffrage and an elective judiciary. Whether this be regrettable or no, it is impossible to deny that the men who were responsible for the change sincerely believed in it. They were drawn, too, as a general thing, from a class competent to form an opinion on the basis of suffrage; and the conventions which incorporated the change into the fundamental law were guided by the same traditions and notions of the foundations on which society rests as their predecessors had been.

The next change in the spirit of constitution making which attracted notice was that which made its appearance in several constitutions ten years or more ago - most noticeable, perhaps, in the constitution of Illinois of 1870 - in the direction of placing great restrictions upon the power of the legislature and upon the sovereign right through the legislature to incur debt. In the old constitutions the branch of the government which had been restricted in its functions was the executive. Almost all the grievances from which the American colonies had suffered in the last century (as may be seen from the long list of the "repeated injuries and usurpations" which are enumerated with each recurring Fourth of July by every village orator who is charged with the duty of reading the Declaration of Independence to his fellow townsmen) were laid by them at the door of the King, and consequently, in the old constitutions, the official who was most hedged about with definitions and restrictions was the governor. The purpose in view was entirely accomplished.

There has probably never been in the history of the world any executive who has made so few encroachments upon popular rights as the governor of the American state. But in carefully guarding these rights from encroachments in one quarter they had omitted to protect them from assaults in another; and it soon became clear that the legislature might become by means of special legislation, and its power of saddling the state with debts, quite as dangerous to popular government, although in a different way, as kings had been in their own. Consequently, in the later constitutions, of which the Illinois constitution is a type, the power of incurring indebtedness and of special legislation is limited in every way. These new safeguards have been found to work well, and in the states in which they have been longest in operation have improved the tone and character of legislation and strengthened the public credit.

A comparison of the earlier constitutions with those recently adopted, however, shows that in one important respect there has been a decline in the art of constitution making. The point to which we refer is this: In the older constitutions, as has been shown, the framers of the instrument were always careful to incorporate provisions affecting life, liberty, and property, which formed a fundamental part of the common laws of England and America; and the great advantage which was gained by incorporating them into a written constitution was that they were removed from the power of the legislature and made irrepealable except by constitutional amendment. They became part of a law which is superior to all mere legislative acts, and, in case of conflict, overrides them.

Of late years, however, it has become more and more common for demagogues to attempt to make use of constitutional conventions, just as the legislature is made use of every year, by getting them to adopt, for the purpose of appeasing some popular cry, a mass of heterogeneous provisions applicable to the law of persons and property, concocted on the spur of the moment and embodying no fundamental economical or legal principle tested by the experience of generations, but forming a sort of popular pronunciamento on a half-understood subject, the actual effect of which the framers themselves cannot foresee. Illustrations of this tendency might be taken from several of the recent constitutions, but that just drawn up in California is the first one in which it has reached a dangerous climax.

The evils and abuses which the Convention undertook to cure and abate were, first, of course, the Chinese difficulty; second, a number of evils which are not peculiar to California, but have appeared in half the states of the Union within the past ten or twelve years, *e.g.,* the escape of large amounts of personal property from taxation, secret combinations by powerful corporations adverse to public interests, the delay of justice owing to the crowded calendars of the courts, excessive rates of toll or service by railroad, telegraph, and gas corporations, corruption in the legislature, gambling in shares of mining companies. When we examine the new constitution to see how the California Convention has dealt with these questions, we find that its most marked characteristic is that it contains some novel and ingenious provision with regard to each of them.

In the first place, it proposes to bring stock gambling to an end by giving to the legislature power to pass laws either to regulate "or *prohibit* the buying and selling of the shares of the capital stock of corporations in any stock board, stock exchange, or stock market under the control of any association." Excessive charges by gas and telegraph companies are brought to an end by directing the legislature to pass laws "for the regulation and limitation of the charges for services performed and commodities furnished" by such corporations. Even charges for "storage and wharfage" are provided for in a similar way, whether made by corporations or *individuals.* Section 35 of the same article brings the corruption of the legislature to an end by declaring "lobbying" (which is made to embrace the somewhat vague offense of seeking to influence the votes of legislators by "intimidation") a felony.

The judiciary article contains a section intended to prevent any further delay or denial of justice in California. It provides that no judge of either Supreme or Superior Court shall draw his monthly salary unless he make oath that no cause remains in his court undecided *which has been submitted for decision for the period of ninety days.* The labor question is disposed of by making eight hours a legal day's work on all public works. Finally, corporations "other than municipal" are handled without gloves. Stock watering is prevented by declaring any stock issued except for value of some kind received to be "void." For the regulation of railroads, a board of commissioners is created with a general power "to establish freight and passenger rates for all transportation companies"; anyone who charges more than the rate established is liable to a fine of $5,000 or imprisonment for a year.

Citizenship is, of course, restricted to natives or foreigners not of Mongolian blood, and corporations are prohibited from employing Chinese labor. The old provision that taxation shall be "equal and uniform" is struck out, apparently for the purpose of enabling the legislature to impose an income tax increasing with the income. As the new constitution does not prevent the imposition of taxes upon the principal as well, it looks as if the "money kings" of "Nob Hill," as Kearney calls them, would certainly catch it this time. Many of the sections directed against abuses by corporations are so worded as to be almost unintelligible. Railroad companies, for instance, are forbidden to make contracts with vessels plying to California ports, "by which the earnings of one doing the carrying are to be shared by the other not doing the carrying." Whenever a railroad lowers its rates of transportation for the purpose of competing with another railroad, there is to be no increase of rates afterward without the consent of the government.

Such a farrago as this is a novelty in American constitutional law. Of course, it is not difficult to see that much of it will never have any lasting effect upon the social and legal machinery in California, because much of it cannot be carried into effect in any civilized country. Some of it will be explained away by the courts, some of it will be rendered null by the corruption of the officials who are elected to execute it. But as it stands it is not the constitution of a civilized state but of a civilized state, the management of whose affairs has partly fallen into the hands of barbarians. Instead of confining itself, with regard to the ordinary rights of person and property, to a simple declaration of those permanent and settled principles to which, as we have shown, the earlier constitutions always confined themselves, it has embodied in the fundamental law of the state a mass of heterogeneous and confused edicts, representing nothing more substantial than those gusts of popular passion which hitherto have spent themselves in primaries or in the election of party candidates, or at most in laws passed *subject* to overruling by the judicial interpretation of a constitution based on fixed principles.

That they should now have reached and so largely controlled the action of a constitutional convention is a bad sign. So far as such a constitution as that proposed in California fails of the evident objects of its authors, it tends to bring all laws and constitutions into contempt. So far as it succeeds, it marks the first incorporation into American constitutional law of pure communism.[1]

The above article should help us get in touch with the contemporary politics of the time at the state level, and perhaps give us some clues on the context in which the 1874 version of the united order was operating.

## Marx and Greeley

In about 1988, I spoke with a person in the Utah publishing industry who told me that Karl Marx himself had actually visited Salt Lake City. I have never seen anything more on this, and I choose to call this an "historical rumor," but it is an intriguing thought. If true, that might aid those who wish to say that Brigham Young accepted communism, perhaps by entertaining, counseling with, or approving of Marx in some manner.

The rumor is at least semi-plausible. Brigham Young and Karl Marx were contemporaries. Karl Marx would certainly have found it interesting to hear of any large-scale communal society anywhere in the world, and his journalist's curiosity might have led him to actually make the visit. The completion of the transcontinental railroad in 1869 would have made the trip feasible. If the capitalist lender Baron Rothschild of Europe could pay a visit (in 1875), so might the socialist Karl Marx.

Horace Greeley, editor of the *New York Tribune*, visited Salt Lake City in 1859 and interviewed Brigham Young on July 13. Since Karl Marx was then contributing to Greeley's newspaper, could Marx have been in that entourage? Possible, but not likely. His name does not even appear in the *Journal of Discourses*, although the term "communism" does appear about 22 times. Was the *Journal of Discourses* purged of any such references to Marx? It is possible. Marx was such a world figure during that era that it seems unlikely his name would not have been used even once.

If Marx had visited Salt Lake City, it is likely that he would have been disappointed when he got there. He would see nothing of the radical destructive class warfare that he espoused. The level of cooperation among all groups would probably have amazed him. At least some individuals would have scorned him. John Taylor certainly made it clear during his lifetime that any form of communism or socialism was repugnant to him. The godless, anti-religion stance of most communists would make them unwelcome, at least to such as John Taylor.

To Marx, having a group such as the Mormons go directly to the "final phase" of communism without all the interesting intermediate steps probably would be upsetting to him. He would probably have been infuriated to find that religion had assisted a group of people to attain effective economic integration and prosperity without the long-term conflicts he predicted and apparently longed to see. His theory would have been shown to be full of holes. His "opiate of the people" had proved to be a stimulus to the people.

At least in the 1859 time-frame, Horace Greeley, the publisher of the *New York Tribune*, was considered to be an enemy of the Mormons. According to John Taylor in an August 23, 1959, discourse, Greeley was the most rabid "Mormon-eater" one could find. (JD 5:153 JT Aug 23, 1859 SLC). In an August 9, 1859, discourse, John Taylor said that Greeley was corrupt and had been associated with a Free Love society, and was its principle supporter. He said "I believe him to be as dishonest a man as is in existence." (JD 5:118 JT Aug 9, 1859 SLC).

John Taylor gave more on Greeley and socialism in a September 13, 1859 discourse:

> Among the number of social movements in our day, there is that of Robert Dale Owen, who thought he could ameliorate the condition of mankind by a sort of communism, having a fellowship of goods among them —— a sort of common stock principle. Everything pertaining to this speculation, however, has flatted out; and in all his schemes and movements, whether in England or in this country, they have signally failed.
>
> It is so also with Fourierism —— a species of French philosophy, established by one Fourier, a Frenchman, and advocated by Greeley of the New York Tribune. They had tried it in France, and then came over to this country; and not far from New York a society of this kind was established. They had a good deal of property, and I am informed they established something of the nature of what is called the free love principle; but within twelve months back, while I was residing in New York, everything they had was sold under the hammer. (JD 5:237 JT Sep 13, 1857)

Horace Greeley was in Salt Lake City on July 13, 1859, and interviewed Brigham Young for two hours. (Note that John Taylor made his negative comments about Greeley just a few weeks later). Greeley's report of the interview seems balanced and non-hostile, although he objected to some of the LDS doctrine.

> Greeley later commented that the Mormons were not so harmful as the public believed, and though he did not approve of their theology, he regarded their accomplishments highly.[2]

Since he was partially to blame for the public's bad image of the Mormons, such a comment with its backhanded compliment was the least he could do.

It is possible that Greeley became less hostile to the Mormons after his visit there. Greeley is mentioned in eight discourses altogether, four by John Taylor, and four by Brigham Young. In three of John Taylor's discourses, he has ill to say of Greeley. In his other discourse and those of Brigham Young's, the comments are mostly neutral. The later discourses are less negative than the first ones.

As noted above, Karl Marx was linked to Horace Greeley. From 1851 to 1862 Karl Marx contributed articles and editorials to the *New York Tribune*, then edited by Horace Greeley. Marx was living in London during that period. It would be interesting to know if the two shared opinions about the Mormons.

It would be interesting to know why Greeley was against the Mormons. Without doing some research into his actual comments, we might surmise that since he was a foe of both the Mormons and of slavery, it may be that the common element in his mind related to the grouping together of slavery and polygamy, a common idea of the time. That he was wrong apparently was seldom an impediment to his speaking loudly, with the whole nation listening. His political ambitions may have colored his statements, influencing him to give the people (and parties) what they seemed to want to hear. The Mormons were apparently a group whom people loved to hate, so why not get on that bandwagon, since their vote could never be significant in national elections.

It is interesting that Greeley considered the Democrats his foes, those same Democrats being the ones which gave the Mormons so much harassment. This may be another of his inconsistencies.

His support for socialist causes is another interesting point. Would he have favored or disfavored the Mormon efforts at cooperation? How does this relate to his support for Karl Marx, one of his reporters or correspondents? Was he disappointed by the saints' failure to incorporate some of his socialist ideas? Was he angered by their achieving notable success without using any of those ideas? These would be interesting questions to pursue, to better understand the intellectual ambiance of the times.

The term "communism" or its variants is mentioned 22 times in 15 discourses by six different speakers. John Taylor used the word in 8 discourses, Brigham Young in two, George Q. Cannon in two, Lorenzo Snow in one, John Nicholson in one, and Erastus Snow in one.

Below are quoted portions of three encyclopedia articles on Communism, Karl Marx, and Horace Greeley.

**Marx, Karl**

Karl Heinrich Marx, b. May 5, 1818, d. Mar. 14, 1883, was a German economist, philosopher, and revolutionist whose writings form the basis of the body of ideas known as Marxism. With the aid of Friedrich Engels he produced much of the theory of modern Socialism and Communism. Marx's father, Heinrich, was a Jewish lawyer who had converted his family to Christianity partly in order to preserve his job in the Prussian state. Karl himself was baptized in the Evangelical church. As a student at the University of Berlin, young Marx was strongly influenced by the philosophy of G. W. F. Hegel and by a radical group called Young Hegelians, who attempted to apply Hegelian ideas to the movement against organized religion and the Prussian autocracy. In 1841, Marx received a doctorate in philosophy.

In 1842, Marx became editor of the Rheinische Zeitung in Cologne, a liberal democratic newspaper for which he wrote increasingly radical editorials on social and economic issues. The newspaper was banned by the Prussian government in 1843, and Marx left for Paris with his bride, Jenny von Westphalen. There he went further in his criticism of society, building on the Young Hegelian criticism of religion. Ludwig FEUERBACH had written a book called The Essence of Christianity (1841; Eng. trans., 1854), arguing that God had been invented by humans as a projection of their own ideals. Feuerbach wrote that man, however, in creating God in his own image, had "alienated himself from himself." He had created another being in contrast to himself, reducing himself to a lowly, evil creature who needed both church and government to guide and control him. If religion were abolished, Feuerbach claimed, human beings would overcome their Alienation. Marx applied this idea of alienation to private property, which he said caused humans to work only for themselves, not for the good of their species. In his papers of this period (published in 1959 English translation as Economic and Philosophic Manuscripts of 1844), he elaborated on the idea that alienation had an economic base. He called for a communist society to overcome the dehumanizing effect of private property.

In 1845, Marx moved to Brussels, and in 1847 he went to London. He had previously made friends with Friedrich Engels, the son of a wealthy textile manufacturer who, like himself, had been a Young Hegelian. They collaborated on a book, The Holy Family (1845; Eng. trans., 1956), which was a criticism of some of their Young Hegelian friends for their stress on alienation. In 1845, Marx jotted down some notes, Theses on Feuerbach, which he and Engels enlarged into a book, The German Ideology (1932; Eng. trans., 1938), in which they developed their materialistic conception of history. They argued that human thought was determined by social and economic forces, particularly those related to the means of production. They developed a method of analysis they called Dialectical Materialism, in which the clash of historical forces leads to changes in society.

In 1847 a London organization of workers invited Marx and Engels to prepare a program for them. It appeared in 1848 as the Communist Manifesto. In it they declared that all history was the history of class struggles. Under Capitalism, the struggle between the working class and the business class would end in a new society, a communist one. The outbreak of the Revolutions of 1848 in Europe led Marx to return to Cologne, where he began publication of the Neue Rheinische Zeitung, but with the failure of the German liberal democratic movement he moved permanently (1849) to London. For many years he and his family lived in poverty, aided by small subventions from Engels and by bequests from the relatives of Marx's wife. From 1851 to 1862 he contributed articles and editorials to the New York Tribune, then edited by Horace Greeley. Most of his time, however, was spent in the British Museum, studying economic and social history and developing his theories.

Marx's ideas began to influence a group of workers and German emigres in London, who established (1864) the International Workingmen's Association, later known as the First International .... By the time of the brief Commune of Paris in 1871, Marx's name had begun to be well known in European political circles. A struggle developed within the International between Marx and the Russian anarchist Mikhail Bakunin, whom Marx eventually defeated and expelled, at the cost of the destruction of the International.

In 1867, Marx published the first volume of Das Kapital (Eng. trans., 1886). The next two volumes, edited by Engels, were published after Marx's death. The fourth volume was edited by Karl Kautsky. Marx's last years were marked by illness and depression. Marx continued to write treatises on socialism, urging that his followers disdain soft-hearted bourgeois tendencies. He took this stand, for example, in The Gotha Program (1891; Eng. trans., 1922). His wife died in 1881, and his eldest daughter in 1883, shortly before his own death.

At Marx's funeral in Highgate Cemetery in London, Engels spoke of him as "the best-hated and most-calumniated man of his time." The importance of Marx's thought, however, extends far beyond the revolutionary movements whose prophet he became. His writings on economics and sociology are still influential in academic circles and among many who do not share his political views.[3]

## Communism

In their Communist Manifesto (1848), Karl Marx and Friedrich Engels applied the term communism to a final stage of socialism in which all class differences would disappear and humankind would live in harmony. Marx and Engels claimed to have discovered a scientific approach to socialism based on the laws of history. They declared that the course of history was determined by the clash of opposing forces rooted in the economic system and the ownership of property. Just as the feudal system had given way to Capitalism, so in time capitalism would give way to socialism. The class struggle of the future would be between the bourgeoisie, or capitalist employers, and the proletariat, or workers. The struggle would end, according to Marx, in the socialist revolution and the attainment of full communism.[4]

## Greeley, Horace

Horace Greeley was a renowned American newspaper editor who founded the influential New York Tribune. His voice in national affairs was of great significance in the critical years before and during the Civil War. Few issues of the time escaped his notice. On all of them he had strong opinions, which he vigorously expounded in his widely read editorials. "For 35 years Horace Greeley was probably the greatest political force this country has ever known except Thomas Jefferson," said the New York World on the 100th anniversary of Greeley's birth.
....

Greeley was forceful and outspoken on the many causes he espoused, sometimes with apparent inconsistency. He championed equality for women in employment and education but was adamantly opposed to woman suffrage and liberalized divorce laws. He advocated agrarianism but recognized the need for industrialization, and although he believed in free trade, he favored protective tariffs. Favorite targets for his condemnation included monopolies, liquor and tobacco, capital punishment, and the theater. He gave generous space in the Tribune to the socialistic doctrine of Charles Fourier. Above all, Greeley fought unceasingly against slavery.

In 1860, as a delegate to the convention of the new Republican party, which Greeley, long a loyal Whig, had helped form, he was instrumental in securing the nomination of Abraham Lincoln. Later, as the war progressed, he was somewhat erratic in his support of the president's policies. His influence on Lincoln has thus been the subject of much debate. For taking several unpopular stands, Greeley and the Tribune were the targets of much abuse, the most violent being two mob attacks on the Tribune building during the bloody New York draft riots of 1863. After the war ended, Greeley urged universal amnesty and impartial suffrage (male) as the basis for reconstruction. He also personally signed a bail bond for Confederate president Jefferson Davis.

....

Obsessed with politics all his life, Greeley frequently sought, but rarely won, public office. He served a brief term in Congress (1848-49), filling a vacancy, and was twice an unsuccessful candidate for the Senate (1860 and 1866) and twice for the House (1866 and 1870). His political aspirations came to a devastating climax in 1872. Disillusioned with President Grant's administration and the Republican party, Greeley helped form the new Liberal Republican party and received its nomination for the presidency. Oddly enough, he was also endorsed by the Democratic party, his longtime political foes. He was overwhelmed at the polls, carrying only 6 states to Grant's 31. Exhausted by the campaign and from sleeplessly caring for his wife, who had died only a week before the election (Oct. 30, 1872), Greeley collapsed, became demented, and died Nov. 29, 1872. Chief among the dignitaries at his funeral, for which huge crowds thronged the streets of New York, was President Grant.[5]

## Other Observations

As shown in the extensive quotes at the beginning of the chapter, there is relatively little direct mention or discussion of communism/socialism in the *Journal of Discourses.* John Taylor did use the term regularly and was against it. Brigham Young only used the term "communism" once in a discourse and then only to identify a group that later inhabited Nauvoo. In the topic summary or headnotes at the beginning of another Brigham Young discourse, the discourse is said to show that the "UNITED ORDER IS NOT COMMUNISM" but the word "communism" is not used in the actual text of the discourse. The word "Marx" does not appear in the JD, nor does the Commune of Paris of 1871.

There is some indirect use or discussion of ideas of communism/socialism. Orson Pratt expounded and promoted a major aspect of communism, that no individual should own any private property. However, regardless of Orson Pratt's position as one of the Twelve, and his significant influence on current affairs, his program was never accepted. Brigham Young did not support any such radical program. In Brigham Young's mind, property was something to be wisely joined together for business or economic advantage, but any number of ownership methods would do. He was an advocate of careful accounting for individual contributions to economic enterprises and withdrawals therefrom, thus keeping things on a fair and business-like basis. In the Orderville case, where Brigham pressed for individual accountability, George Q. Cannon advised against it.

## Freedom is Indivisible

The question of individual liberty is at the core of this united order question. Some current comments on freedom help demonstrate that individual rights are not really severable or delegable. Property rights and speech rights tend to be closely connected, as argued in a book entitled *Free Speech for Me -- But Not for Thee:*

For most of those who founded Vermont and the United States, protection of individual rights was the highest purpose of government, the chief reason to form a government in the first place. Our ancestors knew from bitter experience what can happen to individuals when those in power decide what is the common good, and what limits to put on individual rights.

Today ... much of our society is losing its grip on the idea of freedom. We don't have the same gut understanding of the importance of liberty that our ancestors did. We think we can trade off some freedoms without losing others. We don't understand what the Bill of Rights is all about.

....

The difference is, early Americans understood what liberty means and they defended it fiercely. They knew exactly what they were doing when they ratified the Bill of Rights.[6]

This "liberty stuff" will never come alive for most of the young if the Constitution continues to have as much personal meaning to them as the average annual rainfall in Wichita. And if the Bill of Rights does not become of passionate interest to them -- and to their children -- it will eventually dissolve into a charming legend of the early years of the Republic when individual liberty -- rather than the will of the majority in all things -- was actually considered the core of democracy.[7]

The church today already has numerous auditors and lawyers to keep its bureaucracy under tight control. Buildings and contributions are about the only functions that need to be watched. If bishops and other leaders had a thousand times more power over money and property, who would supply all the necessary controls? Do we build a massive bureaucracy for that? A priestly bureaucracy? Such controls are not necessary if individuals take care of their own matters. This is a little like the usual priesthood/professional manager/priestcraft problems that come with having (and defending) a social status as a privileged person. One the greatest strengths of the church is that it is not ruled by a priestly class which then has its own vested interests in doctrines and how they affect the members, the priest's income, power, etc. Getting the church involved in all aspects of life would surely put the correctness of the church and the freedom of the members in great danger. It is almost inconceivable to the author how it could not then fall into many of the snares of the socialist paradigm. Putting massive power over individual rights into the hands of any group of mortal administrators, however well-intentioned, has its risks. The flip side of the altruism preached by most socialist groups is the raw power accumulated by the administrators, usually self-appointed and self-perpetuating. See George Q. Cannon's lamentations in his August 12, 1883, discourse quoted above concerning the unwillingness of the members to blindly put their property into the church's hands.

## Utilitarianism and Majoritarianism

On several occasions, the brethren in their discourses on the united order, the Constitution, and other topics, used the phrase "the greatest good for the greatest number of the people" as the dominant and desired principle. (JD 12:113 BY Dec 8, 1867 SLC; JD 17:58 BY May 7, 1874 SLC; JD 17:74 ES May 8, 1874 SLC; JD 22:64 GBG Jan 30, 1881 SLC. See also JD 9:324 WW Apr 8, 1862 SLC; JD 11:301 BY Feb 3, 1867 SLC; JD 26:353 JT Feb 20, 1884 SLC). This altruistic sentiment has its value in many areas, but if followed with too much fervor (or lack of revelation) could easily lead to the majority ignoring the minority and overpowering and oppressing them. The result may be many little tyrants rather than one big one if it gets to be pure democracy with no minority protections. It may allow an intolerance for all but one idea and method, like today's "political correctness" where force is used to limit the ideas expressed.

There is a danger in majoritarianism. Conformity may be as dangerous as communitarianism or communism. The tyranny of one, a small group, or the majority may be equally bad; whether the majority rules or a powerful minority rules, the results may produce much injustice and suffering for the oppressed minority or majority.

Brigham Young's "the greatest good for the greatest number" is a majoritarian idea that can imply that the minority can be sacrificed for the benefit of the majority. Certainly, he did not ever mean that to happen, but if a people accept that as a principle, the opportunity then exists for abuse.

On the constitutional note, we might say that today's church socialists are fighting against the constitution - using sophistry to change that God-given statement of principles to reach a "higher" law. That "higher" law, alas, is a hoax. (Note the parallel case where the "higher" law of communalism was used as a substitute for the truly higher law of tithing.)

This is propaganda, not doctrine. It may be driven by the same incentives that have convinced other intellectuals to start other revolutions for their own benefit. "Uplifting the downtrodden" is the deceptive cry of that class of "reformers." Here they sometimes use manufactured church doctrine to ensnare the unwary.

Accepting socialism or communism within a large segment of the society would represent a great change in the constitution. You cannot keep the old and graft on the new without effecting major changes. The limits on the power of the central government must be maintained, else the language of the constitution loses meaning as we slide towards an autocracy and abuse of individual rights by the government, be it that of a tyrant or of the majority.

## Was There a Specific Revelation?

It was a puzzle to the people of Brigham Young's time (and that puzzle continues today) why such important new "commandments" as those dealing with cooperation and the various versions of united orders, with such potentially drastic effects on society, reconstituting it from top to bottom, were not also given a place in the formal revelations. In Joseph Smith's time, topics of any importance at all were the subject of specific revelations, and the people of Brigham Young's time may have wondered why that stream of tangible revelation ceased.

For example, the Word of Wisdom, a fairly important individual health law, has its own written revelation given during Joseph Smith's time. In contrast, the united order, supposedly containing the rules for setting up an entire society, has no written revelation of its own. Does this make the Word of Wisdom the more important revelation, even though its total effects on one's life would probably be much less?

Some effort was made to take some of the old revelations and stretch them to fit the new situations, but the fit was bad, and the leaders after Brigham Young rejected that attempted rejuvenation and re-interpretation of old verses. Brigham Young once composed the text of a short "revelation" in a speech on the topic, but said at the same time that a separate revelation was not necessary. No other attempts appear to have be made to formalize or canonize that or any other version of a revelation.

There were two competing themes presented by different speakers on the unity topics. One argued for (1) better economic production through cooperation and good business practices, while the other almost ignored good economics and sought to make (2) "better" people through endless humiliation and sacrifice.
Of these opposing goals, I accept only (1) as valid, and I believe Brigham Young would agree. But (2) seems to have had a number of supporters as well, and it continues today to a lesser degree. I consider it destructive and so did Brigham Young.

Some of the events occurring after President John Taylor officially discontinued the united order program in 1882 are interesting on this point of the existence of a specific revelation. The Orderville people were perhaps the most avid supporters and most thorough implementers of what they supposed the united order to be, their version being almost perfect Christian communism by the New Testament Book of Acts account. In 1883, it was recommended that the old system be abandoned:

> [T]he decision to shift to an unequal wage and partial stewardship system in 1883 [split the group]. Some thought that the original provision that the labor of all should be subject to common direction and entitled to equal credit (except for the age and sex groups previously mentioned) had led to inefficiency, sluggardliness, and loss of personal freedom. Others thought the original system was the word of God as relayed to Brigham Young, and that any change would be blasphemous. Viewing the procedural disagreement with alarm, Erastus Snow, as resident general church authority in southern Utah, began to emphasize the experimental nature of the Order. He argued that the various enterprises and departments of the Order were not significantly different from ordinary Mormon cooperative stores; that the system of giving equal credit for unequal labor had been unsound; and that the United Order, as practiced, was not a commandment of God but a financial experiment initiated by Brigham Young. He thought resort to simple cooperation might be the better course.
> ....

A portion of a letter written by one of the directors of the Order on August 18, 1883, shortly after the change was made, gives a particularly revealing comment on the dilemma that faced Order leaders:

> Accumulating wealth was not our object, that was farthest from our minds, our aim was to establish a principle of equality as near that spoken of in the Revelations, as our fallen natures would admit of, striving always to grade upwards towards the mark....
> Now this command from God, as we supposed, was our cement; this is what brought us together, what held us together, what comforted us in all our sorrows, what cheered us up when cast down, and in our vicissitudes we felt to rejoice and put on new determinations to endeavor to surmount every obstacle and make every sacrifice necessary to and consequent upon establishing a new order of things.... We verily believed we were in the line of our duty endeavoring to work out a problem and felt that we were sustained by the General Church Authorities until our last quarterly conference, when we were told by Apostle Erastus Snow that our organization was no more (not

> much more) than Canaan Co-op, Z.C.M.I. or any other co-operative company in the territory, that it was not a commandment of God and never has been, that it was a financial experiment of Brigham Young and that there was nothin[g] binding on the people in that respect.... So you see we are thrown entirely on our own responsibility.... The consequence was many have "drawn out" and have gone and strange to say that no one of our industries have failed yet; but all are moving along as formerly and some of them even more prosperous than formerly.

> Finally the Order came to substitute, albeit with considerable hesitancy, a system of limited individual stewardships for the strict common-stock property arrangement under which they had lived for eight years. BCG p. 283-7.

It is easy to see the dilemma described here, since the "is it or isn't it a commandment?" question is still with us. However, after studying the history, I am of the opinion that there never was a commandment to live communally, and that any claim of "communalism as a commandment" is simply untrue and not based on historical fact. There are traditions on that topic, but they apparently were originally generated and continue to be propagated by those who, in their own personal feelings, tend to prefer the arrangement of societal power in the socialist pattern.

In the Orderville quote above, the statement "Accumulating wealth was not our object, that was farthest from our minds, our aim was to establish a principle of equality as near that spoken of in the Revelations" is an interesting one. Brigham always told the people to acquire as much as they rightfully could, so that the church could have the means to bring in more immigrant/converts and to care for its own. If all were so inward-looking that mere subsistence was sufficient to fulfill their ambitions, they were of little use to the president in his enormous duties.

Brigham Young always counseled the keeping of careful individual accounts in all economic endeavors, making them "business-like" in operation. Where no accurate and long-term accounts are kept, but the results are split evenly regardless of input, the lazy are assured of living off the efforts of the industrious, at least for the short time until they catch on and cease to be industrious. (Of course, with no reliable feedback, even the lazy have some justification for their relative inaction.)

One practical reason for keeping good accounts was to be able to pay off people in the correct amounts if they left the project for any reason, but it was more than merely for fighting off dissidents and doing damage control. It also kept the incentives just and proper for everyone involved.

## Fervor

The book BCG presents a wealth of historical data on various united order efforts and projects throughout the Utah area, and is an important book for the serious student. It does not attempt to cover all examples of economic cooperation, but focuses on the 1870's.

I have no basis to challenge any of the historical data presented. However, interpretation or extrapolations are made from that data and in some cases I would take issue with those interpretations, or at least desire to see other theories compared with the data. For example, in the case of the Kanab united order, the data presented seems to indicate that the members of a united order had more valuable property, on average, than those who were not members of the order. This is taken as an indication that the more wealthy had more fervor for the united order program than did those with less, since, presumably, they had more to risk, and therefore more commitment would logically be required for them to be willing to proceed. This may be well be true.

However, it seems just as possible that religious fervor in Kanab was not the difference at all, but that, for example, either the united order business project was run on good economic principles, and so made the participants more wealthy, or perhaps they just took better measures of the city folk's property and did not attempt to value carefully the rancher's lands.

What I am really resisting here is the argument that religious fervor has an important part to play, or is a necessary ingredient, in getting the economic arrangements right. If someone has to act against their ordinary good sense in order to support such a project, there is probably something wrong with it. If the fervor is brought about by propaganda or misinformation or disinformation, as it often is, then there is great opportunity for harmful errors to be made. Scams are born this way. "You can't cheat an honest man" is an old saying, which I interpret to mean that thoroughness and level-headedness will keep a man from inadvertently cheating another or being cheated. Fuzzy thinking has not been shown to be good for basic economic success (except in Hollywood).

There seems to be a general antagonism between religious fervor and economic good sense. John Taylor said that he was against any kind of fanaticism, referring to the comparison between the socialist projects of the time and the gospel. This fervor or fanaticism can lead men to do foolish things and may let some take advantage of others in the process. Fantasies and fairy tales can lead to devastating failures like the so-called "Great Leap Forward" of China's Mao Zedong.

It appears that Brigham Young had little interest in artificially induced religious fervor on economic matters, or fervor for its own sake, but always and only sought for actual positive economic results. See especially the chapter containing Brigham Young's denials of the "all things common" language in the Book of Acts.

## Social Philosophy

In debates of social philosophy, it seems difficult to keep the terms of discussion clear. For example, however strange it may seem, it appears to be common socialist practice to use the word "fairness" in contrast to "justice." To accomplish that feat of verbal magic, they define "fairness' as being a requirement that everyone get equal rewards for unequal efforts. That seems completely unjust and therefore "unfair." But by redefining "fairness" to exclude justice and contain only "mercy" (or more accurately, forced mercy, another twisting of terms) they make the topic difficult to discuss. They win arguments, not by good logic, but by warping the words, making crisp debate more difficult.

"Fairness" thus becomes what many would call injustice or non-justice or mercy or charity or forced-charity. "Fairness" can then become a codeword for legalized theft, or legalized assumption of otherwise illegal power. This use of the term "fairness" is completely contrary to efficiency which requires clear justice to work. Thus "fairness" can come to mean economic inefficiency, resulting in "unfairness" for all. Without the predictability of action/reaction and reward/punishment in the world, effort wanes.

Fear and envy seem to be the negative emotions used to drive this leveling ideology. The argument against strict individual economic justice, and for the pooling of all, and ignoring the unique contributions of the individual, seems to be a fear that if people are given their just due, they will not have any charity and will let everyone else starve. This is a choice-destroying and very negative attitude, hardly calling forth the best in men, but basing all government on *a priori* suspicion, wherein all are guilty before proven innocent, but the chance to prove their innocence is taken from them by force.

Orson Pratt's idea of the ideal society was much like Russian communism - no one would be allowed to own any property. Luckily his plan was not accepted. It would have been terribly inefficient, and would not have let us join well or easily with the United States.

Such systems wreck individual choice and responsibility. It does not breed success, although in a temporary and desperate tribal setting it may prevent failure (death). Instead of everyone being responsible in different degrees for economic decisions, only the top few make all significant decisions - all new ventures, etc., because only they have any resources. They can never process enough information to make all such decisions for a large and complex economy; they tend to depend on fuzzy ideologies, not facts for many crucial decisions. The usual result is that only a few areas can be emphasized, at the expense of all others. In Russia it was steel and military weapons.

Joseph Smith said that a church that cannot save its members temporally cannot save them spiritually. Usually we think of one person at a time, but here Brigham Young was saving the whole church at once. He could not afford to do anything that was not the most effective available. Silly experiments would only confuse and impoverish the saints. We should recall again that Joseph Smith fought these socialist ideas all of his days.

## Historical Sources and Viewpoints

The book BCG presents much good and interesting data on both sides, but whether from a sense of duty to tradition or personal preference, seems to struggle to find support for the "communism as a commandment" tradition. They seem almost to be implying that those who discontinued the Brigham-Young-period communal projects were somehow themselves possible apostates from the original (oral?) commandments, and that the commandments will be re-activated at some point. This position does not seem to be supported by the bulk of the history.

While I find much to commend, admire, and agree with in BCG, still there is an element that I find disturbing, and that is what I consider to be an excess of zeal to find support for communism as a commandment of God. For example, the Orderville united order from 1874 to 1885 (p. 268) was gradually changed into a more individually just system and less of an undifferentiated communal system. To the authors of BCG this seems to be a pity, something to be deplored. In other places they speak of "the more ideal communal order" (p. 253). But the question is, ideal by whose standards? The ideal in their minds seems not to have been in Brigham Young's.

In other words, I am unwilling to let BCG be the last and only word on the subject, and wish to argue that it was not a commandment of God and never had been. I contend that Brigham Young never gave that commandment and that thousands have misunderstood what he did say. The "misunderstanding" in some cases being evidence of a personal preference rather than being based on solid data. If this difference really is just a matter of opinion, then the opposing opinion needs to be aired as well.

## Chapter notes

[1] Edwin L. Godkin, "Communism in California," *The Annals of America*, 10:401.

[2] *Annals*, 9:132.

[3] "Marx, Karl," *The New Grolier Electronic Encyclopedia* (Grolier Electronic Publishing, Inc., 1991)

[4] "Communism," *Grolier.*

[5] "Greeley, Horace," *Grolier.*

[6] Nat Hentoff, *Free Speech for Me -- But Not for Thee: How the American Left and Right Relentlessly Censor Each Other* (New York: HarperCollins Publishers, Inc, 1992), p. 388.

[7] Ibid., p. 371.

# CHAPTER 25

# Latter-day Prophets on Welfare Topics

An important goal of this book has been to make the policies from older eras comprehensible in today's terms. Whether that purpose has been accomplished can only be determined by the reader. As a help in the process, some comments from more recent prophets on these temporal topics should be interesting. In October 1977 welfare session of Conference, President Spencer W. Kimball expressed these thoughts:

> Singing this song ["Improve the Shining Moments"] takes me back some generations. My beloved mother, who died early in my life, used to hum this song, as she went about the house preparing the meals and taking care of our home. So it's very dear to me.
>
> It's good to meet with you again in conference--to consider our covenants, our duties, our blessings, and to learn the mind and will of our Heavenly Father.
>
> As I considered my remarks for this welfare session, I was struck by the thought that if we measure a generation as forty years, then a generation has passed since the reestablishment of this great welfare work in October of 1936. In my mind's eye the great leaders of this effort passed in review: Presidents Heber J. Grant, J. Reuben Clark, Jr., David O. McKay, Henry D. Moyle, Harold B. Lee, Marion G. Romney, and many more too numerous to review. So also their counsels and their teachings of the scriptures have been recalled to mind.
>
> As I recounted their contributions and the Church's splendid growth in Welfare Services, I encountered this question: Do our people today, and more particularly do our regional, stake, and ward leaders today, *have the same grasp of welfare principles and the same commitment to welfare services work* as did those of this previous generation?
>
> I am constrained to agree with President Romney's assessment of this, when in an instructional session of General Authorities several years ago he stated:
>
> "As 'There arose up a new king over Egypt, which knew not Joseph' (Exodus 1:8), so there has arisen in the Church a new generation of bishops and stake presidents who have not been taught and trained as were their predecessors." (Marion G. Romney, *The Basics of Church Welfare*, March 6, 1974.)
>
> Because of the overriding significance of this great welfare plan, I thought it appropriate to restate the fundamental truths of this work and to emphasize how we should apply these in this generation. My hope is that we may intensify, if possible, our spiritual heritage in this work and, building on their foundation, lengthen our stride in its present implementation.
>
> Since the first dispensation of time on this earth the Lord has required his people to <u>love their neighbors</u> as themselves. Of Enoch's generation we are told that "the Lord blessed the land, and they were blessed upon the mountains, and upon the high places, and did flourish.
>
> "And the Lord called his people Zion, because they were of one heart and one mind, and dwelt in righteousness; and there was <u>no poor among them</u>." (Moses 7: 17-18.)
>
> All through the Book of Mormon we see leaders teaching and generations learning this truth as spoken by that benevolent king, Benjamin:
>
> "And now, for the sake of these things which I have spoken unto you--that is, for the sake of retaining a remission of your sins from day to day, that ye may walk guiltless before God--I would that ye should impart of your substance to the poor, every man according to

that which he hath, such as <u>feeding the hungry, clothing the naked</u>, visiting the sick and administering to their relief, both spiritually and temporally, according to their wants." (Mosiah 4:26.)

In Fourth Nephi we witness the blessings of the Nephites as they subdue selfishness and prosper in perfect righteousness for four generations. Who does not thrill to this picture of the ideal of Zion?

COMMENT: Note here that the above scripture about giving to the poor and the "all things common" scripture below are treated as equal in meaning.

"And they had <u>all things common among them</u>; therefore there were not rich and poor, bond and free, but they were all made free, and partakers of the heavenly gift....

"And there were no envyings, nor strifes, nor tumults, nor whoredoms, nor lyings, nor murders, nor any manner of lasciviousness; and surely there could not be a happier people among all the people who had been created by the hand of God." (4 Ne. 3, 16.)

It is now nearly four generations ago in this, the last dispensation, that the Lord again laid down his precepts for modern Zion when he said:

"And let every man esteem his brother as himself, and practise virtue and holiness before me.

"And again I say unto let every man esteem his brother as himself.

"For what man among you having twelve sons, and is no respecter of them, and they serve him obediently, and he saith unto the one: Be thou clothed in robes and sit thou here; and to the other: Be thou clothed in rags and sit thou there--and looketh upon his sons and saith I am just?

"Behold, this I have given unto you as a parable, and it is even as I am. I say unto you, be one; and if ye are not one ye are not mine." (D&C 38:24-27.)

President Joseph F. Smith foreshadowed the reestablishment of <u>welfare work</u> in 1900 when he reminded us:

"You must continue to bear in mind that the temporal and the spiritual are blended. They are not separate. One cannot be carried on without the other, so long as we are here in mortality.

"The Latter-day Saints believe not only in the gospel of spiritual salvation, but also in the gospel of temporal salvation.... We do not feel that it is possible for men to be really good and faithful Christian people unless they can also be good, faithful, honest and industrious people. Therefore, we preach the gospel of industry, the gospel of economy, the gospel of sobriety." *(Gospel Doctrine,* Deseret Book, pp. 208-9.)

Thus you can see that when in 1936 the First Presidency re-enunciated these precepts in the form of the <u>present-day welfare plan</u>, they were merely extending to that generation a more complete opportunity for establishing the ideal of Zion. In this generation their words may have even deeper meaning.

"Our primary purpose," said the First Presidency, "was to set up, in so far as it might be possible, a system under which the curse of idleness would be done away with, the evils of a dole abolished, and independence, industry, thrift and self respect be once more established amongst our people. The aim of the Church is to help the people to help themselves. Work is to be reenthroned as the ruling principle of the lives of our Church membership." *(Conference Report.* October 1936, p. 3.)

There is no mistaking their intent: and while often seen as temporal in nature, clearly we must understand that this work is spiritual at heart! It is people-centered and God-inspired and, as President J. Reuben Clark, Jr., put it, "The real long term objective of the Welfare Plan is the building of character in the members of the Church, givers and receivers, rescuing all that is finest down deep inside of them, and bringing to flower and fruitage the latent richness of the spirit, which after all is the mission and purpose and reason for being of this Church." (President J. Reuben Clark, Jr., special meeting of stake presidencies, October 2, 1936.)

As we travel and visit the people throughout the world, we recognize the great temporal needs of our people. And as we long to help them, we realize the vital importance of their learning this great lesson: that the highest achievement of spirituality comes as we conquer the flesh. We build character as we encourage people to care for their own needs.

As giyvrs gain control of their desires and properly see other needs in light of their own wants, then the powers of the gospel are released in their lives. They learn that by living the great law of consecration they insure not only temporal salvation but also spiritual sanctification.

And as a recipient receives with thanksgiving, he rejoices in knowing that in its purest form--in the true Zion--one may partake of both temporal and spiritual salvation. Then they are motivated to become self-sustaining and able to share with others.

Isn't the plan beautiful? Don't you thrill to this part of the gospel that causes Zion to put on her beautiful garments? When viewed in this light, we can see that <u>Welfare Services</u> is not a program, but the essence of the gospel. *It is the <u>gospel in action</u>.*

It is the crowning principle of a Christian life.

So as to better visualize this process and firmly fix the specific principles that undergird this work, may I rehearse to you what I believe are its foundational truths.

First is *love.* The measure of our love for our fellowman and, in a large sense, the measure of our love for the Lord, is what we do for one another and for the poor and the distressed.

"A new commandment I give unto you, That ye love one another; as I have loved you, that ye also love one another.

"By this shall all men know that ye are my disciples, if ye have love one to another." (John 13:34-35; see Moro. 7:44-48 and Luke 10:25-37, 14:12-14.)

Second is *service.* To serve is to abase oneself, to succor those in need of succor, and to impart of one's "substance to the poor and the needy, feeding the hungry, and suffering all manner of afflictions, for Christ's sake." (Al. 4:13.)

"Pure religion and undefiled before God and the Father is this, To visit the fatherless and widows in their affliction, and to keep himself unspotted from the world." (James 1:27.)

Third is *work.* Work brings happiness, self-esteem, and prosperity. It is the means of all accomplishment; it is the opposite of idleness. We are commanded to work. (See Gen. 3:19.) Attempts to obtain our temporal, social, emotional, or spiritual well-being by means of a dole violate the divine mandate that we should work for what we receive. Work should be the ruling principle in the lives of our Church membership. (See D&C 42:42; 75:29; 68:30-32; 56:17.)

Fourth is *self-reliance.* The Church and its members are commanded by the Lord to be self-reliant and independent. (See D&C 78:13-14.)

The responsibility for each person's social, emotional, spiritual, physical, or economic well-being rests first upon himself, second upon his family, and third upon the Church if he is a faithful member thereof.

No true Latter-day Saint, while physically or emotionally able will voluntarily shift the burden of his own or his family's well-being to someone else. So long as he can, under the inspiration of the Lord and with his own labors, he will supply himself and his family with the spiritual and temporal necessities of life. (See 1 Timothy 5:8.)

*Fifth is consecration,* which encompasses sacrifice. Consecration is the giving of one's time, talents, and means to care for those in need--whether spiritually or temporally--and in building the Lord's kingdom.  In Welfare Services, members consecrate as they labor on production projects, donate materials to Deseret Industries, share their professional talents, give a generous fast offering, and respond to ward and quorum service projects.  They consecrate their time in their home or visiting teaching.  We consecrate when we give of ourselves. (See ENSIGN, June 1976, pp. 3-6.)

Sixth is *stewardship.*  In the Church a stewardship is a sacred spiritual or temporal trust for which there is accountability.  Because all things belong to the Lord, we are stewards over our bodies, minds, families, and properties. (See D&C 104:11-15.)  A faithful steward is one who exercises righteous dominion, cares for his own, and looks to the poor and needy. (See D&C 104:15-18.)

These principles govern welfare services activities.  May we all learn, obey, and teach these principles.  Leaders, teach them to your members; fathers, teach them to your families. Only as we apply these truths can we approach the ideal of Zion.

*Zion* is a name given by the Lord to his covenant people, who are characterized by purity of heart and faithfulness in caring for the poor, the needy, and the distressed. (See D&C 97:21.)

COMMENT: Note that the emphasis here is on making sure there are no poor.  This is quite a different focus than trying to make the kingdom strong.  One is preventing or eliminating an undesirable condition, removing a negative, while the other is more positive and aggressive and could be politically sensitive.

"And the Lord called his people ZION, because they were of one heart and one mind, and dwelt in righteousness; and there was no poor among them." (Moses 7: 18.)

This highest order of priesthood society is founded on the doctrines of love, service, work, self-reliance, and stewardship, all of which are circumscribed by the covenant of consecration.

May I turn now to some of the activities and programs that represent ways to live these principles.

As you know, in the recent past we have placed considerable emphasis on personal and family preparedness.  I hope that each member of the Church is responding appropriately to this direction.  I also hope that we are understanding and accentuating the positive and not the negative.

I like the way the Relief Society teaches personal and family preparedness as "provident living."  This implies the husbanding of our resources, the wise planning of financial matters, full provision for personal health, and adequate preparation for education and career development, giving appropriate attention to home production and storage as well as the development of emotional resiliency.

I hope that we understand that, while having a garden, for instance, is often useful in reducing food costs and making available delicious fresh fruits and vegetables, it does much more than this.  Who can gauge the value of that special chat between daughter and Dad as they weed or water the garden?  How do we evaluate the good that comes from the obvious lessons of planting, cultivating, and the eternal law, of the harvest?  And how do we measure the family togetherness and cooperating that must accompany successful canning?  Yes, we are laying up resources in store, but perhaps the greater good is contained in the lessons of life we learn as we *live providently,* and extend to our children their pioneer heritage.

Think of the learning that accompanies a family council on the family budget.  How do Mom and Dad feel when a teenage son who, because he is included and understands the budgeting process, volunteers part of his summer's income to help replace that tired refrigerator?

We speak of literacy and education in terms of being prepared for a better occupation, but we cannot underestimate the present pleasure of our reading in the scriptures, Church magazines, and good books of every kind. We teach of emotional strength in terms of family prayer, kind words, and full communication, but we quickly learn how pleasant life can be when it is lived in a courteous and reinforcing atmosphere.

In like manner we could refer to all the components of personal and family preparedness, not in relation to holocaust or disaster, but in cultivating a life-style that is on a day-to-day basis its own reward.

Let's do these things because they are right, because they are satisfying, and because we are obedient to the counsels of the Lord. In this spirit we will be prepared for most eventualities, and the Lord will prosper and comfort us. It is true that difficult times will come--for the Lord has foretold them--and, yes, stakes of Zion are "for a defense, and for a refuge from the storm." (D&C 115:6.) But if we live wisely and providently, we will be as safe as in the palm of his hand.

I hope that in our priesthood quorums and Relief Society meetings the concepts of personal and family preparedness are being properly taught and with the kind of positive approach that we all respond to.

Let's also teach our obligations relative to the law of the fast. Each member should contribute a generous fast offering for the care of the poor and the needy. This offering should at least be the value of the two meals not eaten while fasting.

"Sometimes we have been a bit penurious and figured that we had for breakfast one egg and that cost so many cents and then we give that to the Lord. I think that when we are affluent, as many of us are, that we ought to be very, very generous....

"I think we should ... give, instead of the amount saved bv our two meals of fasting, perhaps much, much more--ten times more when we are in a position to do it." *(Conference Report,* October 1974, p. 184.)

Fast offerings have long constituted the means from which the needs of the Lord's poor have been provided. It has been, and now is, the desire and objective of the Church to obtain from fast offerings the necessary funds to meet the cash needs of the welfare program; and to obtain from welfare production projects the commodity needs. If we give a generous fast offering, we shall increase our own prosperity both spiritually and temporally.

Now, turning from personal and family responsibilities to the Church's formal welfare activities--sometimes referred to as Church preparedness but perhaps better understood as the Storehouse Resource System--let me emphasize briefly several points.

1. Make adequate provision for those who receive Church assistance to work or serve, according to their ability, for what they receive.

2. Use good judgement in acquiring and managing your welfare production project. Be businesslike and frugal, recognizing that we are growing people--both givers and receivers---more than food and merchandise.

3. Follow the Spirit in knowing to what extent individuals and families can and should care for themselves on their own.

4. Use local resource persons to the fullest extent possible.

5. Finally, regularly hold effective Welfare Committee meetings at all administrative levels.

Brothers and sisters, with these thoughts in mind may I urge you to go forward in this great work. So much depends upon our willingness to make up our minds collectively and individually, that present levels and performance are not acceptable, either to ourselves or the Lord.

You leaders presently serving are as great as or greater than those of this past generation.

Learn your lessons well. Emulate the Savior in your life by serving and consecrating, by overcoming temporally so that you might more fully achieve spiritually.

If we all so labor, then it will eventually be written of us that "surely there could not be a happier people among all the people who had been created by the hand of God."

It is wonderful to be associated with this work and to be given the inspiration of it. I bear my witness of it in the name of Jesus Christ. Amen.

### President Marion G. Romney followed President Kimball in the welfare session:

My beloved brethren and sisters, I invite you to join in a prayer with me that while I speak we will all enjoy the Spirit of the Lord. What I have to say I was taught between thirty and forty years ago, principally by President J. Reuben Clark. Much of what I say will be in his language, and much else, while not directly quoted, will be the substance of his teachings.

In these remarks I shall emphasize three things concerning Welfare Services: first, the bishop's role; second, the responsibility, of priesthood quorums; and third, the distinction between Church welfare and other types of welfare.

*The Bishop's Role*

In December of 1831, before the Church was two years old, the Lord said that it is the responsibility of the bishop "to keep the Lord's storehouse; to receive the funds of the church" which are to "be consecrated . . . to the poor and needy." (D&C 72: 10, 12.)

Ten months later He added that it is the duty of the bishops to search "after the poor [and] administer to their wants by humbling the rich and the proud." (D&C 84:112.)

President Clark thus summarized the bishop's role: "To the bishops is to be paid the tithing." He is "to administer all temporal things. . . . In his calling he is to be endowed with the spirit of discernment to detect those 'professing and yet be not of God'; he is to 'receive the funds of the church', and to 'administer to the . . . poor and needy'; he is to search 'after the poor to administer to their wants.' . . .

"To the bishop is given all the powers and responsibilities which the Lord has specifically prescribed in the Doctrine and Covenants for the caring of the poor. . . . No one else is charged with this duty and responsibility, no one else is endowed with the power and functions necessary for this work....

"By the word of the Lord the sole mandate to care for and the sole discretion in caring for, the poor of the Church is lodged in the bishop.... It is his duty and his only to determine to whom, when, how, and how much shall be given to any member of his ward from Church funds and as ward help.

"This is his high and solemn obligation, imposed by the Lord Himself. The bishop cannot escape this duty; he cannot shirk it; he cannot pass it on to someone else, and so relieve himself. Whatever help he calls in, he is still responsible." ("Bishops and Relief Society," J. Reuben Clark. July 9, 1941.)

Now a whole generation has passed, as President Kimball has said, since these instructions were given. But in our current handbooks and other literature they are taught. In the *Bishops Guide* the duties of the bishop are outlined under five major categories; one of these is entitled "Director of Welfare Services." On paces 24 to 26 of this guide, the specific duties of bishops are listed. They, together with the instructions in the *Welfare Services Handbook,* should be read, studied, and implemented bv every bishop.

In order to adequately care for the spiritual and temporal needs of his people through the facilities of Welfare Services, a bishop must know the needs of each ward member. With respect to the importance of so knowing, President Clark said in the October 1944 Conference:

"A bishop could hardly say he was doing his duty ... if ... he did not take stock of his whole ward to see about how much he is going to require to care for those who need help and sustenance. This could not be a mere cursory operation.... To be effective, [it] must be one that involved the visiting, by some proper authority, . . . every household in the ward, and for a final check, a visit by the bishop himself, to determine the proper help he must be prepared to render to every needy person in the ward." ("Fundamentals of Church Welfare Plan," Bishops Meeting, October 6, 1944, p. 567.)

The effective bishop will be adequately informed on the condition of his ward members, physically, emotionally, economically, and spiritually.

To obtain this information, you bishops may call upon any organization in your ward or any member of the ward. Particularly you should use your ward Relief Society presidents, the Relief Society visiting teachers, and, of course, your priesthood home teachers.

In addition to knowing their needs, *the bishop should determine to what extent individuals and families can solve their own problems.* That this be done is fundamental to Welfare Services work.

We do not bless anybody when we do for them what they can do for themselves. The purpose of Welfare Services is to promote "independence, thrift, and self-respect," and every individual should value his or her independence and labor with all their might to maintain it by being self-sustaining.

Next to himself, the responsibility for sustaining an individual rests upon his family--parents for their children, children for their parents. It is an ungrateful child, as President Kimball has said, who, having the ability, is unwilling to assist his needy parents.

Finally, the individual having done all he can to maintain himself, and members of his family having done what they can do to assist him, the Church, through Welfare Services, stands ready to see that such members, *who will accept the program and work in it to the extent of their ability,* are cared for, each "according to his family, according to his circumstances and his wants and needs." (D&C 51:3.)

Having determined the need, the bishop must marshall the required resources. The Ward Welfare Services Committee has been provided to help him do this. The Ward Welfare Services Committee can be of inestimable value. I remember President Lee's saying that an inactive bishop is one who does not hold his weekly Ward Welfare Services Committee Meeting. I hope that we do not have inactive bishops in the Church today. If there are such, they should repent and become active during this coming week and continue to be active.

With respect to social services--an important part of Welfare Services--President Lee, at the Regional Representatives Seminar in October 1970, said:

"[This] program has already been a great blessing to our Church members. [It] seeks to respond to many problems that beset our members in an affluent society, and it will no doubt increase in its importance, because so many of the problems which this cluster of agencies deals with are symptomatic of our time. Members may need counseling more than clothing, and members, who, through bishops, are referred to any agency in our social services program should feel no more hesitancy in asking for help of this kind than they should in requesting help through the priesthood [production] program.

*The Responsibility of Priesthood Quorums*

Having reviewed now the role of the bishop in Welfare Services, I remind you stake presidents particularly that priesthood quorums have an important role in Welfare Services. They do not, of course, have the obligation prescribed to the bishop, although they should and do assist in the production and gathering of materials.

But the relationship of the priesthood, the spirit of lofty, unselfish brotherhood which it carries with it, does require that they individually and as quorums use their means and energy in rehabilitating spiritually and temporally their erring and unfortunate brethren.

In his temporal administrations, the bishop looks at every needy person as a temporary problem, caring for them until they can help themselves. The priesthood quorums must look at their needy brethren as a continuing problem, until not only their temporal needs are met but their spiritual ones also.

As a concrete example: a bishop extends help while the artist or craftsman is out of work and in want; a priesthood quorum sets him up in work and tries to see that he goes along until fully self-supporting and active in his priesthood duties. Much, much more attention must be given to this aspect of our welfare work.

Now, third, I call attention to a most significant fact. Specifically, it is that help given by a bishop is far different from help given for political, social, or economic considerations in which moral and spiritual considerations play only a secondary part. The welfare of the state, not the welfare of the individual, is the measure by which that kind of relief is gauged and its amount determined. In such relief special favors are frequently given in exchange for some special favor--usually political support--to be given in return. Such a prostitution of relief is destructive of the state and of the individual and must be carefully guarded against.

Relief by private nonchurch agencies and individuals is often motivated by the highest considerations; it is given responsive to general religious commandments and admonitions. But in this giving, the emphasis is rather on the giver than the receiver. There can be a distinct element of selfishness in this--one may give, because to do so makes him truly religious.

But the help given by the bishop is wholly different.

In the first place, the Church is expressly and directly to care for its poor and needy, and the bishop is charged with the responsibility of carrying out that command and is given all the rights, prerogatives, and functions necessary therefor.

In the next place, the standard of care has been indicated. The bishop has been directed "to keep the Lord's storehouse; to receive the funds of the church . . . and to administer to [the] wants" of his people. (D&C 72:10-11.)

To the Church the Lord gave this law:

"Women have claim on their husbands for their maintenance ....

"Children have claim upon their parents for their maintenance....

"And after that, they have claim upon the church, or in other words upon the Lord's storehouse....

"And the storehouse shall be kept by the consecrations of the church; and widows and orphans shall be provided for, as also the poor." (D&C 83:2, 4-6.)

The Lord has authorized exceptional measures to secure the materials to care for these unfortunate members. He has directed the bishop to search "after the poor to administer to their wants by humbling the rich and the proud." (D&C 84:112.)

On another occasion He said:

"Wo unto you rich men, that will not give your substance to the poor, for your riches will canker your souls; and this shall be your lamentation in the day of visitation, and of judgment, and of indignation: The harvest is past, the summer is ended, and my soul is not saved!" (D&C 56:16.)

Neither in public relief nor in private charity is any duty, restraint, or inhibition placed upon the needy recipient of help. He may take and take, and grasp for more. It is quite otherwise in the Church. The Lord has said to the unworthy poor:

"Wo unto you poor men, whose hearts are not broken, whose spirits are not contrite, and whose bellies are not satisfied, and whose hands are not stayed from laying hold upon other men's goods, whose eyes are full of greediness, and who will not labor with your own hands!" (D&C 56:17.)

Under the Lord's plan, the reward coming to those who help is not so much that a blessing will be added to those helping the poor, as a declaration that blessings shall be lost by those who do not help them.

"And remember in all things the poor and the needy, the sick and the afflicted, for he that doeth not these things, the same is not my disciple." (D&C 52:40.)

"I prepared all things, and have given unto the children of men to be agents unto themselves.

"Therefore, if any man shall take of the abundance which I have made, and impart not his portion, according to the law of my gospel, unto the poor and the needy, he shall, with the wicked, lift up his eyes in hell, being in torment." (D&C 104:17-18.)

But the real end of all help to the poor and the needy, under the Lord's plan, is not the mere temporal help, for after warning the poor against pride, covetousness, thieving, greediness, and laziness--none of which things enter into public relief and rarely into private charity--the Lord says:

"But blessed are the poor who are pure in heart, whose hearts are broken, and whose spirits are contrite, for they shall see the kingdom of God coming in power and great glory unto their deliverance; for the fatness of the earth shall be theirs.

"For behold, the Lord shall come, and his recompense shall be with him, and he shall reward every man, and the poor shall rejoice;

"And their generations shall inherit the earth from generation to generation, forever and ever." (D&C 56:18-20.)

The prime duty of help to the poor by the Church is not to bring temporal relief to their needs, but salvation to their souls.

Thus, the bishop is to "visit the poor and the needy and administer to their relief," as a husband to the widow, as a parent to the orphan. And for temporal needs he is to draw from the storehouse. Spiritually he is to see that they are or become the pure in heart, that their spirits are contrite, that their "hearts are broken."

These things cannot be achieved by dollars and cents; therefore all cannot be brought to the same living standards; more help must be given here and less there, to fit the needs of those in want; and all must be measured by the ultimate spiritual uplift.

It is my prayer that all bishops and stake presidents will thoroughly inform themselves of their duty and carry this great work to its ultimate achievement in the redemption of Zion in preparation for the second advent of the Lord. This is my prayer, in the name of Jesus Christ. Amen.

In general, the above discourses are consistent with the approach taken in the rest of this book. The scriptural injunctions are interpreted to require only the normal welfare goals and processes of today, and do not require any more grandiose or extreme interpretation or application.

## CHAPTER 26

# Summary and Conclusions

## The Issue

The major issue addressed by this book is whether the gospel doctrinally requires any particular economic organization for spiritual salvation. I argue that it does not. There ARE economic and legal principles that work well in certain circumstances, but use of them or failure to use them is irrelevant spiritually, except as the use or non-use illustrates wisdom and experience on the part of those involved, and illustrates and accomplishes the desire to do the Lord's work in an efficient and appropriate way.

The major relevant historical experience comes from the Brigham Young era. If it can be shown that the economic programs of the times were *ad hoc* adaptations to the needs of those times, instead of eternally prescribed and required forms, then the major point will have been established.

## The Problem and Solution

In this book I have wished to show that the united order teachings of Brigham Young's time, and numerous subsidiary teachings, can all be related to an overriding goal of making the saints powerful enough to withstand the unceasing onslaughts of the world. They had not been able to do so in the past, coming near extinction in more than one setting. Having established the reason for Brigham Young's programs, the saints' 50-year life-and-death struggle for survival, then the means used will be seen to be appropriate.

The underlying conclusion for application in the present and future is that there is no doctrinally mandated and pre-set way to provide for the needs of the saints, but that every setting has its own required reaction. Living the law of consecration can be accomplished through an infinite variety of temporal-religious arrangements, all dependent on the specific needs and possibilities of the times.

As evidenced by the sending of one army and the continuous threat of others, the saints needed all the power they could muster of every possible sort including economic, military, and political. To meet the economic part of that need, Brigham Young employed innovative economic programs with a goal of maximizing economic growth and GNP. He mostly aimed at concentrating wealth, seeking for efficiencies and economies of scale. He sought to avoid economic dependence on a hostile outside world, or to be subject to exploitation by them. He did not encourage equality, as is often thought. Men of greater skill and experience were expected to direct the use of the available property. Those with less abilities were to help, watch, and learn.

Polygamy's goal was the maximum growth of the saints in terms of population to help ensure ultimate survival. It was thus a very practical matter, not some abstract commandment aimed particularly at the self-improvement or humiliation of the people.

## Anomalies

Many of the unusual teachings of Brigham Young, including polygamy, blood atonement, and the united order itself, can be classed as Gospel "anomalies," that is, topics that are so out of the ordinary, and basically unexplained or seemingly unexplainable, that one must simply ignore them in the usual study of the Gospel. In this work I have tried to identify these unusual teachings and demonstrate that they were all related and were caused by a single set of circumstances.

## A Conclusion

I am of the opinion that the usual traditions from the Brigham Young era are not merely interesting history but can actually be destructive today. I argue that through our ignorance we have allowed the depredations of our political enemies and the rigors of a hostile environment to define for us what we should regard as the best of all possible future worlds, when in fact it was among the worst of situations. The saints were effectively under martial law for at least thirty years trying merely to survive. Who would willingly desire that sorry state to be replicated for our future? Why should we do this to ourselves, and willingly seek to restrict our freedoms, our economic prosperity, and our opportunity for positive influence on the world, based on some supposed, but misunderstood, "golden age" of the past? We have made a virtue of necessity, and then carried it into realms of doctrine.

In the event that we might again come under attack from the general populace, or are forced to live in primitive conditions, then those early lessons of adaptation and protection might again serve us well. But if we are spared those tribulations, we should rejoice, not mourn or seek self-flagellation.

## Summary of Teaching Pattern

The graph depicted on the next page gives a very general overview of the pattern of teaching of the ideas of required pooling of resources and labor – communalism. Notice that there are times when the idea is positively rejected – a negative number on the graph. Today we seem a little more ambivalent, less negative on the theme than Joseph Smith was.

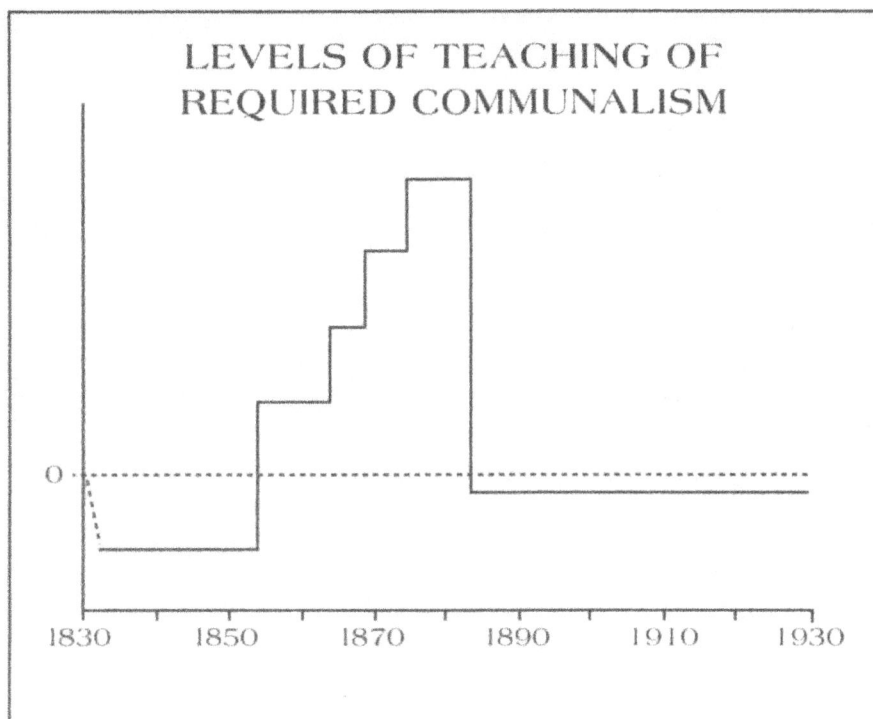

LEVELS OF TEACHING OF REQUIRED COMMUNALISM

The important dates begin with 1830 when the church was organized, after which Joseph declared regularly and in many ways that the church was not a common stock organization. In 1854 Brigham Young first taught the principle, and it was re-emphasized in various ways in 1864, 1869, and 1874, when it reached its most complex form. The program was terminated in 1882 by John Taylor. Ideally, we would have graphs showing both intensity of teaching and complexity of organization. This graph favors the complexity of organization over the intensity of teaching. Actually, in many ways, the emotional intensity decreased as the complexity of organization increased, perhaps indicating that as the goals were close to being accomplished, the anxiety levels went down.

# BRIGHAM YOUNG'S UNITED ORDER
## A Contextual Interpretation
Volume 2 – Related Anomalies and Side Issues
### TABLE OF CONTENTS

# BRIGHAM YOUNG'S UNITED ORDER
## A Contextual Interpretation
Volume 2 - Related Anomalies and Side Issues

## CHAPTER SUMMARIES

### INTRODUCTORY SECTION

Preface

To facilitate economical publication, two-thirds of the lengthy original edition was moved to a second volume.

1. Introduction to Related Anomalies.
   Various practical and theoretical teachings were presented to enhance the power of the saints and their leaders. These teachings have been discontinued and some have even been shown to have been inaccurate when first given.

### GENERAL CONSIDERATIONS

2. A Philosophy of Doctrinal Anomalies.
   Many of Brigham Young's unusual teachings involved modifying the idea on heaven, how one gets there, and how one behaves when there, to get the desired behavior here and now on earth.

   Various techniques were used to make religion support or substitute for other societal institutions. Making one's salvation the basis for action in economic matters replaced the more common economic interests that drive business activity. Brigham Young was denied all the usual government and economic means of giving stability to property and other relationships. In the absence of better institutions, he used what he had or could create.

3. Time Distribution and Clustering of Anomalous Doctrines.
   These unusual doctrines, used for motivational purposes, tend to be taught together in the arguments and rhetoric to promote a certain result.

### BRIGHAM YOUNG'S UNITED ORDER

4. Early Theories - Orson Pratt.
   See next chapter summary.

5. Early Theories - Brigham Young.
   Brigham Young and Orson Pratt presented early theories that seemed to require "dead level" equality. Their theories were evidence of frustration and confusion and are a possible source of myths and troublesome traditions. Brigham Young soon abandoned those ideas, and then strongly resisted them, but Orson Pratt continued on for decades to teach the same ideas and theories.

## MULTIPLE CONTEMPORARY VIEWPOINTS

6. Multiple Views: Introduction.
   The leading brethren were not all in agreement on the nature of the economic problems or their solutions.

7. Multiple Views: Erastus Snow.
   Erastus Snow presented the most complete description of the 1874 version of the united order, which proposed to unite and control all land, capital, and labor.

8. Multiple Views: Orson Hyde.
   In 1853, Orson Hyde proposed the theme of a "common salvation" and further taught that "self-preservation is the first law of nature." This is a good practical statement of the principles that Brigham Young later taught under the united order topic. He seemed skeptical and concerned that the united order rhetoric of centralization would damage many worthwhile local projects.

9. Multiple Views: John Taylor.
   John Taylor was skeptical of any ideology beyond the simple principles of the gospel, such as faith and repentance. He studied communism and socialism and warned against them.

10. Multiple Views: Wilford Woodruff.
    Wilford Woodruff recognized the value and efficiency of cooperation, but said little about the doctrine of the united order.

11. Multiple Views: Wilford Woodruff's Journal.
    Wilford Woodruff's journal shows some of the details of administration and of seeking support from the populace. It confirms the teaching of the anomalous doctrines and gives examples of "united order" planning and behavior.

12. Multiple Views: Orson Pratt.
    Orson Pratt devised theoretical schemes for maintaining the perfect equality of the saints, but later stated that he did not understand the united order.

13. Multiple Views: George Q. Cannon.
    George Q. Cannon pressed for communal farming and equality. He was restrained somewhat by Brigham Young.

14. Multiple Views: George A. Smith.
    He accepted and transmitted all the incorrect traditions concerning Joseph Smith and the united order. He promoted the idea that the saints had the means and talent to care for themselves.

15. Multiple Views: Heber C. Kimball.
    Heber C. Kimball seemed to focus on the "do what you are told" aspects of the united order. He seemed to accept or to be indifferent to "common stock" ideas.

16. Multiple Views: Lorenzo Snow.
    As leader of the Brigham City Cooperative, Lorenzo Snow was a strong advocate of a tightly controlled economy which permitted no internal competition among business institutions.

## OTHER RELATED ANOMALIES

17. Blood Atonement: Introduction.
The "doctrine" of blood atonement is not just one idea, but a class of loosely connected ideas, having something to do with wrong-doing and punishment.

18. Blood Atonement: Law Enforcement in Nauvoo.
After the Nauvoo charter was dissolved, the saints were left without constitutionally supported law enforcement in Nauvoo, and had to improvise.

19. Blood Atonement: Law Enforcement in Utah.
Until statehood in 1896, Utah had no adequate constitutionally supported law enforcement system, and improvisation was necessary. Individuals were expected to avenge crimes against their family and property.

20. Blood Atonement: God's Vengeance for No Law Enforcement.
Failure of the gentiles to give justice to the saints in the criminal courts is likely to lead to an exercise of vengeance on the Lord's part.

21. Blood Atonement: Reformation in Utah.
As part of a revival atmosphere, some extreme statements were made about shedding the blood of some sinners and backsliders. Others recognized that the rhetoric had gone too far.

22. Blood Atonement: Conflict with the Real Atonement.
The blood atonement teaching appeared to redefine and constrict the Savior's atonement, and to itself go beyond the Savior's atonement in some areas.

23. Blood Atonement: God's Vengeance on a Wicked Nation.
In some cases, the Lord must chastise the wicked for their mistreatment of the saints, or to humble them so they can accept the gospel.

24. Blood Atonement: Joseph Smith's Testimony: A Sacrifice or Offering to the World.
Joseph Smith's testimony, sealed with his blood, was a blessing to some, and a curse to others.

25. Blood Atonement: Summary and Conclusions.
A complete society has many aspects. Blood atonement deals with criminal law aspects of society while the united order deals more with the economic aspects. Both are necessary and complementary.

26. One-Man Power, No Independent Thoughts on Earth, No Freedom in Heaven.
Brigham Young sought to be the saints' lawgiver for all purposes, to help them solve their huge problems. His teachings supported this goal. In support of centralized, one-man power, he and others extended the idea of God's power to include being the source of all new thoughts on earth, and the control of all details of life in heaven.

27. The Prophet as Dictator.
In conjunction with the "One-Man Power" idea, the concept of Prophet as Dictator (or leader or instructor of the people) was often mentioned.

28. Adam-God.
   The Adam-God teaching was an adjunct to the one-man power doctrine, describing how God might wish to keep His children under His direction, being unwilling to delegate.

29. Polygamy.
   Polygamy is a power doctrine that helped the saints grow and protected their women from outsiders.

30. Theocracy and Constitution.
   Various comments were made on the nature of the government within the temporal Kingdom of God, and its relationship to other temporal kingdoms.

31. Annihilation of Identity. The Second Death - The Dissolution of the Spirit.
   The annihilation doctrine, the possible total extinction of identity, was used to frighten the saints into obeying their lawgiver.

32. Shortcuts to Heaven.
   Various concepts about short-cuts to heaven have been used to encourage certain specific behaviors of believers. One example is the Muslim idea of a warrior going straight to heaven if killed in battle. A Utah example was boys who saved people at a river crossing and then died themselves. The second endowment may be another variation.

33. Negative Consequences of Using These Anomalous Doctrines.
   The anomalous doctrines taught may have had a short-term benefit, but many have had a bad long-term effect.

34. An Atonement Dilemma: A Plausible "Anomaly."
   Today's teachings have a single savior over an infinity of worlds. Brigham Young assigned one savior to each world, a much simpler arrangement.

## MODERN INTERPRETATIONS OF TEMPORAL ISSUES AND TERMS.

35. Comments on 1930's Welfare Programs.
   The welfare program of the 1930s did not reconfirm or re-institute any of the traditions about the 1800s united order. The welfare program does not affect the mainline economic system, but is an adjunct to it.

## APPENDIX

Statistics on the contents of the *Journal of Discourses*: counts by year, speaker, and topic; complete index of citations used in this book.

www.ingramcontent.com/pod-product-compliance
Lightning Source LLC
LaVergne TN
LVHW011342080426
835511LV00005B/105

*9 780975 583159*